HISTORY OF BURMA

HISTORY OF BURMA

FROM THE EARLIEST TIMES TO 10 MARCH 1824
THE BEGINNING OF THE ENGLISH CONQUEST

BY

G. E. HARVEY

INDIAN CIVIL SERVICE

WITH A PREFACE BY

SIR RICHAR CARNAC TEMPLE, BR.

WITH SEVEN ILLUSTRATIONS AND
FIVE COLOURED MAPS

GYAN

Published by

GYAN

Gyan Publishing House
5, Ansari Road
Daryaganj, New Delhi-110002
Phone: 011-47034999, 9811692060
E-mail: books@gyanbooks.com

Distribution Network
gyanbooks.com
India, USA, Canada, UK, Australia, France

ISBN : 978-81-212-3505-1 (PB)
First Published, 1925

2nd Impression 2020

Printed at: Gyan Press, Delhi.

HISTORY OF BURMA

FROM THE EARLIEST TIMES TO 10 MARCH 1824
THE BEGINNING OF THE ENGLISH CONQUEST

BY

G. E. HARVEY

INDIAN CIVIL SERVICE

WITH A PREFACE BY

SIR RICHARD CARNAC TEMPLE, BT.

WITH SEVEN ILLUSTRATIONS AND FIVE COLOURED MAPS

LONGMANS, GREEN AND CO.
39 PATERNOSTER ROW, LONDON, E.C. 4
NEW YORK, TORONTO
BOMBAY, CALCUTTA, AND MADRAS

PREFACE

By Sir RICHARD CARNAC TEMPLE, Bt.

I PROMISED Mr. Harvey to write the Preface to his book on the History of Burma, and now that I have his typescript before me I fulfil my promise. It is well over fifty years since I first landed in Burma, when Thayetmyo and Toungoo were on the British frontier, when it used to take three weeks by boat to reach the latter from Rangoon, what time the bore in the Sittang served. It took one fourteen days to reach Thayetmyo from Rangoon up the Irrawaddy in the rains of 1871. Circumstances have changed the amenities of travel almost inconceivably since then. At that time the corners in the Irrawaddy stream were rounded by fastening hawsers on to trees on the bank and steaming round by degrees with their help, as the current was stronger at such spots than the horse-power of the river steamers.

It is now also approaching forty years, after a long absence in India after the Thayetmyo days, since I first saw Mandalay in the war of 1885 onwards. It had been well known to me by reading as a place of romance in the distance beyond the frontier, approachable only by the favoured few, and it was as to a land of romance that I approached it in the greatly improved means of travel reached by the middle eighties of the last century—finding my way through the miles of complicated streets from the river shore to the walled and moated city and the stockaded palace in its midst. For three years, April, 1887, to December, 1889, I was the first Cantonment Magistrate and the first Vice-President of the new Municipality—and to me it fell to dismantle the great city and change its features, within and without its walls, into the Cantonment of Mandalay. To commence also at the same time the fashioning of the great modern provincial town of the British Indian Government variety out of what was virtually a mediæval Burmese capital was a work of absorbing interest and an unforgettable experience.

I was necessarily in close touch with the greater personalities of the King's régime and had to learn much of the recent history of his rule and his people, which created in my mind a strong desire to ascertain all that the scant leisure hours during my many duties permitted of their origin and earlier story. I have therefore long taken an absorbing interest in Burmese History and in all works which purport to teach it.

A great deal has been written on Burma, and there are valuable monographs on her history and anthropology. But of the two, it is history which has been the less studied till quite lately. The reason for this has been the difficulty of finding such material as exists—though there is a great deal of it—and rendering it intelligible. Of late years the Burma Research Society, founded in 1910, has begun to collect material of all kinds, and this book may be regarded as one of the first-fruits, for it is written by an office-bearer at the instance of one of the Society's founders, Monsieur Charles Duroiselle, who is himself responsible for much of the most enduring work that is being done on Burma and her archæology.

Up to this year the only full length History of Burma, based on original sources, has been Sir Arthur Phayre's, which was published in 1883, but excellent as that great work is, much that was not available to him has naturally come to light since then; thus, he had not access to the inscriptions, or to Chinese sources.

In the length of time that circumstances of government service and health have made it necessary for Mr. Harvey to consume in bringing out the result of his many labours, Sir George Scott has also produced a general History of Burma, published this year under the title of *Burma from the Earliest Times to the Present Day.* He has clearly consulted the authorities, and he has written his book with all the literary skill which distinguishes his former writings. But I agree with his own statement in his preface "that parts of the narrative are flippant," and taken altogether it is a light book. It does not interfere with a work like that before me. There is plenty of room for both, and the student would do well to study Mr. Harvey after running over Sir George Scott, if he would dive seriously into Burmese history.

Mr. Harvey's book presents us with a mass of original work and incorporates the results of research up to the date of going to press. But it is something more than a work of scholarship; it is also a singularly sympathetic study of the peoples of Burma; it is a book written with the heart as well as with the head. I venture to stress this point, because I am old enough to remember the seamy side of native rule. Things which sound incredible to-day were commonplace under native rule two generations ago, yet anyone who records them now is dismissed as a hostile critic—so short is human memory, so rapid has been the growth of nationalist sentiment. Burmese, like all oriental, and indeed most general, history, is a sombre record, a fact that many modern Burmese "patriots," as those of other nations, are apt to forget; the tendency is to regard the past as a golden age, and even Thibaw now has his halo.

People who want tendencious writing will have to look elsewhere, for this book glozes over little. But the beauty of the ancient world is described with equal vividness. Thus, Mr. Harvey writes of the Pagān Dynasty: "The legacy of their fleeting sway enriched posterity for ever. It was they who made that sun-scorched wilderness, the solitary plain of Myingyān, to blossom forth into the architectural magnificence of Pagān. If they produced no nation-builder like Simon de Montfort, no lawgiver like Edward I., they unified Burma for more than two centuries, and that in itself was an achievement. But their rôle was æsthetic and religious rather than political. To them the world owes in great measure the preservation of Thēravāda Buddhism, one of the purest faiths mankind has ever known. Brahmanism had strangled it in the land of its birth. In Ceylon its existence was threatened again and again. East of Burma it was not yet free from priestly corruptions. But the Kings of Burma never wavered, and at Pagān the stricken faith found a city of refuge. Vainglorious tyrants build themselves sepulchres, but none of these men has a tomb. . . . These men's magnificence went to glorify their religion, not to deck the tent wherein they camped during this transitory life." It is a kindly and just judgment.

After quoting the early European visitors' accounts of Pegu in its days of power, which read so extravagantly to modern eyes, Mr. Harvey makes the following illuminating remarks: "These men saw the East in all her glory, such as we no longer see her. We have lost that vision and are the poorer. Yet we have lost it because we have grown richer. Our standards have altered. We no longer accept the pinchbeck and bone which even kings among our forbears were fain to wear as gold and ivory. Our Europe is no longer the little Christendom of Gothic times, living on the scanty produce of grey skies, trembling at every rumour of Saladin or the victorious Turk. She is sovran Europe who holds the East in fee and the whole world beside. We have come to know that all that glitters is not gold, but these first voyagers did not know it. They came from evil-smelling walled towns, where folk dwelt in kennels and died like flies of epidemics caused by their own insanitation. To men who lived in the cold and changed their clothes but once a year and went unwashed for months, the sunshine and the clean water, the children splashing all day in the creeks, the girls at the well, were one long delight. Ordure vanished quickly under the tropical sky, and instead of fetid narrow streets and overhanging houses, they saw the airy spaciousness of Pegu city in its heyday, and wide ways sweeping out of sight towards the four main gates. Men who had wrung a fourfold crop, at best, from the hard northern soil, saw a miracle in rice with its forty-fold out-turn, and in the mango a rare and refreshing fruit. They did not stray inland far from the capital, these simple sailormen. They saw little but the wealth of a kingdom heaped together on one man, the prince who peacocked it in his palace, and they took such vestures, such jewels, such pomp and circumstance, to be a type of the whole country."

Mr. Harvey ends a well-told account of the death of Alaungpayā (Alompra), during his last expedition to Ayuthia in Siam, with the burning words: "So he was buried with the ritual of the kings in the palace city [Shwebo] which once had been his lowly village, and the mourning of an entire people. They would never see his like again, the village headman who had made himself lord of Burma and received the homage not only of the tribes, but also of French and English captains kneeling to receive his orders in respectful silence. . . . He had reigned only eight years and was under forty-six when he died; but men are remembered by the years they use, not by the years they last."

Speaking of another great man of the past, Anawrahtā, the founder of the Pagān Dynasty, Mr. Harvey writes of the effects of Buddhism on Burma: "His chief monument, the Shwezigon Pagoda, built in A.D. 1059 and still unfinished at his death, is a solid pagoda of the kind so common all over Burma. Yet it attracts worshippers daily, while finer temples built by his successors are deserted. Its popularity is due to the exceptional sanctity of the relics (Buddha's collarbone, his frontlet from Prome and his tooth from Ceylon), and to the shrines of the entire pantheon of the Thirty-Seven Nat spirits, who, as it were, have come circling round in homage to these relics. If anyone doubts the debt Burma owes to Buddhism, or wishes to see what she would have been without it, let him wander here and contemplate these barbarous images of the heathen gods. Asked why he allowed them, Anawrahtā said: 'Men will not come for the sake of the new faith. Let them come for their old gods and gradually they will be won over.'" The local oral tradition which Mr. Harvey here quotes shows that a Buddhist leader was influenced by the same feelings as the early Christian missionaries in Europe. The images at the Shwezigōn Pagoda cannot, however, have been those of the

Thirty-Seven Nats as they now exist, as so many of them were living human beings long after Anawrahtā's date. The illustrations of my own collection of images and drawings of this order of Burmese supernatural beings (see *The Thirty-Seven Nats*, 1906) will also show how the all-pervading faith in the Buddhist religion in Burma has changed the old barbarous representation of the Nats into something that is noble in expression and beautiful in feeling.

The first successes of the village headman of Shwebo, Alaungpayā, are told with a swing, a raciness and an insight into the Burman character that make instructive reading: "The deficiency of the races of Indo-China in power of combination on a large scale is natural to people whose inherited instincts were formed in a country of great distances and bad communications. But when roused to enthusiasm they have shown considerable capacity for combined action. Among the Burmese the years 1752-7 are a model instance. Alaungpayā was not the only prominent man in Upper Burma. Independent attempts to form centres of resistance [to the Talaing invaders] had been made at Mōgaung in Myitkyinā district and Salin in Minbū district. Some of the leaders were men of better birth [than Alaungpayā], who had not to go back nine generations to claim royal blood. They were masterful men with considerable followings, who could have ruined the common cause by insisting on their rights. Not one of them did so, and the hereditary nobles ended by placing the territorial cadres at the disposal of Alaungpayā."

One more quotation and I have done with this particular point. Writing of the doings in 1823 during the days of Bāgyîdaw, "the Impossible" from the British point of view, Mr. Harvey remarks that the Assamese campaigns, "waged amid strange races and magnificent scenery, powerfully affected the imagination of the Burmese, as they swarmed through the passes, or floated for hundreds of miles down the Brahmaputra river on rafts. They marched with the tread of conquerors, and the earth seemed to tremble under their feet. The succession of victories confirmed the opinion they had of themselves and whetted their appetite for further conquest. Among the commanders who thus won fame was Mahābandūla," of whom much was heard in the first British war with Burma in 1824. Mr. Harvey's account of Mahābandūla is just and discriminating, and the following remark shows that in historical judgment he rises above racial feeling: "He was an imperialist of the most aggressive type, yet it is unjust to regard him as responsible for the war of 1824. He did, indeed, force it on, but in advocating it he was merely the mouthpiece of the entire people."

There is one criticism which it would not be difficult to level at this book in places. At times it reads almost like a jumble, in which the wood cannot be seen for the trees. That is not the fault of Mr. Harvey but of his subject. Except when Burma has happened to come under the rule of one man or of one dynasty, or say under two or three definitely separable rulers whose careers can be clearly followed, its history is a jumble very difficult to disentangle. It has in fact been the prey for centuries at a time of small tribes, or even cliques, ruling over small areas, always fighting and for ever getting the better of each other alternately. It is a disheartening matter for the historian to try and give a clear view of the various happenings under such circumstances. The hierarchy of the Thirty-Seven Nats is closely connected with personages of historical consequence, and I soon found, in trying to trace out the stories in historical sequence, how difficult it was to fix the place in history of the individuals concerned. Much of Burmese history is necessarily the relation of the small doings of princelings and mere raiders, and yet if the story of the country is to be rightly presented it must be all told. But it cannot help being confused to the rapid reader, and anyone wishing to understand history in such conditions must in fact be patient and careful.

But however insignificant these local ambitions, fights and victories were in the world's view, they were mighty happenings to the inhabitants of Burma. The war with the Chinese in the thirteenth century was to the great Emperor of China an affair with a small people beyond his boundaries—a matter to be left to the discretion of one of the officers on his frontiers. To the Burmese, however, it was a struggle between two mighty peoples, to be recorded with the same attention to the actual facts and the same perception of proportion that they subsequently bestowed on their fights of the same description with the great British Empire.

The Burmese nevertheless have always been happy tellers of tales. Their capacity for relating a story well is remarkable and makes their historical records enticing reading, apart from their high or low value as history. Many a page of the *Hmannan* or *Glass Palace Chronicle* is a delight to peruse, and the same may be said of almost any other Burmese Chronicle one may consult—the narrative is so vividly and so humanly told. Mr. Harvey has been therefore wise in drawing largely on the legends of Burmese history and so made his work more thoroughly of the soil than would otherwise have been possible. The story, for instance, of the end of Narathīhapate, the last king of the Pagān dynasty—the Tarōkpye Min, the king that fled from the Chinese—as quoted from the *Glass Palace Chronicle* in this book—is told with the fascinating skill and power of the born story-teller.

The happenings in most history are so frequently horrible that one often wonders how life could have been tolerable. Much greater is the wonder as to how so much that is beautiful in art, that is wonderful in philosophy and noble in religion, could have come into existence. Burma is no exception. Much that happened there has been terrible, and simple devastation went on for long periods together so constantly and so completely as to constitute a nightmare.

Such periods are to be found in all Eastern history and in Western history as well, and yet philosophy, religion and the arts of peace have flourished exceedingly. How was it? Anyone who has experience of street riots knows that the trouble is confined to the streets in which it occurs. Life in the rest of the town—even in a street or two away from the riot and outside it—passes on quietly as usual. So it is with war. In the area actually concerned it is terrifying, all-absorbing and destructive of every amenity. Elsewhere the countries concerned are affected, of course, but private life goes on quietly in much the usual way, and when communications are long or difficult it is not affected at all. So the poet can write, the philosopher can think and study, the priest can preach, and the artist work, just as they have always done. Thus it was possible for the great philosopher-historian Al-Bīrūnī and the equally great poet-historian Firdūsī to produce their world-renowned works at the court of such a raider and restless warrior as Mahmūd of Ghaznī. It is in fact a mistake to suppose that because a man has been a cruel invader and conqueror, he was therefore a man of low intellectual attainments and cared nothing for the arts and the higher living. Tīmūr Lang (Tamerlane) was anything but an illiterate man caring nothing for the beautiful things of life, for all his shocking sack of Delhi and many other similar deeds. So it was in Burma. The greater rulers, cruel as they frequently were, were mighty builders, and under them the arts and religion flourished. Under such men there were constant periods of general peace. When the country was divided up among petty local fighters, however complete the anarchy supervening in one locality, there was peace in another at the same time. Like all other countries, Burma has always been a good place for the top dog to dwell in, but even he has had his bad times as well: a condition that is apparently inseparable from human life.

Anyone who has worked, like myself, in the same field, will quickly realise the labour which has gone to the making of these few hundred pages. It has involved ransacking Chinese and Portuguese records, Dutch and English State Papers, and working through native Burmese material of which much is unprinted and in defective languages. How valuable such research can be the transcript *verbatim* of the Chinese General Staff Report on the invasion of Burma in 1765-9, in the days when Hsinbyushin sat on the throne of 'Alaungpaya, is a strong instance. Often it is the very virtue of a piece of historical research that leads to its overthrow by those who come after, but whether Mr. Harvey's conclusions endure or not—and I think that they are generally sound—his book will form a starting-point for searchers of the coming generation. It has blazed a way through the jungle so that others may build the road. The great feature of the book is the flood of light it throws on the still many dark places of Burmese history. It constitutes distinctly a step forward in our knowledge of the subject.

R. C. T.

AUTHOR'S INTRODUCTION

MR CHARLES DUROISELLE, Superintendent, Archæological Survey, Burma, suggested in 1918 that I should write this book. Since then he has guided my reading and given me access to his notes—the accumulated notes of a lifetime—so that the first half of this book is largely his, and the only reason his name does not appear on the title page is that he has not seen the final draft.

Next to him my chief collaborators were J. S. Furnivall, H. F. Searle and J. A. Stewart, members of my own service, and Professor G. H. Luce, Rangoon University; with these four I have been in regular consultation for several years. My thanks are also due to Mg San Shwe Bu (Honorary Archæological Officer), Mr Justice May Oung, Maung Mya (Archæological Assistant), Mg Po Kye 2 (Subordinate Civil Service), C. K. De (Secretariat Librarian, Rangoon), R. Grant Brown (Indian Civil Service), Miss L. M. Anstey, Arthur Waley, W. A. R. Wood (His Britannic Majesty's Consul-General, Chiengmai), G. W. Wheeler (Bodleian Library), George Cœdès (Librarian, Vajirañana National Library, Bangkok), and many others.

The reader will find the footnotes intelligible if he remembers that authorities are referred to by means of abbreviations or keywords which are printed in italics and are explained in the alphabetical bibliography at p. 373. Only the italicised portion of a reference is given in the bibliography; thus p. 95 refers to *ARASI* 1915-6 Duroiselle "The Ari of Burma and Tantric Buddhism"—the bibliography expands *ARASI*, the periodical containing Duroiselle's article, but does not give the article, even s.v. *Duroiselle*.

I have taken advantage of long leave in Europe to consult unpublished state papers in the India Office, and the usual Dutch and Portuguese sources. Chinese sources have been translated in the files of the Political Department. As to the native sources, they are so little known outside Burma that explanation is necessary.

It has too long been the fashion to deny the existence of historical material in Burma. But it is a question of standard, and the native material, though modest in both quantity and quality, is better than in the rest of Indo-China. Inscriptions may be rare in the fifth to the tenth centuries, but from the eleventh there is literally a deluge of them; and whereas in Campa, Cambodia and Siam, scripts have in the course of centuries undergone such profound changes that the compilers of later chronicles could not read the earlier inscriptions, in Burma inscriptions from the eleventh century onwards are in what is practically "square Pali," which is still used in the *kammawasa* (ordination service). Hence after the eleventh century the chronology of Burmese chronicles is reliable. Unfortunately the inscriptions used by historians were often copies containing dates which had been seriously miscopied (*Duroiselle*, "List" v, vi); this, and the tendency of the chroniclers to overlook inscriptions such as the Myazedi (p. 43), which did not happen to be in the collection near the palace (p. 268), resulted in the chronicles often being several decades out from the eleventh to the thirteenth centuries. Some 1,500 inscriptions have long been printed in the six volumes of *Inscriptions*, which are useless to philologists because the spelling has been modernised and the copying is defective—there is one page which contains eighty-two mistakes; this is now being rectified, for the major inscriptions, in *Epigraphia Birmanica*, issued by Mr Duroiselle, which retains the original spelling and gives a large photograph of each text.

Second to these, and inferior, are the vernacular chronicles. One of them, the Yazawingyaw, goes back to the fifteenth century (p. 104). Other early works are the sixteenth century *Razadarit Ayedawpon* (p. 170), and the curious *Pawtugi*

Yazawin (p. 188), written probably within a generation of De Brito's death (1613) by some burmanised Portuguese captive. But the standard chronicles are eighteenth and nineteenth century lucubrations, such as the *Hmannan Yazawin*, compiled by a royal commission in 1829; linguistic criteria show them to be based on material which is clearly late; save for quotation of archaic songs, their style reveals no archaisms of so marked a type as to suggest that their basic MSS. date from before the sixteenth century. Indeed it could hardly be otherwise. Although some sort of palace records were kept in the Pagan and Pegu palaces before that date, the country possessed no developed civilisation with diffused private or institutional papers. Vandals like Thohanbwa 1527-43 and Alaungpaya 1752-60, rebels like those who in 1564 burnt down Bayinnaung's capital, helped to destroy such records as there were. Changes of dynasty would lead to their neglect and dispersion. For such as survived, there were no proper record-room methods; mildew, white ants, and the accident of fire prevented MSS. from reaching any great age, especially those which were not strictly religious. It is the rarest thing in Burma to find MSS. as much as two centuries old even in the imagination of the possessor.

The chronicles abound in anachronisms (p. 340) and in stock situations which recur as regularly as in a yellow back. But it was not the eighteenth century compilers who started the fashion of romancing; they were only following precedent, for close study will show that perhaps as much as half the narrative told as historical down to the thirteenth century is folk-lore (pp. 315, 316, 327, 329). When a standard history of Burma comes to be written, it will be necessary to divide the reigns of such kings as Anawrahta into two parts; the first part will be The Evidence, e.g. inscriptions showing him to have actually existed and what he did, and the second part will be The Anawrahta Legend. Such division is not feasible within the limits of this little pioneer work, and although critics trained in the history schools of the West will be shocked at my treatment of the Pagan period, anyone familiar with the atmosphere of Further India will be able to supply his own comment on these pages, which reproduce the miraculous narrative objectively. Nor is it practicable to produce a lucid and well arranged book at the present stage, when the chief desideratum is to collate and record evidence much of which is scattered and untranslated or unprinted.

The chroniclers regard general conditions in early times as being the same as in their own day, the eighteenth century. The only evidence we have as to what they really were consists of exiguous inferences from mediæval inscriptions and of occasional references by foreign travellers; so far as it goes, such evidence gives one the idea of a stationary civilisation, the same in the Middle Ages as at the time of the English Conquest in 1824. What the English found is so easily ascertainable in print that, in the interests of space, I have omitted it, and refer to general conditions only when the narrative contains contemporary evidence to show what they were.

The main Burmese record is the *Hmannan Yazawin* down to 1752 and thereafter the *Konbaungset;* both are official. Local histories such as *thamaings* are frequently late, some, such as *Ko Hkayaing Thamaing*, being written a decade ago; written by individuals, they have not the range and accuracy of the great official compilations, but some, such as the *Shwemawdaw Thamaing*, must have been maintained at pagodas for centuries and record valuable traditions.

Alaungpaya, as his behaviour at Pegu in 1757 indicates (p. 235), destroyed many Talaing records; tradition says his successors did so, and the Talaings after they were conquered had neither the heart nor the means to maintain archives. I have used a Burmese MS. version of *Razadarit Ayedawpon;* the British Museum MS. "History of Pegu," by *Sayadaw Athwa*, used by Sir Arthur Phayre; Burmese MS. translations of the *Thatonnwemun Yazawin* and the *Paklat Talaing Chronicle;* and *Schmidt's* German translation of "Slapat ragawan datow smim ron."

The best Arakanese records, Maharazawun (148 *angas*), Do We "Rahkaing Razawun" (48 *angas*), Nga Me "Maharazawun" (24 *angas*), are practically unobtainable, being in palm leaf copies which are few and far between. San Shwe Bu has given me a few notes from Do We, Nga Me and others, and I have used Phayre's Arakanese MS. in the British Museum. *Dinnyawadi Yazawinthit*, the only printed Arakanese history I know, is a third hand piece of work. An admirable though slender check on Arakanese chronology exists in the dated medallions issued by the rajas of Arakan from the fifteenth if not the tenth century onwards (p. 137).

For Siamese chronicles I am mainly indebted to Mr. W. A. R. Wood, who furnished me with a précis. Shan chronicles are so consistently reckless with regard to dates, varying a couple of centuries on every other leaf, that I have disregarded them. As for the remaining races, such as Karens, Chins, Kachins, they were illiterate, and there is no record.

Hence our main authority is the standard Burmese chronicles. It is impossible to study these, especially in conjunction with the other native records, without acquiring considerable respect for them. No other country on the mainland of Indo-China can show so impressive a continuity. The great record of substantially accurate dates goes back for no less than nine centuries, and even the earlier legends have a substratum of truth. But that which gives continuity also gives false perspective; the record is that of the Burmese, the energetic and dominant minority who possessed an abiding palace and a continuous tradition. Written in the shadow of the throne, the chronicles tell little of general conditions, and their story is not that of the peoples of Burma, or even of the Burmese people, but simply that of the dynasties of Upper Burma. In a land of centrifugal tendencies, facts are distorted to fit into a centripetal scheme, and the Burmese capital is made to occupy the whole of the canvas, while races such as the Shans, who for centuries were of at least equal importance, and the Talaings, who were probably the leaders of civilisation to the very end, are scarcely mentioned save as a foil.

The Pagan period appears to have unity, but, apart from inscriptions, material is lacking; the Shan period is seen to be chaotic, because the chronicles were becoming fuller with the growth of the monastic system and the diffusion of literacy. Thibaw 1878-85 is notorious; yet if our only evidence were the Burmese court records, he would appear as a model monarch who spent his time uttering sublime sentiments, making ideal arrangements for religion, abolishing monopolies, etc., etc. The chronicles for the period of Pagan, which read so charmingly, were written by men who thus describe the First Anglo-Burmese War, 1824-6 (B.E. 1186-7):—

> In the years 1186 and 1187 white strangers from the west fastened a quarrel upon the Lord of the Golden Palace. They landed at Rangoon, took that place and Prome, and were permitted to advance as far as Yandabu; for the King, from motives of piety and regard to life, made no preparations whatever to oppose them. The strangers had spent vast sums of money in their enterprise, so that by the time they reached Yandabu their resources were exhausted, and they were in great distress. They then petitioned the King, who in his clemency and generosity sent them large sums of money to pay their expenses back and ordered them out of the country. (*Crawfurd* I. 304.)

It is difficult to see the history of Burma in its true colour and orientation, because material is lacking. Weakness is the predominant feature of central government in the East, and in Burma most of our material is that of the central government; hence the story told in this book is sombre. But it is less depressing than that of many eastern countries, and it would not be depressing at all if only we could get out of the palace and among the people. It is a people which must sometimes have wondered whether its government did not emanate from a vampire rather than a king, and yet it never lost its buoyancy or missed its hold on the essentials of civilisation. The clergy may have been recluses, but they not only lived beautiful lives: they fearlessly maintained the Law of Mercy. When greater races bound the feet or veiled the face of their women, or doubted if she had a soul, the Burmese held her free and enthroned her as chieftainess and queen.

Perhaps some better equipped writer will tell this story and portray the life of which we catch glimpses in many an old song. When he appears, much that is ugly will recede into the background; at present it clogs the foreground. Those who would have it omitted forget that a historian has no power to suppress an integral part of the record; neither the rules of his craft nor the dictates of his conscience allow it, for, in the words of one of the greatest of Liberals, John Morley: "The law of things is that they who tamper with veracity, from whatever motive, are tampering with the vital force of human progress."

G. E. H.

EXETER COLLEGE,
OXFORD.

TABLE OF CONTENTS

LIST OF ILLUSTRATIONS

LIST OF MAPS

CHRONOLOGICAL TABLE

YEAR.	EVENT.	PAGE.
500 *circ.*	Earliest inscription in Burma	4
	Ari Buddhism in Myingyan District	17
754	Nanchao becomes suzerain over Northern Burma	13
Eighth Cent.	Vikrama dynasty at Prome	12
800-02	Pyu envoys at the Court of China	13
Early IXth	Fall of Prome	12
Middle IXth	Arab sea traders reach Lower Burma	10
849	Foundation of Pagan	15
1057	Anawrahta conquers Thaton and introduces Hinayana Buddhism to Upper Burma. Decline of the Ari	27
1058	Earliest inscription in Burmese	29
1059	Anawrahta begins the Shwezigon pagoda	33
?	Anawrahta reduces North Arakan	29
	Visits Yünnan	30
	Builds Kyaukse canals	25
1071	Cingalese missions	32
1084	Talaings raid Pagan	35
1090	Kyanzittha builds the Ananda, the first of the greater temples	40
?	Burmese mission to Buddhagaya	42
1103-4	Burmese envoys visit Yünnan	43
1106	Burmese embassy at the Court of China	43
1112	The Myazedi inscription	43
1115 *circ.*	Death of Shin Arahan	44
1115	Burmese envoys visit Yünnan	48
1118	Letyaminnan, restored to the throne of North Arakan, repairs Buddhagaya	46
1144	Alaungsithu builds the Thatpyinnyu temple	47
1180	Cingalese raiders sack Bassein	57
1190	Chapata returns from Ceylon. Rise of Cingalese religious influence on Burma	56
1200 *circ.*	The Dhammavilasa *dhammathat*	59
1210	Kyaukse weir built	57
1218	Nantaungmya builds the Htilominlo, the last of the greater temples	59
1273	Narathihapate slays the ambassadors of Kubla Khan	64
1277	Battle of Ngasaunggyan	65
1280	Foundation of Toungoo	123
1281	Wareru becomes lord of Martaban	110
	The Wareru *dhammathat*	111
1287	Tartars enter Pagan	69
	Disruption of the Pagan kingdom	69
1289-98	The chiefs of Hsenwi, Mohnyin, Myinsaing, Pagan, Martaban, receive recognition from China	75, 110
1299	Shans sack Pagan	77

YEAR.	EVENT.	PAGE.
1301	Chinese fail to take Myinsaing	77
	Thindwe canal built	77
1312	Foundation of Pinya	78
1324	Ari in use as retainers	79
1356 *circ.*	Mission from Martaban to Kandy Temple	112
1362	Binnya U increases the height of the Shwedagon pagoda to 66 feet	112
1364	Shans sack Pinya and Sagaing	80
	Burmese migrate to Toungoo	80, 124
1365	Foundation of Ava	80
1368	Zidaw weir built	81
	Meiktila lake embankment repaired	81
1369	Martaban palace moved to Pegu	112
1374	North Arakan asks for a Burmese regent	86
1390-1	Death of Bawlawkyantaw and birth of Minrekyawsa	86
1404-30	Narameikhla an exile in Bengal. Thereafter the rajas of Arakan bear Mahomedan titles in addition to their own	139-40
1406	Razadarit raids Ava	88
1407	Talaing expedition restores an Arakanese claimant in North Arakan	91
1417	A generation of attacks from Upper Burma ends in the devastation of the Delta, especially on the Bassein side	94
1433	Foundation of Mrohaung	139
1435 *circ.*	Nicolo di Conti	98
1437 *circ.*	After this time Sandoway is usually subject to North Arakan	137
1446	Thonganbwa surrendered to China	99
1450	Binnyakyan increases the height of the Shwedagon pagoda to 302 feet	117
1453	Turks capture Constantinople	130
	Birth of Shin Uttamagyaw and Shin Thilawuntha	104
	Early vernacular literature	103
1456, '74	Missions from Ava to Kandy Temple	100-01
1460	Shinsawbu embanks the platform of the Shwedagon pagoda	118
1472	Dammazedi's mission to Buddhagaya	119
1475	Dammazedi's mission to Ceylon	119
	The Kalyani inscriptions	119
1496	Hieronimo de Santo Stephano	121
1498	Vasco da Gama finds the sea route to India	131
1503	Kyaukse ceded to Toungoo	105
1507	Ludovico di Varthema	121
1503	Shwebo district ceded to Mohnyin	105
1519	Portuguese establish a trading station at Martaban	121
1527	Thohanbwa *sawbwa* of Ava	107
1539	Tabinshwehti captures Pegu	154
	The palace is set up there	154
1541	Tabinshwehti captures Martaban	155
1544	Tabinshwehti annexes central Burma up to Myingyan	158
1546	Ngakyi canal built	109
1547	Minbin repels the Burmese expedition against Mrohaung	158
1548	First siege of Ayuthia	159
1550	Assassination of Tabinshwehti	161
	Talaings drive Burmese out of Pegu	162
1551	Bayinnaung regains Pegu	163
	Execution of Smim Htaw	164
1555	Bayinnaung sends a mission to Kandy Temple	172

YEAR.	EVENT.	PAGE.
1555-9	Bayinnaung annexes Upper Burma and the Shan states from Manipur to Viengchang. He abolishes animal sacrifice at Popa Hill and human sacrifice in the Shan states	165-7
1564	Second siege of Ayuthia; fall of the city. Tenasserim becomes subject to Burma for a generation	167
	Pegu is burnt by the peasantry	177
1567	Famine in the Delta	177
1569	Third siege of Ayuthia; fall of the city	169
1574-6	Bayinnaung receives a princess and a Buddha tooth from Colombo	173
1580 *circ.*	*Dhammathatkyaw* and *Kosaungchok*	171
1587-93	Fourth siege of Ayuthia—a series of abortive sieges	181-2
1595 *circ.*	Talaings flee to Siam	180
1596	Famine in the Delta	181
1600	Arakanese and Siamese sack Pegu. Famine in the Delta. Disruption of the kingdom	182-4
	De Brito makes Syriam his stronghold	185
1609	Tibao makes Sandwip his stronghold	142
1613	Anaukpetlun restores the monarchy and captures Syriam	185
1617	Minhkamaung captures Sandwip	142
	Beginning of the Magh-Portuguese raids on Bengal	143
1619	English East India Company's representatives visit Pegu	190
1625	Magh-Portuguese sack Dacca	143
1627 *circ.*	Dutch and English East India Companies open branches in Burma	191
1628	The last year for which the Chinese claim that a tribute mission came from Burma	184
1630	Talaings flee to Siam	193
1630 *circ.*	Manusarashwemin or Maharaja *dhammathat*	195
1635	Capital moved to Ava	193
1638	Thalun's revenue inquest	194
1658-62	Chinese brigands ravage Upper Burma	197
1658	Talaings flee to Siam	198
1660	Arakanese use coined currency	146
1661	Shah Shuja slain at Mrohaung	146
1662	Surrender of Yung-li	200
1666	Moghuls capture Chittagong. End of the Portuguese share in the Magh raids on Bengal	147
1677	Dutch and English East India companies close their branches in Burma	191
1683	Dutch send Arakanese monks to Ceylon. They close their branch in Arakan	146
1687	English massacred at Mergui	202
1688	Mergui temporarily garrisoned by the French royal troops	202
	French East India Company's branch at Syriam	203
1695	Mission of Fleetwood and Sealey to Ava	203
1709	English East India Company reopens branch at Syriam	206
1721	Foundation of the Catholic mission	207
1724-50	Manipuris raid Upper Burma	208-9
1725	Burmese lose Chiengmai	207
1740	Talaings expel Burmese from Pegu, Syriam, Martaban	212
1742, '53	Upper Burmans take refuge in Arakan	210
1742-51	Talaings ravage Burma as far as Ava	212-6
1743	Burmese take Syriam but are driven out. Talaings burn the English East India Company's buildings there	212-3
1744	Death of Gallizia and De Sconenville	214
1747	Gwe Shans of Okpo combine with Madaya Talaings	211

YEAR.	EVENT.	PAGE.
1750	King of Ava appeals to Yünnan	215
	The Manu Ring *dhammathat*	233
1751	Talaings occupy Kyaukse	216
1752	Talaings take Ava	216
1753	English East India Company occupy Negrais	213
1753	Talaings evacuate Ava	222
1754	Alaungpaya repels the Talaing grand attack on Ava	222
	Talaings execute captive Burmese king	223
1755	Alaungpaya occupies Prome, Myanaung, and Rangoon	223-4
	English ships are seized and fire at Rangoon	224-5
	Captain Baker's mission	225
	The "First Devastation" of Manipur	228
	Shan states pay homage	228
1755-6	Siege of Syriam	229
	Capture of French ships	231
1756 *circ.*	Manu Kye *dhammathat*	238
1756-7	Siege of Pegu. Overthrow of the Talaings	232-6
1757	Ensign Lester's mission	227
	English agreement with Alaungpaya	227
1758-9	Alaungpaya overruns Manipur	238
1759	The Negrais massacre	240
1760	Fifth siege of Ayuthia	241
	After this time Tenasserim remains in Burmese hands	241
	Captain Alves' mission	244
	East India Company at Rangoon	246
1763	Letwethondara's *Meza taungche*	249
1764	Raid on Manipur	248
1765	Capital moved to Ava	248
	The *Vyakarana*	249
1767	Sixth siege of Ayuthia. End of the city	251-3
1765-9	Chinese invasion	253-8
1773	Talaing mutineers flee to Siam	259
1774	Hsinbyushin raises the Shwedagon to its present height, 327 feet	260
	Execution of captive Talaing king	260
1768-75	Paya Tak expels the Burmese from Siam	261
1775-82	Manipur campaigns	261
1775-7	Cachar and Jaintia campaigns	261
1776	*Alphabetum Barmanorum*	346
1780 *circ.*	Birth of Mahabandula	300
1783	Capital moved to Amarapura	265
	Talaings temporarily seize Rangoon	265
1784-5	Conquest of Arakan	267
	Collection of inscriptions at the Arakan Pagoda, Mandalay	268
1784	Bodawpaya's revenue inquest	269
1785-6	Invasion of Siam	270
1787	Sino-Burmese missions	279
1790-7	Mingun pagoda	275
1794	Arakanese revolt. Burmese cross the Chittagong frontier	281
1795, 1802	Captain Symes' missions	285-6
1797	Nga Chin Pyan's revolt	282
	Migration of Arakanese to Chittagong	282
	Captain Cox's mission	285
1802	Cingalese monks seek ordination at Amarapura	277
1803	Siamese raid Kenghung and deport the people of Kentung	271
1803, '09, '11	Captain Canning's missions	286
1807-16	Famine in Upper Burma	272
1809-11	Burmese raid Isthmus of Kra and Junkceylon Island	272

YEAR.	EVENT.	PAGE.
1810	Burmese mission to Buddhagaya	277
1813	Expedition to Manipur	283
	The Judsons arrive in Burma	278
1814	Talaings rebel at Martaban and flee to Siam	272
1815	Death of Nga Chin Pyan	283
1816	Burmese overrun Assam	283
1818	Burmese claim Bengal	292
1819	Burmese annex Manipur	296
	Burmese annex Assam	297
1823	Capital moved to Ava	295
	Burmese seize Shahpuri Island	301
1824-6	First Anglo-Burmese War	304
	Annexation of Arakan and Tenasserim	270
1852	Second War. Annexation of Pegu	315
1857	Foundation of Mandalay	321
1885	Third War. Annexation of Upper Burma	4

CHAPTER I

BURMA BEFORE 1044

BURMA ABOUT 700 A.D. (Conjectural)

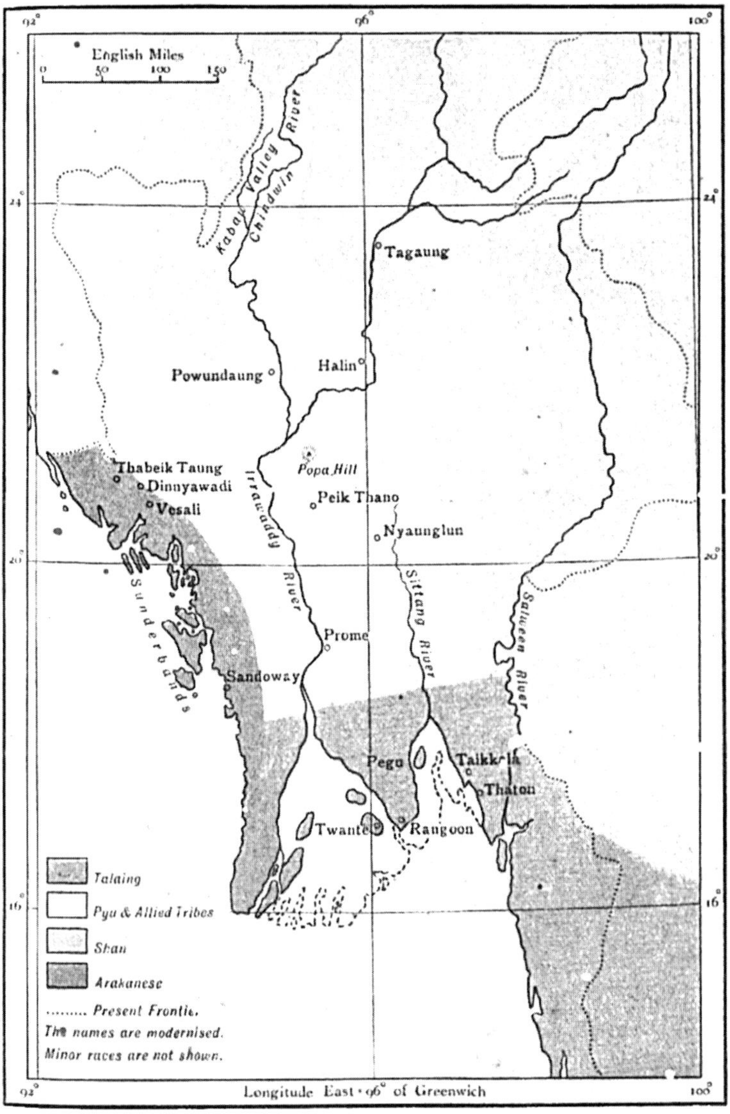

Emery Walker Ltd. sc.

Longmans, Green & Co. London, New York, Toronto, Bombay, Calcutta & Madras.

CHAPTER I

BURMA BEFORE 1044

BURMA,[1] being little more than the valleys of a river system shut off from the outer world by hills and sea, is fitted to be the home of a unified people. But even now the process of unification, though accelerated, is incomplete; and when history began, the country was a medley of tribes.[2]

Perhaps the earliest inhabitants were Indonesians but they have left scarcely a trace and in any case they were displaced by Mongolian tribes whose home was probably in western China. These were the Mon and the Tibeto-Burman tribes from eastern Tibet. Doubtless they came down the great rivers, but the routes, order, and dates at which they came are purely conjectural. The Mon (Talaings) spread over Burma south of Henzada. The traditional names of the Tibeto-Burman tribes are Pyu, Kanran, and Thet; perhaps the Thet are the Chins, and the Kanran the Arakanese; the Pyu, now extinct, may be an ingredient in what afterwards became the Burmese, and they seem to have been pushed inland from the Delta coast by Talaing pressure from the south-east, as if the Talaing route into Burma was down the Salween. The Karens may have been earliest of all.

These races came, owing to causes such as drought and ethnic pressure, in successive infiltrations, each driving its predecessor farther south. Down from the north they came,

[1] *Myamma* is the same word as *Mien* the Chinese name and *Man* the Shan name for Burma. The derivation from Brahma is on a level with the derivation of English from angels. The mediæval scribes with the name Brahma before them write not Brahmadesa (land of Brahma) but Myammadesa (land of Myamma), and an eleventh century Talaing inscription (*RSASB* 1920 21) calls the Burmese *Mirma*.

[2] See the current Census Report, Imperial Gazetteer, *Lowis*, *Halliday*, *Smeaton*, *JBRS* 1911 Gilmore "Karen Folk-Lore" and Grant Brown "Origin of the Burmese" *ibid.*, Temple "The People of Burma" in Journal of the Royal Society of Arts 1910 with which read *Vincent Smith* "Oxford History of India" 47.

tribe after tribe of hungry yellow men with the dust of the world's end upon their feet, seeking food and warmth in tiny homesteads along the fertile river banks, seeking that place in the sun which has been the dream of the northern races in so many ages. The infiltration lasted centuries. The Shans did not enter the plains till the thirteenth century and the Kachins were penetrating Upper Burma when the English annexed it in 1885. Many of the immigrants must have been settled in before the Christian era. They lay thinly scattered over the country, illiterate animist tribes with little political organisation. Men dwelt in isolated units, divided by forest and hill, a scanty population whose hut-fires sent up smoke here and there above the jungle. The unit was doubtless the village, with communal tenures and rigid clan customs.[1] If after a time kings came into existence they were little more than tribal chiefs

> . . . in times long passed away,
> When men might cross a kingdom in a day,
> And kings remembered they should one day die,
> And all folk dwelt in great simplicity.

We read of seven kings who went up to do battle against Taikkala (Ayetthima in Thaton district); but as their realms were all pressed in between the mouths of the Salween and Sittang rivers, each kingdom must have been no larger than a township.[2]

Indeed there can hardly have been political units of any size before writing came into use.[3] Although it was not unknown before A.D. 500, no inscriptions of earlier date have yet been found. It was brought, probably about A.D. 300, from South India to the Pyus first of all, as part of the great Hindu expansion overseas; the earliest Pyu inscription contains Kadamba letters which were in use at that date near Goa on the Bombay coast. Hindus had come long before but it was not till this time that their cultural influence took root; they brought writing, customary law, and other elements of civilisa-

[1] *Forchammer* "Jardine Prize," *Clayton*, *Hertz*, *Furnivall* "Myingyan Settlement," his "Syrian Gazetteer," and his "Land as Free Gift of Nature" in Economic Journal 1909. As late as 1794, out of 8500 parishes in England 4500 were farmed on the common field system.

[2] *IA* 1893 and 1894 Taw Sein Ko "Kalyani inscriptions."

[3] See note "Inscriptions the Touchstone" p. 307.

tion.[1] They founded kingdoms in Java and Sumatra, and dotted the coast from Bengal to Borneo and Tonkin with little trading principalities such as Prome, Rangoon, and Thaton. Their coming was generally peaceful, for if they came as individual traders they would be welcomed; and if they came in numbers to set up independent communities, there was usually room in so thinly populated a land. But as time went on there was less room, at any rate in the places most worth having; and a few traditions such as the following suggest that at times there was petty fighting:—

THE STORY OF THE TALAING HERO KUN ATHA.

Thamala king of Pegu [A.D. 825-37] made his younger brother successor to the throne and, promising to welcome him on his return, sent him to learn wisdom from a famous teacher at Taxila. Now on the border between the realms of Pegu and Thaton there dwelt an aged Karen couple working their *ya* fields, and they had a daughter and Thamala the king made her his chief queen. And the months and the years went by, and she conceived in her womb, and the king forgot his brother Wimala.

Now Wimala, having learned wisdom, bade farewell to his teacher, and returned home. But because his brother the king forgot his promise and welcomed him not, forthwith in anger he slew his brother the king. And inasmuch at that very time the queen gave birth to her son, he ordered that the new-born babe also be slain. But the queen, with grief in her heart, hid the babe outside the town near a pasture where buffaloes graze; and the *nat* fairies guarded him, and day by day he grew in wisdom and strength.

When he was sixteen years old, Hindu strangers came to the land. They were angered because the Talaings had driven them out, and they came back saying "We will fight and regain Hanthawaddy." Led by Lamba, a giant seven cubits high, they came in their ships and surrounded Pegu town and sent a letter to Wimala the king. And when he had the letter, Wimala the king sent out messengers to seek a champion; but though the messengers searched, they found no champion.

Now at that time a certain hunter went hunting in the forest, and he came to where the wild buffaloes graze, and lo! among the buffaloes there stood a valiant youth. And the hunter returned home, and he told his wife, and she said "Husband, if this be true, tell it to the king, and he will reward thee." And the hunter told the king, and Wimala the king sent ministers to fetch the youth. And when they brought him, at once Wimala the king knew him for his nephew,

[1] See also *IA* 1891 Temple "Burmese Arithmetic," 1886 Phayre "Notes on Early History of Pegu," 1897-8 Temple "Currency and Coinage among the Burmese," *Hobson-Jobson* s.v. "Viss."

> and he ennobled him and called his name Atha-kumma, because he should conquer his enemies. Then Wimala confessed his sin, and in that moment Atha-kumma plighted his troth to fight the Hindu strangers. But first he waited seven days, and sought the buffalo who was his foster-mother to ask her leave, and she gave him leave and shewed him how to fight and conquer. Then he returned to Pegu town and did battle there,[1] and speared the Hindu giant in the side, and took prisoner seven ships and three thousand five hundred Hindu strangers. He built Kyaikatha [the pagoda of Atha, in Thaton district]. And Wimala the king made him successor to the throne. (*Nanda-thara.*)

The Burmese are a Mongolian race, yet their traditions, instead of harking back to China, refer to India. Their chronicles read as if they were descended from Buddha's clansmen and lived in Upper India. Even their folk-lore is largely Hindu. Most of their towns have two names, one vernacular, the other classical Indian,[2] just as the Latin Church made it the fashion for every city in Europe to have a Roman name whether the Romans had been there or not. A few of these classical names are due to actual immigration from the original namesake in India; thus Ussa, the old name for Pegu, is the same word as Orissa, and Pegu was colonised from Orissa. The surviving traditions of the Burmese are Indian because their own Mongolian traditions died out. The only classes who could read and write and keep traditions alive were their ruling class, the Indian immigrants.

In Upper Burma these immigrants came overland through Assam; in Lower Burma they came by sea from Madras. In some localities, such as Thaton, Prome, Pegu, Rangoon, and in many a town in Arakan, Indian immigrants doubtless formed a large proportion of the population; indeed the name "Talaing" is probably derived from Telingana, a region on the Madras coast whence so many of them came.[3] Like

[1] Tradition points to a stone pillar near a monastery at Hinthakan, half a mile north-east of the Shwemawdaw pagoda, as commemorating the site. See p. 113.

[2] The name of the Irrawaddy (Sansk. *Iravati* = "giver of refreshment") happens to be also the ancient name of the river Ravi in the Panjab. See *RSASB* 1915 31 and 1917 26, 35.

[3] This derivation of Phayre's is still the best. See *Halliday*, *Hobson-Jobson* s.v. "Talaing," *JBRS* 1914 Blagden "Talaing." The ætiological tale that Alaungpaya christened the people Talaing meaning "downtrodden" is disproved by the occurrence of the name Talaing in Burmese inscriptions as early as 1107 (*Inscriptions* 1913 18).

good Hindus, they built little shrines; and it is probably these shrines that form the original strata of such pagodas as the Shwemawdaw at Pegu, the Shwedagon at Rangoon, and the Shwezayan at Thaton, all of which may well date back, in some shape or another, to before the Christian era. They brought their clergy with them, just as chetties and European merchants do now in Rangoon, and with as little result on the people at large. As a rule their religion was a domestic matter, but in the course of centuries they became so numerous as to effect peaceful penetration. Moreover, their Hinduism begun to include Buddhist elements after 261 B.C. when Asoka conquered the Kalinga and introduced Buddhism into South India. Its spread there doubtless took some time—the absorption of a religion is a slow process—and its spread to Lower Burma probably took longer still. What must have been a decisive factor was the rise, in the fifth century after Christ, of a great Hinayana centre at Conjeveram in Madras under the commentator Dhammapala; ancient Talaing writings frequently mention Dhammapala and Conjeveram, and the earliest Talaing inscription is in the Pallava alphabet used there in his time.

The faith existed side by side with Brahmanism. What the excavator[1] finds in Burma is often Hindu rather than Buddhist. In some sculptures Buddha appears as an incarnation of Vishnu. The legend of Duttapaung,[2] the Pyu chief, is tinged with Sivaism, for he is described as having three eyes; and what look like phallic emblems have been found at Pegu.

Doubtless these changes affected for the most part only the towns, the trade centres, and the rulers who, if not foreigners, intermarried with foreigners. The bulk of the people outside went on in their old quiet way worshipping stocks and stones—the usual animism and spirit worship of simple races. Religious strife is scarcely mentioned; but that there were occasional struggles between Hinduism and Buddhism is indicated by traditions such as

[1] See note "Ancient Sites" p. 309.

[2] *IA* 1893 Taw Sein Ko "Folk-lore in Burma—the three-eyed king."

THE STORY OF THE TALAING HEROINE BHADRADEVI (TALAHTAW).

Tissa [A.D. 1043-57] was a heretic king [of Pegu]. He . . . made no obeisance to Buddha, to the Law he hearkened not, he honoured the Brahmans. He threw down the images of Buddha, he cast them away into ditches and marshes.

Now there was a certain merchant's daughter who clung to true religion. Bhadradevi was this maiden's name. From her tenth year up she went out to listen with her parents and she hearkened continually to the Law. She had exceeding great joy in the Three Gems. Daily she said the Three Names of Refuge with care. And it came to pass that the time when she was in her first youth was the time when the king cast down the images of Buddha. At that time the maiden went down to bathe, and by chance she thrust her hand against an image of Buddha. And she drew it up, and it glistened with gold. She asked "Who has caused this image to be cast away?" And the old slavewomen made answer "Lady, this king follows the word of false teachers. Verily it is the king who has caused this image of Buddha to be cast away. Whoever greets, honours, or bows before Buddha at the pagodas, him the king causes to be slain and to be brought to naught." Thus said the slavewomen. When the maiden had heard their words, she spake on this wise "I obey the Three Gems. I can endure death. First wash the image clean, then set it up at a pagoda." She herself and the slavewomen washed it and set it up at a pagoda. . . . Now as she was setting up the image, these things were told to the king. And he sent runners to call her. The maiden, that ring adorned with gems beyond price, spoke to the king's runners saying "Let me abide here before the image." And she made haste to wash every image of Buddha as many as were there, and to set them up, every one. And after a time the king sent more runners. When the maiden came before the king, she spake unto him. But he listened with anger, and spake in this wise "Take her to the elephants that they may trample her to death." Then the maiden caused gentleness to soften the king and the elephants and the elephant-men, and continually she said the "I take refuge in the Lord" and she called on the Three Names of Refuge. And the elephant dared not tread on her, but he roared with his voice, neither could the elephant-men make him run at her. Many times they brought other elephants, but no elephant dared tread on her. So men told the king in fear. When the king heard these things, he spake in this wise "Cover her with straw for the funeral pyre." But the maiden caused gentleness to work again, and she called on the Three Names of Refuge. Men stirred themselves to burn her, yet she burned not. So they told the king in fear. Thus spake the king "Bring her here." They brought her to the king, and he said "O maiden! When I see the image of Buddha thy teacher fly up into heaven, then mayest thou live. But if from the image of thy teacher there fly not up seven images, eight images, I will have thee cut into seven pieces." And he had her led to the foot of the ditch . . . and she prayed on this wise "O image of the Lord of Bliss! I thy handmaiden set up thy images. Buddha is lord everywhere, his Law is lord everywhere, his Church is lord everywhere. As Buddha, his Law, his Church are everywhere lord, so may eight images of Buddha fly up into heaven at the king's hall!" And in the twinkling of an eye there flew eight images up into heaven . . . towards the king's hall. And the maiden returned and pointed them out to the king. With many men he saw them, it was a wonder far and wide. Then said the maiden "O earthly king! Buddha my teacher is gone to Nirvana. Thou hast been able to see only his images fly up into heaven in his stead. Thou hast followed false teachers and called them better. Let thy handmaiden see *them* fly up." Then the king commanded them to fly. But the false teachers could not fly. And the king drave them away . . . and he caused the maiden to bathe and he raised her to be his chief queen . . . and he returned thanks and followed true religion ever after. (*Schmidt.*)

Civilising influences were strongest round the coast and in the Delta. Upper Burma lay inaccessible; true, it was nearer to China, which from the second century before Christ used trade routes through Burma,[1] but China's interest seems to have been limited to these routes, for traces of any influence of hers are hard to find (p. 73). Tagaung in Mogok subdivision received civilisation from Upper India, but not till some time later than the Talaings, judging from the fact that the earliest writing so far found there is in North Indian script of the tenth century.[2] Again, in the seventh century a Talaing princess married a Tibetan king. But though instances such as these show that the tedious overland route was in use, it was round the sea-coast that development centred, and especially in the south where the river mouths brought down the produce of the interior. Roman shipmasters,[3] trading in Ceylon and Madras, heard of Sobanas River (Irrawaddy, Salween, cf. Suvannabhumi), and Golden Land (the Delta, Malaya and Sumatra).[4] Ptolemy, the Greek geographer, writing

[1] Two were along the Irrawaddy and Salween rivers; the third, down the Chindwin river and through Manipur, took the caravans a three months' journey to Afghanistan where the silks of China were exchanged for the gold of Europe (*BEFEO* 1904 Pelliot "Deux itinéraires" and *Hunter* I. i).

[2] See note "Führer's Inscription" p. 310.

[3] See note "Eastern Shipping" p. 310.

[4] See note "Golden Land" p. 310.

in A.D. 140 even mentions a Tugma Metropolis, in a spot curiously like Upper Burma, as if it were Tagaung. But it is to Prome that the Chinese pilgrims chiefly refer when, in their travels, they speak from hearsay of Burma; and to the Arabs, whose shipping predominated in the eastern seas from the eighth to the sixteenth century, Burma was Arakan and Lower Burma:—

> They say that the king of Rahma [Lower Burma] has fifty thousand elephants. His country produces cloth made of velvety cotton, and aloe wood of the sort called *hindi.* (Ibn Khordadzbeh, years 844-8, Persian traveller from Basra, in *Ferrand.*)
>
> The king of Rahma enjoys no great repute . . . His troops are more numerous than those of Ballahra, Gudjra and Tekin. They say that when he marches to battle he is accompanied by about fifty thousand elephants. He campaigns only in winter; indeed his elephants cannot stand thirst and so they can go forth only in winter. They say that in his army the washermen amount to between ten and fifteen thousand. In his states are found cloths not found elsewhere; a dress made of such cloth is so fine and light that it can pass through a signet ring. It is of cotton. We have seen a sample. For barter the people use cowries, which form their currency. But gold, silver, aloes are also found, and a stuff called *camara* [yak hair] whereof flyflaps are made. The same country produces . . . the rhinoceros, an animal which has on his forehead a single horn, and in this horn is a human figure. . . . We have eaten the flesh. He is numerous and lives in the woods. He is found in other parts of Ind, but here the horn is more beautiful, often containing the image of a man, peacock, fish or anything else. The Chinese make girdles of this horn and pay high prices among themselves, up to three or four thousand *dinar* and even more according to the figure's beauty. These horns are bought with cowries. (Sulayman, year 851, traveller from the Persian Gulf, *ibid.*)
>
> In Ind lies a realm called Rahma, bordering on the sea. Its ruler is a woman. It is ravaged by the plague, and any man who comes from elsewhere in Ind and enters the country, dies there. Yet many come by reason of the great profits to be made. (Ibn al Fakih, Persian traveller, year 902, *ibid.*)

The above exports, to which ivory must doubtless be added, contrast curiously with the rice, teak,[1] and oil by which Burma is known to-day. But the scanty populations of the ancient world were self-sufficing and had no need to import rice; their consumption of oil was small, for it was not used industrially till after the development of power-plant in the eighteenth

[1] See note "Teak" p. 311.

century; their own forests had not yet been cleared, and sufficed for housing and shipbuilding. Power transport did not exist until the nineteenth century; consequently articles of heavy bulk could not be exported, and commerce was confined to luxury articles such as precious metals, jewels, ivory, pepper, silk and aromatic woods. As the above extracts show, few of these were found in Burma, and traders therefore ranked her below many other parts of Asia. Indeed most of the country was uncleared jungle. What is now the fertile Delta had not yet silted up; it lay beneath the tides, and the higher land was an archipelago of tree-clad islets. Thaton was on the coast, and the earliest traditions refer to Pegu town as an island in a shallow sea.[1]

The imports included piece goods from the Chola kingdom in Madras and Buddhist images from Upper India. Possibly there was a regular manufacture of such images for the Burma market long after Buddhism had died out in Upper India—

> In Benares land there was an ancient pagoda on the top of the river Ganges' bank. When the bank washed away, men picked up the relics and holy images that had been enshrined there, and gave them to their children to play, for there was no longer anyone to worship them. Now Nga Dula a ship's captain saw this, and he thought "The folk of the east country deem these images divine and worship them. I shall get gain if I sell them to the folk of the east country." So he bought them for a fitting price and came with them to the landing stage of Pegu. . . . Men told king Tissa [1043-57] . . . and he rewarded Nga Dula richly and ennobled him. (*Shwemawdaw Thamaing* 81.)

Probably every town of any size went its own way, receiving propitiatory homage from the surrounding villages and yielding it to some larger town whose chief happened to be masterful. The races inhabiting them were those which we see to-day and probably their appearance was much the same save that intermarriage had not yet produced the present uniformity of type. Perhaps the most interesting are the Pyu, now extinct.[2] Their language still existed in the thirteenth century; up to that time the Arakanese, and the Chinese till the tenth century, knew the people of Burma as the Pyu. The Chinese describe Burma in the ninth century as containing

[1] See note "The Ancient Coastline" p. 311.
[2] See note "Pyu Physiognomy" p. 312.

eighteen states and nine walled towns all of which were dependent on the Pyu. Their chief town was Prome but traditions of them survive as far north as the Kabaw valley. Their elimination, leaving so few traces, renders it unlikely that they had a very noticeable civilisation but doubtless it was equal to any other in Burma at the time. They burned their distinguished dead and buried the ashes in large urns. The writing on these urns indicates the existence, at Prome in the eighth century, of a dynasty named Vikrama who may well have been rajas of Indian or half Indian blood. Prome was overthrown, probably not long after A.D. 800, by internal dissensions among the tribes. The chief town in Burma, it was a port not far from the sea which in those days came farther north. Its pagodas, such as the Bawbawgyi, Payama and Payagyi, are of a curious type not found elsewhere. It is the most extensive site in Burma, larger than any city the Burmese ever built, possibly because the whole population dwelt inside the wall. The remains of this massive wall at Hmawza show that, where seven or eight villages now stand amid brushwood and rice-swamp, there was once a great and powerful city.

> When the P'iao king goes out in his palanquin, he lies on a couch of golden cord. For long distances he rides an elephant. He has several hundred women to wait on him. The wall of his city, built of greenish glazed tiles, is 160 *li*[1] round, with twelve gates and with pagodas at each of the four corners. The people live inside. Their house tiles are of lead and zinc, and they use the wood of the *nephelium litchi* [*kyetmauk*] as timber. They dislike taking life. They greet each other by clasping the arm with the hand. They know how to make astronomical calculations. They are Buddhists and have a hundred monasteries, with bricks of glass ware embellished with gold and silver vermilion, gay colours and red kino. The floor is painted and is covered with ornamented carpets. The king's residence is in like style. At seven years of age, the people cut their hair and enter a monastery; if at the age of twenty they have not grasped the

[1] The present *li* of 631 yards would make this 58 miles, but the *li* has varied greatly. The distance round the wall is actually 8½ miles, twice as much as Mandalay. Mr Taw Sein Ko at *RSASB* 1908 13 says, "The ruins consisting of earthen ramparts, walled enclosures, burial grounds, stone sculptures, and pagodas in all stages of decay, are found scattered within, roughly speaking, an area of 400 square miles, that is to say, within a distance of about 10 miles in the direction of the cardinal points from the Railway Station as the centre." But 10 miles to the east is across an old river bed (probably the old Irrawaddy), 10 miles to the west is across the Irrawaddy, the walls are quite clearly defined, and the area is 5·52 square miles.

doctrine, they return to lay estate. For clothes they use skirts made of cotton, for they hold that silk should not be worn as it involves the taking of life. On the head they wear gold-flowered hats with a blue net or bag set in pearls. In the king's palace are two bells, one of gold, the other of silver; when an enemy comes, they beat these bells, and burn incense to divine whether their fortune is good or evil. There is a huge white elephant-image a hundred feet high; litigants burn incense and kneel before the elephant, reflecting within themselves whether they be right or wrong, and then they retire. When there is any disaster or plague, the king kneels down before the elephant and blames himself.

They have no fetters. Criminals are flogged on the back with five bamboos bound together, receiving five blows for heavy, and three for light offences. Murder is punished with death. The land is suited to pulse, rice, and the millet-like grains. Sugar-cane grows as thick as a man's leg. There is no hemp or wheat. Gold and silver are used as money,[1] the shape of which is crescent-like; it is called têng-ch'ieh-t'o [dingadaw] and tsu-tan-t'o [sudandaw]. Having no grease for oil, they use wax and various scents for lighting. In trading with the neighbouring states they use porpoise [? skin], cotton, and rock-crystal and earthenware jars as barter. The women knot their hair on top of their heads and ornament it with strings of pearls; they wear a natural-tinted skirt and throw pieces of delicate silk over themselves; when walking they hold a fan, and the wives of great personages have four or five attendants at each side carrying fans. (Chronicles of the T'ang dynasty of China A.D. 618-905, chapter on "Southern Barbarians," at *Parker* "Burma, relations to China" 12 slightly amended.)

The eighteen chieftainships mentioned by the Chinese were probably in Central Burma and the Delta. In the third century the Khmer kingdom of Funan[2] held most of Indo-China outside Burma and included the present Tenasserim division among its feudatories. As for the north of Burma, the tribes there were dependent on Nanchao (Yünnan). The people of Nanchao, probably Shans, combined, in the middle of the eighth century, into a considerable state which defeated Chinese attempts at conquest until 1253. About 754 the Nanchao chief conquered the tribes of the upper Irrawaddy. In 800-2 two deputations of P'iao (Pyu), the latter of which was headed by their chief's son Shunant'o (?? Shwenandaw), accompanied a Nanchao mission to the court of China at Hsi-an-fu; there the Pyu retinue sang songs containing Sanskrit

[1] Until 1861 the Burmese had no coined money, see *IA* 1897-8 Temple "Currency and Coinage among the Burmese."

[2] *Aymonier*.

words and went through spelling dances, lining up in a pattern which read "Nanchao sends Holy Music"; the Emperor was quite amused and he bestowed minor honorary offices at court on Shunant'o and his father. But the secretary who drew up the patents gave vent to his private feelings in the following

POEM BY PO-CHÜ-I THE IMPERIAL SECRETARY ON THE OCCASION OF A BURMESE PWE AT THE CHINESE COURT A.D. 802.

Music from the land of P'iao, music from the land of P'iao!
Brought hither from the great ocean's south-west corner
Yung Ch'iang's son Shunant'o
Has come with an offering of southern tunes to fete the New Year.
Our Emperor has taken his seat in the courtyard of the Palace.
He does not press his cap strings to his ears, he is listening to you!
At the first blast of the jewelled shell their matted locks grow crisp.
At one blow from the copper gong their painted limbs leap.
Pearl streams glitter as they twist, as though the stars were shaken in the sky,
Flowery crowns nod and whirl, with the motion of dragon or snake.
When the dance was ended the king's son addressed our holy Monarch:
"My father desires to be your servant, beyond the realms of T'ang."
From left and right a shout of joy bursts from all the court:
"How far is spread the virtuous name of our All-Highest Lord!"
A moment later the whole Cabinet was assembled in the Chamber of State.
Here it submitted documents to the Throne, counselling the Sovran Lord
That such an occasion as an Emperor watching the P'iao presenting new tunes
Ought to be recorded in the state annals, to be handed down to future generations.
At that time there was an old farmer who hoed the earth and sang.
Secretly he sounded his Prince's heart, speaking quietly to himself:
"They say that you intend to exercise a wise and enlightened rule,
That you wish to move men's hearts towards bringing about complete peace.
Moving hearts is done from within, it cannot be done from without.
Complete peace comes from realities, not from mere names.
If the state be regarded as a human body, the state may be well ruled.
The Emperor is that body's mind, the people are its limbs.
If the limbs are ailing, the mind also will be ill at ease.
If the people are at peace, the Emperor will be happy.
But the people of this era Chêng Yüan are far from enjoying peace.
Although he listen to P'iao music, surely the Emperor must be sad?
Hearken, Lord! If the people of Chêng Yüan were healed,
Even if no music came from P'iao, the Emperor would be hailed as a saint."

Music of P'iao, in vain you raise your din.
Better were it that my Lord should listen to that peasant's humble words.

(Translation, sent me by Mr Arthur Waley, from Po Chü-i's works, British Museum Chinese supplementary catalogue 15315.d.2, the Japanese edition printed in 1618.)

In 808-9 the Nanchao chief styled himself P'iaohsin (Pyushin), "Lord of the Pyu." He cannot have had any authority over Prome, but he overshadowed Upper Burma to the extent that whenever he wanted slaves he could make a foray and carry off people, as in 832 when he deported 3,000 Pyu people to populate Yünnan Fu; and they took care to placate him, as in 858 when they presented him with a gold Buddha in gratitude for having helped them against raiders. Upper Burma tribes such as the Kachins seem to have furnished levies for his great attack on Hanoi in 863. Several northern towns have Shan names—Tagaung is Takawng "Drum Ferry," Mogaung is Mëngkawng "Drum Town." Pyusawti, the title of a traditional chief at Pagan, is Shan Chinese, and his five successors bear names formed in the same way as those of the Mêng dynasty 649-902 of Nanchao.[1] Probably Upper Burma was half Shan by race and under Nanchao influence. Such influence was non-cultural, for Nanchao was not a civilising centre, and her existence as a barrier state furnishes a reason, in addition to China's remoteness, for the absence of Chinese influence on Burma during these formative centuries.

After the fall of Prome (p. 12) its people migrated to Pagan merged with the local tribes, and thereafter were known as the Burmese. A cluster of nineteen villages,[2] Pagan developed, into a town which became the capital of all Burma from the eleventh to the thirteenth century. The situation is good, near the confluence of the Chindwin and Irrawaddy rivers, and it was probably here that a trade route from the Shan states joined one from Yünnan on their way to Assam; yet so arid a spot seems singularly unsuited for a capital, and to-day the soil could not feed the population of any considerable city. But riverine islands doubtless yielded fertile crops and there are reasons for believing the climate of the Upper Burma dry,

[1] See note "Nanchao" p. 312.
[2] *JBRS* 1911 Furnivall "Foundation of Pagan."

zone to have been humid and fertile.[1] It is difficult otherwise to account for the presence of forests which must have existed to provide fuel for the countless millions of pagoda bricks, for the tradition of the Myingyan folk that in past times they grew their own rice, and for mediæval inscriptions dedicating extensive rice fields in land at Pagan where now no rice could grow (p. 78).

To an early chief at Pagan, Popa Sawrahan 613-40, is attributed the introduction of the present Burmese era (Kacchapancha), starting in March 638. Siam uses it under the name Chulasakaraj. Doubtless it was drawn up by Hindu astrologers at one of the courts in Burma.[2] Popa Sawrahan's name suggests wizards and primitive beliefs at the volcanic peak of Popa, and perhaps it was about this time that the noble Mahagiri myth took its present shape—

> This is the story of Mahagiri, brother and sister. Nga Tin De, son of Nga Tin Daw blacksmith of Tagaung, was famous for his vast strength. It is said that once he wrenched even the tusk of a grown male elephant. When the Tagaung king heard of it he commanded his ministers saying "This man will rob my prosperity. Seize and do away with him!" So Nga Tin De fearing to lose his life ran away a far journey and lived in a deep jungle. And the king was afraid; so he took the young sister of Nga Tin De and raised her to be queen. Long after, the king said to the queen "Thy brother is a mighty man. Send for him straightway, and I will make him governor of a town." And Nga Tin De came, thinking "He hath raised my sister to be queen, and now he sendeth for me desiring me to enter his service." But the king had him seized by guile and bound to a *saga* tree [*Michelia Champaca*], and he made a great pile of wood and charcoal and caused the bellows to be blown. And the queen descended into the fire saying "Because of me, alas, my brother has died!" Men say that the king clutched her by her hair, but rescued only her head and face, for her body was burnt. After their death brother and sister became spirit brother and sister and dwelt in the *saga* tree. Any man horse buffalo or cow who entered so much as the shade of that *saga* tree, died. And when this verily befell, they dug up the *saga* tree from the root and floated it in the river Irrawaddy. Thus it reached Pagan; and they carved images of the spirit brother and sister and kept them on Popa Hill. And king, ministers and people visited them once a year. (*Hmannan* I. 211.)

[1] *Carey* 10, *JBRS* 1913 Mackenzie "Climate in Burmese History." Yet the Talaing inscriptions of Kyanzittha 1084-77 call Pagan *Tattadesa*, "torrid country."

[2] *JBRS* 1912 May Oung "Burmese Era."

They became the mightiest of *nat* spirits next to Thagyamin himself. Throughout Burmese history their seat on Popa was a delphic oracle, kings making pilgrimage there and submitting to them in matters of conscience.

Pagan was a backward hinterland compared with Prome or Thaton. Still, northern Indian influences not only came along the coast, leaving the Mahamuni[1] shrine in Akyab district, but also penetrated overland through Assam to Pagan, bringing, in the fifth century, Mahayanism and architecture of which the surviving witness is the lower structure of the Kyaukku Onhmin near Pagan.[2] To stand in this ancient refuge, looking up at the great stone vault, is to regret the supersession of north Indian influence, with its stonework and orderliness, by the Talaing brick and shoddy which swamped Burma after the eleventh century.

The Mahayanism thus introduced was of a low type; indeed Burmese chroniclers will not face the fact that it is Buddhism at all, and pass on with a few shocked references to "infidels." But the teaching of the Ari[3] priesthood, who held sway for many generations down to the eleventh century in Upper Burma, is distinctly recognisable as one of the developments of Tibetan Buddhism. They centred at Thamahti village a few miles south-east of Pagan and they fostered a *naga* snake cult in which a Buddha and his *sakti* wives figure. They were bearded, grew hair four fingers long, wore robes dyed blue-black in indigo, practised boxing, rode horses, went into battle, and drank intoxicants (p. 314).

> Now the farmer [Nyaung-u Saw-rahan 931-64] became king and was great in glory and power. At his cucumber-plantation he made a large and pleasant garden, and he wrought and kept a great image of Naga Dragon. He thought it good thus to make and worship the image of Naga because Naga was nobler than men and his power greater. Moreover he consulted the heretical Shin Ari regarding the Zigon pagodas in the kingdom of Yathepyi [Prome] and Thaton, and he built five pagodas—Pahto-gyi, Pahto-nge, Pahto-thamya, Thinlin-pahto, Seitti-pahto. In them he set up what were neither spirit images nor images of the Lord, and worshipped them with offerings of rice, curry and fermented drinks, night and morning. . . . The teaching of the Ari lords at Thamahti was in general adopted, and in the reign

[1] See note "Mahamuni" p. 313.

[2] *Forchammer* "Report on the Kyaukku temple."

[3] See note "Ari" p. 313.

of king Saw-rahan the king and the whole country held that teaching. . . . The Ari lords, in order that the people might believe their doctrine, made manuscripts to suit their purpose and placed them inside a *tha-hkut* tree [*Dolichandrone Rheedii, Seem.*], and when the tree became covered with scales and bark, they sought and seduced fit interpreters of dreams and made them read and publish the manuscripts found in the tree, so that the king and all the people misbelieved. . . . Now the kings of Pagan for many generations had been confirmed in false opinions, following the doctrine of the thirty Ari lords and their sixty thousand pupils who practised piety in Thamahti. It was the fashion of these Ari monks to reject the Law preached by the Lord and to form each severally their own opinions. They wrote books after their own heart and beguiled others into the snare. According to the law they preached, a man might take the life of another and evade the course of *karma* if he recited the formula of deprecation; nay, he might even kill his mother and his father and evade the course of *karma* if he recited the formula of deprecation. Such false and lawless doctrine they preached as true doctrine. Moreover kings and ministers, great and small, rich men and common people, whenever they celebrated the marriage of their children, had to send them to these teachers at nightfall, sending, as it was called, the flower of their virginity. Nor could they be married till they were set free early in the morning. If they were married without sending to the teachers the flower of their virginity, it is said that they were heavily punished by the king for breaking the custom. This sending of the flower of virginity meant an act of worship. (*Hmannan* I. 227, 204, 241.)

They did nothing for the people. They had pretensions to clerkly lore, with books of magic and a Mahayana canon in Sanskrit;[1] but they treated writing as a secret art with which to fake tree oracles. Pagan first became of importance in 849 when the chief, Pyinbya, enclosed it in a wall the remains of which still exist in the Sarabha Gate. The simplicity of the little state may be imagined from the manner in which Nyaung-u Sawrahan 931-64 came to succeed Theinhko—

This was the manner of king Theinhko's death. He rode abroad for sport in the forest, and being hungry he plucked and ate a cucumber in a farmer's field. And because he plucked it without telling him, the farmer struck him with the handle of a spade that he died. . . . Theinhko's horsebreaker came up and said "Ho, farmer, why strikest thou my lord?" He answered "Thy king hath plucked and eaten my cucumber. Did I not well to strike him?" And the horsebreaker spake wheedling words saying "Farmer, he who slayeth a king becometh a king." But the farmer said "I will not be king. Have not my cucumbers grown in my garden like pups sucking milk?" Then

[1] *Epigraphia Birmanica* I. i. 7.

spake the horsebreaker with wheedling words "Farmer, not only shalt thou have thy cucumbers, but also thou shalt flourish as a king. To be a king is exceeding glorious. Verily kings have fine raiment, victuals in abundance, gold, silver, elephants and horses, buffaloes, oxen, goats, pigs, paddy and rice!" So at last the farmer consented and followed him. And the horsebreaker, letting no man know, brought the farmer within the palace and told the queen all, and she praised him for his wisdom. And the queen, fearing lest the country and villages be cast into turmoil, let none come in or go out, saying "The king's body is not whole." And she instructed the farmer and made him bathe in warm water and cold, and rub himself with bath powders to remove all dirt and disease. . . . And on the day before the seventh day she sent causing a brazen gong to sound throughout the kingdom saying "To-morrow the king walks abroad. Enter, all ministers both high and low. Let none be absent." So at dawn all ministers and captains went up to the palace. And when they were met, the door of the throne was suddenly opened, and the ministers and the followers raised hands and did obeisance. (*Hmannan* I. 225, see note "Cucumber King" p. 315.)

Nyaung-u Sawrahan was overthrown by a pretender Kunhsaw Kyaunghpyu who in his turn was overthrown by Nyaung-u Sawrahan's two sons—they enticed him to a new monastery of theirs on the pretext of invoking his blessing, and then forced him to take the robe. He lived in the monastery with his wife and their son Anawrahta. Of the usurping brothers, Kyiso[1] was accidentally killed with an arrow while hunting *thamin* stag in his favourite haunt, Bangyi in Monyua district; Anawrahta raised a following at Popa Hill, challenged the surviving brother Sokka-te to single combat, slew him at Myinkaba near Pagan, and seized the throne in 1044. Burmese history now begins to be less conjectural.

[1] A mighty hunter, he became the Yomashin Mingaung Nat spirit, *Temple* 50. Kunhsaw Kyaungbpyu became the Htihpyusaung Nat, *IA* 1906 Temple "A native account of the Thirty-Seven Nats" 225.

CHAPTER II

THE KINGDOM OF PAGAN OR THE DYNASTY OF THE TEMPLE BUILDERS 1044-1287

THE KINGDOM OF PAGAN 1044-1287 A.D.

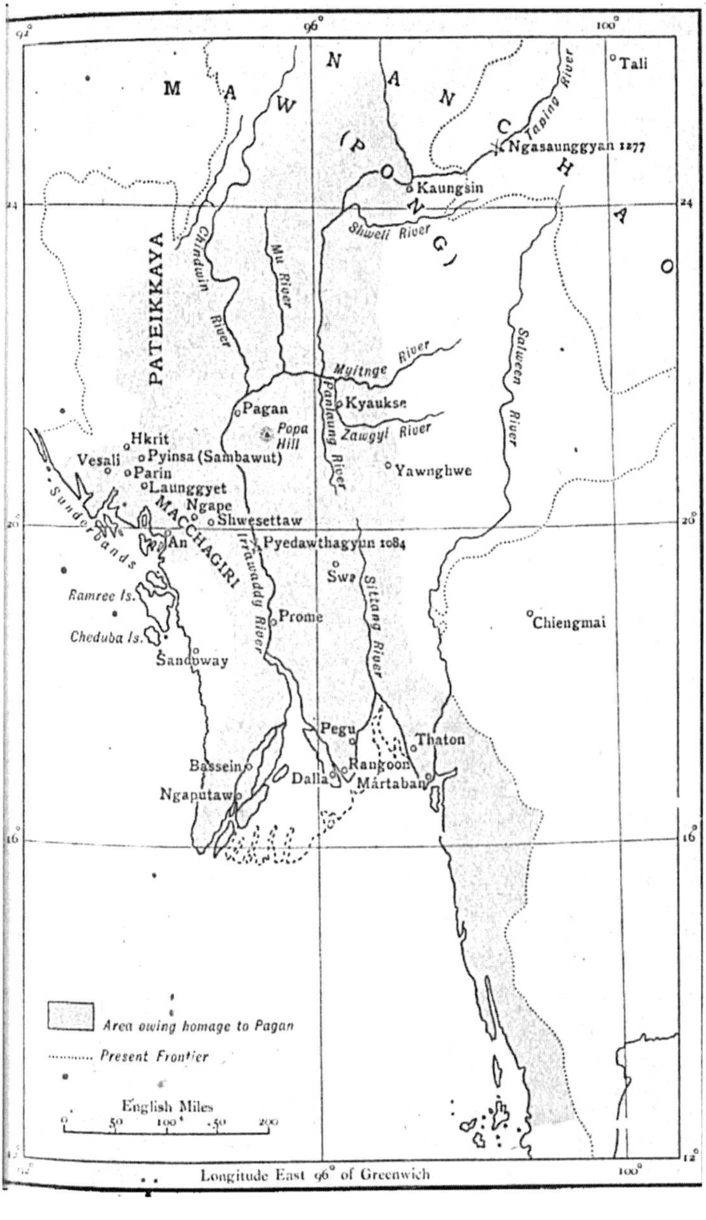

Emery Walker Ltd. sc.

Longmans, Green & Co. London, New York, Toronto, Bombay, Calcutta & Madras.

CHAPTER II

THE KINGDOM OF PAGAN OR THE DYNASTY OF THE TEMPLE BUILDERS 1044-1287

ANAWRAHTA 1044-77. His first act was to offer the throne to his father and, when he refused it, to invest him with kingly state; the old man lived as a royal monk for four more years, and his women waited on him in his monastery. Anawrahta's sleep was troubled for months with remorse at the slaying of his foster-brother, Sokka-te, until Thagyamin, the King of the Spirits, appeared to him in a dream saying "O king, if thou desirest to mitigate thine evil deed in sinning against thine elder brother, build many pagodas, caves, monasteries, and rest houses, and share the merit with thine elder brother. Devise thou many wells, ponds, dams and ditches, fields and canals, and share the merit with thine elder brother."[1]

Anawrahta already had a wife and their son was Sawlu. But now, being king, he desired greater state and sent a lord to search the world for a princess to be his bride. The lord found a fitting princess, Panchakalyani, at Vesali in the Indian land (p. 316). Her father consented and sent her away on a palanquin with eighty handmaidens. On the return journey the lord made love to her and then, to remove the witnesses of his guilt, scattered her retinue in remote villages. He waited discreetly until after her marriage with Anawrahta and then worked on his feelings by raising doubts as to whether she could be a genuine princess. Anawrahta saw in the unhappy girl's lack of retinue proof that she was spurious, and banished her to the quiet Sagaing countryside where, at

[1] *Hmannan* I. 234. Cf. Mass for the Dead, and the doctrine that any member of the Communion of Saints can pray that the merit of his good deeds may be transferred to any other member, drawing on the common Treasury of Merit. Another parallel—with this passage in an inscription at Pagan, year 1408 (*Tun Nyein* 34) "Poison cannot be said to be very destructive to life, because it can kill only one; but the poison of the monkhood can destroy all monks and laymen and send them to the *avici* hell," compare Bellarmine's justification of persecution (De Laicis III. xxi. 22) "Heretics do more mischief than any pirate or brigand, because they slay souls."

Payeinma on the banks of the Chindwin river, she gave birth to a son, Kyanzittha. Scandal said that Kyanzittha's father was not the king but the lord who went to Vesali. He was brought up under a cloud, and indeed narrowly escaped death at the hands of the king who, hearing from soothsayers that a child was born who should become king, thrice ordered a massacre of children (p. 316): the first time of over seven thousand in the womb, the second time of over six thousand sucklings, the third time of five thousand children of the age of cowboys—hence the name Kyanzittha, "he who survived the search." His youth was passed at a monastery, but Anawrahta, learning that he should be king only in the second generation, relented and employed him as a soldier.

Anawrahta's principality was a small area which remained till the end the homeland of the kings, where their writ always ran. It was barely 200 miles from north to south and less than 80 from east to west, comprising roughly the present districts of Mandalay, Meiktila, Myingyan, Kyaukse, Yamethin, Magwe, Sagaing and Katha east of the Irrawaddy, and the riverine portions of Pakokku and Minbu. To the north lay Nanchao, to the east hills uninhabited save by a few Shans, to the south and west the Pyus, and farther south still the Talaings.

Anawrahta graded every townlet and village according to the levy it could raise, and gathered round him a band of chosen henchmen. Kyanzittha when he grew to manhood, with Nyaung-uhpi the great swimmer of Nyaung-u in Myingyan district, Nga Htwe Yu a toddy climber of Myinmu in Sagaing district, Nga Lon Letpe a ploughman near Popa Hill in Myingyan district—these were the paladins who rode at the head of his levies. Byatta the swift runner was a Mahomedan[1] shipwrecked at Thaton whose chief Manuha oppressed him so that he fled to Pagan. Shwepyingyi and Shwepyinnge were the two warrior sons born of Byatta's secret love in the forest at Popa Hill whither he ran daily on magic feet to gather fresh *saga* flowers for the court.

Anawrahta repaired Meiktila lake, and visited the eastern hills, where he founded the Bawrithat pagoda near Yawnghwe

[1] Perhaps an Arab seaman. See note "Byatta" p. 317.

and received the homage of the nearer Shans. The wild scenery of the passes wrought on his feelings as he returned down the Panlaung river. He had seen Shan irrigation, and now as he stood on the summit of Pyetkaywe Hill (Kayut-taung), the sight of the waters swirling at the foot of the Shan hills, suggested a work of merit which would atone for the death of his foster-brother Sokka-te; and he constructed the irrigation system which still enriches Kyaukse. When beginning the work, he dreamt[1] one night of three snakes. The southern snake he cut into four—signifying the four weirs and canals (Kinda, Ngalaingzin, Pyaungbya, Kume) which he built on the southern river, the Panlaung. The middle snake he cut into three—signifying the three weirs and canals (Nwadet, Kunhse, Nga Pyaung) which he built on the middle river, the Zawgyi. The northern snake eluded him without a wound—and all his efforts failed on the northern river, the Myitnge, which is still uncontrolled.

The work, supervised by the king himself, lasted three years and there were many casualties from fever. When, according to custom, a human victim was about to be taken for each weir, one of Anawrahta's queens, sister to a Shan chief, asked whether her death would not suffice for all. So she was slain, and became the guardian spirit of the weirs. Her brother, the chief of Myogyi (Baw in the Myelat), was summoned to do homage. Sooner than drag his people into war, he set out for court; but on the way, horror overcame him, and when he reached the whirlpool in the Zawgyi river, where it enters Burma, he threw himself in and was drowned. To-day you can see little images of the brother and sister in many a way-side shrine.[2]

Anawrahta peopled the area with villages which, under royal officers, served the canals; known as Ledwin, "*the* rice country," it became the granary, the economic key of the north country. History shows that he who gained control of Kyaukse became king-maker in Upper Burma.

Shin Arahan, son of a Thaton Brahman, came to Pagan in

[1] *Ko Hkayaing Thamaing*. *GUB* II. i. 504 gives a variant. See note "Burmese irrigation" p. 318.

[2] *Grant Brown* "The Lady of the Weir" and his "Pre-Buddhist religion of the Burmese." *GUB* II. i 517 gives a variant. See note "Myosade" p. 320.

1056. He was a Talaing monk of the Theravada school of southern Buddhism, who burned to evangelise the heathen land of Upper Burma. He dwelt in a solitary hermitage in a glade near Pagan, until one day a woodman, wondering what this strange being in a yellow robe might be, led him away to court. Anawrahta saw him and realised that here was one whose purity and restrained power were in utter contrast with the leering vacuity of the corpulent Aris. He told him to be seated, and to all men's wonder, Shin Arahan seated himself on the throne. Anawrahta asked "Master, of what race art thou? Whence comest thou? Whose doctrine dost thou follow?" Shin Arahan told him and Anawrahta entreated saying "My lord, teach me somewhat, yea, though it be a little, of the law preached by the Lord, the Master." Before long, the apostle's first step was accomplished: he had won authority to his side.

Anawrahta had long waited for a helper; he had him now, and the power of the Aris was broken. The new thought filtered down to the countryside, bringing release from bondage, for men knew that the court would no longer heed if they ceased to yield their children to the priests. Arahan sent for helpers, and soon missionaries began to arrive from Thaton. The offerings of strong drink vanished and, finding his livelihood gone, many an Ari turned villager and worked for his bread; some were compelled by the king to become scavengers, others conformed to the new fashion. But the greater men, who had wielded power so long, were not minded to yield without a struggle, and fearing for Shin Arahan's life, Anawrahta banished them in numbers; many went to the Shan States, brawling[1] with the royal guards who convoyed them.

Yet they did not die out; although no longer able to impose their yoke on others, they lingered here and there, especially at Popa Hill and at Thamahti near Pagan. Even Shin Arahan in extreme old age went to Tenasserim to fetch a relic for the Nandaminnya chapel built near Pagan just after 1112; and the Nandaminnya, like its neighbour the Payathonzu,

[1] Arizingagamyogyi tradition at Thabyewa in Meiktila district. Cf. also traditions in Kyaukse district concerning Sheinkyaw west of Paleik, Yuabo east of Mekkaya, and Minhla reservoir on the Minye canal.

is covered with frescoes which are patently Ari. They are probably the best of such frescoes as exist in Burma, and their technique is of a Nepalese or north Bengali type.

Shin Arahan had brought no sacred books, for writing was still a rare gift. His mission could not thrive without them, and he urged Anawrahta to procure copies from Thaton where there were thirty complete sets of the Tripitaka, the Three Scriptures. Envoys were sent but returned with an insulting refusal. Stung to anger, Anawrahta marched on Thaton with all his men. Kyanzittha, though still in his early teens, rode with the levies. They went down the river, foot, horse, and elephants. The land forces crossed the Sittang river, and the boats went by the Hlaing river and along the coast. Thaton was decaying but any walled town was impregnable save to starvation, and the Burmese had to undertake a three months' siege; moreover, the town was guarded by the spirit of a dead Indian brave and fell only after Anawrahta had exhumed his remains and cast them into the sea.[1]

'Now the king of Arimaddanapura [Pagan] mustered his army and rode his horse . . . and came to the city of Thaton in the land of Thudammawadi. He compassed it round about and beleaguered it for three months straitly. And those within could get neither food nor drink, and they were exceedingly afamished, and so great was their hunger that they ate one another; and many perished thereby. The four warriors [Kyanzittha, Nyaung-uhpi, Nga Htwe Yu, Nga Lon Letpe] entered the city on their flying horses, and slew many. Then the folk could no longer abide such sufferings; and on the morning of Monday the eleventh waxing of Nayon, the moon being in the mansion of Visakha, in the year 42, king Manuha rendered himself. And the king of Arimaddanapura, having possession of king Manuha, took away the saintly monks, who were full of learning and piety; he took away the monks who knew the Three Scriptures and the Four Books of Divination . . . he took them all to the land of Arimaddana. He chained king Manuha with golden chains and led him captive. From that time henceforth Thaton was desolate, but Pagan that is called Arimaddana flourished like unto a heavenly city.' (*Paklat Talaing Chronicle.*)

In the beginning, in the lifetime of the Lord, Thiharaja was king of Thaton. From Thiharaja to Manuha there were eight and forty kings in Thaton, famous and mighty kings, and they kept the faith of our Lord God; and their people followed the command of

[1] See note "Byatta" p. 317.

> almsgiving and all other commands of righteousness, and the land was glad and flourished like unto a heavenly city. And Manuha, this great king of so high and joyous and excellent a realm, this lord of thirty-two white elephants, merely because he answered king Anawrahta's messengers in discourteous wise, came to utter destruction, he himself and all the people that were his. (*Hmannan* I. 251.)

This is the end of Thaton as a royal city, and she could not recover her prosperity by sea trade because the receding coast-line left her high and dry. Anawrahta rode back in triumph to Pagan. Like some great glittering snake the victorious host uncurled its long length and set out through the Delta creeks with a captive chief and court, all the monks, and an entire population,[1] numbering 30,000; but the pride of the Burmese was Manuha's thirty-two white elephants, each laden with scriptures and relics. On all sides chieftains hastened to make submission to the new power; he razed the walls of Prome and stripped its pagodas of the relics enshrined since the days of the traditional chief, Duttapaung—he would have no rival fortress, he would teach the Pyus to look to Pagan alone for religion.[2]

After arriving at Pagan, Manuha was at first treated with consideration. At Myinkaba, south of the city, he built the Nanpaya; it contains his throne room and is of good stone-work with interesting bas-reliefs in which Hindu deities are so prominent as to leave no room for doubt that Thaton Buddhism was largely Hindu. Feeling anxious as to his future, he looked at the great jewelled ring[3] on his finger and thought "It will not be mine for long. They will take this too when they like." So he sold it to a Myinkaba merchant for six cartloads of silver which he spent in building the Manuha temple there. Soon after, his foreboding came true, for Anawrahta dedicated him and his family as slaves to the Shwezigon pagoda, thus rendering them outcaste for ever. To this day the headman of Nyaung-u West village, close under the pagoda, is believed by his followers to be of Manuha's line and is treated with unusual deference (p. 35[7]).

The influx of Thaton captives, many of them craftsmen,

[1] See note "List of Captives" p. 321.

[2] See note "Cholas in the Delta" p. 322.

[3] Manuha temple inscription, *Inscriptions* 1913 7. One of his family died of leprosy and became Nyaungyin Nat, the leper spirit, see *Temple* 53.

helped to civilise the north, and there were three immediate results. Firstly, Shin Arahan gained many helpers from the Thaton clergy, and got all the scriptures he wanted, housing them in the Tripitakataik library building which is still to be seen at Pagan. Secondly, Pali supersedes Sanskrit as the normal language of sacred books, and Hinayana teaching supersedes Northern Buddhism. Thirdly, the Burmese adopted the Talaing alphabet and for the first time wrote their language —the earliest inscription[1] in Burmese is dated 1058, the year after the conquest. But none of the great temples of Pagan were built till a generation later (p. 40), and it was not the actual captives so much as the intercourse with the outer world given by the conquest which civilised Upper Burma.

Anawrahta's next conquest was north Arakan (p. 138). He marched over the pass from Ngape in Minbu district to An in Kyaukpyu and subjected the prince, whose capital was at Pyinsa in Akyab district. He failed to bring home the ponderous Mahamuni image, probably because he had not sufficient men to furnish relays and to clear a proper road; he contented himself with taking away the gold and silver vessels of the shrine, burying its magical figures and uprooting its magical trees, lest the charms should aid an Arakanese raid into Burma.[2]

He had received homage from several of the nearer Shan chiefs, but their allegiance was nominal and he had to establish forty-three outposts along the eastern foot-hills; thirty-three still exist as villages, or at least as tract names:—

Bhamo	*Kyaukse*
Kaungton	Mekkaya
Kaungsin	Ta On
Shwegu	Myinsaing
Katha	Myittha
Yinhke	*Meiktila*
Moda	Hlaingdet
Katha	Thagaya
Htigyaing	Nyaungyan

[1] *Inscriptions* 1913 1. There are earlier ones in Burmese, but this is original, whereas they are copies and their dates are miscopied.

[2] *JBRS* 1912 Chan Htwan Oung "The Mahamuni Shrine," *RSASB* 1918 12. The order of events in Anawrahta's reign is uncertain, no dates being given for the Kyaukse canals or the Nanchao visit. San Shwe Bu at *RSASB* 1919 56 assigns the conquest of Arakan to 1057.

Mogok

Myadaung
Tagaung
Hinthamaw
Kyanhnyat
Sampanago

Mandalay

Singu
Konthaya
Magwetaya
Yenantha
Sonmyo
Madaya

Mandalay—concld.

Thetkegyin
Wayindok
Taungbyon
Myodin

Yamethin

Shwemyo

Toungoo

Myohla
Kelin
Swa.

He now made some of those curious expeditions which recur throughout Burmese history, roving about with an armed host to pray or prey as opportunity offered. Thus he visited "the Indian land of Bengal," perhaps Chittagong, and planted magical images of men there.[1]

Again, taking his force by land and river, he advanced beyond what is now Bhamo and entered the Nanchao kingdom. The Utibwa[2] of Nanchao shut the gates of his capital, Tali, against this strange visitor, and Anawrahta sat down outside. After a long pause, the two potentates exchanged presents and conversed amicably. The Burmese went sight-seeing and conversed with the Nanchao primate, asking questions about the great brazen image, a fathom square, of a god called Sandi; the primate explained, "We have two religions, one of this world, the other of the next world. For this life we worship the idol Sandi; for the next life we worship Buddha." But although the Burmese say they made an overwhelming impression on Nanchao, they could not induce the Utibwa to give up a Buddha tooth of which he was the proud possessor, and they had to rest content with a jade image which had come into contact with the tooth. With this trophy Anawrahta returned home, visiting the Shan states on the way and receiving

[1] See note "Byatta" p. 317.

[2] Utibwa is the name by which the Burmese knew the ruler of Yünnan or China, two areas which they confused. It was actually one of the official t[illegible] the Nanchao kings and is from *udi* = (Pali) *udaya* = rising sun + *bwa* (as in *sawbwa*) = chief, i.e. "King of the East." *BEFEO* 1904 Pelliot "Deux Itinéraires" 162-4 takes the title to indicate Hindu influence, through Burma, on Nanchao.

the homage of their chiefs. Maw,[1] the largest state, presented a daughter Sawmunhla who had a romantic career as Anawrahta's consort, being driven into exile by Burmese rivals who hated her as a Shan witch. She built the Shwezayan pagoda in Mandalay district and her story is still acted on the stage.

He returned home down the Irrawaddy on a barge of barbaric splendour. While halting near Wayindok in Mandalay district, he built the Taungbyon pagoda and put his henchmen Shwepyingyi and Shwepyinnge to a cruel death because they were remiss in bringing each a brick, as the others did, for the construction of the pagoda. They are now spirits, worshipped at the annual festival there, and the religion of their father (p. 24) is indicated by the fact that nobody connected with the shrine will touch pork.[2]

In none of the great events of the reign is mention made of Anawrahta's son Sawlu who, born in 1048, wasted his days with a favourite, Yamàn, the son of his wet nurse. Yaman enjoyed the revenues of Dalla and, being blind in one eye, was called Yamankan.[3]

Lao Shans from the direction of Chiengmai raided Pegu. The people asked for help, and the king sent Kyanzittha with a small body of men. Seeing how few they were, the people clamoured saying they would not be properly protected. But the detachment were picked Indians, not the ordinary levy; Indians are several times mentioned among Anawrahta's palace troops[4] but their origin and status is not given. Kyanzittha and his men dazzled the people of Pegu by wondrous feats at practice among the cucumber beds, and then defeated the raiders who flung away their arms and fled, leaving their four leaders to be taken prisoner. After this Kyanzittha was a hero among the Talaings. They sent him home with presents for the king—four hair relics in a golden casket, a *chinthe* gryphon image, and the lady Hkin U, daughter of the lord of Pegu. She was borne in a curtained litter. Kyanzittha rode at her

[1] See note "Pong and Koshanpye" p. 322.

[2] *GUB* I. ii. 23 and II. ii. 105; *Grant Brown* "The Taungbyon Festival" Stewart at *Ridgeway* 387.

[3] The name is, with equal probability, Rahman Khan.

[4] See note "The Guards" p. 323.

side, and during the long journey they fell in love with each other so violently that the matter had to be reported to Anawrahta.

That was the end of Kyanzittha's career under the great king. He was brought bound into the presence and Anawrahta taunted him for a time until, his anger rising, he hurled his fairy spear Areindama. But Kyanzittha's hour was not yet come. The spear missed, grazing his skin and severing the ropes which bound him. He picked it up and fled from the presence never to return. Sawlu and Yamankan, rejoicing in their rival's downfall, joined in the persecution. His flight over hill and dale still forms a favourite subject on the stage. At one time he was fain to earn his living by tending horses, and finally he found rest at Kyaungbyu (? in Sagaing district); here he wandered into a monastery garden to pluck lime fruit and rest in the heat of the day; Thambula the monk's niece saw him and with her he lived in happy obscurity for the remaining years of the reign.

Ceylon was now undergoing one of its periodic invasions from the Indian mainland during which Buddhism suffered severely from Hindu persecution. Vijaya Bahu I. king of Ceylon sent ships to ask Anawrahta for aid against the Cholas of Madras;[1] but finally he drove them out himself and in 1071, to repair their ravages on religion, he asked Anawrahta for scriptures and monks, since there were so few monks left that it was hard to convene a chapter (p. 56) and make valid ordinations. Anawrahta gladly sent the monks and scriptures, and added a white elephant as a present for the king of Ceylon; in return he asked for the Buddha Tooth of which Ceylon is the proud possessor. His envoys failed to get the tooth but were given a duplicate, for Buddha's teeth possessed the faculty of miraculously reproducing themselves in order to cope with the needs of a growing religion. The duplicate was placed in a jewelled casket and was taken on board ship. The ship

[1] Vijaya Bahu I.'s regnal years 1065-1120 are yet another blow at the traditional Burmese chronology for the eleventh to thirteenth centuries, e.g. *Hmannan* assigns his contemporary Anawrahta to 1017-59; but they tally with Jatapon and with the Myazedi inscription (p. 43). *Müller* 61 shows that the date of Vijaya Bahu's request for monks was 1071 or just after. His request for troops was fruitless and Anawrahta sent only costly stuffs instead of men. See *Hmannan* I. 264, Mahavamsa LVIII. 8 and LV. 4.

crossed the seas and came up the Irrawaddy to Lawkananda, the landing place three miles below Pagan, where the whole countryside came out to meet it. Anawrahta himself waded into the river up to the neck and bore the casket on his head in solemn procession to its shrine.

His chief monument, the Shwezigon pagoda, begun in 1059 and still unfinished at his death, is a solid pagoda of the kind so common all over Burma; yet it attracts worshippers daily while the finer temples built by his successors are deserted. Its popularity is due to the exceptional sanctity of the relics (Buddha's collar-bone, his frontlet bone from Prome, and his tooth from Ceylon), and to the shrines of the entire pantheon of the Thirty Seven Nat spirits who, as it were, have come circling round in homage to those relics. If anyone doubts the debt Burma owes to Buddhism, or wishes to see what she would have been without it, let him wander here and contemplate these barbarous images of the heathen gods. Asked why he allowed them, Anawrahta said "Men will not come for the sake of the new faith. Let them come for their old gods and gradually they will be won over."[1]

The site of the Shwezigon was chosen by setting the tooth in a jewelled *pyatthat* shrine on a white elephant and letting the animal roam; where he rested was chosen as the site. By the same method, sites were chosen for the Tuywin Hill and Lawkananda pagodas in Myingyan district, the Tankyi Hill pagoda in Pakokku district, and the Pyetkaywe in Kyaukse district; all these contain Buddha teeth which, in answer to Anawrahta's prayer, were miraculously reproduced from the Ceylon tooth. For the hair relics presented by Pegu he built the Shwehsandaw (Mahapeinne) south of Pagan. Farther afield he built other pagodas such as Shweyinhmyaw, Shwegu, Shwezigon, in Meiktila district.

While in camp[2] in 1077 he was warned by his soothsayers that he would die before reaching home. He cast them into fetters. He reached Pagan and was actually entering the Sarabha Gate when a hunter came with news that a wild buffalo was terrorising Myitche in Pakokku district. He turned back and crossed the river to Myitche. There he was

[1] Oral tradition.

[2] The spot is marked by the Palinbo pagoda in Kyaukse district.

gored to death by the buffalo while his followers fled; his body was never recovered from the jungle.

The first king, as apart from chieftains, to appear in Burma, Anawrahta has passed into legend and many an institution is fathered on him. Bricks bearing his "seal," a Sanskrit text, have been found as far apart as Paunglin in Minbu district and Twante west of Rangoon.[1] His portrait in the chronicles is shadowy and conventionalised, but he must have been a great character. In a single lifetime he established true religion and expanded a petty chieftainship into what was, if not a kingdom, at least an overlordship comprising the main portion of what is now Burma—the Irrawaddy valley from Bhamo to the sea, the nearer Shans on both sides, north Arakan, and north Tenasserim (pp. 44, 57).

SAWLU 1077-84 on ascending the throne married[2] his father Anawrahta's Talaing queen Hkin U and recalled Kyanzittha from banishment. Kyanzittha heard the summons gladly and rode away leaving Thambula a ring and saying "If thy child be a girl, spend this ring on her nurture; but if it be a boy, bring ring and child to me." But he did not stay long at court and was soon banished again for renewing his old intimacy with Hkin U; this time he was sent to Dalla near Rangoon. Sawlu did not continue work on the Shwezigon but built two pagodas called Shwesawlu, one at Myogyi in Monyua district, the other at Paunglin in Minbu district.

> He gave the town of Pegu to Yamankan. One day he played at dice with Yamankan, and Yamankan won and rose up and clapped his elbows. Said king Sawlu, "Thou hast won a mere game of dice, dost thou arise and clap thine elbows? If thou art a man, rebel with thy fief of Pegu!" "In sooth?" asked Yamankan. "We kings," quoth the king, "Should we utter aught but sooth?" Now Yamankan had been plotting already, and he returned to Pegu. (*Hmannan* I. 278.)

Before long he was back again, but this time it was at the head of his Talaings. Sawlu recalled Kyanzittha and gave him the

[1] *RSASB* 1906 10, 1912 19, 1915 15.
[2] See note "Married his father's queen" p. 324.

command. They marched south and halted at Myingun in Magwe district where the Shwenanbauk pagoda marks the site of Sawlu's royal camp. Yamankan lay at Pyedawthagyun just below Minhla in Thayetmyo district, on a stockaded island with water on three sides and heavy mud on the fourth and west side. They marched on him. Kyanzittha arrived at sunset and decided that the position was too strong to be attacked.[1] Sawlu, arriving a little later, was furious at the delay and would not listen to the argument that it would be better to wait till Yamankan moved towards the capital, and then fall on his line of march. They attacked at once. Yamankan had erected dummy elephants and soldiers in the most treacherous part of the marsh. The Burmese advanced in the moon-light to the beat of drum, attacking from east and west. Coming in open boats, or sticking in the mud, they suffered severely from the missiles of the Talaings who fought under cover. Sawlu fought at the head of a thousand men with gilded helms and shields. He made no headway. Then, catching sight of a richly caparisoned dummy elephant in the dim light, he mistook it for Yamankan and rode madly up to it. He never came within sixty feet, for his own elephant stuck in the mud while his followers were driven off. Only such of the Burmese as were fortunate escaped.

Sawlu took refuge in a hollow banyan tree and was captured through his own act: being famished he had to beg a woodcutter for food, and in exchange gave his royal ring asking the man to tell nobody. The man showed the ring to every one asking how much it was worth. The Talaings suspected that Sawlu could not be far away, for his elephant was in their hands; they now seized the ring and submitted it to Yamankan who recognised it at a glance. The woodcutter at first refused to say anything but told all he knew when they put him to torture.

As for Kyanzittha, he turned away with rage in his heart at the stupid defeat, crossed the Irrawaddy to Taunghkwin in Magwe district, and rode unattended the sixty-five miles to Pagan in a single night. Behind him lay death and disaster, before him lay complete uncertainty, for a defeated prince usually found his city gates closed against him. He reached

[1] *Pagan Yazawinthit.*

the moat in daylight, anxiously scanning the walls to see what welcome awaited him. The people saw that he was alone, but they knew their man, and the gates rolled open. The ministers met hurriedly. All guessed that the king must be dead. They offered Kyanzittha the crown. But he was obdurate in refusal, saying "Our Lord the King lives yet." The Talaing horde poured on and camped at Myinkaba a mile south of the city.

Kyanzittha determined to rescue the king. He entered the enemy camp at night and found Sawlu. Seated on Kyanzittha's shoulders and well on the way to safety, Sawlu reflected "My father harmed this man, and I also have harmed him. Belike he is stealing me to kill me. Rather will I trust Yamankan, who sucked the same breasts with me as a child. He at least will do me no harm." So he called out "Kyanzittha is stealing me!" The Talaings came hurrying up. Kyanzittha, exclaiming "Then die, thou fool, die the death of a dog at the hands of these Talaing scum!" flung him down and ran for dear life. The nearest way to safety lay in the Irrawaddy. He plunged in and swam out into the darkness. The river at this point is a mile broad even in the dry weather. He could see nothing and was well-nigh exhausted when he heard a *myit-htwe*[1] bird cry on an island. Thus guided, he reached safety, seized a fisherman's canoe, paddled across to the Pakokku bank and rested at Aungtha. His return was cut off, for the Talaings were all round the city. He therefore fled north, crossed the Chindwin near Kyahkat and Waya, turned east, and finally reached Htihlaing (Wundwin) in Meiktila district; but before he was come there Yamankan had executed Sawlu.

KYANZITTHA 1084-1112 though a fugitive became king by the death of Sawlu, for the offer of the court still held good. Yamankan summoned Pagan to surrender but the people refused saying "There cannot be two buffaloes in one wallow. Settle with Kyanzittha before you treat with

[1] *Esacus recurvirostris*, the great stone plover.

us." Unable to do anything against a walled town which his men were too few to blockade, Yamankan drifted north and stockaded himself in the locality where Ava was subsequently built.

Meanwhile men rallied round Kyanzittha so that soon he had a force which required for billets all the eleven villages of Ledwin, the Kyaukse rice area; it was his natural base, for it must have been the most prosperous and thickly populated region in Upper Burma. He called in Shin Popa, a wizard of Htihlaing, who had studied at Chiengmai[1] and was probably an Ari. Shin Popa moved among the levies, reciting incantations and inscribing magical signs of the sun and moon on the elephants' heads, on the horses' withers, and on the warriors' spears and shields.

When all was ready, Kyanzittha marshalled his men and set out for Pagan. The news that he was present in person spread dismay among the Talaings marching eastward to bar his road; they remembered his exploit against the Laos—he had been with them then, he was against them now. They were beginning to tire of the long separation from their fields and families. Kyanzittha left them little time. He had the choosing of his own measures now, and was no longer thwarted by incompetents like Sawlu; his men burned to avenge Pyedawthagyun and free their homes, broke the Talaings at the first rush, and sent them racing back to their stockade. Kyanzittha made it untenable, and they retreated to Myinkaba, but here again he gave them no breathing space and pressed on the attack. This time the Talaings did not wait; saying "Kyanzittha will eat our flesh," they fled before he could bring them to battle. Blazing with gold and gems, Yamankan's barge sped down the Irrawaddy; close to the bank at Yuatha in Myingyan district, he heard the strange call of a bird in a tree, put his head out of the window to look, and fell back dead with an arrow through the eye, for the call was mimicry from the king's archer Nga Singu who had hidden himself in the branches of a *yethahpan* tree.[2]

Thus ended the Talaing attempt to shake the Pagan

[1] *Pagan Yazawinthit.*

[2] *Ficus glomerata*, one of the *Moraceae*, the red swamp fig-tree. Singu in Mandalay district was the archer's home.

monarchy, and after many wanderings Kyanzittha came into his own at last. To share his gladness were Abeyadana who had married him as a young captain, with their daughter Shwe-einthi; Hkindan the bride he had recently taken when campaigning with her father, his right-hand man the Htihlaing *myothugyi;* and Hkin U, whom he now hastened to marry. He had twice endured exile because of her, and she now became queen to the third monarch in succession.

He was crowned[1] according to the great ritual in the pavilion of the Lion Throne. Shin Arahan the primate led him by the hand, maidens of noble birth bore the holy water, the coronation exhortations were uttered, the white umbrella was held over him, he was fanned with the yaktail, on his head was set the crown, the sword of state was slung to his side, and the golden sandals were bound to his feet. He who had been an outlaw was now king of them all by divine right of birth and the still diviner right of proved capacity. He built a new palace to replace the barbaric wreck which had served Anawrahta, and he set up a series of inscriptions some of which rank as literature—

> With loving kindness . . . shall king Kyanzittha wipe away the tears of those who are parted from their trusty friends . . . his people shall be unto him as a child to its mother's bosom . . . he shall soften the hearts of those who intend evil . . . he shall exhort to speak good those who speak evil. With wisdom, which is even as a hand, shall king Kyanzittha draw open the bar of the Gate of Heaven, which is made of gold and wrought with gems. Kings' daughters, fragrant with the fragrance of jasmine flowers, splendid with the splendour of Alambusa, spouse of king In, shall wait upon him. Kings' daughters from seven cities, adorned with gems of divers kinds, shall wait on him, bearing white umbrellas. King Kyanzittha shall sit upon a throne of gold adorned with gems, and he shall enjoy the splendour of royalty. . . . He shall offer treasures of three kinds, with images in a gold reliquary, like a lamp that glows; so brightly shall it shine. (The great Talaing inscription of the Shwezigon pagoda, Pagan, *Epigraphia Birmanica* I. ii 90.)

The language of most of his epigraphs is Talaing, doubtless because scribes were as yet commoner among the Talaings than among the Burmese; he kept a Talaing scholar at court.[2]

[1] See notes "Coronation and Palace" and "Primate" pp. 325, 326.
[2] See his Payeinma inscription, *Inscriptions* 1913 18.

Perhaps, too, he liked the Delta folk, and had made friends during his exile at Dalla.

His only child was a daughter, Shwe-einthi. The son of the chief of Pateikkaya[1] came to ask for her hand. Kyanzittha's ministers objected to the match, saying it would deliver the realm into the hands of an Indian prince, and they hastened her marriage to Sawlu's son Sawyun although he was lame. Shin Arahan broke the news to the prince of Pateikkaya, who committed suicide. Before long Sawyun's child by Shwe-einthi was born; it was a boy, Alaungsithu, and Kyanzittha was so delighted that he crowned the infant as king and presented him to the people saying, "Behold your king! Henceforth I reign only as his regent."

While the quaint ceremony was in progress, there arrived Indian prisoners captured in a raid at Thandaung and Ngathonpinle;[2] they were settled in places such as Singu, Ngathayauk, Kalade, Nwahta, and Seiktein, in Myingyan district. Anawrahta's expedition to Arakan affected only the north, and Thetminkadon, a lord of the south, now came raiding the Burmese border villages. Kyanzittha sent a levy with elephants and horses to hunt him down. But Shin Arahan, and the Mahagiri spirit in a vision, counselled the king not to slay him, saying that they, together with the king, Thetminkadon, and little Alaungsithu, had been five friends in a previous existence. Therefore the king recalled his forces after admonishing Thetminkadon; before leaving, they destroyed[3] the Mahamuni shrine but could not remove so heavy an image. Kyanzittha believed the Mahagiri spirit to be his patron, who had preserved him through all his miseries, causing Anawrahta's spear to cut the ropes which bound him, guiding him in his desperate ride from Taunghkwin, and speaking to him in the voice of the *myit-htwe* bird when he was nearly drowning.

Kyanzittha had declared the infant Alaungsithu to be his successor because he thought he had no son. He had forgotten the days in quiet Kyaungbyu and was soon to regret his mistake—

[1] See note "Pateikkaya and Macchagiri" p. 326.

[2] Perhaps Thandaung and Ngapathonpinle in Ramree township, Kyaukpyu district. *Hmannan* I. 284 calls the prisoners Kyekala, i.e. Tamils. See *Carey* 2.

[3] *JBRS* 1912 Chan Htwan Oung "The Mahamuni shrine," *RSASB* 1918 12.

> In the second year of his reign Thambula came to Pagan with her seven year old son. And when she was come to the palace she dared not enter, for the king was granting audience to his captains. And she walked up and down in front of the palace holding her son. Then said the pages "Woman, bide not here. Our Lord the King is about to come forth. Get thee hence." And they drave her forth. But she said "I have a boon to crave. Let me be." And they told the king, and he sent for her. And when he saw that it was Thambula and her son, he cried aloud "How great is my debt to this lady!" And he called the child and took him to his bosom in the midst of the court and said "Men say that a son cometh first and a grandson last. But I have crowned my grandson, I have made him the first and my son the last." (*Hmannan* I. 286.)

Kyanzittha could not go back on his consecration of little Alaungsithu, but he made Thambula's son titular lord of north Arakan and the Seven Hill Tracts, and he made Thambula herself his fourth queen, with the beloved title U-hsaukpan.[1]

Devout Buddhists, fleeing from persecution in India, were now migrating as far as Siam; some came to Pagan,[2] for its fame as a religious centre was growing. Eight Indian monks were entertained for three months by Kyanzittha who fed them with his own hand and listened to their tale, especially the description of their great cave temple of Ananta in the Udayagiri hills of Orissa. He built the Ananda temple in imitation.

Still in daily use as a house of prayer, the Ananda, with its dazzling garb of white and its gilt spire glittering in the morning sun, is to-day one of the wonders of Pagan. It is the earliest of that series of great temples to which Pagan owes her undying appeal. Such temples are called by the people "caves," and caves they are—masses of brick in which the aisles, pillars, and mysteriously lit recesses are as it were hewn out of some deep hillside. The sun never penetrates there, and in the gloom at the end of the western aisle two life-size statues kneel at the feet of a gigantic Buddha; they have knelt there for more than eight centuries. One is a king, the pious founder Kyanzittha, the other a monk, his teacher Shin Arahan. Here in the stone, large as life, can be seen the clear-cut features and strong chin of the hero-king; his face is not Burmese—his mother was an Indian lady.

[1] See note "Thambula" p. 327. [2] *Schiefner* 255.

Photo Duroiselle

STATUE OF THE FOUNDER, KING KYANZITTHA,
IN THE ANANDA TEMPLE, 1090 A.D.

On the outside of the temple are fifteen hundred plaques[1] illustrating the *jataka* stories of Buddha's previous existences, each explained by a short inscription in Pali or Talaing. Inside the aisles are eighty niches with sculptures[2] of Buddha's own life; these, by Indian artists, possibly journeymen imported for the purpose, are of a conventional mediæval type, but a wealth of labour and devotion has been expended on them and the detail is frequently good.

Kyanzittha, riding a white horse at the head of a great procession of monks and people, dedicated the temple in 1090. With its tender beauty, its wealth of sculpture, its mingling of races and languages, the Ananda shows forth the kingship's undivided sway over the upper reaches of the Irrawaddy and the Talaings of the Delta, in the days when Pagan was a religious centre far and wide, and men came even from India to worship at her shrines.

The building so entranced Kyanzittha that he broke the mould by executing the architect.[3] At the foundation a child was buried alive to provide the building with a guardian spirit;[4] the temple slaves still claim to show the place where the victim's mother rolled on the ground in grief.

Of the six villages he dedicated to the Ananda, four—Payeinma, Kyaukyit, Kyahkat, Waya, all in Sagaing district—are associated with incidents in his career. He built[5] some forty smaller pagodas such as the Payeinma at his birthplace, and the Shwedwinaung to commemorate his hiding in a pit, in Sagaing district; three at Yesagyo in Pakokku district; and in Myingyan district—the Nagayon, the Hlanpyangyet to commemorate some of his best spearcasts, the Minochantha to contain nine relics sent by a prince of Ceylon, and the Pusittok to commemorate the spot where his mother, when

[1] *Epigraphia Birmanica* II. i. and ii.

[2] Reproduced with a full account of the temple in *ARASI* 1913-4 Duroiselle "Stone Sculptures in the Ananda Temple at Pagan." The statues of Kyanzittha and Shin Arahan are probably the only portrait statues in Burma.

[3] Oral tradition.

[4] See note "Myosade" p. 320.

[5] At Nyaungu the Kyanzittha Onhmin, named after him and dating from his dynasty, contains frescoes some of which, like those at Minnanthu, appear from their technique to be the work of Nepalese or north Bengali craftsmen. Among the Kyanzittha Onhmin frescoes is one of a Tartar officer in helmet, boots, and uniform with a hawk on his wrist.

brought as a bride to Anawrahta, knelt in homage to the palace. He completed Anawrahta's unfinished pagoda the Shwezigon, using blocks of stone three spans by one quarried at Tuywin Hill from which they were handed to the pagoda by two rows of men lined up all the way. He endowed Shwesettaw in Minbu district; he exhorted a Chola lord[1] to Buddhism; and he was the first Burmese king to restore the shrine at Buddhagaya where grows that Holy Tree in whose shade the Buddha was made manifest:—

> King Kyanzittha gathered together gems of divers kinds and sent them in a ship to build up the holy temple at Buddhagaya and to offer lights which should burn for ever there. Thereafter, king Kyanzittha builded anew, making them finer than before, the great buildings of king Asoka, for they were old and in ruins. In this respect no other king is like king Kyanzittha. Thereafter he presented all the Lords of the Church who dwelt in the city of Arimaddanapur [Pagan] with the four necessaries on every occasion. In that respect, too, no other king is like him. Thereafter, many persons from all the provinces came into his presence to attend him. At that time king Kyanzittha heard that a Chola lord had arrived, and he bethought him that apart from the Three Jewels there is no other single thing that can give great happiness in this world or in the worlds to come, or confer Nirvana upon all beings: the Three Jewels alone can give it. Therefore he wrote concerning the grace of the Jewel of the Lord, the Jewel of His Law, and the Jewel of His Clergy, with vermilion ink upon a leaf of gold and sent it unto the Chola lord. Thus hearing of the grace of Buddha, the Law, and the Clergy by reason of king Kyanzittha's sending word unto him, the Chola lord with all his retinue cast off his adhesion to false doctrine, and adhered straight away to the true doctrine; he saw, he was pleased, he was happy. And he came to offer unto king Kyanzittha pearls, an awning of pearls, a *padeitha* tree adorned with the seven kinds of gems, together with a virgin daughter of his who was perfect in form and with ornaments of divers kinds, who was shaded by a white umbrella, a peacock umbrella, a peacock set with the seven kinds of gems. And of these things, too, no other king possesseth the like. (Third Talaing inscription at the Shwehsandaw pagoda, Prome, *Epigraphia Birmanica* I. ii. 153.)

The Chola lord was probably travelling on some mission, for the Chola dynasty of Madras fostered maritime trade. Their conquest of Kedah in the Malay states brought them into subordinate relations with their own colony, the flourish-

[1] See note "Cholas in the Delta" p. 322.

ing Hindu kingdom of Palembang in east Sumatra. Therefore when their envoys attended the Chinese court in 1077, they were addressed only on strong white paper in a plain silk envelope, instead of the gold-flowered silk used for a sovereign power such as Palembang whose envoys were present on the same occasion. When Burmese envoys appeared at the Chinese court in 1106, they appear to have insisted on precedence, for the Board of Rites, after inquiry, reported that Pagan was a sovereign state entitled to superior ceremony.[1] Previous missions, the earliest recorded, from Pagan to China were in 1103-4 but they do not appear to have gone further than Yünnan, and they presented elephants which the Chinese regarded as tribute. Conceivably these missions, and Anawrahta's relic quest to Tali, were intended to facilitate overland trade, which probably revived after 866 when Nanchao subsided in defeat and was no longer in a position to block the road.

The long romance of Kyanzittha's life now drew to a close. He was nearly seventy, and as he lay dying it was his only son, the love-child born in exile, who made solemn offerings and set up the inscribed stone post, still in its place, at the Myazedi pagoda south of Pagan. Its chronological and linguistic importance is considerable. It fixes the dates of the early kings of the Pagan dynasty, which were previously doubtful. Bearing on each of its four faces the same matter in a different language—Pali, Talaing, Pyu, Burmese—it has enabled us to decipher Pyu which until 1911 was an unknown tongue; and it shows that this numerous tribe, who have left so few traces, were not identical with the Burmese.

> Glory and honour be to Buddha! In the one thousand six hundredth and twenty-eighth year of religion [A.D. 1084] Kyanzittha became king in this city of Arimaddanapur [Pagan]. The beloved wife of this king was named Thambula, and she had a son named Yazakumar. The king gave unto her three villages of slaves, and after her death he gave her ornaments and the three villages of slaves unto her son Yazakumar. Now the king having reigned twenty-eight years, fell sick unto death. Then Yazakumar the queen's son, remembering the benefits wherewith the king had nourished him, made a golden Buddha and went into the presence and showed it to the king saying "This golden Buddha have I, thy

[1] *Chau Ju-kua* 59, *Sainson* 101, *Gerini* 624 and 819.

slave, made to assist my Lord. The three villages of slaves which my Lord gave unto me, I now dedicate unto this Buddha. May my Lord approve!" Then was the king well pleased and said "Well done! Well done!" And in the presence of the image, of the Primate, of the Venerable Lords Muggaliputtatissa, Sumedha, Brahmapal, Brahmadiw, Son and very learned Sanghasena; in the presence of all these Venerable Lords the king made offering of poured water. When it was done, the son of the beloved queen made this cave-temple with a golden spire and enshrined therein the golden Buddha. And in dedicating this shrine and Buddha, the queen's son brought up the men of Sakmunalon, one village, Rapay, one village, Henbuiy, one village, all those three slave villages, and made offering of poured water for the gold Buddha and the shrine wherein he had enshrined it; and thus he prayed "May this act of mine be unto me for the attainment of divine wisdom! If any hereafter, be it my son, grandson, kinsman, or any other, oppress the slaves whom I have dedicated unto this Buddha, may he never behold the most high Buddha Arimittiya!" (Myazedi inscription, A.D. 1112, *Epigraphia Birmanica* I. i. A duplicate is in the museum at Pagan.)

ALAUNGSITHU 1112-67 spent his early years quelling rebellion in places such as Bassein. In 1114 dacoits, numbering over a hundred, raided his palace, and when they were cut down the throne room resembled a shambles. Levies had to be sent once more against Thetminkadon, lord in south Arakan, who was again raiding the border villages; he was caught and his head was sent to Alaungsithu. The Mahagiri spirit appeared to Alaungsithu and blamed him for permitting the death of one who in a previous existence had been a fellow worshipper; therefore Alaungsithu begged pardon of the head and placed it in a jewelled casket on the top of Tuywin Hill where people worshipped it in annual festival. He had to suppress a rising in Tenasserim himself: a Pali inscription[1] set up in Mergui by one of the Pagan kings shows that the dynasty ruled there.

It was just after Alaungsithu's return from this Tenasserim campaign that Shin Arahan died at the age of 81, about the year 1115.[2] His eyes had witnessed much since the days when,

[1] *RSASB* 1919 25, footnote 9. [2] *RSASB* 1919 23.

THE MYAZEDI INSCRIPTION, 1112 A.D.
The Burmese face.

The Talaing and Pali faces are in the same script as the Burmese, i.e. the Talaing script.

The Myazedi Inscription, 1112 A.D.
The Pyu face.

a youth with his vows still fresh upon him, he had dwelt alone in a woodland hermitage near Pagan. He was now primate of a kingdom, the acknowledged head of a thousand monasteries whose network spread religion over many a land and many a people. He had seen a chieftainship expand into the wide dominion of Pagan. He had been the trusted adviser of four sovereigns and had assisted at the coronation of three. He had witnessed and directed the overthrow of the dread Ari and their abominations, while in their place sprang up a purer faith and a people liberated from the bondage of dark creeds. He had seen the glittering spire of the Ananda soar to heaven, heralding the new movement which inspired the age's highest art and pressed it into the service of religion. The great work he had done was speeding beyond him, but he could go to his rest knowing that the light he had kindled would never die, that the work no longer depended on the thread of a single life, for devoted disciples stood ready to take the torch from his failing hands.

In Kyanzittha's reign a usurper had seized the throne of north Arakan and the rightful heir with his son and daughter fled to Pagan. There he lived several years, and died charging his son Letyaminnan to recover his throne. To attract attention Letyaminnan wore his hair at the back, after the Arakanese fashion, during Alaungsithu's head-washing ceremony.[1] Alaungsithu, saying "Showest thou scant ceremony at a time of ceremony?" dragged him forth to slay him, but relented on hearing his story, and arranged to re-instate him. He sent levies, Burmans by land, Talaings by sea. The Talaing warboats were severely defeated, for the Arakanese were as usual better at sea, and in consequence the Burmans also had to withdraw. Alaungsithu reinforced them and sent them back. Finally in 1118 they were successful, executed the usurper, and pillaged the Mahamuni shrine. The Burmese set the image on fire with a pair of bellows and stripped the gold off its back; the Talaings took away a leg and were drowned at sea for their impiety; the remaining portion of the image fell into neglect for fifty years.

[1] Cf. *Shway Yoe* 351. The kings of Persia and the Mauryan kings of ancient India also washed their heads ceremonially once a year, Herodotos ix 110, Strabo xv 69. The head is a great taboo, *Frazer* "Taboo and the Perils of the soul" 252.

Letyaminnan was restored to the throne of his fathers and in gratitude asked what he should do; Alaungsithu told him to render thanks by repairing the shrine at Buddhagaya; therefore, under guidance from Panthagu, son of the lord of Seinnyet, who had succeeded Shin Arahan as primate, he sent an envoy with funds to Bengal, and on the stone at Buddhagaya may be read to-day, inscribed in antique characters, how "the lord of a myriad Pyus" repaired the holy place, keeping troth with his liege. Owing to this and subsequent Burmese missions, the detail of the Buddhagaya temple, especially in the basement images, is unmistakably Burmese.[1]

In his pride, Alaungsithu thought himself the greatest of kings, greater than his ancestors even. For this sin of impiety he was bereft of sight until he cast golden images of his ancestors and bowed down before them; then alone, in that moment of humility, his sight returned.[2]

One reason why Alaungsithu was troubled with rebellions was that he spent much of his time travelling. A king felt secure only so long as he stayed inside the ramparts of his palace city; if he stayed away too long, he ran a risk of finding somebody else in possession when he came back. Alaungsithu built works of merit wherever he went, for instance:—

Minbu

Shwepanmyaing
Shinbinkuni
Paungdaw-u

Thayetmyo

Payabaw
Paungdaw-u

Mogok

Paungdaw-u

Shwebo

Shwegugyi

Monyua

Shwedaung-u

Mandalay

Nandagan and
Maungmagan lakes
Shwemale pagoda.

He worshipped at Shwesettaw and restored Kyaungdawya in Minbu district. But his chief claim to gratitude is the

[1] *Rajendralala Mitra*, *Fergusson* I. 78, *RSASB* 1911 18, *JBRS* 1912 Chan Htwan Oung "The Mahamuni shrine." Letyaminnan calls himself the lord of a myriad Pyus because till the thirteenth century the Arakanese called the Burmese "Pyus."

[2] See note "Ancestor worship" p. 327.

noble Thatpyinnyu temple, built in 1144, which dominates all others at Pagan in majesty of line. Nearby is the Shwegu temple in which he was destined to die; it was built in seven months, and on its walls may still be seen the inscription containing his great prayer in Pali verse :—

By this my gift, whatever boon I seek,
It is the best of boons, to profit all;
By this abundant merit I desire
Here nor hereafter no angelic pomp
Of Brahmas, Suras, Maras; nor the state
And splendours of a monarch; nay, not even
To be the pupil of the Conqueror.
But I would build a causeway sheer athwart
The river of Samsara, and all folk
Would speed across thereby until they reach
The Blessed City. I myself would cross
And drag the drowning over. Ay, myself
Tamed, I would tame the wilful; comforted,
Comfort the timid; wakened, wake the asleep;
Cool, cool the burning; freed, set free the bound.
Tranquil and led by the good doctrines I
Would hatred calm. The three immoral states,
Greed, hate, delusion, rooted all in self,
O may they die, whenever born in me!
Won not by oppression may my wealth remain
Nor yield to fire nor robbers, life by life.
Longing of sense for all delicious things,
Sound, sights, and touches, odours, relishes,
Pregnant of immorality, begone!
May sense of shame, fear of reproach (declared
By the Sun's kinsman Guardians of the world)
Cover me alway! As the best of men
Forsaking worldly wealth and worthless fame
Fled, for he saw their meaning . . . so would I
All worldly wealth forsaking draw me near
Religion and the threefold course ensue.
I would fulfil hereafter, great and small,
Those rules the Teacher gave for our behoof.
Borne through the elements the spotless moon
Outdazzles all the constellated stars:
So I delighting in the Master's lore,
The saint's religion, virtuously yoked,
Would shine among disciples. I would know
Sutta, and Abhidhamma, Vinaya,
The Master's mind, his ninefold doctrines fraught
With words and meaning. By the Conqueror's Law

I would do good to others and myself.
What the Great Sage forbids I would not do.
May I be always conscious and aware
Of kindness done me. Union of ill friends
Be far from me. Beholding man's distress
I would put forth mine energies and save
Men, spirits, worlds, from seas of endless change.
By merit of this act I would behold
Mettayya, captain of the world, endued
With two and thirty emblems, where he walks
Enhaloed on a rainbow pathway fair
Like Meru King of mountains, and sets free
Samsara's captives by his holy words.
There might I hear good Law, and bending low
Offer the four things needful to the Lord
And all his monks, till clad in virtues eight,
Informed by such a Teacher, I become
A Buddha in the eyes of spirits and men.

(*JbRS* 1920 Mg Tin and Luce "The Shwegugyi pagoda inscription, 1141.")

Sailing from Bassein, Alaungsithu journeyed to Malaya, to the isles of Arakan, and to "the Indian land of Bengal" where he found the images set up by Anawrahta (p. 30). Men said he even went to the Zambuthabyebin, the fabulous Rose Apple Tree which groweth at the World's End; in its shade came Thagyamin, King of the Spirits, bearing celestial gifts, and the rustling of the wind through the leaves, the plash of the fruit falling into the sacred rivers, suggested new notes which Alaungsithu introduced into Burmese music.

He made five images of the holy wood given him by Thagyamin, and enshrined them in five pagodas; four are in the neighbourhood of Pahkangyi in Pakokku district, the fifth and most picturesque is at the Thihadaw on an Irrawaddy island in Shwebo district. The Shinhla and Shinpyu images given him by Thagyamin he enshrined at Sagaing. All these pagoda sites were chosen by the wandering of the white elephant or by the flight of birds.

He hunted elephants in the Mahton, Pandaung, Talok and Ngasaunggyan forests of Bhamo district. In 1115 he sent an embassy offering gold and silver flowers, rhinoceros horns, and elephant teeth, to Nanchao;[1] and later himself wandered

[1] *Sainson* 102.

there with a great host, seeking in vain to obtain the Tooth. He tried to introduce uniformity of weights and measures by fixing the tical, the basket, and their subdivisions (p. 171). The rulings given at his court, perhaps by himself, once existed in a collection, the Alaungsithu *pyatton*.

The chief of Pateikkaya[1] paid him the tribute of a daughter, and she became the delight of his old age. One day his three sons, coming to pay their respects, saw that she remained seated by their father's side after their entry. The face of the eldest, Minshinzaw, lowered, and exclaiming "Shall this foreign wench remain seated in my presence?" he strode from the room; he was sent for but pleaded indisposition. Again, the king gave a robe, such as princes of the blood wore, to a certain lord's son; one day the youth arrayed himself in it and attended a council. Minshinzaw stripped it off him, saying "Thou art not of the blood." For this act the king placed him under arrest. The queen and ministers entreated but the king said "If he is like this while I am alive, what will he be when I am dead? He will be like a cat among you chickens." Again they entreated and at last he yielded, saying "So be it. But he has sulked in my presence. Let him abide not here." Minshinzaw was given back his revenues and his retinue, and was sent to live at Htuntonputet, east of where Mandalay now is; there he ruled in state, building the Shwekyimin pagoda and reaping three harvests a year, for he constructed the Aungbinle and Tamokso lakes with a system of irrigation channels. His brother Narathu became the king's deputy.

But now, in his eighty-first year, king Alaungsithu fell sick. Narathu was not the man to hesitate, least of all when everything was in his favour. Minshinzaw might be senior, but he was in his province ninety miles away. Narathu held the palace, with the court and the Guards under his immediate orders. He had the dying king removed to the Shwegu temple, and set about securing the throne. But the peace of the temple revived Alaungsithu; he regained consciousness and, looking round, said "This is not my palace. Where am I?" A handmaid answered "My lord, thou art not in thy palace. Thou art in thy holy temple, the work of thy hands." He

[1] See note "Pateikkaya and Macchagiri" p. 326.

asked shortly "Whose trickery is this?" and on learning that it was Narathu's command he burst out in anger—his whole body burned like fire. Nearby in the palace, Narathu heard that his father was recovering. Fear seized his heart—he had not allowed for this, it meant the end of all his dreams, it was unthinkable. In haste he went to the temple. He found his father sitting up; the old man's anger had vanished; his face was calm, his dim eyes seemed to linger on golden spire and sacred portal, on the beauty of the buildings he had dedicated to religion; he looked very frail. What difference would it make? He could not live much longer in any case; to speed his going would not be such a very great sin, for his last thoughts were holy; and if he recovered, though only for a few days, there would be utter ruin, there would be no forgiveness from the princes. Narathu hesitated for a moment and then, seizing the bedclothes, held them down firmly and smothered the gentle face.

NARATHU 1167-70. Minshinzaw marched on Pagan with all his men. Narathu thought for a while. Then he approached Panthagu the primate, saying "Make peace betwixt my brother and me. Tell him I will yield the throne. Let him come alone, with only his horse and his sword." Panthagu answered "Bethink thee well. I am a monk and may not meddle with falsehood. What if he come and thou abide without raising him to the throne?" Then said Narathu "I speak truth. Make him believe me"; and he swore a great oath "Freely will I set him on the throne and bear his sword in the crowning." So Panthagu went to the camp where Minshinzaw lay amidst his men, and told him all; and Minshinzaw, having the archbishop's word and trusting his brother, came alone in a boat to Pagan. And Narathu met him, and bore his sword, and set him on the throne. But that same night Minshinzaw the king died of a poisoned dish.

Next day Narathu received the homage of the court. But there was one who would pay no homage. Although past seventy, an age when most men let things slide, Panthagu was primate and the direct successor of Shin Arahan. He came before the king and said "Thou foul thing! Thinkest thou thy body shall not wax old, thinkest thou to escape the doom of eternity?" Narathu stirred on his throne, but he answered coldly "Sir monk, I have kept my troth with thee. I swore to carry my brother's sword and to set him on the throne. Have I not accomplished these things?" But Panthagu was beside himself, and exclaiming "A king more damned than thou there is not in all the world!" he strode from the palace; and after a little time, unwilling to abide in a blood-stained realm, he departed to Ceylon.

Narathu did not find the crown so light to wear as he had expected. Men shunned him. He had a simple remedy for that. Princes and queens, secretaries and kinsmen, he slew them day after day. He ground the poor and persecuted the monks, pressing them into the levies regardless of their vow to spill no blood. He killed the lady of Pateikkaya because, being used to Hindu ablutions which he disregarded, she grew disgusted and would live with him no longer.

Then remorse seized him. To the loneliness of power was added the loneliness of sin. To make amends he built the Dammayan temple, the largest pile at Pagan. Its grim mass slowly towered aloft. The workmen complained of the noonday heat, of the torrential rain which made the bricks slippery. He hounded them on. Yet for all his haste he would have no imperfect work. Men say he executed master-masons because a needle could be inserted between two of the bricks and this much is true that the brickwork is among the finest in Pagan. The temple is built on the same ground-plan as the Ananda, but has nothing of its serenity or grace; the building's whole soul is sullen.

Yet all his prayers, his mighty masonry, were in vain. He had scarcely reigned three years, and retribution was already at hand. It came from the dead lady of Pateikkaya's father, the chieftain of Pateikkaya. Calling for volunteers, he selected eight of his best guards, made provision for their families, and sent them over the hills with secret orders. They entered Narathu's palace dressed as Brahmans. He sent for the holy men to receive their blessing. They drew near in a circle round his throne, with arms outstretched in benediction; but once within striking distance they drew concealed daggers from under their robes and plunged them into his body. Then—for they were but common men, and had spilt the blood of a consecrated king—they carried out their master's final orders and killed each other where they stood.

NARATHEINHKA 1170-3. Narathu was succeeded by his son Naratheinhka one of whose three queens, Taung-pyinthi, was great-granddaughter of Anawrahta's paladin Nyaung-uhpi.

> And again, the king saw his brother's wife, how fair she was to look on, and his soul was dazed, and he could not stand upright. And he thought on this wise "I will cause mine heir to march, telling him that war hath broken out in Ngasaunggyan [in Bhamo district]. When he hath set forth, I will take his wife and raise her to the throne." So he put words into the mouth of a minister and caused him to come saying "War hath broken out in Ngasaunggyan!" And the king called Narapatisithu and commanded him to march to Ngasaunggyan.
>
> Now his brother Narapatisithu was a prince of nimble wit and discernment, and he commanded Nga Pyi his equerry saying "If any ado arise in mine house, take the horse Thudawsin and come quickly!" Then he marshalled his men by land and water, and went up country with his councillors and captains, circle and village headmen, and all his host. When he reached Thissein [in Shwebo district], lo! there was no trouble soever at Ngasaunggyan; and he weighed the matter in his heart saying "My brother hath duped me with a false excuse." And he gathered and conferred with his councillors and captains, his circle and village headmen, and bound them with a solemn oath. And his councillors and captains said "Minyin Naratheinhka is without a son, verily he hath made his brother Narapatisithu heir." The more gladly, therefore, with one heart they leagued with Narapatisithu.
>
> When Minyin Naratheinhka heard that his brother had reached Thissein, he took his sister-in-law and raised her to the throne. Nga Pyi the equerry crossed over to Aungtha [in Pakokku district] at the stroke of the morning bell and rode his horse at a soft and easy pace. It was not yet noon, they say, when he reached Chindwin Payeinma [in Sagaing district]. Crossing to Payeinma he made straight for Halin [in Shwebo district] and reached the stream of Ngapat [in Shwebo district] at sunset. And because night was drawing on and the royal horse was tired, he watered it and fed it with grass and slept that night at Myinhli Hill [unidentified].

Now when the horse Thudawsin had rested, he neighed loudly, for he scented his master. And the prince knew his horse's neigh and could not sleep saying "Verily it is the sound of mine horse, neighing." Then he made a solemn vow and said "If it is indeed the sound of my horse neighing, may this pillow be pierced with a hole, and fail not!" And he struck the royal pillow with his hand, and lo! a hole was pierced. The place is still known as Malwe-onpauk [in Shwebo district]. . . . When Nga Pyi the equerry had slept and it was early morning, he came at the stroke of morning bell and told all his tale. And when he heard that matter prince Narapatisithu was in high dudgeon and waxed wroth and cried "My beloved queen Veluvati! My brother hath taken and raised her to the throne!" Then he asked Nga Pyi the equerry "Where didst thou sleep yesternight?" "I slept," said Nga Pyi, "at the stream of Ngapat, for the horse was tired and I refreshed it." "What!" said prince Narapatisithu, "Thou didst sleep not far from the place where I lay. Didst thou well to sleep? We princes might accomplish much, had we hours to plan it." And in his royal pride he slew Nga Pyi. The place is still known as Kuttawya [unidentified].

Then the prince cried "Our enemy is behind us!" And he called minister Aungswa-nge and commanded him saying "Bear my yoke though it cost thee thy life! See thou catch my brother unawares and slay him. When that is done I will make thee great and give thee whom thou wilt of my three sisters-in-law." So Aungswa-nge chose four score mighty men of valour and took them in a fast *hlawga* boat and went in furious haste, not knowing day and night.

Prince Narapatisithu marshalled his men by land and water and came downstream. When he reached Kyetyet [Shwekyetyet pagoda in Mandalay district] he made a solemn vow saying "If my brother shall verily be slain, at the moment I spread this cloth at the pagoda in the south, may the Lord himself bow down and take it!" And when he spread the cloth, behold! the image of the Lord himself bowed down and took it. When he saw that thing he came downstream marshalling his troops by land and water.

But the body of Nga Pyi whom he had slain floated not far from the royal raft. And the prince saw it and asked "Whose body is it?" His ministers answered "The body of Nga Pyi whom thou hast slain." And he commanded them saying "Bury the body at the head of yon island, and let it be worshipped by all people in this place. See that ye build a goodly spirit-house." So the ministers did as the prince commanded, and built a spirit-house. The isle where Nga Pyi was buried is still known as the isle of Shwepyishin. The village headmen are fain to worship there.[1]

[1] There is a Shwepyishin at the mouth of the Mu river, and nearby is Aungzwa village. Nga Pyi is Myinbyushin Nat, the spirit Rider of the White Horse, see *Grant Brown* "The Lady of the Weir" and *GUB* II. i. 518.

When Nga Aungswa-nge, the royal servant sent by prince Narapatisithu, reached the palace, he entered with his four score mighty men of valour hugging sword in scabbard. Now it so befell that Minyin Naratheinhka was entering a privy; and Nga Aungswa-nge followed after as far as the privy. And the king asked him "Who art thou?" He replied "Thy servant, Nga Aungswa-nge. O king, thy brother sent me." And the king looked, and lo! he was hemmed in by white and gleaming blades. And he besought them saying "Slay me not! Let me only serve my brother as his watcher of crows, his scarer of fowls!" But Aungswa-nge replied "O king, my lord thy brother hath not so ordained it." And he slew him even in the privy, and he died. A ruby earring that he wore fell from the privy to the ground. Thirty-two years in the nether house, three years he flourished; he passed at the age of thirty-five.

[NARAPATISITHU 1173-1210]. His younger brother Narapatisithu became king. He was anointed with his queen Veluvati.[1] When his sisters-in-law heard that he would give them to Aungswa-nge, they clasped his knees and besought him with meek and piteous words "O king, are we women known to covet so many husbands? We have done no sin. We are not mere sisters-in-law. We are all daughters of thine aunts, Chit-on and Eindawthi. We are all wives of a king." So the king called Aungswa-nge and commanded him saying "Nga Aungswa-nge, I made thee a promise indeed, but if I were to give thee one of my sisters-in-law it would be held a sin against my grandsires and great-grandsires. I will make thee great, and give thee a daughter of a great nobleman." "Pish!" said Aungswa-nge. And the king slew him[2] saying "He hath braved me to my face."

Then he seized Anantathuriya, tutor to his brother Minyin Naratheinhka and gave him over to the executioners to slay him. Now Anantathuriya was of a brave and constant heart; about the time of his death he spake four stanzas of *linka*, and gave them saying "Offer them, I pray thee, to the king." Nevertheless the executioners tarried not but slew him, and afterwards gave the writing to the king. These are the four verses of that *linka*:—

Yes, he is one who, wealth attained,
Shall pass away and disappear;
'Tis Nature's Law.
Within his golden palace hall,
Surrounded by his lords in state,
He sits serene.
But kings' delights, like eddies small
On ocean's face a moment seen,
Are but for life.

[1] She built the Shwethabeik pagoda in Myingyan district.

[2] Nga Aungswa-nge is the Aungswawamagyi Nat, see *Temple*, and is confused with the Myinbyushin Nat, Nga Pyi.

Should he show pity, and not slay,
But set me free, my liberty
  Is Karma's work.
Of mortals here the elements
Last not, but change and fall away;
  It is the Law.
The sure result of suppliant acts
Or prayers, I wish not to transfer
  To future lives:
T' escape this fate, past sins' result,
Is my desire. Calmly I'll wait.
  My heart is firm.
Thee, gentle lord, I blameless hold,
Freely to thee I pardon give,
  'Tis not thy deed.
Danger and death are constant foes
And in this world must ever be:
  It is the Law.

Now when these four stanzas were read before the king and he heard them, he commanded saying "Set him free." But the executioners spake into his ear and said "The deed is done." And the king slew those executioners saying "Ye should have offered the writing before ye killed him; but behold, ye killed him first and offered the writing after." Now when he heard the writing the king had great remorse. Again and yet again he gasped and swooned away. Ever afterwards he refrained and checked his anger; and he commanded the chief executioner, kinsman of the king, saying "Hereafter when I am wroth, though I give thee the order to slay a man, keep him alive for a month of weeks and look to the matter. Let him die only when he ought to die. If he ought not to die, release him." (*Hmannan* I. 316. Verse translation by R. F. Andrew St. John.)

The reason why Panthagu, when shaking off the dust of Narathu's kingdom in 1167, had chosen Ceylon as his refuge was that religion there was once more flourishing after yet another Hindu persecution. He returned home soon after Narapatisithu's first regnal year 1173 and was treated as primate; he was then ninety and did not live much longer.

His successor as primate was the Talaing monk Uttarajiva, who attained fame by his pilgrimage to Ceylon in 1180, earning the title "First Pilgrim of Ceylon." Panthagu's visit shows the importance of Ceylon as a religious centre, and Uttarajiva's title suggests that this importance was new. The island no longer had a rival in Conjeveram (p. 7) where Brahmanism had at last triumphed. Uttarajiva sailed from

Bassein with many other monks, and after a comparatively short stay they returned. But one of them, Chapata, a Talaing novice, born near Ngaputaw in Bassein district, received ordination in Ceylon and stayed there ten years; he returned to Burma in 1190 and was known as the "Second Pilgrim of Ceylon." He brought with him four learned foreign monks, also ordained in Ceylon; one was Ananda, a native of Conjeveram, and another was a prince, son of the king of Cambodia. All five of them settled just north of Pagan, building at Nyaung-u the Chapata pagoda which is of Cingalese pattern. It takes five monks to form a chapter *pañcavagganā* able to perform valid ordination *upasampadā* and all other rites; and that is why Chapata brought four other monks with him, as he was minded to regard the ordination of the Burmese clergy as invalid, saying it was not in accordance with canon law, *Vinaya*. He and his companions refused to perform the duties of the Order with the Burmese clergy, and in 1192 set up a schism or rather three schisms, for they disagreed among themselves as to the precise nature of holiness, and one of them even had to be expelled for losing his heart to a dancing girl. The original Burmese clergy, who derived their succession from Shin Arahan and Thaton, were called the Former Order; others who derived from the newcomers and Ceylon, were called the Latter Order.

Narapatisithu was impressed by the foreign lore of these monks who had gone all the way to study in Ceylon, and he encouraged their ordinations. The mission of the two Talaings, Uttarajiva and Chapata, is of great importance, for whether the Burmese doubted the validity of their own orders or not, they took to meeting the new movement on its own ground and sent clergy to Ceylon for ordination by the monks at the Mahavihara (p. 119); and such intercourse led to the establishment of Ceylon as the chief foreign influence on Burmese religion. Thaton Buddhism, probably from Conjeveram, had been just one and a third centuries in Upper Burma when in 1192 Ceylon Buddhism was introduced and finally predominated to such an extent as to obliterate even the memory of Conjeveram.

It is not stated in what ships the intercourse took place, but there was an appreciable volume of seaborne trade all round the southern coast of Asia from China to Egypt and Madagascar. Most of it was in the hands of Arab shipmasters, but Chinese junks predominated east of Malaya and still went as far west as Ceylon.[1]

Doubtless it was in connection with such trade that the Cingalese king kept what seems to have been a resident agent in Burma, probably at Bassein, then the most important port. The Burmese, as was the custom in several eastern countries, supplied him with rice and quarters. But Narapatisithu stopped the grant of these supplies, forbade the export of elephants to Ceylon save at exorbitant rates, ceased giving the customary present of an elephant to every ship which bore royal gifts, imprisoned Cingalese merchants, seized their goods, flung the king of Ceylon's envoys into prison or drove them out to sea in a leaking ship, and finally carried off a Cingalese princess on her way to Cambodia. To avenge all this, the king of Ceylon despatched an expedition in 1180. It suffered from storms and several ships were wrecked; but one ship reached Crow Island near Moulmein and carried off the inhabitants, while five reached Bassein, and others landed elsewhere, killing a governor, burning villages, massacring the inhabitants and carrying off a number into slavery. The Burmese then sent a conciliatory message to Ceylon through the monks, and friendly relations were resumed.[2]

Narapatisithu founded the Guards.[3] His greatest works are the superb Gawdawpalin and Sulamani temples at Pagan, with the Mimalaunggyaung, Dammayazika, and Chaukpala nearby. His lesser pagodas are the Myatheindan and Swedaw in Thayetmyo district, Zedihla in Monyua, Paungdaw-u in Kyaukse, and Shwetaza in Shwebo town; the Zetawun in Mergui district, and a Talaing inscription[4] he erected at the Shwe-indein pagoda near Yawnghwe in the Shan states, show the extent of his rule. Others, such as the Shinbinsagyo in Myingyan district, were each built from the value of gold weighed against one of his sons, according to the widespread Hindu custom.[5] He built the Kyaukse weir at Kyaukse, started the Mu canals in Shwebo district, and tried to make a

[1] See note "Eastern shipping" p. 310.
[2] See note "Cingalese raid 1180" p. 328.
[3] See note "The Guards" p. 323.
[4] *RSASB* 1920 16.
[5] See note "Tula-dana" p. 328.

canal system on the Mon in Minbu district, but had to abandon the project after repeated failures.[1]

He made Nadaungmya, greatgrandson of Nyaung-uhpi, chief justice; but the office is not mentioned elsewhere and may have been personal. His chief minister was Anantasuriya, a mighty man of valour, who continually hunted dacoits and even presented them alive to the king. Anantasuriya built the Lemyethna temple at Minnanthu near Pagan, inscribing a curse on all who should injure his dedication. Such curses are usual in Burma as elsewhere, but this particular curse is so dreadful that it is still used as the oath-book in law courts throughout Burma.

The king had a *hkuna* whitlow on his hand, and one of the lesser queens used to keep her mouth on the spot to lessen the pain: once while he was sleeping she swallowed the humour rather than wake him, and in gratitude he made her son Zeyatheinhka his heir.[2] Though Zeyatheinhka was the youngest son and he was born of a lesser wife, his elder brothers acquiesced, and the white umbrella confirmed the selection by miraculously inclining towards him alone out of all his brothers. Therefore, when he came to the throne, he was called Htilominlo, "He whom the umbrella wished to be king." Narapatisithu died in the thirty-seventh year of his reign and the seventy-fourth of his age. On his death-bed he placed the hands of his five sons on his bosom and enjoined them to rule with mercy and justice and to live together in brotherly love.

HTILOMINLO 1210-34 was also called Nantaungmya, "many entreaties for the throne," because his mother had so often entreated that he might succeed to the throne; and a collection of the judicial rulings made at his court was called the Nantaungmyamin *pyatton*. It is not likely that these rulings were his own, for, like some of his successors, he was happier praying at a pagoda than ruling a realm. One reason why his

[1] See note "Burmese irrigation" p. 318.
[2] See note "The Whitlow" p. 329.

brothers loyally accepted his succession was that he virtually abdicated all power into their hands. The four of them met daily and transacted the affairs of the kingdom. Thus was founded the Hluttaw Yon, the Court of the Royal Commission, which remained till the end the council of the ministers.[1]

The king built the Sittana pagoda near Pagan on a Cingalese pattern, completed the Gawdawpalin which his father left unfinished, and built the Mahabodhi and Htilominlo temples. The Mahabodhi is a second-rate piece of work but possesses interest as being a copy of the temple at Buddhagaya. The Htilominlo, a magnificent creation built on the spot where the white umbrella had bowed down before him as a youth, is the last of the series of great temples at Pagan, although smaller ones of merit, such as the Thambula, built in 1255, continued to be constructed for a generation or so.[2]

Though built in brick, a material of fatal facility, these temples are among the noblest monuments in Indo-China, and they are the one positive contribution Burma has made to humanity. There was indeed in places such as the Kyaukku Onhmin at Pagan a crowded monastic life which, especially after the Ceylon mission in 1180, produced voluminous Pali treatises on grammar and prosody and a law-book, the Dhammavilasa *dhammathat*,[3] by a pupil of Ananda (p. 56). But, like later Burmese writings, this monastic literature was not creative, and fares poorly in comparison even with other clerical literatures. Thus, it contains nothing like the constructive thought of the mediæval Catholic writers, notably St. Thomas Aquinas, to whose powerful advocacy human freedom owes so much.

KYASWA 1234-50 succeeded his father Htilominlo and was even more devout. He resigned all business to his son Uzana and spent his hours with the monks memorising the Tripitaka scriptures and writing devotional works for the palace

[1] See note "Hluttaw and Kingship" p. 329.

[2] See note "The Temples and their Builders" p. 330.

[3] Dhammavilasa was a Talaing of Dalla. His law-book, the first in Upper Burma, was in Pali and it was based on Talaing or Pali sources attributed to Manu (p. 111). It does not survive but quotations show that it was similar to the Wareru *dhammathat*, see *Forchammer* "Jardine Prize" 35-6.

ladies. The following, however, indicates that even under so pious a king religion retained Ari survivals:—

> The minister commanded that these things be dedicated to the monks . . . two potfuls of rice, two baskets of betelnut betel leaf, one and a quarter *viss* of meat, one 10 quart pot of long-fermented liquor. . . . This offering was made in the presence of my lord the king. (Inscription dated 1248, Itzagawna monastery near Pagan, *Inscriptions* 1892 251. See note "Drink" p. 314.)

At Sagu in Minbu district he built a monastery for Sihamaha-upali who had succeeded Uttarajiva as primate. There is a poem, Myagan-bwe-linga, about the Myagan, the "Emerald Lake" which he made; it was famed for its crystal water, and on its shore you can still see a crumbling inscription and a stone building, probably his own retreat:—

> He dammed the water falling from the foot of Tuywin Hill, and made a great lake. He filled it with the five kinds of lotus and caused all manner of birds, duck, sheldrake, crane, water fowl, and widgeon, to take their joy and pastime there. Near the lake he laid out many cultivated fields; men say he reaped three crops a year. Hard by the lake he built a pleasant royal lodge, and took delight in study seven times a day. (*Hmannan* I. 339.)

UZANA 1250-54 succeeded his father Kyaswa. He was a merry person, given to jesting, to liquor, and to hunting elephants at Dalla near Rangoon. One of his favourite wives was a village girl whom he found when ascending Popa Hill to hold the annual Mahagiri spirit festival; another was a village carpenter's daughter. He went to see a kheddah capture, riding his Katha elephant, but the captured elephant was must, ripped the girth ropes of the royal elephant, and trampled the king to death.

NARATHIHAPATE 1254-87. The late king left a son Thingathu by a queen and one other, Narathihapate, by a concubine. The latter had no conceivable claim against a queen's son. But Thingathu was not acceptable to the chief minister Yazathinkyan, a descendant of Anawrahta's paladin Nyaung-uhpi. Once he had come walking behind Yazathinkyan who did not notice him and so failed to pay proper respect.

Thingathu thereupon spat betel on Yazathinkyan's sleeve. Yazathinkyan said nothing but went home and laid by the jacket carefully without cleaning it. Now that the king was dead he summoned a large meeting of ministers and headmen and held up the soiled jacket before them all. At his bidding they decided that a man who while yet a prince behaved like that to his elders, would be unbearable as a king, and they made Narathihapate king instead.

Yazathinkyan the king-maker looked forward to a long spell of power, as Narathihapate was only sixteen years old. But he grew up and showed a will of his own. Yazathinkyan was inexpressibly shocked, and so far forgot himself as to twit the king with the fact that his mother was not a queen but a village carpenter's daughter. At once the king rounded on him :—

> "Grandfather, when they crown a pagoda with a spire, wherewith do they raise it?" He replied "Son of my Lord, they raise the spire by first making a scaffold." Said the king once more "When the spire is set on the top of the pagoda what do they do with the scaffold?" Yazathinkyan replied "Son of my Lord, when the spire is set on the top of the pagoda, it is not graceful until the scaffold is destroyed." Then said the king "I am as the spire, Yazathinkyan as the scaffold. As the spire reaches the top of the pagoda, so have I reached kingship. And the spire will not appear graceful until the scaffold, that is to say Yazathinkyan, be destroyed. Ho! ministers, seize his office, his elephants and horses, his minions and retinue, and off with him to Dalla town!" And they did as the king had ordered and sent him away.
>
> As Yazathinkyan journeyed a great wind arose, and lo! the big trees brake and split, but the waterplants only leaned and swayed, and so brake not. And seeing it he was taken with remorse and said "I, a servant of the king, have not been as wise even as a waterplant. Because I have acted as a big tree it has come to this!" When his escort returned the king asked what words Yazathinkyan had spoken. So the escort reported them "O Lord of glory, a great wind arose and the big trees brake and split, but the waterplants only leaned and swayed and so brake not. And when Yazathinkyan saw it he said 'I have not been as wise even as a waterplant.'" And the king abode in silence. (*Hmannan* I. 344.)

Martaban and Macchagiri[1] revolted. The king sent levies against Macchagiri and, at the advice of Saw his queen,

[1] See note "Pateikkaya and Macchagiri" p. 326.

recalled Yazathinkyan to deal with Martaban. Yazathinkyan speedily crushed the rebellion there, set up a governor, Aleimma, and returned to Pagan. But the levies sent against Macchagiri fled back to Minbu in panic; therefore the king ordered the commanders to be executed. But Yazathinkyan gained them a reprieve, pacifying the angry king by producing a long string of Martaban prisoners. Then he took over the Macchagiri campaign himself, quelled the rising, and sent the leading men to Pagan where they repented and were pardoned. But he himself never returned. He died at Dalla, worn out with faithful service at the age of sixty-two; and "when the king heard thereof, he recalled all that Yazathinkyan had done of old, and now in the latter days, and his heart was stricken."

The king made a concubine splash Sawlon, one of his queens, while they were bathing in the river from the palace wharf. Therefore Sawlon nursed a grudge and tried to poison him. The attempt failed and he ordered her to be burnt alive. The executioners made an iron frame. She bribed them to wait seven days and when the seven days were accomplished, she ascended the burning fiery furnace, telling her beads. Thrice the flames died down, and only when she desisted from prayer were they able to burn her. Not long after, the king would shriek her name aloud in his sleep, crying "Sawlon, come and watch beside me!" The primate told him not to publish his remorse thus, lest men should laugh at him. So he restrained his grief and issued instructions that his death sentences should always be suspended for a fortnight to allow his anger to cool.

He made his sons live in the palace, fearing lest they should rebel if they were left to themselves in the provinces. He ate together with them, and used to distribute the food, a pig's hind trotters to his son Thihathu, lord of Prome, and front trotters to the elder sons. Thihathu's mother took this as an insult and paid the cook to give her son a front trotter, leaving hind trotters to the other queen's sons. When the king discovered this, he punished the cook and continually teased Thihathu, calling him "son of a stealer of pig's trotters." Thihathu therefore nursed malice. The king built the Mingalazedi pagoda and set up this inscription :—

> King Narathihapate, styled Siritribhavanatityapavaradhammaraja, the supreme commander of a vast army of thirty-six million [1] soldiers, the swallower of three hundred dishes of curry daily, being desirous of attaining the bliss of Nirvana, erected a pagoda. In it he enshrined fifty-one gold and silver statuettes [2] of kings and queens, lords and ladies, and over these he set up an image of Gaudama Buddha in solid silver one cubit high, on the full moon of Kahson 636 [A.D. 1274]. A covered way was made from the palace to the pagoda, with bamboo matting, whereon were laid rush mats, and on these again were spread pieces of cloth each twenty cubits in length, and at each cubit's distance on the way there was a banner. During the ceremony the princes princesses and lords cast pearls among the statues. (Mingalazedi pagoda inscription near Pagan, year 1274, *Inscriptions* 1892 199.)

The pagoda took six years to build, because work was not continuous. After it was started, a prophetic rumour spread abroad, "The pagoda is finished and the great country ruined!" Soothsayers confirmed the rumour, saying "When this pagoda is finished, the kingdom of Pagan will be shattered into dust." Therefore the king abandoned the work. But the primate upbraided him, saying that this life is transitory, nor could the kingdom abide for ever even if the pagoda were not built. So the pagoda was completed, a large stupa of the sort so common all over Burma. Its coarse execution seems to symbolise the exhaustion of a realm: it was built in blood and sweat. For two centuries Pagan had witnessed the spectacle of a whole population filled with a passion for covering the earth's surface with pagodas, and now she was perishing to the drone of prayer.

The kingdom had been in existence two and a quarter centuries, a long time for any government which is purely dynastic. Narathihapate was a pompous glutton who boasted three thousand concubines, and for generations his predecessors had been self-indulgent nonentities, unlike the founders of the dynasty. Yet, although the Shans were beginning to migrate southwards, the kingdom, left to itself, might have endured for some time, for the people were placid, vast stretches of country were uninhabited, and the scattered population in remote areas had no need to rebel against a rule which was little more than nominal. But the kingdom could not expect to be left to itself for ever.

[1] See "Numerical Note" p. 333. [2] See note "Tula dana" p. 328.

The Tartar hordes swept across Asia from Mesopotamia to the China Sea. They boasted, not without truth, that they had wiped out the cities of Russia and Poland in 1241 so utterly that they could gallop over the sites without encountering an obstacle big enough to make their horses stumble. Had they tried, they could probably have overrun Christendom, for she was rent asunder by the struggle between the Empire and the Papacy; and although they were deficient in constructive ability, so that their rule inevitably collapsed as quickly as it arose, yet the splendour of their court so amazed European travellers that it has passed into a fable. This was the power which the Burmese monarchy persisted in insulting.

In 1253 the Tartars annexed Yünnan. In 1271, under instructions from the Emperor Kubla Khan, the Yünnan government sent envoys to the Burmese demanding tribute as paid by Narathihapate's predecessors (pp. 14, 43, 48). This was not a summons to surrender, for, provided they paid nominal tribute, the Tartar empire often left its remoter vassals alone. Narathihapate deigned not to grant the envoys an audience, and kept them waiting long at the beck and call of subordinates, but finally sent them back with one of his lords to express friendly sentiments and to worship a Buddha tooth at Pekin. In 1273 an imperial ambassador, First Secretary to the Board of Rites, with three colleagues, came to Pagan with a letter from Kubla Khan. In the letter, Kubla Khan, after pointing out that he himself had received the Burmese envoy, says—

> If you have really decided to fulfil your duties towards the All-highest, send one of your brothers or senior ministers, to show men that all the world is linked with Us, and to enter into a perpetual alliance. This will add to your reputation and be in your own interests; for if it comes to war, who will be victor? Ponder well, O king, upon Our words.

As the ambassadors who bore this letter refused to take off their shoes[1] sufficiently often, Narathihapate ordered their immediate execution. The minister Anantapyissi, who still retained his senses in that atmosphere of insane adulation, remonstrated, saying "Sire, protest at Pekin against their lack of ceremony, but do not slay them. The kings of old were

[1] See note "The Shoe Question" p. 336.

never wont to slay ambassadors." But Narathihapate would not listen, and the ambassadors with their numerous retinue were executed.

The Yünnan government reported to Pekin that the embassy did not return, the Burmese evidently had no intention of submitting, and the only way to bring these people to their senses was to make war at once. The order the Emperor passed on this was that the case should come up again later. But in 1277 the Burmese proceeded to invade the "Gold Tooth" state of Kanngai, on the Taping river, seventy miles above Bhamo, because its chief had submitted to China. He asked for protection, and Kubla Khan thereupon sanctioned early action.

What follows was in Burmese eyes a titanic war in which the whole resources of the Chinese Empire were strained to the uttermost, pouring in millions of men to destroy Burma. But it was really a frontier affair, disposed of by the Yünnan government. The Emperor had his hands full of other campaigns, some of which ended disastrously; the matter was not of sufficient importance to require a headquarters expedition, and in any case he had no intention of invading Burma. From start to finish the affair was left to the provincial garrison, with such levies as they could raise among the Chinese Shans. But the native levies did not count: the real work was done by the regular garrison—Mahomedans of Turkish race, the race which time after time has stood up to European troops and held its own. They proceeded to clear the intruders out of Kanngai in a battle which the Burmese call the Battle of Ngasaunggyan 1277. The Venetian traveller Marco Polo, who served as a Privy Councillor on the Emperor's staff, doubtless heard the tale from officers who took part in the action:—

> The king of Mien [Burma] had, let me tell you, 2,000 great elephants, on each of which was set a tower of timber, well framed and strong, and carrying from twelve to sixteen well-armed fighting men. And besides these, he had of horsemen and of footmen good 60,000 men. In short, he equipped a fine force, as well befitted such a puissant prince. It was indeed a host capable of doing great things.
>
> And what shall I tell you? When the king had completed these great preparations to fight the Tartars, he tarried not, but straightway

marched against them. . . . And when the Captain of the Tartar host had certain news that the king aforesaid was coming against him with so great a force, he waxed uneasy, seeing that he had with him but 12,000 horsemen. Nevertheless he was a most valiant and able soldier, of great experience in arms and an excellent Captain; and his name was Nasr-uddin. His troops too were very good, and he gave them very particular orders and cautions how to act, and took every measure for his own defence and that of his army. And why should I make a long story of it? The whole force of the Tartars, consisting of 12,000 well-mounted horsemen, advanced to receive the enemy in the Plain of Vochan, and there they waited to give them battle. And this they did through the good judgment of the excellent Captain who led them; for hard by that plain was a great wood, thick with trees. And so there in the plain the Tartars awaited their foe. Let us then leave discoursing of them a while; we shall come back to them presently; but meanwhile let us speak of the enemy.

After the king had halted long enough to refresh his troops, he resumed his march, and came to the Plain of Vochan, where the Tartars were already in order of battle. And when the king's army had arrived in the plain, and was within a mile of the enemy, he caused all the castles that were on the elephants to be ordered for battle, and the fighting men to take up their posts on them, and he arrayed his horse and his foot with all skill, like a wise king as he was. And when he had completed all his arrangements he began to advance to engage the enemy. The Tartars, seeing the foe advance, showed no dismay, but came on likewise with good order and discipline to meet them. And when they were near and nought remained but to begin the fight, the horses of the Tartars took such fright at the sight of the elephants that they could not be got to face the foe, but always swerved and turned back; whilst all the time the king and his forces, and his elephants, continued to advance upon them.

And when the Tartars perceived how the case stood, they were in great wrath, and wist not what to say or do; for well enough they saw that unless they could get their horses to advance, all would be lost. But their Captain acted like a wise leader who had considered everything beforehand. He immediately gave orders that every man should dismount and tie his horse to the trees of the forest that stood hard by, and that then they should take to their bows, a weapon that they know how to handle better than any troops in the world. They did as he bade them, and plied their bows stoutly, shooting so many shafts at the advancing elephants that in a short space they had wounded or slain the greater part of them as well as of the men they carried. The enemy also shot at the Tartars, but the Tartars had the better weapons, and were the better archers to boot.

And what shall I tell you? Understand that when the elephants felt the smart of those arrows that pelted them, like rain, they turned tail and fled, and nothing on earth would induce them to turn and face the Tartars. So off they sped with such a noise and uproar that you could have trowed the world was coming to an end! And then too they plunged into the wood and rushed this way and that, dashing their castles against the trees, bursting their harness and smashing and destroying everything that was on them.

So when the Tartars saw that the elephants had turned tail and could not be brought to face the fight again, they got to horse at once and charged the enemy. And then the battle began to rage furiously with sword and mace. Right fiercely did the two hosts rush together and deadly were the blows exchanged. The king's troops were far more in number than the Tartars, but they were not of such metal, nor so inured to war; otherwise the Tartars who were so few in number could never have stood against them. Then might you see smashing blows dealt and taken from sword and mace; then might you see knights and horses and men-at-arms go down; then might you see arms and hands and legs and heads hewn off; and besides the dead that fell, many a wounded man, that never rose again, for the sore press there was. The din and uproar were so great from this side and from that, that God might have thundered and no man would have heard it! Great was the medley, and dire and parlous was the fight on both sides; but the Tartars had the best of it.

In an ill hour indeed, for the king and his people, was that battle begun, so many of them were slain therein, and when they had continued fighting till midday the king's troops could stand against the Tartars no longer; but felt that they were defeated, and turned and fled. And when the Tartars saw them routed they gave chase, and hacked and slew so mercilessly that it was a piteous sight to see. But after pursuing a while they gave up, and returned to the wood to catch the elephants that had run away, and to manage this they had to cut down great trees to bar their passage. Even then they would not have been able to take them without the help of the king's own men who had been captured, and knew better how to deal with the beasts than the Tartars did. The elephant is an animal that hath more wit than any other; but in this way at last they were caught, more than 200 of them. And it was from this time forth that the Great Khan began to keep numbers of elephants. (*Yule* "The Book of Ser Marco Polo" II. 99. See note "Ngasaunggyan 1277" p. 336.)

The Chinese advanced with 3,800 men to Kaungsin in Bhamo district, and having destroyed a large number of abandoned stockades, found the heat excessive and returned. But the Burmese were unteachable, and again raided the frontier. Therefore the Chinese advanced in 1283, and smashed a Burmese army at Kaungsin, inflicting 10,000 casualties and leaving garrisons in the area.

Such events made a deep impression on the Burmese, who

record that the very gods fought in heaven, and that, long before mortal messengers could arrive, the guardian spirits of the city gates, bleeding from arrow wounds, wakened the sleeping palace with the news of doom. Narathihapate had pulled down hundreds of pagodas to build defences for the capital. But he did not wait to see whether the Chinese were really coming or not. He fled in panic and is therefore known as Tarokpyemin, "the king who fled from the Chinese." There were not sufficient boats to accommodate the whole palace, and he ordered the slave-women to be bound hand and foot and thrown into the river lest they should fall into the enemy's power; but the primate protested, so they were allowed to stay and take their chance. The court fled to Dalla and thence to Bassein, where the king's eldest son, Uzana, loyally received them. The rest of the country south of Prome was openly in revolt, and the outlying vassals such as Arakan paid no more worship to a setting sun. The Tartars, of course, did not advance on Pagan, for the Emperor consistently refused to sanction an invasion; Narathihapate might have saved himself the trouble of running away and ruining whatever little prestige he had left; and when he sent a celebrated monk of Thitseinggyi in Shwebo district to Yünnan admitting defeat and offering humble submission, he received a sympathetic reply.

> And the King took counsel with Queen Saw and others saying "Shall we go up to our royal city of Pagan, or shall we tarry here and collect our armies?" Queen Saw spake into his ear "'Tis easy to say, we shall go up: but how are we to go? Consider the state of the realm. Thou hast no folk nor people, no host around thee. If thou enter thy city without them, it will go hard with thee if thou fall into the enemy's hand. Thy country men and country women tarry and will not enter thy Kingdom. They fear thy dominion; for thou, O King, art a hard master. Therefore I, thy servant, spake to thee of old. . . . Bore not thy country's belly—that is, cast not reproach upon the rich when they are guiltless, for they are as the belly of thy Kingdom. Seize not nor spoil them of their goods and gold and silver. When rich men died, though they had sons and daughters to inherit, they gat not their inheritance. To seize their goods and squander them till all is gone, this is to bore thy country's belly. Abase not thy country's forehead—that is, deal not harshly in thy reckless choler with thy chief counsellors, thy faithful captains, who are as thy country's forehead. Fell not thy country's banner—that is, wax not wroth nor rage blindly against the wise men, monks and hermits, who are as thy country's banner. Pluck not out thy country's

eye—that is, be not wroth and furious as a devil, without let or thwarting of thine anger, against thy wise chaplains learned in the Pitakas and Vedas, who are as thy country's eye. Break not thy country's tusk—that is, do not chafe and fume, regardless of the future, against the members of thy family, who are as thy country's tusk. Sully not thy country's face—that is, take not by force another's son or daughter who are as the mirror of their parents, their husbands, or sons, for such are as thy country's face. Cut not thy country's feet and hands—that is, kill not in anger, regardless of the future and the present, thy soldiers who are as thy country's feet and hands." And the King said "My Queen, thou didst not tell me all these things before!"

And the Queen continued saying "O King, this is not all. Even now Thihathu hath reached Prome, his province. Doubt not but Thihathu will be thy bane." But the King said "Nay. Did I not alone save his life? When his brother held him in iron fetters and led him away to die, I took and saved him alive. He at least will do me no harm. I will get me to Prome and gather mine army, and thence will I go up to my royal city of Pagan."

So they went upstream in disarray, without union or order. And when they reached the port of Prome, Thihathu stopped the royal raft, and putting poison in food he offered it and said "O King, eat!" But the King wist that there was death in the dish, and he would not eat. When Thihathu heard it he caused three thousand soldiers to go and stand around the royal raft with gleaming swords unsheathed within their hands. And Saw the Queen spake into his ear "O King, all this hath befallen because thou wouldst not hearken to my words of old. And now it is nobler for thee to eat of the poisoned dish and die, than to meet a fearful death with thy blood gushing red at point of sword and lance and weapon." Then he took the ring from off his finger, and poured libation of water over it, and gave it to Queen Saw. And he made a solemn vow saying "In all the lives wherein I wander through eternity until I reach Nirvana, may I never have man child born to me again!" And he took the food and ate; and even as he ate, swift death seized him and he passed beyond. (*Hmannan* I. 361.)

Now that Narathihapate was murdered and the country was in disorder, the Yünnan commanders would no longer be baulked of their prey. They had living among them, to strengthen their disregard of imperial orders, Kubla Khan's spirited grandson, and with him at their head they fought their way down to Pagan with a loss of 7,000 men, occupied the city, and received the homage of the kingdom, sending out detachments one of which reached Tarokmaw below Prome.

Thus perished Pagan amid the blood and flame of the Tartar Terror. Her wide dominions were parcelled out into Shan satrapies owing fealty to China and Siam, her kindly peace fled before the advancing shadows of internecine strife. If the men whose day-dreams became incarnate in the temples of Pagan were also swarthy tyrants whose peevish frown spelt death, whose harems were filled with slave-women, that is only to say they were as other kings of their time. But whatever they were, the legacy of their fleeting sway has enriched posterity for ever. It was they who made the sun-scorched wilderness, the solitary plain of Myingyan, to blossom forth into the architectural magnificence of Pagan. If they produced no nation-builder like Simon de Montfort, no lawgiver like Edward I., they unified Burma for more than two centuries, and that in itself was an achievement. But their role was æsthetic and religious rather than political. To them the world owes in great measure the preservation of Theravada Buddhism, one of the purest faiths mankind has ever known. Brahmanism had strangled it in the land of its birth; in Ceylon its existence was threatened again and again; east of Burma it was not yet free from priestly corruptions; but the kings of Burma never wavered, and at Pagan the stricken faith found a city of refuge. Vainglorious tyrants build themselves lasting sepulchres, but none of these men has a tomb. It is a mistaken sentiment which contrasts the old-time splendour of Pagan with the mat huts of to-day. Then as now hut jostled temple and housed even the great; the two were not antithetic but correlative: these men's magnificence went to glorify their religion, not to deck the tent wherein they camped during this transitory life. Those who doubt the reality of a populous city given up to the spiritual, should read the numberless inscriptions of the period, richly human and intensely devout; contemplate the sixteen square miles at Pagan, all dedicated to religion; contrast each separate brick from the depths of a great pile with the rubble of Norman pillars; reflect that each temple was built not in generations but in months; remember how short was the period when Pagan was inhabited; think of the literary activities of the Kyaukku Onhmin; add to all this our natural preconception of the conditions necessary to the production of great religious art; and then say whether those campaigns for a tooth, those heart searchings over the loss of a white elephant, at which we smile, are not rather possessed of a significance as deep to men of the age as the quest of the Holy Grail had for Arthurian knights.

CHAPTER III

SHAN DOMINION 1287-1531

SHAN DOMINION 1287-1531

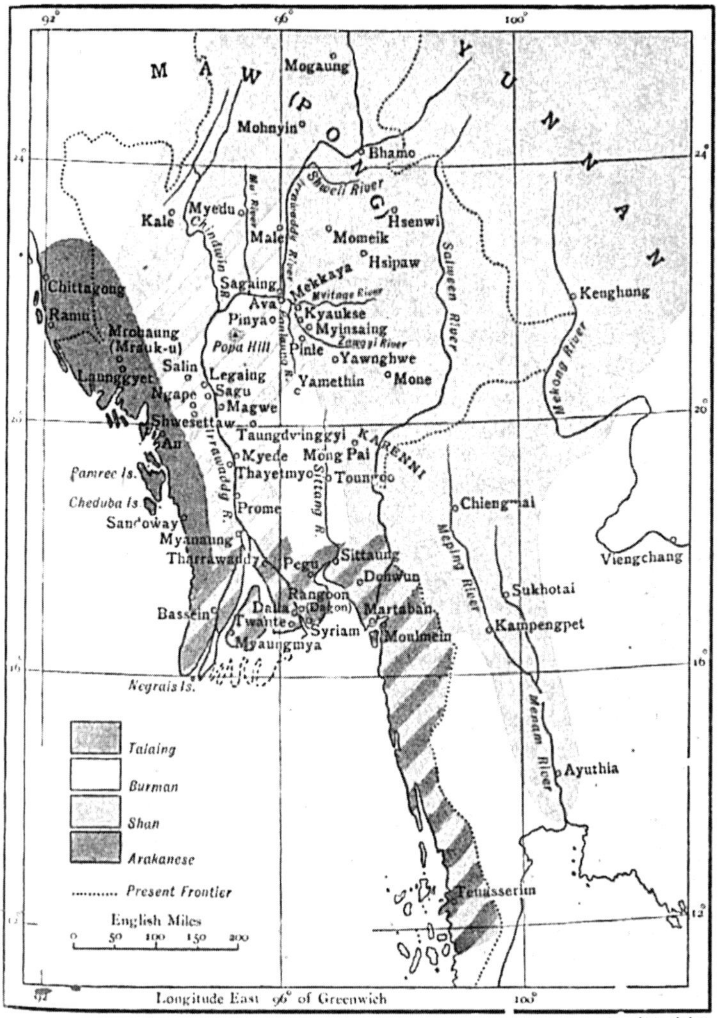

Longmans, Green & Co. London, New York, Toronto, Bombay, Calcutta & Madras.

CHAPTER III

SHAN DOMINION 1287-1531

THE Great Khan accepted the conquest of Burma now that it was an accomplished fact, and for the next two and a half centuries the princelets who ruled the various parts of Upper and even of Lower Burma usually held authority under the Chinese seal. Technically they were Chinese governors; actually they were the native chieftains who would have ruled there in any case, and they did as they pleased.

Since the Nanchao barrier states (p. 13) were henceforth the Chinese province of Yünnan, the road lay open and there was no longer any impediment to communication with Burma. That being so, we should now witness a marked advance in Burmese culture, for China possesses the greatest civilisation in the East. What we actually witness is the exact opposite: for the next two and a half centuries there is a marked decline. Instead of the great dynasty with the refining influence of the palace, we have half a dozen squabbling little courts, all of them, even when not positively barbarous, busily engaged in degrading the country with civil war. Sacred literature languishes, and if pagodas continue to be built, most of them are of a sort which might just as well remain unbuilt, while even the best cannot be mentioned in the same breath as the temples of Pagan. When at length the darkness lifts, it is from the opposite direction to China that two rays of light appear: one is a religious revival from Ceylon, the other is the birth of vernacular literature.[1]

Indeed it was not the Tartars who destroyed the Pagan

[1] See note "Chinese inscription" p. 337.

monarchy. It collapsed temporarily under the defeat but could have risen again had it been a real government. The Tartars did not wish to upset existing conditions, and gave the royal family every support in re-establishing itself. It was washed away by a wave of migration which was beyond the control of a purely dynastic government. What we are now to witness is not so much a series of internal squabbles as a racial movement affecting all Indo-China: the Shans swarm south, east, and west. In 1229 they founded the Ahom kingdom of Assam along the Brahmaputra river, about the same time they made themselves felt in Tenasserim, in 1294 they raided north Arakan, and in 1350 they founded the kingdom of Siam—Siam is the same word as Shan, and she is simply the greatest of Shan states. In Burma they overran the entire country, swamping Burman and Talaing alike. To-day they are the most numerous race in Indo-China, numbering eighteen million.

CHAPTER IIIA

AVA 1287-1555

AFTER murdering his father, Thihathu did not go to Upper Burma, for he knew it was no use trying to murder Tartars. He murdered three of his brothers—the nearest he could get to the Massacre of the Kinsmen (p. 338)—and then tried to recover the Delta. He went to Bassein but instead of trying to make common cause with its lord, his eldest brother Uzana, he hacked him in pieces as he lay ill in bed. He then attacked his other brother Kyawswa at Dalla but was driven off. So he went to Pegu where Tarabya, the lord who had rebelled, shut his gates and stood on the wall hurling insults which stung Thihathu into coming out with a bow to shoot him in such fury that he succeeded only in making the arrow hit himself, with fatal results.

The surviving son Kyawswa returned to Pagan where he paid annual tribute and in 1297 sent his eldest son to receive investiture from the Emperor himself, not as king of Burma, for the kingdom had ceased to exist, but as prince of the Upper Burma state. This state lasted till 1555 and ran from Myedu in Shwebo district and Bangyi in Monyua district to below Prome, and from Laungshe in Pakokku district to Kyaukse; sometimes its authority was real in this area, but sometimes it was not, and from the first the rulers of places such as the recently founded Toungoo (p. 123) were independent chiefs rather than governors.

At the same time as he invested Kyawswa, the Emperor sent a seal to Athinhkaya as prince of Myinsaing in Kyaukse district; Hsenwi had been similarly recognised in 1289, and Mohnyin[1] in 1296. Athinhkaya was eldest of the Three Shan Brothers who now became the real rulers of Upper Burma;

[1] *Parker* "Précis."

the second was Yazathinkyan chief of Mekkaya, the youngest Thihathu chief of Pinle. Their towns, all in Kyaukse district, command passes into the Shan hills and were exactly where a chieftain ruling over hill and plain would fix his stronghold —to command the plain and afford easy escape to his ancestral highlands. They were sons of a hill chief[1] who owing to a family quarrel had fled in 1260 to Myinsaing where there was already a Shan colony; he settled and proceeded to have these three sons and a daughter who married Thihathu, the parricide prince of Prome, for the family rose in favour and Narathihapate entrusted them with the Kyaukse area. The Three Brothers were not quite such savages as some of the later Shan rulers of Upper Burma, for they had been bred at Narathihapate's court. Probably they were loyal so long as the monarchy was unshaken; but when it fell they went their own way and had every temptation to do so because, being in power at Kyaukse, the granary of Upper Burma, they could control the kingdom through its food supplies.

When Kyawswa received the investiture brought back from the Chinese court by his son, he was so pleased that he summoned a great meeting of all his lieges to hear the reading of the imperial rescript. But the Shan brothers would not attend, and in 1298 they plotted with the dowager queen Saw, who thought Kyawswa was not paying her sufficient attention.

> Queen Saw spake unto the king saying "My Lord's ancestor Anawrahta founded eleven villages in the Kyaukse rice land, and the fields thereof are fair as the fields of Pegu. Let my Lord go and see them, and worship at the pagoda on Pyetkaywe Hill." And the king believed her and went with a host of all four arms, and when he was come to Kyaukse he ascended to the Thalyaung pagoda and looked forth from the top of the hill, and lo! he beheld the monastery[2] built at Myinsaing by the Three Shan Brothers. And he asked "What is that shining there?" And queen Saw, being of one mind with the ministers, answered "It is the offering made by us and the Three Brothers on behalf of my Lord. Let my Lord go there and ask a blessing on it." And the king went there unheeding to ask a blessing on it, for he believed her. But when he was come to Myinsaing the Three Brothers made him wear the yellow robe and shave his head and dwell under a guard in that monastery. (*Hmannan* I. 368.)

[1] "Chief of Beinnaka town" says *Hmannan* I. 366. But *GUB* I. i. 198 says *beinnaka* simply means "a man."

[2] Together with it the Three Brothers built the Nandawye pagoda.

Having set up his sixteen-year-old son Sawhnit they reported to Yünnan that Kyawswa was justly deposed for asking Chiengmai to send an army into Burma, and for intercepting envoys whom the new Talaing state of Pegu was sending to Yünnan.

What had really happened was that they had murdered Kyawswa with his eldest son, his monk and a hundred principal followers, alleging him to be in league with the Chinese to enslave the country. He was chained by the leg in a pigsty while they seized his harem; at his death he said "None of my ancestors were ever executed with the sword. Either throw me into the river or strangle me." So they strangled him, and buried him under the palace threshold; but a tempest raged for seven days and his ghost appeared complaining of such ill treatment; so they cremated his remains and cast them into the river; then the tempest subsided.[1] They also burnt Pagan, killed such Chinese as were settled there, killed some more princes, forcibly seized the princesses, and went raiding beyond Male (in Shwebo district), then in the area occupied by the Yünnan government.

Scions of the fallen house applied to the Emperor for protection. The Yünnan commandant asked leave to march with 6,000 men, but the Emperor, in granting sanction, authorised up to 12,000, remarking that it was best to be on the safe side, as the rumour about Chiengmai sending help might turn out to be true. The expedition marched in 1300 and besieged the Brothers in three walled towns at Myinsaing. On their walls the Brothers mounted balistae, and in one assault the Chinese lost 500 men through the arrows, blocks of stone, and beams which were hurled down on the stormers.

Finally the Brothers bought off the commanders with 800 taels of gold and 2,200 taels of silver (66 lb. of gold and 183 of silver), and they withdrew to Yünnan after letting their men help on the Kyaukse irrigation works, constructing Thindwe canal. At the high feast that followed their departure, Thihathu the Shan Brother danced and sang in triumph; the words of the song[2] were his own and they ran:

[1] See note "Royal drowning" p. 338. Kyawswa blends with the warrior prince Minrekyawswa (p. 95) to form the Minkyawswa Nat spirit, *Temple* 56.

[2] *Anthology O.*

တရုပ်လာသည်။	The Chinks came down the passes,
ရိုင်ရိုင်လော။ရိုင်ရိုင်။	Roaring, boys, roaring ;
မြားမိုဃ်းရွာသည်။	The rain of their arrows
ဖြိုင်ဖြိုင်လော။ဖြိုင်ဖြိုင်။	Pouring, boys, pouring.

This is the end of Chinese interference resulting from the 1287 expedition, but none the less there was trouble for those commanders when they reached home. This is the relevant extract from the Chinese record:

> The civil councillor and the pacificator had already surrounded the city, and the food and fuel were exhausted. The Burmese were just on the point of capitulating when these two individuals accepted a heavy bribe to withdraw their troops, the pretext being that the climate was hot and malarious. Let them be executed.

Men now deserted Pagan, for she was clearly ill-omened. But there were probably other reasons as well. Whether the climate had hitherto been fertile or not (p. 15), it was certainly unfertile now, and the soil of Myingyan district assumed its present desolate and barren aspect. Denudation of the forests to provide fuel for pagoda bricks had doubtless lessened the rainfall, and extensive irrigation at Kyaukse might attract rainfall thither from Pagan.

Crops grow there, but not in such quantity as to supply a city of some 50,000 inhabitants who eat rice. There was rice in the Delta, but it was far away and in any case it was not to be had, for the Delta was now under a hostile chief. There was rice in Kyaukse, but a capital there would be too far from the country's one highway, the Irrawaddy river. It was necessary to find a site which should be on the Irrawaddy and accessible to the rice of Kyaukse.

The obvious site was Ava in Sagaing district, where the Myitnge river brought down the grain boats from Kyaukse. But the omens were adverse to Ava, and as the ancients in their wisdom knew better than to disregard omens, Thihathu the Shan Brother ceased to consider Ava and in 1312 set up his Golden Palace at Pinya nearby. He had only himself to consider now, for one of his elder brothers had died and he had just poisoned the other. The opening of the palace was a great event, and at the feast the dowager queen Saw presented a golden belt and a golden tray which had been handed down in the royal family since the time of Anawrahta 1044-77.

She had no children and she had long accepted the Shan as one of the family. He was worth accepting, for he had all power, and the Three Brothers certainly became part of the family when they seized the harem.

Thihathu built pagodas and shared the merit with the son of Kyawswa, the master he had murdered. This son **Sawhnit 1298-1325** and his son **Uzana 1325-69** continued to rule Pagan as *myosa* governors, and with them the dynasty of Anawrahta ended, save on the distaff side where it merged with the new rulers.

The only specific mention of the Ari after their overthrow by Anawrahta (p. 26) occurs in connection with Thihathu's son Sawyun who in 1314 enumerated Ari among his armed retainers; apparently they were like the warrior abbots of contemporary Christendom.

Unlike some of his successors, Thihathu was a Buddhist, with a monk as his teacher, and the 1829 chroniclers regard him as a wise ruler; thus, he would tell one of his sons to attack another in his fief, and meanwhile warn the second son that the first was marching against him. His family ruled till 1364. His son Sawyun set up at Sagaing in 1315 a line which held the north and west independently of the elder branch at Pinya.

The Shans, having dwelt so long in isolated valleys, seem to have inherited centrifugal instincts, and for the next two centuries Burma was the victim of separatist tendencies. Taungdwingyi, with Toungoo, probably under Burmans, and Kyaukse, probably under Shan invaders, revolted. Yet amidst such revolts the following inscription occurs:—

> This realm of Pagan is so named because it is the fairest and dearest of lands. It is also called Arimaddana because its people are warriors who vanquish their foes, and even its name is terrible. Its folk are free from pain or danger, they are skilled in every art, they possess the tools of every craft, they are wealthy, the revenues are past telling and the land is full of useful things. Verily it is a land more to be desired than fairy land. It is a glorious realm and its people are famed for their splendour and power. The monastery I have built stands to the east of the capital. (Year 1343. *Tun Nyein* 134.)

The memory of Pagan must have seemed like a golden age to the donor of the inscription, Narathihapate's daughter Mi Saw U, who was queen to her brother Kyawswa 1287-98 and to his supplanter **Thihathu 1312-24.** Of her sons, one resigned the crown in high dudgeon and entered a monastery on finding that his brother and successor,[1] **Ngasishin 1343-50,** had collected no fewer than five white elephants.

At Sagaing the family assassinated each other and finally the state there passed to a kinsman by marriage. Then Narathu, chief of the Pinya state, angry at an outsider's elevation in Sagaing, asked the Maw Shans to oust him. The Maw Shans had long been in their states to the north, but now they were doubtless greatly strengthened by immigration. They accepted the invitation and swarmed down on Sagaing. Its lord made his elephant drunk on fermented rice, opened the gate, and let it loose on the Shans. But, maddened by their darts, it ran back into the town, knocking down the houses. What with the Shans outside and the elephant inside, the townfolk all stampeded into the jungle, so that when the Shans entered they found nothing but two old men. But they remembered that there were plenty of people in Pinya to carry off as slaves, so they crossed the river, looted Pinya, and went home rejoicing with three white elephants. Narathu regretted his invitation, for they carried him away also. Crowds of Burmans fled to Toungoo,[2] and with this year 1364 such migrations became a regular feature during the Shan irruption into Upper Burma, so that Toungoo became the stronghold of the Burmese race.

After the Maw Shans had departed, **Thadominbya 1364-8,** one of the Sagaing family, killed off his kinsmen (p. 338) who stood in his way there and at Pinya, drained the swamps round Ava, and built the town. It was usually the Burmese capital during the next five centuries; till two generations ago the English, like the Chinese, referred to Burma as Ava, and for the Shans the king of Burma was till the end "The Lord of the Golden Palace at Ava."

On his mother's side Thadominbya was descended from the Three Brothers and his father was a Shan notable of Tagaung through whom he claimed descent from the primitive Pyusawti lineage. He proved his primitive origin in various

[1] He is the Ngasishin Nat spirit, *Temple* 57.

[2] *Tun Nyein* 149.

ways, such as killing a Toungoo rebel and eating a meal on the corpse's chest. One of his right hand men was a dacoit whom he captured and raised to high office instead of torturing him to death as he had originally intended; however, this method of selection was occasionally used as late as 1885.

His country was in uproar to the south. In 1359 Toungoo had raided Kyaukse and still went its own way. He reduced Taungdwingyi in Magwe district, but while trying to take Sagu he was seized with small-pox. As he lay dying at the age of 25, a pagan who had no respect for Buddhism, he told an officer to return to the palace and kill his queen Saw Umma lest she should pass to another man. The officer went upstream to the palace and told her his orders, so she then and there married him. She was of the fallen Pagan house, and, as part of the regalia, had already passed through the hands of four Pinya chiefs in succession. The couple now executed everyone who opposed them, crossed over to Sagaing, and ruled there. But the ministers would not have them, and hawked round the crown, till at last

Minkyiswasawke 1368-1401 accepted it. He drove out the Sagaing couple; the husband absconded and Saw Umma was given to the officer who captured her. Minkyiswasawke was descended from the parricide Thihathu's union with the Shan sister, and so could claim from both Narathihapate 1254-87 and the Shan Brothers. As a child of two he had been carried away into captivity with his brothers and father, the lord of Thayetmyo, when king Minhti of Arakan raided it in 1333. So he was brought up in Arakan; on his release he became *thugyi* of Amyin in Sagaing district and when he became king he made an Arakanese monk his primate.[1]

He now built the Zidaw weir in Kyaukse district and repaired the embankment of Meiktila lake. While superintending work on the lake he met a villager of Wunzin and finding him learned in ancient traditions called him to court where he became famous as the wise minister Wunzinminyaza and lived till 1422.

In 1371 Minkyiswasawke met Binnya U, king of Pegu;

[1] *Tun Nyein* 146, 159. He also built Shwethetlut pagoda at Thayetmyo in 1373 to commemorate the saving of his life when carried away as a child.

they exchanged their betel boxes, spittoons, and such like articles of pomp, and delimited the frontier together. But when Razadarit ascended the throne of Pegu in 1385, his uncle wrote to Minkyiswasawke offering to hold Pegu as a vassal state if he would help to oust Razadarit :—

> I, Laukpya, lord of Myaungmya, bow at thy feet, O king of the Golden Palace at Ava, and pray that thou march against Razadarit before he is firm upon his throne. I will bring men by water. When we have conquered him, do thou keep the heart-wood and leave me the bark (*Razadarit Ayedawpon*).

This started a war between the Upper Burma and Talaing states which lasted a generation. Although Pegu town was never captured and finally held its own, the fighting was almost entirely in the Delta. Possibly it was a war of migration, in that the main avenue of Shan pressure was from the north and the Ava state, thus reinforced, was able to swarm down on Pegu. The Burmese base was Prome and their usual line of advance was down the Hlaing river to Dagon, sometimes with another string of levies going down the Sittang valley from Toungoo. With them marched contingents from allied states, such as Mohnyin, Kale, Yawnghwe; indeed the Talaings sometimes refer to their adversaries as simply "the Shans." The total strength of the invaders would usually be about 12,000.[1] This went on every other year or so, both sides going home for the rains, and there was no warfare in any sense understood by the regular soldier. Now, as to the end of time, it was desultory irregular fighting, consisting largely of ambushes and skirmishes. Occasionally some determined leader would bring about a battle in which there would be real fighting, and then men could be brave and destructive. But the casualties mentioned are seldom more than a decimal per cent. of the numbers engaged and it is difficult to avoid the impression that most of the fighting was of the type not uncommon in mediæval countries, when there was as much shouting as killing and the wretched villagers were the chief sufferers. Not improbably it resembled the fighting which a professional soldier[2] witnessed between

[1] Partly because the *Hmannan* figure is usually 120,000 and the chronicles habitually overestimate by ten, see "Numerical Note" p. 333.

[2] *Crawfurd* II. 39.

Burmans and Talaings in 1827 when "the courage and conduct of both parties were on the very lowest scale."

The energy which should have been directed to reaching a decision was dissipated on tortuous strategems. Thus, a commander would desert to the enemy, complaining of oppression, and fight bravely on their side until the critical moment arrived when he would reveal his true colours with great effect. An ambassador would be arrested and held as hostage. A lord would ask the enemy prince to receive him and his wife as they were in fear of their lives; and when the enemy prince came by boat to meet the distressed lady at the appointed place, her curtained barge would suddenly disgorge a band of armed men. One side would invite the other to discuss terms at a pagoda, and ride up on elephants with daggers concealed in their clothes, but on the way one of the lords would relent and shout a warning to the enemy lords as they came riding along; he is called upon by the infuriated king to explain why he gave away the plot, and the delighted chronicler is thus enabled to put into his mouth a noble reply on the imperative necessity of honourable dealing. A besieged commander forges a letter from his king announcing his early arrival with overwhelming forces, sends men out with this letter and they pretend to get in again through the lines of the besiegers who capture them, read the letter, and beat a terrified retreat. A leader challenges the enemy's best commander to single combat in war canoes, and when his canoe is fully engaged, three other war canoes, which have been concealed, dart out and finish him.

The ideal of Burmese warriors was cunning. Yet there are less unattractive stories, some of which probably happened at one time or another, and in any case they mirror the mind of the people. The commanders and even kings sometimes challenge each other to single combat, and actually fight, though seldom with serious results, partly no doubt because they felt due respect for their august skins, but also because it was mainly an affair of elephants, and one of the two elephants would find the other too strong for him, unlock his tusk, and turn tail. Or take the following Burmese account of a Talaing exploit in 1415 when Minrekyawswa, the famous

Burmese prince, is besieging Dalla, defended by prince Binnyadala, son of king Razadarit. The town starves and Razadarit sends gold so that the besieged may buy food—how, the chronicler does not explain. The gold is smuggled into the town by Emuntaya, a Talaing officer from Pegu, who deserts to the Burmese until they let him fight close up to the walls, whereupon he slips into the town.

> Then prince Minrekyawswa shouted out to prince Binnyadala "Emuntaya spake untruth and hath done me disrespect. By guile hath he entered the town. But if he can come out and return to his king, I will give him great gifts." When prince Binnyadala told these words to Emuntaya, he said "Son of my glorious master, tell them that Emuntaya will go up to Pegu to-morrow." And the Burmese shouted "Hath Emuntaya wings to fly above? Or is he a snake that can creep beneath? He entered the town by guile only." And Emuntaya answered them "I shall win forth, keep what guard ye please." And prince Minrekyawswa charged his captains saying "To-morrow Emuntaya will come forth, saith he. Keep ye watch to take him." And they kept double watch by land and water. But Emuntaya gave unto the king's son Binnyadala the five *viss* of gold that the king had entrusted unto him, and then he made the counsellors and captains go far away, and before dawn he caused men to make a raft of plantain trees, and he thrust his sword inside one of the trees. And he made himself appear like a corpse, smearing his cheeks and ears with turmeric, and wrapping his body round with old matting. And four or five women let down their hair and beat their breasts and wept as they wailed "Other husbands cleave to wife and child through good and ill, and forsake them not in war or famine. But thou hast forsaken us and gone away. What shall we do, thy wife and orphans, in this cruel war, this cruel famine?" Thus wailing they lifted up the corpse, while the Burmese soldiers who were near the Shan-Death gate of the town looked on. Gently the women laid the body on the plantain raft, with an earthen dish and a cup of rice and a chicken; and they lit oil lights and placed them at the head, and pushed forth the raft into the middle of the stream. And the women followed it beating their breasts and weeping and crying aloud "Shalt thou forsake us thus?" But the raft floated along and came near to a Burmese boat, and the Burmese said "See! It is a corpse," and they pushed it away with a bamboo. And the raft was carried up stream by a strong flood tide, and when it was come to Ta-paw-ta-ngauk [in Pegu district near Kyauktan], because it was now far from the Burmese boats, Emuntaya took his sword from out the plantain log and went up to Pegu. . . . And prince Minrekyawswa sent a messenger to Pegu . . . and the messenger asked king Razadarit saying "My master asks if it be true that Emuntaya hath returned to thee, as men say." And king Razadarit

> called Emuntaya and he came before the messenger. And when the messenger saw him, he gave him a horse with golden trappings and a velvet robe from prince Minrekyawswa. (*Hmannan* II. 44.)

Minkyiswasawke attacked such places as Pankyaw north of Pegu, Hmawbi, Dalla, Dagon, and the then town of Hlaing, and after succeeding in some cases in spite of the mosquitoes,[1] would withdraw for the rains. In 1390 Razadarit captured Myaungmya with its rebel lord whose son Nawrahta and son-in-law Pyanchi fled to Minkyiswasawke. Nawrahta was made lord of Salin and Pyanchi lord of Prome and henceforth they are prominent leaders on the Burmese side. In 1391 Razadarit cleared the Burmese out of their frontier garrison Myanaung (Lunhse, Kudut) in Henzada district. Minkyiswasawke tried to recapture it but was beaten off with the loss of his own golden barge, which the Talaings returned, with a chivalrous letter. Also, contrary to usual practice, they treated the Burmese wounded humanely and even returned them, for Razadarit made several efforts to stop the war and live on friendly terms; but the Burmese always insisted on renewing the struggle.

In 1371 the *sawbwas* of Kale in the Upper Chindwin district and Mohnyin in Katha district each applied to Minkyiswasawke asking him to help oust the other and promising to become tributary. The wise minister Wunzin-minyaza said "Temporise and let them fight it out till they are exhausted and then you can get both." The king did so, and secured a nominal supremacy, but in 1373 Mohnyin raided the frontier at Myedu in Shwebo district and the king had so much trouble that he sent an embassy to Yünnan in 1383. China thereupon graciously appointed him governor of Ava and ordered Mohnyin to behave.[2] In 1393 Mohnyin came again in spite of the homily; the lord of Legaing in Minbu district marched to Tagaung against him but was driven headlong into Sagaing town while the Shans burnt the houses and monasteries outside the walls until Thilawa of Yamethin came up and broke them, pursuing them as far as Shangon (20 miles N.W. of Sagaing town) where he heaped their corpses in piles. Thilawa was a great character. He was brother-in-law to the king and had refused the crown in 1368, saying "I do not

[1] *Hmannan* I. 430. [2] *Parker* "Précis."

open my mouth to speak three words a day. You had better choose Minkyiswasawke." He laughed only thrice in his life, one occasion being at Yamethin when his wife interrupted a cock-fight he was watching to tell him that the Shans were rushing the town; she was so dishevelled that even he smiled; but he finished the cock-fight before driving off the Shans.

In 1374 the throne of Arakan was vacant and some of the faction-ridden people asked Minkyiswasawke to send a king. He sent his uncle Sawmungyi, charging him to cherish the people and rule justly. On Sawmungyi's death in 1381 he sent his own son by the daughter of the wise minister Wunzinminyaza; but this son oppressed the Arakanese and soon came fleeing back to Ava.

Like every other chief of Ava, Minkyiswasawke had even less control over Toungoo than over other outlying areas. But when he found its chief, Pyanchi, becoming friendly with Pegu in 1377, he told his brother, lord of Prome, to inveigle Pyanchi into a visit and kill him. The king's brother carried out instructions with the skill of an artist. He wrote to Pyanchi "Come and marry your son to my daughter." Pyanchi accepted the invitation and came with his son to Prome, staying just outside at Nawin where during the night his host fell on him unawares, did him to death, and seized his retinue and much booty. The king rewarded this exploit with rich presents, and the 1829 chroniclers who record the incident classify him as a king with a most upright heart.[1] He died at the age of 70, and after some palace murders was finally succeeded by a younger son.

Minhkaung 1401-22 had been married by his father to Shinminauk, a daughter presented by the chief of the Maw Shans during a friendly mood at the time when the Talaing king Razadarit put to death his own son Bawlawkyantaw (p. 114). A year later, during her first pregnancy, she longed for strange food from the Delta, so the family asked Razadarit, though a foe, to send some. Razadarit consulted with his ministers and they perceived that the unborn child must be Bawlawkyantaw himself taking flesh again according to his dying prayer; they sent the food, such as mangoes from Dalla, having bewitched it.

[1] *Hmannan* I. 420, 440.

The child, prince Minrekyawswa, was born in 1391 and was already campaigning at the age of thirteen when he accompanied the 1404 expedition to Arakan. This expedition was a reprisal for an Arakanese raid on Yaw and Laungshe in Pakokku district. It was completely successful, for the Burmese, marching from Minbu up the An Pass where they broke the enemy at Hnanwin Hill[1] and killed the leader, probably the lord of An, occupied the capital Launggyet and drove out the king Narameikhla who fled to Bengal. They returned after leaving behind as king Anawrahtaminsaw, who next year was sent the five regalia and a bride aged thirteen, Sawpyechantha, the sister of Minrekyawswa.

The Onbaung (Hsipaw) and Yawnghwe *sawbwas* entered into friendly relations with Minhkaung, partly owing to the tact of Wunzinminyaza. In 1406 the Burmese, siding with Kale, occupied Mohnyin in Katha district, overrunning the state and killing the chief. China sent an envoy[2] to expostulate with the Burmese, who withdrew as they would doubtless have done in any case. In 1407 Minhkaung, who had for years been recognised as governor by China, sent a mission to Yünnan. In 1413 the northern Shan state of Hsenwi ravaged the Ava villages and sent some prisoners to Pekin, but Minrekyawswa broke the Hsenwi host at Wetwin near Maymyo, himself killing their leader in single combat on his elephant; in the next year Hsenwi made another foray at the instigation of Razadarit, whose envoys travelled via Chiengmai, carrying a considerable weight of gold as an inducement. Two Shan brothers, chiefs of Mawke and Mawdon in Shwebo district, attacked Myedu until Minrekyawswa drove them off in 1414; in 1415, while he was away in the Delta, they came back and ravaged up to the walls of Ava, which they invested for a time.[3]

Taking advantage of the palace troubles which attended Minhkaung's accession, Razadarit made several raids, and in 1406 he came up the Irrawaddy river. It is characteristic of Burmese warfare that though he failed to reduce the Burmese

[1] Sanwingaing Hill in Ngape township, Minbu district.

[2] *Parker* "Précis," *BEFEO* 1904 Huber "Une embassade chinoise en Birmanie en 1406."

[3] See note "Smim Payan" p. 339.

garrisons at Prome Myede and Pagan, he simply left them in his rear, pressed on straight to Sagaing and camped there, raising the white umbrella and beating his drums. Minhkaung was taken at a loss and called a great council. Nobody dared speak, for after all there was nothing to be said. But at last an eminent monk of Pinya came forward saying he had eloquence enough to persuade any king in the universe, and he would undertake a parley. Minhkaung consented and the monk went forth riding a tall elephant with a golden howdah, attended by 300 *thadinthon* (fasting elders) robed in white, 300 old men bearing presents, and many elephants also loaded with silks and rich gifts. They met Razadarit on his great barge moored at O-hteinmaw village, north of Shwekyetyet in Mandalay district. There the monk spoke holy words on the sin of bloodshed and Razadarit inclined his ear. It was the most graceful thing to do, for he could not stay for ever in Upper Burma, and although he might have devastated as many villages as he liked, he could hardly reduce the walled town of Ava. He consented to withdraw on the return of a detachment which had gone ravaging up to Tagaung; he even rebuked his men for taking the heads of forty of the Shwekyetyet pagoda slaves.

Having broken up his state barge and built therewith a *zayat* at the pagoda, he went down-stream with all his host and many prisoners from the villages. He had only reached Kyauktalon, the landing stage below Ava, when, looking back, he saw the smoke ascend from his *zayat* which the Burmese were already burning; and when, lower still, he received news of his daughter's capture he could with difficulty be restrained from returning. She had been taken by the Prome garrison under the son-in-law of his enemy Laukpya and was now sent to the Ava harem.

Razadarit executed her husband for failing to prevent her capture, and as soon as the rains were over he invested Prome. On hearing that Minhkaung was coming in great strength along the east bank of the Irrawaddy, the Talaing commanders Byat Za and Deinmaniyut wished to withdraw all forces to the west bank where the majority already lay at Thalesi lower down. But the commander of three stockades at Nawin, just north of Prome, insisted on being left where he was, and

Razadarit consented, over-riding his two senior commanders. Minhkaung arrived before he was expected, for his men covered the last forty-five miles down the river from Myede in a single night, planted their scaling ladders at dawn, and were swarming inside the three stockades before the Talaings had rubbed the sleep out of their eyes.

But although Minhkaung killed or captured them all, from the commander downwards, the enemy main body was still intact on the west bank and now proceeded to send 300 war canoes upstream to ravage the villagers as far as Thayetmyo and cut his communications. His men had brought nothing but what they slung on their shoulders; in a few days they were starving, and he had to ask for terms. Meeting with a refusal, he promised his liberty to the captive Talaing commander, who was father to two of Razadarit's queens, if he could get them to work on Razadarit's feelings. The captive commander sent this letter to the two queens in Razadarit's camp:—

> Suffer me not to die a captive in my old age, without my two daughters to close my eyes. If I die in a foreign land, my regret will drive me to the four hells. I shall never rest till the two kings are at peace. Dear daughters, entreat His Majesty to make peace. (Year 1406, *Hmannan* I 467.)

They came weeping into Razadarit's presence. He consulted Byat Za, who said "He went his own way. He let himself be taken. It is all one whether he lives or dies." Razadarit said to his queens "I overrode Byat Za once, and see the result. I cannot override him again." They therefore sent Byat Za rich presents, including a *viss* (3·65 lb.) of gold, which he promptly returned without an answer. They worried the king again, and he again asked Byat Za, who said "I am concerned with my king's victories, not with women's feelings."

But at last, day after day, clinging to Razadarit's knees, the two queens had their will and he granted terms. In spite of his victory he consented to evacuate Myanaung, although he had won it and it was really a Talaing town. Both sides exchanged prisoners and the frontier remained as before below Prome. The armies fraternised, and Byat Za received especial honour in the camp of his Burmese enemies.

The two princes sent each other richly caparisoned elephants, they exchanged their white umbrellas and plate, and they ate together in high festival. Before going their several ways, they worshipped at the Shwehsandaw pagoda, holding each other by the hand as they mounted the steps, and plighting their troth to eternal love and friendship.

Next year, Minhkaung even acceded to Razadarit's request for a marriage alliance and sent his sister in charge of the minister Wunzinminyaza to Kawliya in Pegu district where she was married to Razadarit amid great rejoicings. Razadarit granted Minhkaung the customs revenue of Bassein. This, and the fact that throughout the fifteenth century Tharrawaddy was subject to Prome and was held by a governor who was appointed, at least nominally, by Ava, suggests that one cause of the war was the need of Ava to trade along the Irrawaddy as far south as possible.

Razadarit could hound his devoted wife into her grave, he could murder his son and wretched suppliants, but when it was necessary to be hard with a purpose he sold his country for a woman's tears. At Prome he had held in the hollow of his hand the young manhood of the Burmese race, with their men of mark from the dynasty downwards. It was his duty to end the struggle for at least a generation. The numbers that would have fallen or passed into captivity there would have been fewer than those who fell during the succeeding years of dreary warfare, and meanwhile his people would have had peace. How little the unctuous promises at the Shwehsandaw pagoda were worth was soon to appear.

After the king of Arakan had fled to Bengal (p. 87), his son fled to Sandoway, where, hearing that Razadarit was at Bassein, he came to pay homage at Bassein and started working on Razadarit's feelings so as to get reinstated in Arakan. Again, there came Minhkaung's younger brother Theiddat (p. 96); he had loyally helped Minhkaung to his throne, going out to do battle in his stead when he wavered, and killing a rival claimant for him; when in 1407 Minhkaung passed him over and appointed Minrekyawswa *yuvaraja* (crown prince), he was naturally furious, rebelled, fought Minhkaung hand to hand on his elephant, and fled to Pegu where Razadarit gave him great state. Minhkaung now sent a cavalcade of a hundred men with a letter to the chief of Chiengmai. But south of Toungoo they missed their way and strayed into the territory of the Talaing governor of Zayatmyo who sent them under arrest to his king. Razadarit took their papers and read

> Letter from Minhkaung, Lord of the Golden Palace, to the King of Chiengmai. Razadarit hath broken the oath he sware in the holy presence of the Shwehsandaw pagoda. . . . He hath received my younger brother who fled because I corrected him for ill-using me. He sendeth no more his tribute of thirty elephants and the customs revenue of Bassein. Whereas he hath thus proved ungrateful and faithless, I will march against him. Do thou also, cousin, march by way of Sittaung. And when I have had my will on Pegu I will give thee its virgin daughters and great elephants and horses and all that thy heart desireth. (*Hmannan* I. 480.)

Razadarit said nothing but released the envoys and sent them back to Minhkaung with the letter, its seals broken. He also told the refugee Arakanese prince to have his way. The prince marched home with Talaing commanders whose levies had strict orders to refrain from the usual excesses and to explain to the population that they made war not on the country but on the Burmese intruders. The people were delighted and came to join them on the way. The townsfolk of the capital Launggyet deserted to them, leaving Anawrahtaminsaw in the palace with only his Burmese guards round him. The Talaings took altogether 3,000 Burmans, probably including the garrison's families, and deported them to the Delta. On arrival there, Anawrahtaminsaw[1] was executed and his little queen Sawpyechantha passed into Razadarit's harem, not however as a concubine but as a full queen.

When her father Minhkaung heard the news he burst into fury and called a council. He might as well not have called it, for he would listen to nothing it said. In vain did Wunzinminyaza and the commanders point out the madness of marching now, for by the times the levies were raised and had reached the Delta, the rains would be on and the Talaing land would be a swamp. Minhkaung would not listen. Raging through the May heat he marched down from Toungoo with crowds of levies who swarmed over the hapless country like

[1] He merges with Nawrahta (p. 105) into the Shwenawrahta Nat spirit, *Temple* 56.

locusts, ravaging villages by the score. But at Pankyaw, north of Pegu, he was checked and had to stockade himself. The rain never ceased night nor day, his communications were cut, he had no supplies, and soon he was asking for terms again and proposing more marriage alliances. The Talaings took good care that his envoys should see Sawpyechantha waiting humbly on her new lord, but they granted no terms, and proceeded to devise a series of tricks which the chroniclers regard as profound strategy. Once they nearly ambushed Minhkaung with the aid of his refugee brother Theiddat and though Minhkaung got away, Razadarit executed Theiddat for having relented at the critical moment and shouted a warning. The series ended with his sending Lagunein, one of the Talaing heroes throughout these years, to slay Minhkaung while asleep.

Lagunein chose twelve brave men. They took swords and spears and after the second hour of the night they came to king Minhkaung's camp and went round spying it. On the north side they saw where the moat was shallow and the guards few and the fence weak. Now there was an *okhne* bush [Streblus asper, Lour.] outside, so they hid thereunder, and took two stakes out of the fence and entered in. Three men he left at the *okhne* bush; three he left behind, charging them "If the captain riseth up, cut him down"; three he left at the elephant sheds, charging them "If men wake, cut the elephant fastenings"; three he took with him and they went in under the royal hut. And Lagunein stood on the shoulders of his two companions and cut the fastenings and opened the floor and went up on to the hut. There he took the betel box of king Minhkaung and handed it down to the men below. Then he took the king's ruby sword, but when he was about to smite him, the concubine who was set to watch during the night saw him in the light of a lamp and cried aloud "Talaing thief!" and the king awoke and the attendants arose in confusion. But the three men cut the elephant fastenings and many elephants ran loose so that the Burmese said "It is but a false alarm, it is but the elephants breaking loose!" And Lagunein and those with him escaped, and when they arrived outside he counted his men and they were twelve complete, and they returned. But in the Burmese camp there was noise for about the space of two hours. And when Lagunein and his men were come, Razadarit asked "Is it done?" and Lagunein answered saying "My father and mother taught me that he who taketh the life of a consecrated king, his life is not long neither hath he honour among the children of men. Therefore I slew him not, that my days may be long to serve thee. And lest thou believe not that I came to his side, see here his betel box and his ruby sword." And when the betel box and ruby sword were shewn to king Minhkaung's daughter

Sawpyechantha, she wept saying "They are his." And Razadarit was well pleased and he said to Lagunein "I give thee thy life." (*Hmannan* I. 487.) Cf. I Samuel xxvi 6-21.

Next day Minhkaung knew it was not a scare among the elephants, for his betel box and sword were missing. He proceeded to cut his way out. The devoted men around him saw that he got safely through, but his wretched levies were shattered "as a bundle of bamboos is broken and scatters." His queen Shinminauk[1] the Maw Shan mother of Minrekyawswa was captured in the rout, and the south queen Shin Bo-me fell off her elephant and was wandering hopelessly by the banks of a stream when the Master of the Elephants luckily found her. Minhkaung could not be troubled with what became of his queens or his men, many of whom, including all his sick and wounded, were captured; he was busily engaged in performing the remarkable feat of reaching Ava in seven days. There he was in such a state of nerves that he would jump at hearing a drum, and even *nat* spirit dances had to be stopped. He said "They've got the Maw girl. If they have taken Shin Bo-me also, I do not wish to live longer." When, some days later, the Master of the Elephants appeared with Shin Bo-me safe and sound, the king was beside himself with joy and overwhelmed him with rewards. But subsequently Shin Bo-me, vexed at dropping her betel-cutter, happened to utter the Master of the Elephants' name. The king at once became suspicious and questioned him.

And the Master of the Elephants answered "My lord, from the moment I found the queen wandering by the stream I knew that I must die. If I saved her not, she would fall into the enemy's hand, and when she was restored she would tell my lord that though I saw her I saved her not, and then not only myself but my wife and children also would die the death. But if I saved her my lord would never believe me, and I knew that I should die. Yet in very truth, from the day I found her, if when we came to rest it was a wood, I built her a sleeping place on a tree, with branches tied together, but I and the mahout kept watch on the ground till it was dawn, and we placed her on the elephant and continued on our way; and if when we came to rest it was a village, we put her on a house to sleep, but we slept on the ground." And the king said "Fine words!" and they executed him. Thereafter he called the mahout and questioned him and he said

[1] She is the Anaukmibaya Nat spirit, *Temple* 56.

> even as the Master of the Elephants had said. And the king repented him exceedingly saying "I have slain a faithful servant" and he gave unto the dead man's son his father's villages and made him Master of the Elephants in his stead. (*Hmannan* I. 490.)

Minhkaung's treatment of the Master of the Elephants reached the ears of the Talaings, and they made a proverb[1] about it —"If you find a man down, leave him down, unless you want to be down yourself."

After this defeat Minhkaung seldom accompanied an advance into Lower Burma but left the war to Minrekyawswa. Now that not only his sister Sawpyechantha, but also their mother, Shinminauk the Maw Shan, was a prisoner in Razadarit's harem, Minrekyawswa became a fiend. "As a crocodile eats his victims, so will I rend the flesh of the Talaings" he said. Sometimes his men, Shans and Burmans who had never seen the sea, lost heavily by being lured into tidal swamps. Sometimes both sides would march into Arakan and fight round Sandoway. In 1412 Minrekyawswa ousted the Arakanese prince whom the Talaings had restored, and in 1413 the Talaings as promptly marched back and turned out the Burmese governors.

But even when Minrekyawswa was recalled to Ava to deal with the Shan trouble which Razadarit had stirred up (p. 87), the Talaings were too exhausted to follow him, and he ended by making their lives unbearable. Numbers of them were deported to Upper Burma. Their great captain Byat Za aged and ended his days in his fief of Myaungmya, other old leaders died off one by one, no fields could be worked in Myaungmya and Bassein for terror of the Burmese, and in 1415 the whole west side paid Minrekyawswa homage. Eastwards he came ravaging almost within sight of the Shwemawdaw pagoda and things were in such a pass that a hundred Talaings would turn tail at the sight of a couple of Shan-Burmans. He kept writing to his father for support, but Minhkaung was ageing and said he was a young hot-head who overestimated the chances of success. None the less Razadarit had only Pegu and Martaban left him and clasped his knees in despair, saying "Why, when I was a lad of sixteen with only two score men at my back, I had won half my kingdom. Minhkaung has a real son, but you sons of mine are useless."

[1] *Razadarit Ayedawpon.*

Yet finally he had his revenge when in 1417 the raging re-incarnation of Bawlawkyantaw (p. 86) came to an end. Razadarit, choosing a day when the omens were favourable, and trusting to Minrekyawswa's impetuosity, set out from his stockade at Kyattale near Twante, lured Minrekyawswa out of his besieging lines at Dalla till he was separated from his men, and then, himself heading some thirty lords on their elephants, dashed out on him. Minrekyawswa's elephant, maddened with a hundred gashes, shook him off and crushed his thigh; he crawled away under an *okhne* bush (Streblus asper, Lour.), but was found and taken to Razadarit's camp. There he refused Razadarit's chivalrous advances and died during the night, uttering hatred with his last breath.[1]

The news of his death spread consternation among the Burmese garrisons in the Delta. Some of the levies collapsed and fled back to Ava. Minhkaung came down to Dalla and exhumed his son's bones from where Razadarit had given them honourable burial. The whole court knelt by the grave-side while they were placed in a gold pot and then, shaded by the white umbrella, they were borne solemnly away and dropped into the water at Mahtiwa (Pathiwa), the river mouth near Twante. There was little more fighting, and the Delta was free from the Burmese.

The Ari-gyi-do-ahnwe (descendants of the Ari) frequented Minhkaung's palace and drank there, sometimes ending in such a condition that they had to be carried back to their monasteries in palanquins.[2]

After Minrekyawswa's death, Minhkaung was heart-broken, and spent his remaining years in piety. He was succeeded peacefully by his son, born of the Maw Shan queen.

Thihathu 1422-6 took over his father's queen Shin Bo-me (p. 93) and was so fond of her that his first wife retired into religion. But he marched into the Delta to help in a quarrel among Razadarit's sons, and when he came back it was with their sister Shinsawbu (p. 116) as bride; he crowned her queen consort in great state and grew so fond of her that Shin Bo-me

[1] He blends with Kyawswa 1287-98 (p. 77) into the Minkyawswa Nat spirit, *Temple* 56.

[2] *ARASI* 1915-16 Duroiselle "The Ari of Burma and Tantric Buddhism 93. See notes "Ari" and "Drink" pp. 313, 314.

sent a message to the *sawbwa* of Onbaung (Hsipaw). The *sawbwa* hid in the wood with a bow near where the king was making a canal at Aungbinle in Mandalay district, and shot him dead.

But the court would not set the *sawbwa* on the throne and instead appointed the dead king's nine year old son; him Shin Bo-me poisoned in three months and brought in a cousin of the royal house, **Kalekyetaungnyo 1426-7**, who was supported by Onbaung. A senior lord, Mohnyinthado, drove off the Onbaung levies and began to encircle Ava. The lords deserted Kalekyetaungnyo and withdrew to their fiefs. Shin Bo-me, seeing she had too few men to resist, fled with her lover to Arakan. They went in a single boat to Salin and then started overland for the An Pass. But when near Shwesettaw, Kalekyetaungnyo[1] sickened and died. Shin Bo-me, in despair, thought of fleeing to the Talaing country. But the one faithful lord who still attended her said "Many men have seized the throne but none has ever harmed the crowned queen of his predecessor. Abide here and await events." So there in the woodland, by the holy hill, she took her rest.

Mohnyinthado 1427-40 had as good a claim as anyone, because recent kings had few sons by recognised queens, and he was of semi-royal blood. He had had a romantic career. Saying their lives were not safe in the palace because of their elder brother, Minkyiswasawke 1368-1401 had turned out his little sons Minhkaung 1401-22 and Theiddat (p. 90) in the care of some attendants. They lived as wandering minstrels and *nat* spirit dancers, one of the older attendants playing a drum, another a horn, and so on. Thus they strayed down to Taungdwingyi, and then, crossing over to Minbu district, lived at Ngape and Padein. Later the father recalled them, saying the lads could take their chance in the palace. When Minhkaung 1401-22 came to reign, he remembered the companions of those early days; he who blew the horn became Letyagyi lord of Toungoo 1409-12 and then, being old, was transferred to a less arduous charge away from the Talaing frontier. A little boy who had followed the two young princes to wait on them became Mohnyinthado; he was one of Minrekyawswa's

[1] He restored the Shwepaunglaung pagoda in Sagaing district, built in the twelfth century by the monk Paunglaungshin Kathapa.

best captains, winning fame in 1406 when he fought his way into Prome with pack-ponies carrying rice, and having provisioned the garrison fought his way out again through the Talaing lines; thereupon the king gave him one of his own queens together with Mohnyin, which had just then happened to come under the influence of Ava. He was forty-seven when he ascended the throne. His braves celebrated the event by sacrificing horses and cattle to the Mahagiri spirit on Popa Hill, but after they were flayed the carcases stood up and bellowed as if alive. He allowed nobody but himself to interpret the omen, and he interpreted it to mean that his seed should reign for seven generations; and they actually reigned until 1527.

Shin Bo-me had not long to wait at Shwesettaw before he sent for her. Men called her fair, but it would have mattered little had she been plain. No king could afford to weaken his claim by omitting to unite his blood with his predecessor's queens. He was her fifth crowned consort but she died childless.[1] In delight at getting her he built the Chanthagyi pagoda at Minbu town.

He took Shinsawbu (p. 95) from the lord of Pagan to whom she had been given during the recent upheavals, but she tired of Upper Burma, as he bestowed his principal affections elsewhere. She had two Talaing monks to teach her letters, and in 1430, at the age of thirty-six, she managed to get out of the palace on the pretext of being ill, and fled down the river to Pegu with her two monks whose presence facilitated her flight, as, by benefit of clergy, a boat carrying monks could not be challenged.

Mohnyinthado's reign was spent trying to maintain his throne. Taungdwingyi, Yamethin, Pinle, and above all Toungoo, under princes of much the same standing as himself, went their own way and treated him as at best a senior. When he tried to reduce these towns, he found some of them defended by Shans, possibly recent immigrants; and Onbaung (Hsipaw) and Yawnghwe made common cause with them. He was so weak that he had only intermittent control of the Kyaukse canals on which his granaries depended. Onbaung attacked

[1] See note "Married his father's queen" p. 324.

Myedu and the northern frontier in Shwebo district, and even for eight months drove him out of his palace, withdrawing only on payment of a large sum. Binnyaran, the prince of Pegu, retained his exiles and was in league with Toungoo but never actually invaded the Ava state; when he sent envoys to Ava asking for a princess as the price of extraditing a fugitive lord and of ceasing to besiege Prome, Mohnyinthado was so angry that he kept the envoys waiting three months without audience and had to be dissuaded from killing them;[1] but finally he gave the princess.

About 1435 the first European wandered into Burma. This was Nicolo di Conti, a merchant of Venice—

> He arrived at the city of Ternassari [Tenasserim] which is situated on the mouth of a river of that name; this district abounds in elephants and a species of thrush. Afterwards having made many journeys he entered the mouth of the river Ganges . . . and departing thence he arrived at the mouth of the river Racha [Arakan], and navigating up the river he came to a large city of the same name. Quitting this city he travelled through mountains void of all habitations and then through open plains and arrived at a river larger than the Ganges. Having sailed up this river for a month he arrived at a city more noble than the rest, called Ava. This province abounds in elephants; the king keeps ten thousand and uses them in his wars. They fix castles on their backs from which eight to ten men fight with javelins and bows. This animal is so intelligent that when he is in battle he frequently receives the javelins of the enemy on the sole of his foot in order that those whom he carries on his back may not be injured. The king of this province rides on a white elephant, round the neck of which is fastened a chain of gold ornamented with precious stones which reaches to its feet. The men are satisfied with one wife. All the inhabitants, men as well as women, puncture their flesh with iron pins and rub in indelible dyes, and so they remain painted for ever. All worship idols, yet when they arise in the morning from their bed they turn towards the east and, with hands joined together, say "God in His Trinity and His Law defend us" [clearly the prayer "I take refuge in the Lord, I take refuge in his Law, I take refuge in his Clergy"]. There is also a tree called *tal* [talipot palm], the leaves of which are extremely large, and upon these they write, for throughout India they do not use paper. There is also an animal [the rhinoceros] which has a head like a pig, a tail like an ox, and on his forehead a horn like that of a unicorn but shorter, being about a cubit in length. In size and colour it resembles the elephant with which it is constantly at war. They say its horn is an antidote

[1] *Hmannan* II. 82.

> against poisons, and it is on this account much esteemed. In the upper part of the country, towards Cathay, there are found black and white bulls the hair of whose tail, fine and light as a feather, is valued at its weight in silver and is made into fans for the service of their idols and their kings. The cavalry also carry the hair at the head of their lances as a mark of nobility. Beyond this province is a land superior to all others in the world, and it is named Cathay [China]. Afterwards he departed from Ava and proceeded towards the sea and at the end of seventeen days he arrived at the mouth of a moderately sized river, and having entered the river, at the end of ten days he arrived at a very populous city called Panconia (= Pago, Pegu. Nicolo di Conti's full text is in *Major*).

In 1430 two monks returned from Ceylon with five relics and though the Talaings stopped them at Bassein they insisted on reaching Ava where the whole court came out to meet them. Mohnyinthado built them a huge monastery of which the site, Kyaungdawgyi, is still to be seen two miles west of Sagaing, and nearby he built a pagoda, Yatanazedi, now called Payabyu, to enshrine the relics. He died shortly after making a minor alteration in the calendar. When the monks cautioned him that kings who alter the calendar die he said, "If I must die, let me die. I will not be put into a song as the king who was afraid to do his duty."

He was succeeded by his sons **Minrekyawswa 1440-3** and **Narapati 1443-69**. Their kinsmen for a time gained Kale and Mohnyin and proceeded to capture the Maw Shan chief Thonganbwa when he was being hard pressed by the Yünnan government. Narapati refused to surrender him, denied his own liability to tribute, and in 1445 drove off the Yünnan levies at Kaungton in Bhamo district. But when in 1446 they appeared in strength before Ava, he yielded. Thonganbwa committed suicide, so only his followers and his body could be given up. The Chinese removed the inside, dried the body in the sun and at the fire, thrust an iron spit through it and took it away.[1]

Before returning they assisted the king in reducing Yamethin which was in rebellion. In 1451 they sent him

[1] Thonganbwa is given at *Hmannan* II. 97, *Parker* "Burma, relations with China" 44 and "Précis," the Burmese and Chinese versions agreeing in essentials. The Shan version in *Pemberton* 111-2 gives date 1333, a mere century's inacurracy being nothing in a Shan chronicle; it misled *Phayre* "History" 61, 85 into recording the event as if it were two events, one at each of these dates.

a golden seal as governor of Ava and in 1454 they gave him some Shan territory in return for the surrender of a Mohnyin chief with whose resistance to China he had previously sympathised. At this time China enumerated in and near Burma eight states held by what she was pleased to consider her "comforters" or governors, of which five can be identified —Ava, Kenghung, Hsenwi, Pegu, and the country round Viengchang (Linzin).[1]

In 1443 king Narapati built the Tupayon pagoda at Sagaing, and the dedication festival was attended by the neighbouring *sawbwas* and by people, probably pedlars who happened to arrive, from Pegu, Tenasserim, Viengchang (Linzin), and Ayuthia. In 1455 he met Ali Khan, king of Arakan, at the Pohkaung-nwe-ngan-taw (Natyegan) Hill up the An Pass in Minbu district, where the two courts camped fraternally for a month and fixed the frontier (p. 140). In 1456 he sent offerings of gold and gems to the Temple of the Tooth at Kandy[2] in Ceylon and bought land there for the support of clergy visiting the shrine.

In 1468 Narapati was stabbed by his grandson whom he had reproved for a love intrigue with his cousin; the wound was not mortal. The king took fright and fled to Prome. His nervousness is explained by the sort of thing he had witnessed all his life; thus, even as a little page he had stood beside Thihathu the king as he lay dying in 1426 from the arrow of the *sawbwa* who hid in the bush (p. 96). Nobody could induce him to enter the palace again, and he died at Prome a year later.

He was succeeded by his son **Thihathura 1469-81** who allowed his boy to marry the girl for whom he had stabbed his grandfather. The queen dowager was shocked, and instigated Toungoo to revolt. Toungoo called in Pegu, but the king suppressed the rebels. He next had to take Prome, and having done so he pardoned his brother who was lord there. It is hardly worth mentioning such troubles, for they were normal.

[1] *Parker* "Burma, relations to China" 60, and *BEFEO* 1909 671.

[2] The Tooth has been in this temple since 1286, see *Gerson da Cunha*. The silver gilt caskets, one within another, which enclose the Tooth, are not unlike a pagoda in shape. The gems which encrust them and the metal of which they are made, are largely the proceeds of Burmese offerings.

In 1474 the king and queen made their hair into a broom, studded the handle with gems, and sent it to sweep the floor of the Temple of the Tooth at Kandy; the envoys took *pahsos* (dresses) of Chinese silk to the king of Ceylon.

In 1475 the king and Hsipaw raided Yawnghwe, securing its submission. In 1476 he raided Kawliya in Pegu district, and Sithukyawhtin, lord of Toungoo, enlarged his town. The ministers perceived that this meant Toungoo was about to revolt but the king showed them they were wrong by telling him to let himself be dragged by the hair to court; he did so, saying "It is my king's command," but the fact that such loyalty created a sensation shows how little power the ruler of Ava had.

In 1472 he asked China to give him Mohnyin and some neighbouring territory. China warned the chief in possession not to obstruct the road from Yünnan to Burma, but she would not give his territory to Ava as he had done nothing to merit eviction. One reason for the consideration shown to Mohnyin may be that he kept on good terms with the Chinese frontier eunuch, presenting him with a jewelled girdle.

Jewels also played a great part in the expansion of Momeik, the Ruby Mine state; founded in 1238, the town was part of Hsenwi but about 1420 it received thirteen villages as a reward for helping Yünnan to raid Chiengmai. In 1465 its chieftainess Nang-han-lung sent ruby tribute separately from Hsenwi and her presents of jewels completely won over the frontier eunuch. She even tried to ally herself with Annam. When she filched most of Hsenwi, and China sent to remonstrate with her, she said "Momeik is the baby elephant which has outgrown the mother elephant Hsenwi and can never enter the womb again," and as, in addition to talking, she presented more rubies to the inquiring officers, they reported sympathetically on her case and she remained in possession in 1484. In 1488, indeed, China told Mohnyin to send troops and prevent Momeik attacking Hsenwi; but he sent only decrepit men, who were of course beaten, and nothing more was done.[1]

Our materials are too scanty to justify more than a guess, but it seems possible that the continuance of Chinese interest

[1] *Parker* "Précis."

in Burma is due to the fact that after Kubla Khan's dynasty 1206-1368 had passed away, China lost control of the route across Asia to Europe. China had to look for other outlets, and the trade route down the Irrawaddy was possibly one of them. Chinese porcelain[1] of the fifteenth century has been found in the bed of the Bassein river near Negrais, and it is recorded[2] that in 1450 the ruler of Ava gave to a favourite "the Chinese customs revenue," probably Yünnan frontier tolls. Her records show that China knew only the roughest outline of what was occurring in Burma, but she none the less tried to see that the road lay open.

The king was succeeded by his son **Minhkaung 1481-1502.** Sithukyawhtin of Toungoo had received his dying instructions, gave him honourable burial by dropping his bones in the river,[3] and loyally assisted his son; but he could do nothing in face of the increasing uproar, and died a captive in the hands of Yamethin and Kyaukse whose revolt he had tried to quell. Hanthawaddy and Prome even came raiding up to Magwe, and the Shans as usual attacked the frontier at Myedu in Shwebo district. Nyaungyan in Meiktila district and Salin also rebelled. In most cases the rebels were of the royal family.

Hearing that Bimbisara, the king of Buddha's day, had raised his son to the throne as joint king, the king determined to do likewise, gave his son the white umbrella, and shared the throne with him.

In 1486 the governor of Toungoo was assassinated by a nephew Minkyinyo who seized the governorship and, to make his peace with the king, sent a present of two young elephants. The king may not have felt strong enough to give him his deserts, but he might have refused him recognition. Instead he took the two young elephants and said "I appoint you governor of Toungoo"; nay more, he afterwards sent him the five regalia, telling him to reign as king. Having thus condoned murder and put a premium on disloyalty, he refused to believe that Minkyinyo was about to attack him, mumbling "He would never dare." But Minkyinyo did dare: whenever he wanted slaves or cattle, he came raiding as far as Meiktila to get them, and his son conquered Ava. The 1829 chroniclers[4]

[1] *RSASB* 1915 35.
[2] *Hmannan* II. 99.
[3] See note "Royal drowning" p. 338.
[4] *Hmannan* II. 127, 185.

cite Minhkaung's treatment of Minkyinyo as an instance of statesmanship.

Hitherto writing had been in the classical languages, principally Pali, but in this age Burmese vernacular literature makes its appearance. Its rise may seem incompatible with the character of the period, but our picture of the period is that given in the chronicles, and the chronicles are a mere list of dates, battles, and official acts. Apart from a few frescoes, and from inscriptions which, though numerous, are narrow in scope, there is nothing corresponding to the private letters, monumental brasses, illuminated manuscripts portraying contemporary dresses and occupations, records of manors and monasteries, official inquests and so forth, which make it possible to reconstruct the daily life of ordinary people in mediæval Europe. Hence it may be that the chiefs who parcelled out Burma in the fourteenth and fifteenth centuries often had too little power to be oppressive outside their immediate neighbourhood, and that the mass of the people away from the track of the armies lived reasonably happy lives. In many a monastery, at least, existence must have been calm and beautiful.

As is usual in secluded countries Burmese literature is narrow in range and, though quite voluminous according to mediæval standards, small in quantity; it shows little development, and no improvement has been made on the earliest poets. Most is unoriginal, consisting of translations and paraphrases of sacred stories; some of these evince a considerable sense of style. Although what would in a developed literature go into fiction, goes in Burma into historical works, the editors of the eighteenth century chronicles are not without a critical sense, and show it in their discussion of authorities. The poetry, marked by a restrained and beautiful diction, is minor poetry of a high order, but the condensation of its style and the obscurity of its dialect militate against its having a wide appeal.

The usually accepted view, that the following are the first vernacular writers, is probably correct, and certainly their poems are the earliest to which a date can be assigned; but the finish of their style indicates that the vernacular had been practised for some generations previously and that its use had not been restricted to the recording of bare inscriptions.

Shin Uttamagyaw was born at Pondawbyi village in the same year as Shin Thilawuntha 1453-1520 and on the same day they entered a monastery school together at Taungdwingyi in Magwe district. As the monk considered poetry profane, Shin Thilawuntha was expelled for writing Paramiganpypo and went to Ava where Minhkaung built him a fine monastery called Yatanabiman; he wrote a grammatical work, poems such as Hsutaungganpyo, Taungdwinlapyo, Tada-u-ti-mawgun, and the Yazawingyaw chronicle, the earliest history extant; had he been content to write a simple account of what was happening around him, he might have left us an invaluable picture of fifteenth century life; but, like a true cleric, he preferred to indite an account of the mythical past, and hence his chronicle is valueless. Shin Uttamagyaw remained twenty years a monk at Taungdwingyi and then went to Ava where he was often invited to the palace for consultation on the scriptures; he wrote only one poem, the famous Tawla.[1] Shin Maharattathara 1468-1529 was descended from the Shan Brother Thihathu 1312-24 and was carried off to Prome when Ava fell (p. 106); he wrote poetry, such as Koganpyo, Hattipala and Meiktilakanbwemawgun. Shin Aggathamahdi, born in 1479 at Kanbya, east of Tabayin, wrote poetical versions of the *jataka* stories of Buddha. Yaweshinhtwe, a maid of honour in the Ava palace, probably at this time, wrote *angyin* verse on the fifty-five styles of hairdressing used by maids of honour under the kings of Ava; most of them are obsolete, but one, *hsabinsuli*, now called *kyettaungsi*, can be seen to-day in little girls aged ten to twelve whose hair is gathered to stand upright with a string tied at the base.

Minhkaung built the Mingalazedi pagoda at Tada-u on the model of the Tupayon (p. 100), and was succeeded by his younger son **Shwenankyawshin 1502-27**, as the elder son, the joint king, had died. The younger son already had a wife whose sister was married to the dead joint king; yet now, when he came to the throne, it was not his own wife, but her sister who became his chief queen, because she was already part of the regalia.[2]

[1] *JBRS* 1917-20 Po Byu "Shin Uttamagyaw and his Tawla" (with translation by Ba Han).

[2] See note "Married his father's queen" p. 324.

In his first regnal year, Shwenankyawshin's life was attempted by order of his kinsman Nawrahta of Yamethin:—

> Nga Thauk Kya came upon the king of the Golden Palace unawares and struck at him with a sword. But the sword struck the pole of the white umbrella so that it covered the king. Then Nga Shwe Kyaing, lord of Yenantha and son of an attendant, rose and seized Nga Thauk Kya. And as they struggled for the sword, they fell. Now Nga Shwe Kyaing, knowing that if he loosed his hold Nga Thauk Kya would kill the king, cried "If I loose him, thou wilt be undone. Master, smite us both." But the king slew Nga Thauk Kya only, so that Nga Shwe Kyaing was freed. (*Hmannan* II. 131.)

Nawrahta[1] lived in the palace so that he was easily caught; and being of royal blood he was drowned. But his party, five lords and seven hundred followers, escaped to Toungoo. The king thereupon gave a daughter in marriage to Minkyinyo of Toungoo, together with Kyaukse as dowry, and a string of villages all the way from Toungoo to Kyaukse (p. 124). He was giving his daughter to the harbourer of his assassins, and in giving away the rice area of Kyaukse he was giving away his crown. But he could not help himself, for the uproar was worse than ever—Prome and Salin were again in revolt, and Mohnyin was attacking the Myedu-Ngayane-Siboktaya-Sitha-Tabayin frontier in Shwebo district. The gift did no good. The only gratitude Minkyinyo of Toungoo showed was to join Nyaungyan and Prome in raiding up stream as far as Sale until the king in desperation called in Hsipaw Yawnghwe and Mone to drive them back. In 1507 he surrendered Tabayin and Ngayane to Sawlon, chief of Mohnyin, on condition that he came no further.

The king had three half brothers whom he had treated well, even refraining from appointing his own son Crown Prince out of consideration for their claims. They might have regarded all this pandemonium as a reason for rallying to his side if only in their own interests, but they preferred to see in it a great opportunity for making a career, and they called in Minkyinyo of Toungoo. Minkyinyo ravaged Myingyan district and then, with the lord of Prome, halted at Magwe till the time came to join the three brothers. The time did not

[1] He merges with Anawrahtaminsaw (p. 91 above) as the Shwenawrahta Nat spirit, *Temple* 56.

come, as the three brothers, after marching with several thousand men and occupying Pahkangyi in Pakokku district, were defeated and captured by the king. Instead of following what had become almost a rule by pardoning them, he reminded them of their father's dying exhortations, and executed all three in 1508.

But it was too late for the kingship to start asserting itself. Upper Burma was a bedlam of snarling Shan states. Ava's only friend was Onbaung (Hsipaw) and the two of them combined could not prevent Mohnyin in 1512 taking sixteen villages from Onbaung, one of which was Bhamo, then in its youth.[1] Year after year rebellions continued at Sagu, Myede and elsewhere. On his Shwebo frontier the king regained for a time Ngayane, perhaps because Mohnyin was busy fighting Kale. But in 1524 Mohnyin wiped out the frontier stockades and drove the Burmese as far as Inpe-Thayaing in Shwebo district.

It was the beginning of the end. Sawlon of Mohnyin overran the west bank and also occupied Thayetmyo, where the king's first cousin, lord of Prome, came to kneel before him, saying "Put me on the throne of Ava and I will hold it as your vassal." The two worthies, after carrying off cattle and elephants in central Burma from Taungdwingyi to Yamethin while the people hid in the jungle, set out for Ava. The king and his *thwethauk*,[2] the chief of Onbaung (Hsipaw), lay camped at Taungbalu, south-east of the city. There the armies met, but the mere sight of Mohnyin Sawlon waving his sword sufficed to make the Shan levies in the Ava ranks desert, and the king fled with Onbaung to Singaung and Wetwin near Maymyo. Ava was all but empty when Sawlon of Mohnyin entered it. He and Prome went home after taking what was left, Sawlon the horses and elephants, Prome a few people and the poet monk Shin Maharattathara (p. 104). When they had gone the king came back, but in 1527 Sawlon of Mohnyin broke into Ava again and the king, fighting on his elephant, was killed by a jingal shot.[3] Such of the Burmese

[1] *Parker* "Précis." Bhamo is not mentioned until the fifteenth century. Before that time the chief place was Kaungsin, "The town at the head of the river."

[2] See note "Thwethauk and Thissa-ye" p. 339.

[3] See note "Firearms" p. 340.

population as could, stampeded southwards, especially to Toungoo.

Sawlon set up as king his son **Thohanbwa 1527-43.** Yünnan sent an officer to ascertain what all the trouble was among the wild tribes round Ava; but the officer found conditions so disturbed that he went home.[1] Sawlon and his son Thohanbwa marched on Prome in 1533 and came back carrying its lord captive. When Sawlon had got past Myedu in Shwebo district his own men murdered him. The lord of Prome was released and returned to find his gates shut against him and his son usurping the throne; so he camped at Nawin and died, and his usurping son gave him most honourable burial. In 1539 Prome, having received Takayutpi, king of Pegu, in his flight from the Burmese conqueror (p. 154), took steps to guard herself against Burmese vengeance by calling in Ava; Thohanbwa went gladly and helped Prome to drive off the Burmese. When the Burmese again attacked Prome in 1542, he marched with his friends Mohnyin, Hsipaw, Momeik, Mogaung, Bhamo and Yawnghwe, but they were badly beaten by Bayinnaung outside Prome and returned, leaving the town to its fate.

Thohanbwa was a full-blooded savage. He said "Burmese pagodas have nothing to do with religion. They are simply treasure chambers," and proceeded to pillage such as were in reach. It is not unlikely that, as on other occasions, the monks led the people in resistance; he said "Monks surround themselves with followers and could rebel if they like. They ought to be killed." Therefore in 1540 at Taungbalu, south-east of Ava, he covered a field with *mandat* pavilions, slaughtered buffaloes, cows, pigs and fowls for a great feast, and invited the monks to feed. When they were all in the pavilions he surrounded them with his braves and massacred them. The survivors fled to Toungoo. Out of 1,300 monks in Ava, Sagaing and Pinya, he succeeded in killing 360, of whom thirty were eminent for their learning. He then proceeded to seize the manuscripts in the monasteries and made bonfires of them. Signs and portents preceded these events, the Shwezigon pagoda at Pagan shedding tears.

Thohanbwa's right hand was Minkyiyanaung, a Burman

[1] *Parker* "Précis."

officer of the old Ava court. He succeeded in dissuading Thohanbwa from attacking Toungoo, the last stronghold of the Burmese race, saying it was quite unnecessary to do so, as Toungoo would pay homage in fear of his glory if he ordered it. The Burmese officers in the palace were subject to continual indignities from their Shan colleagues, who would knock off their head-dress. They appealed to Minkyiyanaung. He hesitated but finally he consented, thinking "He reveres not the Three Gems, he regards not human life, he respects not other men's wives, and the fear of the Lord is not in him. We shall be destroyed unto the seventh generation." In the hot weather of 1543 Thohanbwa moved into a temporary palace, a collection of field-huts; being a true parvenu he was desirous of following the correct procedure of the old court, and asked Minkyiyanaung what it was. Minkyiyanaung explained that one of the customs was that no officers or men wore swords in the summer camp, but everybody took his ease. So Thohanbwa disarmed even his Shan officers. Minkyiyanaung had seen to it, when the camp was pitched, that the Burman attendants lightly buried their swords in the positions they would occupy while waiting in the presence. When all was ready, and he was talking to the king, he turned the subject to swords. Thohanbwa said "They say my predecessor, king Shwenankyawshin, had a fine blade. Once he cut a man down with it and the blade went through the man, through the howdah, and into the elephant even. Did you know that sword?" Minkyiyanaung answered "And who should know it but I, seeing that I was His Majesty's sword-bearer? I could tell it at a glance." The king sent for the old royal swords. When he had the bundle, Minkyiyanaung picked out the blade, and bending low as if to present it, went close to the king and smote him so that the blade went through and out again, severing five bamboos of the dais floor. The Burmans took their swords out of the loose earth and killed the Shan attendants inside, and when the Shans outside, hearing the cries, came running in, they also were cut down. The throne was there for the taking and they all asked Minkyiyanaung to take it. He was only thirty-six and he was kinsman to the fallen Ava house. The friendly Hsipaw *sawbwa* sent congratulations and said he would recognise him as a matter of course. But Minkyiyanaung would have none of that blood-stained throne, and so it passed by general agreement to Hsipaw.

Minkyiyanaung consented to remain in office and advise him for the first year of his reign; when the year was over, he laid aside his pomp, and retired into a woodland monastery near Mekkaya in Kyaukse district, and there ended his days telling his beads. The modern world regards the monastic life as a form of shirking, but in those days of violent contrasts a cloister was the only place on earth where existence was bearable to a man of finer nature.

The Hsipaw chief ruled Ava as **Hkonmaing 1543-6.** He went with six other *sawbwas* (Mohnyin, Momeik, Hsenwi, Bhamo, Yawnghwe, Mone) to regain Prome in 1544 but they were again broken by Tabinshwehti who thereupon permanently occupied the country as far as the north of Minbu and Myingyan districts (p. 158). Hkonmaing was succeeded by his son **Mobye Narapati 1546-52** who constructed Ngakyi weir in Kyaukse. Even with the imminent power of Tabinshwehti staring them in the face, the Shans continued the kaleidoscopic methods so dear to their heart. The various *sawbwas* went on playing at war with each other, and Mohnyin supported Sithukyawhtin, a Shan who had held Salin till Tabinshwehti ejected him, in holding Sagaing and attacking Ava, and was furious on finding that he refrained from hacking the heads off the Ava wounded. Finally Mobye Narapati fled, paying homage to Bayinnaung and leaving Ava to its last *sawbwa*, **Sithukyawhtin 1552-5** (pp. 163, 165).

Indeed for two and a half centuries the rulers of Ava had been *sawbwas* in all but name; yet there was this difference between Ava and the other Shan states, that whereas they were so wild as to leave not even a record,[1] the tradition of the Burmese palace gave Ava a veneer of civilisation, and her numerous monasteries contained monks, who, if not learned, were at least literate; and to them it is due that though the lamp of civilisation flickered and burnt low, it never went out.

[1] There was, however, from the late twelfth century onwards, a school of repute, the Kambojasangha, among the monks of Lai Hka, Southern Shan States. Some of them dwelt in the Delta.

CHAPTER IIIB

PEGU 1287-1539

Wareru 1287-96, a Shan pedlar born at Donwun in Thaton district, took service in the elephant stables of the chief of Sukhotai, a Siamese state, became Captain of the Guard, eloped with the chief's daughter and some kindred spirits from the Guard, and set up at his native village.

He had a fair sister, and made her choose for her bathing place in the river a spot where Aleimma, the Burmese governor of Martaban (p. 62), would see her. Aleimma asked for her hand. Wareru, saying he was overwhelmed with honour, arranged a wedding feast, and when Aleimma came to it, murdered[1] him, seized his governorship and so became lord of Martaban in 1281.

The Pagan kingdom was now breaking up, and Wareru made common cause with Tarabya, the revolting governor of Pegu (p. 75), each marrying the other's daughter. But in 1287 after they had expelled the Burmese governors and occupied the country south of Prome and Toungoo, Tarabya tried to ambush Wareru, and failed. Wareru, calling the spirits of earth and air to witness his innocence, and pouring libation of water from a golden bowl, mounted his elephant, fought with Tarabya in single combat, and took him prisoner. At the intercession of the monks he spared his life. Tarabya again plotted, but his wife, Wareru's daughter, warned her father in time.[2] So Tarabya was executed although she twined her tresses with his and dared the executioners to cut off his head.

Wareru now became sole prince of the Lower Burma state which lasted till 1539. In 1298 it received recognition from China which henceforth chose to regard its rulers as governors

[1] See note "Drink" p. 314. [2] *Paklat Talaing chronicle.*

appointed by herself.[1] Its capital was Martaban till 1363 and Donwun till 1369 when the palace was moved to Pegu.

Wareru received recognition from his old master and father-in-law the chief of Sukhotai, who in 1293 sent him a white elephant because it chose to eat Martaban grass; no sooner did they hear of its arrival than the Shan Brothers[2] of Kyaukse came raiding Martaban to get it, but were driven off. Wareru is responsible for the Wareru *dhammathat*, the earliest surviving lawbook in Burma; the Hindu colonists who came to the Delta a thousand years previously had left traditional laws, ascribed to the ancient sage Manu who found them written on the boundary walls of the world; these laws survived in Talaing monastic writings, and Wareru made his monks produce the collection known by his name. It is Hindu, but not Brahmanical, and the sacerdotal element is ignored, marriage no longer being treated as a sacrament; it forms the basis of Burmese law literature.[3]

Wareru was murdered by his grandsons, the children of Tarabya; they took sanctuary in a monastery but were dragged out and killed by the ministers, who handed over the throne to his brother. For some years the family ruled down to Tenasserim and even received homage from the Lampun villages south of Chiengmai; but after these areas had continued to change hands for a generation, they remained in Siamese possession and the frontier was that of the present province of Burma down to Tavoy.

As usual, there was little real government and the land was in continual uproar. If it was not brigands it was kinsmen who revolted, and there was trouble from Shan immigrants such as the 500 braves who took service under one of the princes and ended by murdering him in 1331. The Sukhotai chief then came raiding to Martaban because his grandson had perished in one of the palace murders.

Binnya U 1353-85 had to repel a formidable raid of several

[1] China called Pegu Kulah, and the prince of Pegu her "comforter" or resident governor of Kulah. *Parker* "Burma, relations to China" 60, *BEFEO* 1909 Huber "Fin de la dynastie de Pagan" 670-1.

[2] *Razadarit Ayedawpon* calls them "Ngawdaw king." Ngawdaw is the Talaing version of Ngedo, the *kwin* lands near Pinle, the town of the third brother Thihathu.

[3] *Forchammer* "Jardine Prize" 37.

thousand men from Chiengmai who destroyed Taikkala, Sittaung and Donwun in Thaton district before they were driven out in 1356; he built a pagoda on the spot where they retreated, enshrining relics which he obtained by sending a mission to Ceylon. The Siamese kingdom, founded in 1350, included in its list of provinces Tenasserim, Moulmein, and Martaban;[1] it certainly held Tenasserim, founding the town in 1373 and building the Wutshintaung pagoda in 1380; but it can have received only nominal tribute from Moulmein and Martaban.

In 1362 Binnya U repaired the Shwedagon pagoda, raising its height to 66 feet (p. 117). But for all his piety he was not to escape tribulation. The white elephant, after being sixty-one years in the palace, died; and while he was devoutly searching the forests for its successor, his kinsmen established themselves in the palace and asked Chiengmai to join them. He bought off the Chiengmai chief by sending him a daughter, but failed to recover Martaban, and for six years had to maintain himself at Donwun. In 1369 his wise minister died, and while his people shaved their heads[2] and sat distracted with grief, the watchful rebels entered Donwun and drove him out; so he moved to Pegu and repaired the walls; thereafter it remained the capital, and his successors continued to repair them. He became reconciled to his rebellious kinsmen and sent them to get his daughter back from Chiengmai, because she was not paid sufficient attention. But he never had peace, as the family was always quarrelling. The eldest son Razadarit (Binnyanwe) stole his half-sister Talamidaw, fled to Dagon (Rangoon) and was pardoned, but was then driven to rebel by the intrigues of the harem and his rival brothers. Razadarit's implacable foes were the chief queen and his uncle Laukpya, lord of Myaungmya, and although he succeeded in maintaining himself in the stockaded town of Dagon, loyally aided by his sister-bride Talamidaw, by some of his brothers, and by Mahomedan shipmen, there was continual fighting and plotting year after year, and even on his deathbed the old king could not induce the queen to be quiet.

[1] *Pallegoix* II. 75.

[2] *Razadarit Ayedawpon*. Shaving the head on the death of royalty is also found in Siam, *Jones* VII. 545.

Razadarit 1385-1423 succeeded in seizing Pegu as the townsmen would not man the walls against him. He was crowned there on the spot where Kun Atha had vanquished the Hindu giant (p. 6); the astrologers said it was an auspicious site which gave victory to those who trod it, so he trod it, and then built the Yanaungmyin pagoda on the site to prevent his enemies from ever treading there. He executed his opponents and was going to include the minister Deinmaniyut but relented on hearing his plea that he had only been true to his allegiance; Deinmaniyut was made lord of Syriam and became one of his most devoted officers. He showed a royal generosity to his father's wife the chief queen, forgiving her and granting her Dagon as a fief. But he failed to catch his raging uncle Laukpya, lord of Myaungmya, who brought in the Burmese (p. 82).

Razadarit had to contend not only with the Burmese but also with treachery and rebellion at home. He reduced Bassein among other revolting towns, but its lord put his treasure on elephants and with 700 followers fled to Sandoway in Arakan. Here Byat Za, Razadarit's best commander, brought him to bay. The Sandoway townsfolk at first shut their gates but finding that Byat Za wished only to get the fugitives, gave them up on receiving his promise to withdraw. The fugitives on being surrendered said to him "The dogs! They were quite unprepared for a siege and had only three days' food left when they gave us up. There was no need for you to make any promise. Attack them now, and you can take the loot of the whole town home to the king." His officers agreed, saying it would be a great triumph, but he curtly refused and returned home with his prisoners who were then executed. Razadarit called upon him for an explanation of his conduct; he answered "Sire, a promise is a promise, and quite apart from that, they would never have trusted us again. It does not pay."

In 1390 he was at the height of his power. He had driven off repeated Burmese attacks, quelled rebellion everywhere,,and had even captured Myaungmya with Laukpya inside. In thank-offering he built shrines at the Shwemawdaw pagoda, feeding a thousand monks throughout a seven days' festival and offering his weight in gold.[1] He even gave Laukpya his life, and contented himself with seeing that he lived safely in a monastery at the Shwedagon. Hearing of this universal success, the king of Ayuthia sent him a white elephant named Gandayaw; Razadarit in delight sent a host of men and elephants in procession headed by his chief lords Deinmaniyut and Byat Za, to meet it at Kampengpet 250 miles away. He also proceeded to be crowned again with a favourite queen; some of his queens were from prominent Shan families in Chiengmai.

He grew weary of his first love Talamidaw the sister who had so befriended him during his unhappy youth; he took away all her jewels down to the family rings bequeathed her by their father, which she tried to hide in her hair, and seeing that she was finally cast aside she poisoned herself with a mixture made from *pon-ma-thein*, a camphor shrub.[2] With her fell her son Bawlawkyantaw. Hearing that he was practising horsemanship and sharpening his elephant's tusks, Razadarit thought "Even as I rebelled at Dagon against my father, so will he rebel against me," and sent two lords to slay him. They announced their duty to the lad.

> And he said "I do but follow the custom of young princes in manly exercise. I do not plot against my father, neither is there any fault in me. My father and mother played together as children. When she grew to womanhood, he took her beauty, and then cast her away. She was a king's daughter, but he used her like a slavewoman and drove her to an evil death. And now he drives me also to an evil death." . . . He entreated the slayers, and they suffered him. And for three days continually at the Shwemawdaw pagoda, he hearkened to the reading of Abidhamma, the holy scriptures. When it was finished, he took off his ruby bracelets, his ruby earrings, and his ruby necklet, and offered them to the pagoda. And thus he prayed "If I have wished ill to my father, yea, even so little as the drop of blood sucked by a midge, then, after leaving this mortal body, may I lie in hell for ever, nor let me behold a coming Buddha. But if I have not wished ill to my father, then, after leaving this mortal body, may I enter the womb among the kings of Burma; so let me be born again, to be the scourge of the Talaings." Thus prayed he, and took the *pon-ma-thein* (it was but three ticals weight) and drank it with juice of the lime, and died (*Razadarit Ayedawbon* and *Hmannan* I. 432).

[1] See note "Tula-dana" p. 328.

[2] *Blumea balsamifera DC.* The kindred *Laurus camphora* is an exotic of comparatively recent introduction.

When this was reported to Razadarit, he said "It is a terrible prayer," and, gilding the pagoda from top to bottom, he prayed "If he become a king in Burma to make war on me, may I on my elephant vanquish him." Both their prayers were fulfilled (pp. 86, 95).

Razadarit had little success after this fatal year 1390. In 1414 he gained a temporary respite by stirring up Hsenwi to attack Ava, but was himself never free from the danger of Shan inroads and on several occasions when he was hard pressed from the north, Ayuthia, Kampengpet, and Chiengmai would raid him from the south.

China sent an embassy to recognise him as her "governor" of Pegu.[1] He was the builder of the Danok pagoda near Twante, and to him is ascribed the division of each of "the Three Talaing Countries" (Pegu, Myaungmya, Bassein) into thirty-two "provinces," i.e. village circles. He must have been a man of considerable character not only to win his throne at the age of sixteen but also to keep it in the face of savage irruptions from Ava and continual rebellions at home. Several times he killed his man in single combat; Minkyiswasawke never dared accept his challenge, and Minhkaung, who did so, turned his elephant and fled within a few minutes.

When the news of Minhkaung's death in 1422 reached Pegu, the queens jeered saying to Razadarit "Now you can pounce down on his palace and capture his harem." But he rebuked them, saying "My sweet enemy is dead. I will fight no more but spend my declining years in piety."

A year later, at the age of fifty-four, while snaring elephants with his own hand in the Labut-tha-lut jungle at the foot of the Pegu Yoma hills north of Pegu, he was caught in the rope and injured so that he died on the way home. His queens came out to meet the body and buried it at Kamathameinpaik (Minkanyo) near Payagyi railway station, north of Pegu. He has a chronicle all to himself, the Razadarit Ayedawpon (p. 170); it ends on the words "This Lion King, so wise, so generous, so mighty in word and deed, could overcome all his enemies, but he too at the last must bow before King Death."

He was succeeded by his son **Binnyadammayaza 1423-6** whose brothers tried to oust him by bringing in the Ava prince

[1] *BEFEO* 1909 Huber "Fin de la dynastie de Pagan" 652.

(p. 95). But the Ava levies, in addition to looting wholesale, captured so many men and women and put them into boats to carry them away as slaves, that the brothers grew disgusted, fell on them and drove them away for a time; they came again and besieged one of the princes so tightly that to free himself he had to present his sister Shinsawbu to the Ava chief. She was a widow aged twenty-nine, with a little son and two daughters. Binnyadammayaza pacified his brothers for a time but finally one of them poisoned him and succeeded as **Binnyaran 1426-46.** Toungoo gave Binnyaran a daughter saying "Put me on the throne of Ava and I will be your vassal." So they besieged Prome together until Mohnyinthado 1427-40 of Ava gave Binnyaran a niece to keep him quiet. Binnyaran found one of his concubines engaged in a love intrigue with a nephew, who thereupon fled with some hundreds of retainers to Ava and was given the revenues of Salin in Minbu district. In 1430 when his sister Shinsawbu returned from Ava (p. 97), where she was childless, her children did not recognise her, for she had left them in infancy and had been away seven years. He treated her with great honour and on his death was succeeded by her son,

Binnyawaru 1446-50, a king famed for his inflexible justice.[1] He said "In Razadarit's time the realm was happy because he was strict. While I reign the realm shall likewise be happy, for everyone who steals or does violence shall be hewn asunder by my sword." Accordingly, when an officer's servant once stole a pedlar's ring, and the officer came with a present of gold to please the king and free his servant, the king scarcely looked at the gold but had both the officer and the servant hewn in two and their bodies exposed at the cross roads. A cat caught a mouse and ate it; she also by royal command was hewn in two and her body was exposed at the cross roads under a guard. The king liked to wander about disguised as a commoner, ascertaining facts at first hand, and while thus disguised he rode his horse carelessly and knocked an old woman's pot off her head; she said "Knowest thou not that we now have a true king in the land? Verily I will hale thee before him and thou shalt die the death!" Thereupon he revealed his identity and paid her the price of the pot.

[1] *Schmidt* 124.

Following the royal example of strictness, everyone who had a son punished the son, everyone who had a slave punished the slave, and everyone who had a pupil punished the pupil. So criminals feared to be criminal, the land flourished exceedingly and men rejoiced, holding *pwe* festivals all day and all night. But the fact that His Majesty in person had time to try the cases of domestic animals helps us to appraise the statements of the chronicles that these were populous kingdoms in a mighty past.

Binnyakyan 1450-3 raised the height of the Shwedagon pagoda to 302 feet (pp. 112, 260). On his death there was, owing to palace massacres (p. 338), no male descendant of Razadarit left alive.

By general consent the throne passed to Razadarit's daughter **Shinsawbu 1453-72.** Village headmanships have been known to descend in the female line,[1] and Shan hill states have been held by chieftainesses (p. 101), but this is the only instance of a major state in Burma being held by a woman. Daughter, sister, wife, and mother of kings, she ruled well, leaving behind so gracious a memory on earth that four hundred years later the Talaings could think of no fairer thing to say of Queen Victoria than to call her Shinsawbu reincarnate.

Once, while being carried round the city in her gorgeous palanquin,[2] sword in hand and crown on head, she heard an old man exclaim, as her retinue pushed him aside "I must get out of the way, must I? I am an old fool, am I? I am not so old that I could not get a child, which is more than your old queen could do!" Thunderstruck at such irreverence, she meekly accepted it as a sign from heaven, and thereafter styled herself "The Old Queen."

Save for a brief escapade on behalf of Toungoo against Ava, there was peace in her time, and even rebellions were fewer than usual. After ruling seven years she decided to retire. The men she admired most were the two monks who had accompanied her flight from Ava (p. 97). In doubt as to which

[1] *JBRS* 1912 Furnivall "Matriarchy in Burma."

[2] *Thatonhnwemun Yazawin.* Palanquins could be of great size; thus the wife of the viceregal governor of Rangoon in 1821 rode one which was carried by no fewer than forty to fifty men, *Mrs. Judson* 289.

she should choose, she left it to providence. One morning when they came to receive the royal rice, she secreted in one of their bowls a *pahso* (layman's dress) together with little models of the five regalia; then, having prayed that the lot might fall on the worthier, she returned the bowls.[1] Dammazedi, to whom the fateful bowl fell, left the sacred order, received her daughter in marriage, and assumed the government. The other monk in his disappointment aroused suspicion and was executed at Paunglin, north of Rangoon. The lords also resented the choice at first but became reconciled owing to Dammazedi's high character; when some of them continued murmuring that he was not of royal race, Shinsawbu had a beam taken out of the floor of a bridge and carved into a Buddha image, and showed it to them saying "Ye say he is of common blood, he cannot be your King. See here this common wood—yesterday it was trodden in the dust of your feet, but to-day, is it not the Lord and do ye not bow before it?"

Shinsawbu spent her remaining years in retirement at Dagon (Rangoon), still interested in public affairs but occupied chiefly with religion. Her additions made the Shwedagon[2] almost what we see now, for she built the terrace, fifty feet high, three hundred yards wide, with a great stone balustrade, a circle of stone lamps, and several encircling walls between which she planted palm trees. She dedicated five hundred prisoners of war as slaves, kept forty-four people occupied in seeing to the sacred lamps, and beat out her own weight (25 *viss* = 91 lb.) of gold for gilding the dome. When her end came at the age of seventy-eight, she had her bed placed where she could see the Shwedagon, and thus, with her eyes fixed on that wondrous spire, she breathed her last.[3]

Dammazedi 1472-92 widened the river at Pegu after one of his favourites had been killed in a collision between two

[1] *Sayadaw Athwa* II. 131.

[2] *Schmidt* 133-35, *Forchammer* "Notes on Early History and Geography. I—The Shwedagon."

[3] *Furnivall* "Syriam Gazetteer" 25 says the ramparts of her residence at Dagon are now the bunkers of the golf course near the Prome Road. But these bunkers seem to be the 1841 wall, see *JBRS* 1920 Fraser "Old Rangoon." She was buried nearby, west of the Prome Road, for there is a monastery on the Windsor Road which within living memory was called the Shinsawbu Tomb Monastery, see *JBRS* 1912 Saya Thein "Rangoon in 1852."

Photo Samarew

SHWEDAGON.

racing boats during a regatta on the narrow stream. Shinsawbu had intended building a new Pegu so as to include the Shwemawdaw, in accordance with a prophecy of Gavampati, the ancient Talaing saint; and Dammazedi proceeded to build a stockade west of the pagoda, set up his elephant stables, and dwelt in a palace there.[1]

Shinsawbu had extended the Shwedagon glebe lands as far as Danok, and finding this excessive Dammazedi reduced them; in compensation he measured his weight and the weight of his queen in gold four times and dedicated that amount to overlaying the pagoda with scroll work and tracery.[2] He also dedicated a great bell there (p. 186).

He made the usual offerings to the Shwemawdaw, including *padeitha* trees, and two huge copper bells. He set up *nat* spirit shrines, and built two large monasteries and many pagodas of which the principal are the Shwegugyi and the Kyaikpon at Pegu. The masonry of his reign is excellent and a mass of pious edifices sprang up on the beautiful plateau between the old and the new towns, men vying with one another in works of merit. He exchanged envoys with Yünnan. In 1472 he sent a mission to Buddhagaya[3] in Bengal to take plans of the Holy Tree and of the temple as a model for buildings at Pegu.

But his greatest work was the religious revival started by his mission of twenty-two monks to Ceylon[4] in 1475. They suffered several shipwrecks and some of them died as castaways in their wanderings on the Madras coast where they reached Negapatam. To the Tooth, the Footprint, and the Holy Trees, they presented a stone alms-bowl studded with sapphires, and reliquaries of gold and crystal; to the Cingalese monks, cloths, and betel-boxes of speckled lacquer made in Chiengmai (p. 166); and to the king of Ceylon rubies, sapphires, Chinese silks, fine mats, and a letter on gold leaf. Their object was to secure valid orders from the clergy of the ancient Mahavihara, the great monastery of Ceylon which, founded in 251 B.C., still exists. On their return they proceeded

[1] *Shwemawdaw Thamaing* 118, 122.

[2] *JBRS* 1915 Furnivall "History of Syriam" 56. See note "Tula-dana" p. 328.

[3] *RSASB* 1914 11.

[4] *IA* 1893 and 1894 Taw Sein Ko "Kalyani inscriptions."

to transmit these orders to the clergy throughout Lower Burma. So valid was this ordination that monks flocked to receive it from all over Burma and even from Siam; and thus religion in Burma, which for three centuries had been split into sects, each with its own ordination, received a measure of unity from the standard Kalyani ordination. It was and is granted at the Kalyani *thein* near Pegu, so called because the original monks were ordained on the banks of the Kalyani stream in Ceylon. Dammazedi recorded these events on ten inscribed stones, called the Kalyani Inscriptions.

One of the principal monks in this mission was Buddhaghosa, who translated the Wareru *dhammathat* (p. 111) into Burmese; he has been merged into his namesake, the Father of the Church a thousand years before (p. 309). Dammazedi was himself a wise judge, and a collection of his rulings survives, the Dammazedi *pyatton*. He died at the age of eighty and was succeeded by his son.

Binnyaran 1492-1526 was revered for his gentleness (p. 121), although his first act was to enforce the Massacre of the Kinsmen (p. 338), putting all the royal offspring to death. In 1501 he went with thousands of armed men up stream; the lord of Prome checked him but he replied "I could conquer both you and Ava but I do not wish. I only wish to worship before the Shwezigon at Pagan," and having worshipped there he returned.

Takayutpi 1526-39 succeeded his father and was the last of Wareru's line, being overthrown by Tabinshwehti (p. 154); the astrologers said he could have reigned till the age of eighty-five had he followed their prescriptions, "but he never looked at a book, he gave himself up to sport in the woods with elephants and horses, he searched for shellfish and crabs, he was like one witless." After abandoning Pegu town to the Burmese he fled to his kinsman the lord of Prome and they made common cause. But within the year, saying he must collect war-elephants, he built a stockade at Ingabu in Maubin district, and while hunting elephants there he suddenly fell ill and died.[1]

[1] At Kangyigon, a mile from Ingabu Inma, there are traces of an old stockade and the fishermen worship a *nat* spirit called Po Yutpi = Takayutpi. There is no local tradition about him, but Smim Htaw (p. 163) is remembered as having taken refuge in the locality.

The years 1423 to 1539 were probably the happiest years in the annals of Pegu. The dynasty was mild. The kings could indulge their peaceful proclivities because the Upper Burma hordes found all the fighting they wanted among themselves, and the states of Prome and Toungoo acted as a buffer. It was the golden age of Lower Burma, and there can be little doubt that its civilisation was higher than that of the savage north. If few traces remain, that is because it was a simple civilisation, the steaming climate of the Delta hastens decay, and the Burmese conquerors touched nothing that they did not destroy.

Nitikin,[1] a Russian merchant from the great emporium of Tver, travelled in the East about 1470 and mentions Pegu as "no inconsiderable port, inhabited principally by Indian dervishes. The products derived from thence are sold by the dervishes." Of course the inhabitants were Talaings, but he was interested in the merchant community, and his remark shows that then as now these were mainly foreigners.

In 1496 an Italian merchant, Hieronimo de Santo Stephano,[1] came to Pegu. He could not go to Ava because communication with Upper Burma was disturbed. Thus he had to sell his stock at Pegu; it was of considerable value, so that only the king could buy it, and the king kept him waiting eighteen months for payment.

In 1505 there came another Italian merchant, Ludovico di Varthema, who also, after going three days inland, found conditions so anarchic that he abandoned the idea of reaching Ava; but he was granted audience in the Pegu palace and sold the king (Binnyaran) some coral. He writes:—

> Do not imagine that the king of Pegu enjoys as great a reputation as the king of Calicut, although he is so humane and domestic that an infant might speak to him, and he wears more rubies on him than the value of a very large city, and he wears them all on his toes. And on his legs he wears certain great rings of gold, all full of the most beautiful rubies; also his arms and his fingers are full. His ears hang down half a palm, through the great weight of the many jewels he wears there, so that seeing the person of the king by a light at night, he shines so much that he appears to be a sun. (*Badger* 219.)

These three Europeans were but forerunners of many more,

[1] *Major.*

for the sea-route from Europe was opened in 1498 and soon the Portuguese came. In 1511 Albuquerque at Malacca sent Ruy Nunez d'Ancunha to make inquiries at Tenasserim, Martaban, and Pegu. In 1519 Anthony Correa on behalf of the Portuguese entered into an official trade agreement with the lord of Martaban; the agreement was sanctified by the presence of Martaban monks, and the Portuguese captain, not to be outdone, made his chaplain put on a surplice and bring a breviary, but the breviary was so tattered that Correa, for the sake of effect, opened an imposing book of church music and read aloud the first passage his eye met; it was *Vanitas Vanitatum*, an appropriate text for a Portuguese pioneer.[1] This branch at Martaban lasted till 1613 and one reason why the Portuguese preferred it to Pegu was that it lay on the sea, their base.

With the insecure condition of the interior there can have been little inland trade, but the Delta itself was peaceful, and the discovery of the sea route from Europe brought Pegu, as well as Martaban and Tenasserim, great prosperity. There was no coinage, but goods were sometimes weighed against *ganza*, an alloy of lead and brass which passed as currency either in odd lumps or in bars of specified weight stamped by merchants of repute but usually false. The native products were not the bulky raw materials of to-day (p. 10) but rubies and other gems from Upper Burma, lac, wax, ivory, horn, lead, tin, Pegu jars, long pepper (*Piper nigrum*) which grew in the moist forests of Tenasserim, and nyper wine made from the *dani* palm (*Nipa fruticans, Wurmb.*) of Tenasserim. What also attracted the Portuguese was the stock of foreign goods brought to the Burma ports for sale—pepper from Achin in Sumatra, camphor from Borneo, scented woods and porcelain from China. Chinese wares came by sea, as the trade of the overland route *via* Yünnan was meagre. The imports were piece goods, velvets and other European wares, and the opium which Mahomedan ships brought from Mecca and Cambay.[2]

[1] *Stevens* I. 227 says the senior monk made oath over the agreement by burning sweet leaves and yellow paper. This suggests the presence of Chinese.

[2] For Pegu jars, etc., see note "Pegu merchants abroad" p. 341.

CHAPTER IIIc

TOUNGOO 1280-1531

In 1280 two brothers built a stockade round their village on the hill-spur *taunggnu*, and thus founded Toungoo; probably ferocious slave-raids from Karenni made the stockade a necessity. The Pagan kingdom was then on its deathbed, and Toungoo grew up without even such slight traditions of loyalty as other towns possessed. In the next two centuries she was ruled by twenty-eight chiefs, of whom fifteen perished by assassination.

Other places, notably Prome, were equally independent, but Toungoo differed in this, that she remained predominantly Burmese. The Shans made life so unbearable in Upper Burma that every now and then crowds of Burmese families would flock south and settle round Toungoo with its stronghold on the hill.

Within a generation of the town's beginning, its lords regarded themselves as people of importance and sported a hundred and fifty elephants. **Thinhkaba 1347-58** styled himself king, built a palace near Gyobinzeik village, saw that tracks were kept clear through the jungle, and went on a foray. This foray was to relieve Yehlwengahkayaing, five of the Kyaukse irrigation circles, of some of their superfluous store; Toungoo always looked longingly on that prosperous hollow, growing three crops a year while she could grow only one, and the stronger she grew the more she encroached there.

Thinhkaba's son **Pyanchi 1368-77** planted groves of toddy palms and built many a pagoda and monastery; there were already numbers of these round the town, showing its importance, and eminent monks are repeatedly mentioned there. He joined the princes of Ava and Pegu in making offerings at Pagan, and it is near the Shwezigon that he and his princess set up an inscription[1] proudly recording how they gave refuge to the Burmans who fled from Shan brutality after the fall of Sagaing and Pinya (p. 80) and how she cut off her hair and twisted it into a torch to burn before the shrine. They prayed that in their next existence they might be man and wife together again, and dwell in the land of Toungoo, and once more rule the people they loved so well. Pyanchi's friendship for the Talaing prince offended Ava, who assassinated him (p. 86).

Sometimes father succeeded to son, sometimes Ava appointed a governor, sometimes Pegu supported the ruler. **Sawluthinhkaya 1421-36** gained divine recognition of his independence, as he found a white elephant. But there was no continuity, for although the rulers sometimes intermarried with Ava, Pegu and Prome, no one family maintained itself for long.

Sithukyawhtin 1471-82 was a murderous brute; he would eat anything, however unclean, short of vulture or human flesh, and he used to have little pigs ripped out just before birth so that he could eat them boiled; but he was the faithful vassal of Ava, and it was in his family that arose

Minkyinyo 1486-1531, father of the kings of Burma, who murdered his uncle and predecessor because he would not let him marry his cousin; thereupon Ava immediately recognised him (p. 102). He secured recognition from Pegu and Chiengmai, and he received propitiatory tribute from Karenni. In 1492 he founded Dwayawadi (Myogyi) near the Lawkoktaya pagoda outside Toungoo and captured Kyaungbya, forty miles south-east, from the Talaings, killing its Shan governor in single combat by jumping on to his elephant and cutting him down. In 1503 he received from Ava the present of a daughter and the coveted canal area of Kyaukse, together with all the country leading up to it from Toungoo, such as the Yamethin villages Taungnyo, Pyagaung (Kyidaunggan), Shwemyo, Kintha, Talaingthe and Petpaing. He deported the population of these to fill his new town Dwayawadi. Nyaungyan in Meiktila district joined him. He drove off the cattle of Meiktila district and raised a cavalry levy there. He joined Prome and the

[1] *Tun Nyein* 149.

rebel princes of Upper Burma against Ava (p. 102) and was going to take Taungdwingyi in 1509 when its lord induced him to make a marriage between their children instead. In 1510 he founded Ketumati, the present Toungoo, digging the lake within the walls and laying out orchards. He continued to sally forth on occasional raids up to Meiktila and to Natmauk in Magwe district, but after founding Toungoo he spent most of his life at home. When he heard the news of the Shans' first entry into Ava in 1525 he went north to see what he could get, but had to return because its own lord Shwenankyawshin regained his city and in retaliation came raiding as far as Toungoo. When the Shans finally took Ava in 1527 he marched out and deliberately devastated the country in the central zone, filling in the wells and breaking down the channels in the hope of making an impassable belt between himself and the Shan terror. The lords of Pinya in Sagaing, Myittha in Kyaukse, and Hlaingdet in Meiktila district, with many a Burmese family, noble and commoner, fled south to take refuge at his feet. In delight he exclaimed "Now I know why the bees swarmed on the gate of Toungoo. It meant that my city was to be populous"; it meant something far more than that, although he did not realise it. He had as commander of the warboats Thondaunghmu, a rimester who wrote courtly verses on the royal family, such as Mintayashwehti-egyin, and was father to Zeyyayandameik (p. 191). Minkyinyo could trace his descent[1] through forbears of rank back to the Pagan dynasty, and dying at the age of seventy-two he bequeathed a great name to Tabinshwehti, his son by the daughter of the *thugyi* of Penwegon, six miles north of Toungoo (p. 153).

[1] See note "Tabinshwehti and Bayinnaung" p. 342.

CHAPTER IV

THE OVERSEAS DISCOVERIES

CHAPTER IV

THE OVERSEAS DISCOVERIES

ALEXANDER'S campaigns resulted in a network of Greek kingdoms on the north-west frontier of India. The road across Asia Minor lay open, and what intercourse there must have been in that old world, so full of splendour and magnificence, so noisy with armies and kings, can be guessed from the fact that the faces which look out at us from Byzantine mosaics have their double in the frescoes of east central Asia, and the casket enshrining Buddha's bones in the Peshawar temple was made by a Greek artist.

Under the Roman Empire, Roman ships went regularly down the Red Sea and as far east as Ceylon. Kings in ancient India issued coinage on the Roman model. Once or twice Roman trade representatives even went as far as China.

But the Germanic tribes overran Europe and overthrew settled government in 455. In the Dark Ages which followed, Europe was reduced to a semi-Asiatic condition, and life was so insecure that intercourse with distant lands died out. But with the lapse of centuries the Roman Church tamed the wild tribes, bishop and king working hand in hand brought order out of chaos; industries, towns, and a middle class developed, and the emergence of stable government once more liberated energy for progress in a hundred fields. One of those fields was the expansion of the races of Europe over the earth. Already in 1245 the first traveller set out for China, and in 1435 the first traveller came to Burma (p. 98).

But no regular intercourse was possible until a sea route could be found. Men set out to find it because it would bring fabulous profits. Before the eighteenth century, when it became normal for individual farmers to possess land of their own, enclosing it in a strong hedge, agricultural conditions in Europe were similar to those in Burma to-day.

The village lands, a wide expanse unbroken by the line of a single hedge, were worked under communal tenures. It was useless for an intelligent farmer to try new methods on his land, for they would require years to bring to fruition, and meanwhile the land would have been allotted to others. The common grazing of the unfenced stubbles, a feature of backward agriculture, spread disease among cattle and prevented the introduction of new crops, for a crop which was not off the ground at the same time as the rest would be trampled down. There was no rotation of crops, eatable fruit and vegetables were rare, and live-stock grew to only half their present size. Cattle were not slaughtered till they were too old or diseased to draw the plough; every autumn saw a selection of those which were not worth the trouble of stall-feeding throughout the winter, and they were killed for the brine-tub. Men had little but salt meat to eat, and it was so insipid as to need spices.

Spices were not produced in Europe but had to be imported from the East. They were brought up the Red Sea and across Egypt, or up the Persian Gulf to Basra and overland to Constantinople; and every time they changed hands, every frontier they crossed, increased their price. Things were made worse when the Turk captured Constantinople in 1453 and blocked the overland route. The idealism of European sailors was reinforced by business necessity, and governments became willing to spend money on exploration which would give them a cheap sea passage to the Indies, a direct route with no profiteering middlemen.

It is difficult to overestimate the heroism of those early explorers, sailing into uncharted seas which, to their belief, might at any moment swarm with dragons; and in point of fact their ships were so frail that sometimes they suffered damage from giant fish. Captains could not get crews, for the men insisted that the world was flat and if they sailed far enough they would tumble over the edge into hell.

In 1492 Columbus landed in the New World and came back announcing that he had found Japan, for to the day of his death he thought he had landed on the east coast of Asia. Most men would now hold that his was the greatest of the discoveries because it led to the finding of North America, but at the time men considered the tropical east to be the greater find. This fell to the Portuguese: in 1498 Vasco da Gama passed the Cape of Good Hope and found a sea route to India.[1]

The first representatives of the races of Europe were not such as to inspire liking. The Renaissance came to the Portuguese late and left them early, and they were below the average of civilisation in sixteenth century Europe. The level of their Catholicism may be imagined from the fact that Vasco da Gama and thirteen of his men, wandering into a Hindu temple at Calicut, mistook it for a Christian church and worshipped there, although they were somewhat puzzled at frescoes of saints with five arms.

They were second-rate soldiers and it was lucky for them that they did not come into contact with the fighting races of northern India, but their equipment was sufficient to annihilate opposition in southern India and Indo-China. It was this fighting superiority that enabled them to give full play to their avarice and persecuting zeal. Their cruel treatment of the natives roused the indignation not only of mission priests like St. Francis Xavier but also of the saner laymen among themselves who, when the downfall came, recognised it as a divine judgment. It came primarily from economic exhaustion. Between 1450 and 1550 they ruled the seas of half the world and tried to build up simultaneous dominions in Brazil and the East Indies. The effort proved too much for so small a nation, numbering barely a million. By 1550 there were not sufficient men left in the country to man the ships, and even the sweepings of the jails did not bring the crews up to complement.

But apart from exhaustion, the Portuguese could never have retained an empire because they had a genius for disloyalty, and consequently no administrative faculty. A Portuguese captain in distress could seldom rely on help from his colleagues for they were probably rejoicing at his misfortune. Crews deserted wholesale and took to piracy against their own countrymen before rejoining.

Yet they were good sailors and brave men. The story of

[1] *Whiteway.*

their voyages is one of the great epics of the human race. What with scurvy, pestilence, and wreck, not 60 per cent. of the men who left Portugal reached India. Their ships were so ramshackle that bombardments sometimes had to be stopped because the recoil from the guns injured the ships more than the shot hurt the enemy. In 1534 one Diogo Botello sailed from India in a boat sixteen and a half feet long, nine feet in beam, four and a half feet to the keel; he had only three white companions and his native crew mutinied out of misery, but he held on his course and finally brought the boat safe into Lisbon harbour.[1] The success of the Portuguese rests on something more than superior equipment: they had a moral superiority. Trained by long apprenticeship in the wars of Europe, hardened by facing the dangers of unknown seas, they stood up with a gay heart to encounter odds that were sometimes literally a hundred to one, and they grew so contemptuous of their native adversaries that they would fling aside their armour and go into action half naked. But their vigour depended on racial purity, and this they destroyed by a professed policy of mixed marriages. Their superior morale depended on their remaining true to their own traditions, and these they abandoned, deliberately imitating the worst type of native diplomacy so that their crookedness became a byword.

Their rule never extended a day's march from their ships. All they wanted was a chain of fortified trading stations, for it took the European courts nearly two centuries to realise the weakness of oriental governments and the ease with which an extensive land empire could be won. Goa on the Bombay coast was their headquarters, and Malacca in the Straits, occupied in 1510, their principal port in the farther east.

Burma attracted them less because she lay off the track, and her goods could be bought in Malacca. Her spices were few, and her civilisation was too backward to produce articles of fine workmanship such as were made in China and Japan. There were only two Portuguese stations in Burma, Martaban and Tenasserim (pp. 122, 202). Martaban was important because it tapped not only the trade of Burma, but also of Siam by the overland route. Tenasserim, held by the

[1] *Stevens* I 379.

Siamese till 1765, was more important still because it commanded an even better overland route direct to Ayuthia, the capital and port of Siam; indeed, Tenasserim was a rival to Malacca. The importance of both Martaban and Tenasserim declined in the eighteenth century when the English gained control of the sea route through the Straits, and it disappeared altogether with developments in navigation which robbed the voyage round Malaya of its last dangers.

The overseas discoveries resulted in a redistribution of power in Europe. Hitherto civilisation had centred round the Mediterranean. But these discoveries reduced the Mediterranean to a lake, and power shifted to the north-west, especially to England. From being a remote power of the second rank lying at the end of the land routes across Europe, she became the starting point of the new sea routes, the centre of the land masses of the globe, and the greatest of maritime powers. It was this command of the seas which enabled her to seize the far places of the earth and to expel rivals of whom some, such as the French, were no whit inferior as colonists but succumbed because support could not reach them from home.

135-49

CHAPTER V

ARAKAN

CHAPTER V

ARAKAN

SHUT off from Burma by a hill range, Arakan has a separate history, but it is the same in kind. Though that wall of hills rendered her immune from attack on the east, the resultant peace did not give her unity, because her territory is a long thin strip of coast intersected by hill torrents. Before 1437 Sandoway was usually independent.

The ease of sea communications renders it likely that Buddhism reached Arakan earlier than the interior of Burma, and the Mahamuni image (p. 313) may well date from the early centuries of the Christian era. But accessibility from the sea brought other things than Buddhism. Thus, Brahmanism is indicated by the word Chandra which ends the name of every traditional king from 788 to 957 and by the fact that medallions ascribed to these kings bear Siva's trident and Nagari script.[1] After the tenth century the country was professedly Buddhist, notwithstanding the spread of Mahomedanism which reached Achin in 1206 and dotted the coast from Assam to Malaya with the curious mosques known as Buddermokan reverenced by Buddhists and Chinamen as well as Mahomedans. Doubtless it is Mahomedan influence which led to women being more secluded in Arakan than in Burma.

The capital was successively Thabeiktaung, Dinnyawadi, and Vesali down to the eleventh century, Pyinsa (Sambawut) till 1118, Parin 1118-67, Hkrit 1167-80, Pyinsa 1180-1237, Launggyet 1237-1433, and Mrohaung (Mrauk-u) 1433-1785. All are in Akyab district, Thabeiktaung on the Yochaung river, the others on or near the Lemro river.

Like the rest of Indo-China, the country suffered chronically from raids. Akyab district was exposed to the hill tribes and in the tenth century Shans temporarily overran it. Settled government was the exception. In the middle of the twelfth century even the famous Mahamuni image could not be found,

[1] For Arakanese medallions, see *Phayre* "Coins" and *Vincent Smith* "Catalogue."

for it had been overgrown with jungle in the prevailing anarchy. But the Arakanese were usually quite able to look after themselves. A Mahamyatmuni pagoda near Mindon in Thayetmyo district was built by them during a successful raid in 1160, and there were many such land raids, although their real aptitude lay in sea raids to the north. The Burmese under the Pagan dynasty 1044-1287 successfully established their suzerainty over north Arakan but not over the south, and even in the north the kings merely sent propitiatory tribute to their stronger neighbour and continued to be hereditary kings, not governors appointed by Pagan.

The reign of **Minhti 1279-? 1374** witnessed a famous sea raid from Bengal. The raiders lay inside the mouth of the Hinya river at Chittagong; the Arakanese secretly sank boats laden with stones so as to block the river mouth and then loosed fire rafts from higher up the river, driving the enemy boats on to the sunken craft and annihilating them.

The length of Minhti's reign is attributed to the superior virtue of the ancients which sometimes increased the span of life. He was beloved for his uprightness. He ordained that masters should be punished for the offences of their servants, husbands for the offences of their wives and children, and teachers for the offences of their pupils. Important cases such as cattle theft, which was punishable with death, he tried himself. He used to wander in disguise among the people, and thus learnt that the crops would not grow because of the misdeeds of his uncle, the powerful minister Anandabaya. Once a rich man's servants stole some cattle at Letma on the bank of the river opposite the capital, and the rich man, knowing that he would be executed along with them, bribed Anandabaya; at the trial, the accused pleaded guilty but claimed exemption from punishment on the ground that they belonged to Anandabaya's household;[1] the king asked if this was so, and Anandabaya in consideration of the bribe said it was so; but the king, taking him at his word, enforced the rule and executed him together with the thieves.

[1] It was the same in Burma. Servants in ruling households were exempt from punishment, and English officers record that they were the worst robbers in the country and no redress could be obtained against them, e.g. *BSPC* despatch 5 Feb. 1813, Canning to Adam. In Upper Burma men still living remember how, by the same law of privilege, a man could not be sued even for an old debt after he entered the king's service.

After chewing betel, men used to clean their lime-stained fingers by rubbing them on the pillars of the hall. When he built his new palace, wishing to keep its gilded posts clean, he ordained that anyone who wiped his fingers on the posts should have his right index finger cut off. Once he wiped his own finger there. A minister noted it down silently. A fortnight later, the king, seated on his throne in full regalia, noticed the stain. In anger he called for the offender, and the minister said " Sire, thou art the man." At once he cut off his own finger. The story made a deep impression on the imagination of the people, and they add that in his wisdom he had done it all on purpose. Nay, at Nanya village in Akyab district there is an image of Buddha with one finger of the right hand missing, erected by the king's order in commemoration of the event.

From the overthrow of the Pagan dynasty in 1287 until 1785 there is not even the pretence of Burmese overlordship, save in the fourteenth century when some of the people, torn with dissension, asked the Ava court to nominate a king (p. 86). From 1374 to 1430 the country was subject first to Burmese and then to Talaing interference, and was raided by both on several occasions (pp. 91, 94).

Narameikhla 1404-34, when ousted in 1404 by the Burmese, fled to Bengal, was well received by the king of Gaur and served him with distinction in the field. After many years in exile he was given a levy from Gaur to regain his throne, and although the Mahomedan commander at first betrayed and imprisoned him in Arakan, he was ultimately reinstated in 1430. His Mahomedan followers built the Sandihkan mosque at Mrohaung and it was under him that a court bard, Adumin-nyo, wrote the historic song Yahkaingminthami-egyin. The turmoil of foreign inroads showed that Launggyet was ill-fated, and the omens indicated Mrohaung as a lucky site, so he decided to move there; though the astrologers said that if he moved the capital he would die within the year, he insisted, saying that the move would benefit his people and his own death would matter little. In 1433 he founded Mrohaung and in the next year he died. A populous[1] sea-port, built on hillocks amid the rice-plain, and intersected by canals which

[1] *Manrique* xxi, year 1630, gives the population as 160,000. See p. 265 below.

served as streets, Mrohaung remained the capital for the next four centuries.

Thereafter it is common for the kings, though Buddhists, to use Mahomedan designations in addition to their own names, and even to issue medallions bearing the *kalima*, the Mahomedan confession of faith, in Persian script; doubtless at first, about this time, the kings had these medallions struck for them in Bengal, but later they struck their own. Narameikhla's brother and successor **Ali Khan 1434-59** (p. 100) annexed Sandoway and Ramu. **Basawpyu (Kalima Shah) 1459-82** occupied Chittagong in 1459 and it was usually in Arakanese hands till 1666; indeed it had occasionally been subject to Arakan for centuries, and according to the fluctuations of power in the middle ages, when Bengal was in the ascendant, some kings, for instance Narameikhla 1404-34, sent tribute to Bengal and when the Arakanese were in the ascendant they received tribute from the Ganges delta, "The Twelve Towns of Bengal." [1]

After 1532 the coast, though poor and largely uninhabited,[2] was liable to pillage by *hpalaung* (= feringhi = Portuguese). It would have been a disastrous period for Arakan, with the aggressive Tabinshwehti on the throne of Pegu, had not king **Minbin 1531-53** been capable. He strengthened the massive stone walls of Mrohaung and dug a deep moat for the tidal waters; and when the Burmese invaders (p. 158) penetrated the eastern outworks of the city, he opened the sluices of his great reservoirs and flooded them out. He retained Ramu and Chittagong in spite of raids there by the Tippera tribes while he was engaged by Tabinshwehti, and coins bearing his name and styling him sultan were struck at Chittagong. He built at Mrohaung the Shwedaung pagoda, the Shitthaung, Dukkanthein, and Lemyethna temples, and the Andaw to enshrine a Ceylon tooth.

Unlike the other races of Burma, the Arakanese maintained sea-going craft [3] and Chittagong bred a race of competent seamen. For centuries they were the terror of the Ganges delta and at times they hampered even Portuguese shipping.

[1] For these, see *JASBengal* 1913 Hosten "The Twelve Bhuiyas or Landlords of Bengal."

[2] *Hamilton* II. 30.

[3] The king could equip as many as two hundred, resembling galleys (Year 1569, Caesar Frederick at *Hakluyt* X. 138).

Finally they united with Portuguese freebooters and thus brought about the greatest period in Arakanese history, circ. 1550-1666. The Portuguese, subject to no control from Goa, had settled in numbers at Chittagong, making it a thriving port, since the middle of the sixteenth century. It was always held by a brother or faithful clansman of the king, with an Arakanese garrison; every year the king sent a hundred boats full of troops, powder, and ball, and then the garrison and boats sent in the previous year returned home to Arakan.

Minyazagyi 1593-1612, the founder of the Parabaw pagoda at Mrohaung, employed De Brito in the expedition against Pegu (p. 183). It comprised land levies which went over the passes, as well as a flotilla from Chittagong and the Ganges delta. On the return journey the wise minister Mahapinnyakyaw, lord of Chittagong, died and was buried, after cremation, near the Hmawdin pagoda at Negrais; he had served the kings from youth up, and his compilation of legal precedents, Mahapinnyakyaw *pyatton*, which placed the interpretation of the Manu *dhammathats* on a definitely Buddhist basis, was thereafter among the most valuable works of its kind throughout Burma.

The Burmese, Talaing, and Siamese prisoners brought back by the expedition were settled at Urittaung and along the Mayu river. Some of the Talaings were at Sandoway, and it is probably they who built the Lemyethna pagoda there; a thousand of them tried to escape and were recaptured; they then plotted with Indians in aid of the *yuvaraja* (crown prince), Minhkamaung, when he came to worship at the Andaw pagoda, Sandoway; they marched on the palace to assassinate the king, and they failed. The crown prince was pardoned but his companion, Ugga Byan, poet and lord of Sindin in Akyab district, was condemned to have his hands struck off and to be dedicated with the Talaings and Indians as slaves to the Mahamuni image.

In 1608 the king offered to let the Dutch trade and build fortifications in return for help in driving out the Portuguese, but their commitments elsewhere were too heavy to allow them to accept the offer.[1]

Fearing De Brito was about to seize Dianga, the port on the bank opposite Chittagong, the king massacred six hundred

[1] *Hague Transcripts* 1607-16 letter 62; *De Jonge* III. 77.

Portuguese settlers there in 1607. Sebastian Gonzalez Tibao, a man of low birth who had made enough money in Bengal salt to buy a boat of his own, was among those who escaped. Though outnumbered eight to one, Tibao and his men exterminated the Afghan pirates of Sandwip island and set up there in 1609; this important island was a trade centre, it commanded the mouth of the Brahmaputra and Ganges rivers, and its neighbourhood provided timber in abundance for shipbuilding. The king quarrelled with his brother, governor of Chittagong, who went over to Tibao and gave him his sister; Tibao baptised and married her. Although they used to plunder Arakan and sell the loot in the Ganges delta, the king leagued with them for a time in order to prevent the Moghul governor of Bengal from taking Noakhali at the Ganges mouth which was then in Arakanese hands. While thus allied to the king Tibao gained possession of the Arakanese flotilla by the simple expedient of murdering its captains at a council. He used to raid villages up the Lemro river and even captured the king's gold and ivory barge;[1] his nephew had been left as hostage with the king who now crucified him on the bank under Tibao's eyes, but even this did not make him desist.

Minhkamaung (Husein Shah) 1612-22, as crown prince, had been captured by De Brito (p. 185). His queen built the Ratanabon pagoda at Mrohaung. On coming to the throne he tried to reinstate Ugga Byan in society, but convention was too strong and he remained an outcaste.

Minhkamaung is famous as the king who broke the power of the Portuguese in his dominions. His first advance on Sandwip was withdrawn because of a raid by the raja of Tippera. He then had to meet a counterstroke by Tibao who, aided this time by official Portuguese ships, attacked Mrohaung in 1615; Minhkamaung with some Dutch ships beat him off and finally in 1617 ejected him from Sandwip. After this the Portuguese ceased to be the king's rivals and became his servants. They centred at Chittagong, becoming ever duskier in complexion, continuing to hear mass devoutly, and occasionally assassinating their priests who, indeed, were little better; with the Arakanese they made a dire combina-

[1] *Stevens* III. 161. The king made long progresses throughout his dominions in this magnificent barge, surrounded by the court in boats, a moving city as it were.

tion, holding Sandwip island, Noahkali and Backergunge districts, and the Sunderbands delta south of Calcutta, and raiding up to Dacca and even Murshidabad, while Tippera sent them propitiatory tribute. After they had sacked Dacca, his capital, in 1625, the Moghul governor felt so unsafe that for a time he lived further inland. For generations an iron chain was stretched across the Hooghly river between Calcutta and Sibpur to prevent their entrance. In a single month, February 1727, they carried off 1,800 captives from the southern parts of Bengal; the king chose the artisans, about one-fourth, to be his slaves, and the rest were sold at prices varying from Rs. 20 to Rs. 70 a head and set to work on the land as slaves.[1] This continued throughout the eighteenth century, decreasing when the English began to police the coast. But even in 1795 they were plundering the king of Burma's boats off Arakan, laden with his customs dues of 10 per cent. in kind.[2] Rennell's map of Bengal, published in 1794, marks the area south of Backergunge "deserted on account of the ravages of the Muggs [Arakanese]." They had forts at Jagdia and Alamgirnagar in the mouth of the Meghna river, and here and there a few of them settled in the delta, for a little colony of 1,500, speaking Burmese and wearing Burmese dress, still survive on four or five islands in the extreme south-east of Backergunge district. They did not occupy the country administratively, they held it to blackmail:—

> The Arakan pirates, both Magh and feringhi, used constantly to come by the water-route and plunder Bengal. They carried off the Hindus and Mahomedans that they could seize, pierced the palms of their hands, passed thin strips of cane through the holes and threw them huddled together under the decks of their ships. Every morning they flung down some uncooked rice to the captives from above, as we fling grain to fowl. On reaching home the pirates employed some of the hardy men that survived such treatment in tillage and other degrading pursuits. The others were sold to the Dutch, English, and French merchants at the ports of the Deccan. Sometimes they brought their captives to . . . Orissa; anchoring a short distance from the coast they sent a man ashore with the news. The local officers, in fear of the pirates committing any depredation or kidnapping there, stood on the shore with a number of followers, and sent a man with money on board. If the terms were satisfactory, the pirates took the ransom and set the captives free with the man. Only the feringhis

[1] *Twenty-four Parganas Gazetteer* 39.
[2] *Symes* 117.

sold their prisoners. But the Maghs employed all whom they had carried off in agriculture and other services. Many high born persons and Saiyads, many Saiyad-born pure women, were compelled to undergo the disgrace of slavery or concubinage to these wicked men. Mahomedans underwent such oppression as they had not to suffer in Europe. As they continually practised raids for a long time, Bengal daily became more and more desolate and less and less able to resist them. Not a house was left inhabited on either side of the rivers lying on their track from Chittagong to Dacca. The district of Bakla [Backergunge and part of Dacca], which formerly abounded in houses and cultivated fields and yielded a large revenue as duty on betel-nuts, was swept so clean with their broom of plunder and abduction that none was left to tenant any house or kindle a light in that region. . . . The governor of Dacca had to confine his energies to the defence of that city only and to the prevention of the coming of the pirate fleet to Dacca; he stretched iron chains across the stream. . . . The sailors of the Bengal flotilla were inspired with such fear of the pirates that whenever a hundred war-boats of the former sighted only four of the latter, the Bengal crew thought themselves lucky if they could save their lives by flight; and when the distance was too short to permit escape, they—rowers, sepoys, and gunners alike—threw themselves overboard, preferring drowning to captivity. Many feringhis living at Chittagong used to visit the imperial dominions for plunder and abduction. Half their booty they gave to the raja of Arakan and the other half they kept. They were known as the Hermad [Armada] and owned a hundred swift *jalia* boats full of war material. . . . Latterly the raja of Arakan did not send his own fleet to plunder the Moghul territory, as he considered the feringhi pirates in the light of his servants and shared their booty. When Shayista Khan asked the feringhi deserters, what salary the Magh king had assigned to them, they replied "Our salary was the Moghul empire. We considered the whole of Bengal as our fief. We had not to bother ourselves about court clerks and revenue surveyors, but levied our rent all the year round without difficulty. We have kept the papers of the division of the booty for the last forty years." (Year 1670 circ., Shihabuddin Talish, soldier and historian, see *Jadunath Sarkar* "History of Aurangzib" III. 224 and *JAS Bengal* 1907 his "The Feringi Pirates of Chatgaon" 422).

Thirithudamma 1622-38 deferred his coronation twelve years because the wise assured him he would die a year after.[1]

[1] To avert this fate, just before his coronation he sacrificed 6,000 human hearts, 4,000 hearts of white cows and 2,000 of white doves (*Manrique* xxxi). The numbers are of course exaggerated, but Arakanese gentlemen tell me the sacrifice is true to type, although they do not cite other instances. A traditional king of Sweden killed nine of his sons to prolong his life; among the Baganda eight men were killed at the coronation, and others throughout the reign, to invigorate the king's life; when a king of Uganda was ill, some of his subjects were selected by the priests and put to death (*Frazer* "The Dying God" 160-1 and "Adonis, Attis, Osiris" II. 220-6).

It took place in 1635, and Manrique, an Austin friar who was present, describes it as a dazzling spectacle—twelve vassal chiefs were crowned at the same time, in the palace was a hall gilded from top to bottom, with massive pillars each composed of a single tree, and the Guards included Mahomedans from Upper India, Talaings, Burmans, feringhi gunners, and even some Japanese Christians.[1]

Thirithudamma raided Moulmein and Pegu town, bringing back, among his loot, Anaukpetlun's bell (p. 191), which he set up at a pagoda near Mrohaung.[2] In 1638 his brother, lord of Chittagong, deserted to the Moghuls. The chief queen, Natshinme, had a paramour, the lord of Launggyet, minister and royal kinsman, who was expert in the deadliest forms of black magic; so Thirithudamma died suddenly. His only direct heir, Minsani, the little son of Natshinme, then fell ill; Natshinme nursed him, and he died.

Her paramour thus became king **Narapatigyi 1638-45**, but as soon as the Massacre of the Kinsmen (p. 338) had been enforced and he was firm on the throne, he would not suffer her in the palace-citadel and made her live at a safe distance outside. Narapatigyi built at Mrohaung the Mingalamanaung pagoda, and, to house some scriptures from Ceylon, the Pitakataik.

Sandathudamma 1652-84 is revered as one of the noblest kings. He built the Zinamanaung, Thekyamanaung Ratanamanaung, Shwekyathein and Lokamu pagodas at Mrohaung. Buddhist missions to and from Ceylon had taken place in previous ages, and now, in the last year of his reign, some forty Arakanese monks went to Ceylon at the request of a mission sent by the aid of the Dutch;[3] the Dutch, fearing a revival of Portuguese influence in Ceylon, wished to strike at Catholicism by reviving upasampadā ordination (p. 56) which was on the way to becoming extinct. One reason why it was

[1] Christianity was undergoing persecution in Japan. Though overbearing, the Japanese were in demand as valiant and faithful mercenaries—thus, the king of Siam had 70 in his bodyguard at this time (*JSS* 1910 Ravenswaay "Van Vliet's description of Siam" 28).

[2] A Hindu officer of irregular horse in the 1824-6 war took it to Aligarh, U.P. The text and translation of its inscription are at *JASBengal* 1838 Wroughton "Inscription of the large Arakan bell."

[3] Similarly in 1753 the Dutch obtained monks from Siam, *Tennent* 223; cf. *Nga Me*.

to Arakan that they sent is that from about 1626 to 1683 they had a branch a mile from Mrohaung; it was closed at times, because they had so many commitments elsewhere; and in 1670 the whole staff was massacred. But while it lasted they found the king of Arakan more business-like than him of Burma, for under the articles[1] of 1653 he admitted their right to claim their own interpreter at audiences and to take away their children by women of the country (p. 350).

Indeed, as might be expected of a people dwelling amid the life of the sea-ports, the Arakanese were in several respects less backward than the Burmese. Thus they permitted the export of rice (pp. 206, 357), under the control of an officer who regulated it so as to prevent a shortage. And about 1660 they began to use coined currency in the ports, striking it themselves; India had done so in Roman times; the Burmese did not do so till 1861, though after annexing Arakan in 1785 Bodawpaya struck some medallions for enshrinement in the Mingun pagoda (p. 275), having learnt the idea from Arakan. The Arakanese had used such medallions since the tenth century for commemorative and religious purposes, usually at a king's accession.

Shuja, brother of Aurangzib, was defeated in his struggle for the Moghul throne, and had to flee in 1660. The people of Bengal regarded the Maghs as unclean savages, but Shuja was in such straits that he asked the king of Arakan to shelter him and provide ships so that he could go to Mecca. The king consented, and Shuja, with his family and followers, were brought to Mrohaung in Portuguese galeasses.[2] Shuja kept aloof from the king, repelled by his table manners. The Arakanese had never seen the like of his treasure, six or eight camel loads of gold and jewels; moreover, the Moghuls offered large sums for his extradition. Eight months went by, yet the king never provided the ships he had promised. Finally he asked for Shuja's eldest daughter, and Shuja, a blue-blooded Moghul of the imperial house, felt that his cup of bitterness was full. He was helpless and could not get away. In desperation he decided to overthrow the king. He had two

[1] *Valentyn* V. i. 140-6.

[2] Half galleys, from early Portuguese *geluas*, a half-decked craft used in the Red Sea and called in Arabic *jalba*, whence *jalia*, and English *jelly-boat*.

hundred faithful men, and he also won over the local Mahomedans; the thrones of Indo-China have been overthrown with fewer men, and good judges on the spot thought he had a reasonable chance. But there were too many in the plot to keep it secret, and the king heard of it in time. Shuja's men fired the city before being overwhelmed, and he escaped to the interior for some weeks but was found and executed. For days it was a sight to see his treasure being melted down and conveyed to the palace strong-room. His daughters were taken into the harem, the marriage of the eldest being celebrated in song and verse which are still greatly admired. A year or so later the king, perceiving a plot, starved them to death, although the eldest was in an advanced stage of pregnancy by himself; and their brothers' heads were hacked off with *dahs.*[1]

Aurangzib himself would have executed Shuja, though not his women, but he did not like outsiders doing it, and also it was necessary to curb the piracy of the Maghs. Shayista Khan,[2] the Moghul viceroy of Bengal, built a fleet, and in 1665 drove them out of their strong stockades on Sandwip island. The news spread consternation, and the king in fear began to distrust the feringhis, who, suspecting that he would exterminate their families, accepted the offers of Shayista Khan and fled with their families in forty-two galeasses laden with munitions; they received fiefs, and their descendants still live at Feringhi Bazaar, twelve miles south of Dacca. In 1666 Shayista Khan's force of 6,500 men and 288 boats took Chittagong after a thirty-six hours' siege, and subsequently Ramu. They sold 2,000 Arakanese into slavery and captured 1,026 cannon, mostly jingals throwing a one pound ball. One hundred and thirty-five ships were taken, the rest had been sunk in action, and two elephants were burnt in the sack. Such of the Arakanese garrison as escaped tried to march home, but on the way they were attacked by their former slaves, the kidnapped Mahomedans of Bengal who had been settled on the land.

[1] *Schouten* I. 228-37, *Bernier* 109-15, *Manucci* I. 369-76, *Bowrey* 139-42, *Hamilton* II. 27-9, *JBRS* 1922 Harvey "The Fate of Shah Shuja."

[2] *Chittagong Gazetteer* 31, *Bernier* 174-82, *JASBengal* 1907 Jadunath Sarkar "The Conquest of Chatgaon," *Jadunath Sarkar* "History of Aurangzib" III. 220-45.

The fall of Chittagong caused indescribable rejoicing in Bengal. It was a decisive blow to the prosperity of the Arakanese, and with it their century of greatness came to an end. They were, indeed, able to continue their sea raids, for the trackless delta of the Ganges afforded scope to them, as to nests of pirates recruited from the scum of every race; but never again did they hold Chittagong or even Ramu, and they lost their sword arm by the desertion of the feringhis. Sandathudamma's long reign saw the power of his race pass its zenith, and his death is followed by a century of chaos. The profits of piracy had gone but the piratical instinct remained, rendering government impossible.

A long coastline exposed Arakan to alien breeds, and a difficult terrain hampered the task of a central government. Shuja's followers in 1661 were retained as Archers of the Guard, praetorians who drew Rs. 4 a month, equivalent to many times that amount of modern currency. They murdered and set up kings at will, and their numbers were recruited by fresh arrivals from Upper India. In 1692 they burnt the palace, and for the next twenty years they roamed over the country, carrying fire and sword wherever they went.

Finally they were suppressed by a lord who set up as king **Sandawizaya 1710-31**; he deported them to Ramree; there, and at Thinganet and Tharagon near Akyab, their descendants still exist, under the name Kaman (Persian *kāmān* = a bow), speaking Arakanese but retaining their Mahomedan faith and Afghan features. He fought the raja of Tippera and raided Sandwip, Prome, and Malun in Thayetmyo district. But his reign was only an interlude of capacity and after his murder the country relapsed.

King after king was murdered, and village fought against village. Earthquakes are for centuries mentioned in the chronicles of the various states of Burma, but those of 1761-2 in Arakan were exceptionally awesome; the whole coastline rose three cubits perpendicular, the king changed his name to evade the pursuit of the unseen powers, and the people felt that they were doomed. When Singu 1776-82 was king of Burma, many of them fled and asked him to intervene; but a more energetic king than Singu might well have felt unequal to calming such a bedlam, and he refused.

Sometimes the lords would induce a hardy spirit to accept the throne, and as often others would combine to make his task impossible.

The last king, **Thamada 1782-5**, bearing as if in irony the name of the first king on earth, had less authority than ever, for he was of slave blood.[1] Another band of lords went to Ava asking for intervention; perhaps they were patriots wishing to see their land at rest; perhaps they wanted the sweets of office. Their request was granted with a vengeance, for Bodawpaya was now king in Burma. Many a village came out with music to greet his armies as deliverers, and there was little fighting because the king had few supporters. But the methods of the Burmese were such that soon the very men who had brought them in were leading insurgents against them. Yet perhaps even a good administrator could have done little better with the only means Bodawpaya had at his disposal (pp. 267, 280).

[1] That is, he was a man of Ramree. The people of Ramree and Cheduba, being rough islanders, occupied in such tasks as woodcutting, are beyond the pale. An Arakanese will not marry among them.

CHAPTER VI

THE TOUNGOO DYNASTY 1531-1752

BURMA UNDER THE TOUNGOO DYNASTY 1531-1752

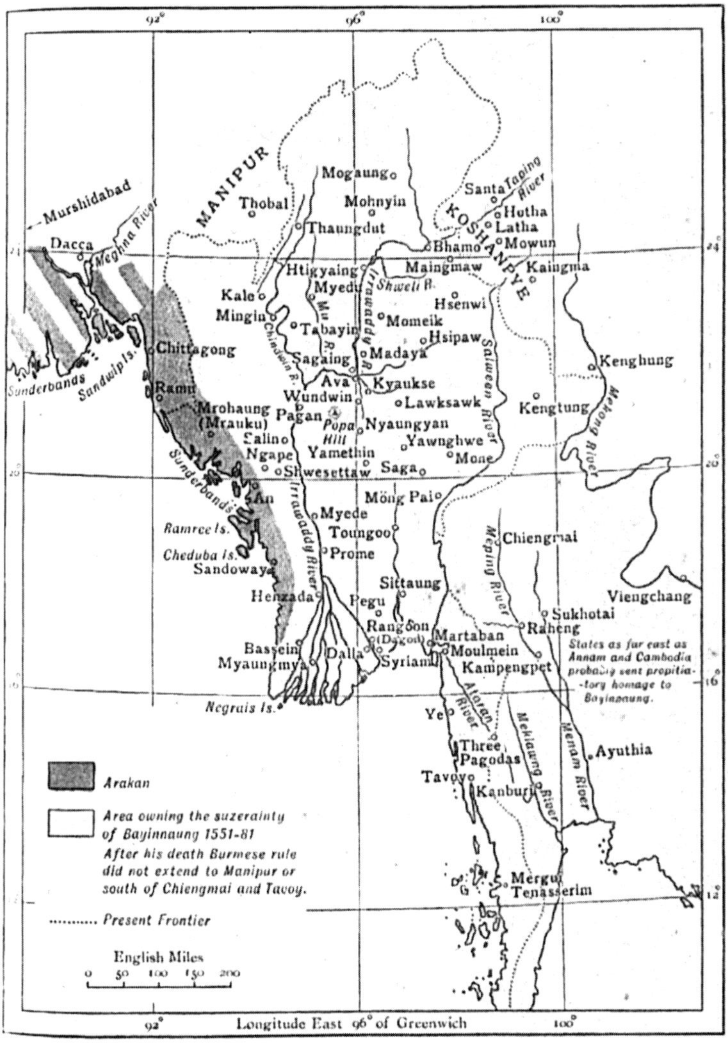

Emery Walker Ltd. sc.

Longmans, Green & Co. London, New York, Toronto, Bombay, Calcutta & Madras.

CHAPTER VI

THE TOUNGOO DYNASTY 1531-1752

Tabinshwehti 1531-50. The Shan migration into the plains (p. 125), a nightmare lasting two centuries, had now ended, but no overlord had emerged. Tabinshwehti was to restore the kingship. He was only fifteen, but the dice were loaded in his favour. The Shan irruption had driven the Burmese south to Toungoo, greatly increasing his man-power; he was in touch with Kyaukse, the richest area in Upper Burma and the key to Ava; and to crown all, his opponents were Shans, a hill-race with a congenital incapacity for combined action.

The Burmese refugees around him included not only simple peasants who had fled in panic, but also men of mark who burned to regain their rightful pomp. He had the faithful lords of Toungoo who had watched him from his cradle, and Bayinnaung,[1] son of his wet nurse, the great comrade to whom he now gave his sister in marriage.

At his accession he decided to have his ears bored at the Shwemawdaw and nowhere else, and he accomplished this surrounded by armed retainers, under the nose of the Talaing king, whose men did not dare gainsay him.

In 1535 he started his career of conquest by attacking Lower Burma, probably because it was prospering on maritime trade and contained more loot than the north country. He reduced the western provinces, Bassein and Myaungmya, with little difficulty. When advancing on Pegu town he was opposed by the Talaing flotilla and a Portuguese craft which happened to be trading in the port; the Burmese drove off the Talaing war canoes and then overwhelmed the Portuguese, who died fighting single-handed.[2] The incident suggests mismanagement or lack of morale on the part of the Talaings

[1] See note "Tabinshwehti and Bayinnaung" p. 342.

[2] *Stevens* II. 10.

who ought to have won easily seeing that they had the best war canoes and boatmen in the country, just as the Burmese had the best infantry and the Shans the best elephantry.

But in spite of several attempts, Tabinshwehti could not take Pegu city. Therefore he had recourse to strategem. The Pegu king's ablest supporters were two commanders, whom he sent to Tabinshwehti with a letter asking for friendly relations. Tabinshwehti pointedly avoided referring to the letter but treated the envoys themselves with unusual honour. After their return he wrote a letter to them by name "When the matter you arranged with me is finished, I will give one of you Pegu and the other Martaban to rule over." The bearers of this letter had instructions to insult the Talaing *thugyis* by demanding food gratuitously and, having thus provoked a quarrel, to run away leaving the letter behind. They did so, and the Talaing *thugyis* forwarded the letter to their king, who at once, perceiving the two commanders to be traitors, put them to death.[1] Thus deprived of their best leaders, the Talaings lost heart, many of them deserted, their king fled to Prome, and Tabinshwehti entered Pegu without striking a blow in 1539.

He then attacked Prome. During the advance we get the first characteristic touch of his great comrade Bayinnaung; it is like a breath of new life after three centuries of mannikins. Bayinnaung's scouts stumbled across a greatly superior Talaing force on the other side of a stream. Other commanders would have promptly retreated, but Bayinnaung had already discovered, as every good leader discovers in a third-rate environment, that numbers do not matter, it is spirit that counts. He improvised rafts and put his men across the stream. Just before the attack he was handed a message from the king that if he found the enemy he should not engage them but wait for the main body. He sent back answer that he had already met and beaten the enemy. His attendant said "You have reported a victory before we have fought, the odds are against us, we shall probably lose, and think how the king

[1] *Hmannan* II. 201-2. This stratagem was the height of technique, and Mahabandula used it against his opponents in 1825, trying to make them get rid of a country-born in their service, to whom he wrote thanking him for information received and asking for more. They filed the letter, *Trant* 164.

will punish us then!" Bayinnaung answered "If we lose? Why then we die here, and who can punish dead men?" He destroyed the rafts after his men had crossed. His officers remonstrated, saying "The enemy are ten to one and we shall never get out of this alive if you destroy the rafts." "Just so," said Bayinnaung, "Friends, we have got to win now."

The attack on Prome failed because the tribes of Upper Burma, headed by the Ava *sawbwa*, came swarming down the river to help the besieged. Tabinshwehti had to return home. But his task was lightened by the death of Takayutpi (p. 120). On hearing of their king's death such Talaings as were still recalcitrant came in to pay allegiance wholesale. He treated them well, giving the men rice and clothes, and confirming the lords in their fiefs. Thus he now had at his back not only his Burmans but also the Talaing levies, under their own lords. Further, he engaged 700 Portuguese, with their ships, under Joano Cayeyro, one of the many Portuguese adventurers who now roamed over the East with his merry men, in great demand among the wrangling rajas; they brought muskets and light artillery, probably the first ever seen in Burma (p. 340).

In 1541 Tabinshwehti proceeded to complete his conquest of the Pegu kingdom by attacking its wealthiest town Martaban. The puny Portuguese artillery was useless against ramparts backed by earthwork, and he could not even get near the water side of the town because it was defended by seven Portuguese ships and a hundred men under a rival adventurer Paulo Seixas. The town repelled him with heavy loss but at the end of seven months it was famished and asked for terms. He would accept nothing but complete submission. The besieged lord would not agree and tried to seduce Joano Cayeyro, secretly sending him this letter:—

> Valiant and faithful Commander of the Portuguese, through the grace of the King of the other end of the world, the strong and mighty lion, dreadfully roaring, with a crown of Majesty in the House of the Sun! I the unhappy Chaubainha [Sawbinnya], heretofore a prince, but now no longer so, finding myself besieged in this wretched and unfortunate city, do give thee to understand by the words pronounced out of my mouth, with an assurance no less faithful than true, that I now render myself the vassal of the great King of Portugal, sovereign

lord of me, and my children, with an acknowledgement of homage, and such tribute as he at his pleasure shall impose on me; wherefore . . . come speedily with thy ships to the bulwark of the chapel quay, where thou shalt find me ready attending thee, and . . . I will deliver myself up to thy mercy, with all the treasures that I have in gold, and precious stones, whereof I will most willingly give the one half to the King of Portugal, upon condition that he shall permit me with the remainder to levy in his kingdom, or in the fortresses which he hath in the Indies, two thousand Portuguese, to whom I will give extraordinary great pay that by their means I may be re-established in this state, which now I am constrained to abandon. (*Pinto* 296.)

Joano Cayeyro was not the king of Portugal's officer but a free lance, and hearing that the lord of Martaban had treasure enough to fill several ships, he wished to aid him in escaping. But his officers were jealous, and threatened to denounce him to Tabinshwehti, so he had to refuse.

In despair, the lord of Martaban allowed Paulo Seixas to depart, paying him off with a pair of bracelets which subsequently sold for a fabulous sum; and with him went his Talaing wife, his two children, and some of his men. But the seven ships remained and the town was far from taken. Tabinshwehti therefore accepted the proposal of one of his commanders, Smim Payu who, being a Talaing, was more expert than Burmans at water fighting. Smim Payu went up stream to Lagunpyin (? Lagun, twenty miles up the Salween river) with a numerous levy, felled huge bamboos by the thousand, and made them into rafts of two kinds. One kind contained jingals mounted on scaffolds higher than the walls of Martaban; the others were fire-rafts and came floating down the river with flames higher than a toddy tree. Fire rafts[1] presented no difficulty to ships of sufficient size to launch several boats manned by competent seamen, but Portuguese craft were tiny things, often only half decked with a single boat apiece, manned largely by Eurasians and slaves. Three of the defending ships slipped their cables and stood out to sea. The remaining four were either burnt or captured. The scaffold rafts, crammed with troops, were then brought alongside the walls and the stormers soon won a foothold.

The sack raged three days. The booty was superior to

[1] The Burmese used them in 1824, containing Pegu jars full of flaming oil. They were flung off and did no damage, see *Havelock*, *Snodgrass*, *Trant*.

anything previously taken in Burma, being the accumulated gold, silver, jewels, pepper, sandal and aloes wood, camphor, silk, and lace which filled the godowns of merchants of many races—Portuguese, Greek, Venetian, Moor, Jew, Armenian, Persian, Abyssinian, Malabari and Sumatran. The palace and town were burnt to the ground. The captive prince with all his family and followers, men and women, were cruelly exterminated in spite of a promise of good treatment. Scores of nobles were flung into the river with stones round their necks, and the remaining property of the merchants, mostly foreigners, was confiscated. Moulmein and the southern territory submitted as far as the Siamese frontier at Tavoy.

Tabinshwehti exercised his royal privilege of putting spires on the Talaing pagodas; to the Shwedagon he offered his queen and redeemed her with ten *viss* (36·5lb.) of gold. In 1542 he marched on Prome. The Upper Burma tribes came down to help it; Bayinnaung went a day's march north, defeated them in an ambush, and drove them back. The lord of Prome had already presented his sister to the king of Arakan and asked him for help against the rising Toungoo power; and the Arakanese sent a force through the Padaung pass and a flotilla along the coast. Bayinnaung sent a forged letter, as from the lord of Prome, to the Arakanese as they came out of the pass, and thus succeeded in ambushing them, after which they went home; their flotilla reached Bassein, heard of this defeat, and also went home. For these services the king gave Bayinnaung the rings off his own fingers, three layers of cushions on which to lie in state, and the appointment of *yuvaraja* (crown prince). After a five months' siege starvation set in at Prome, the besieged deserted in great numbers, and the town was mercilessly sacked, atrocities being perpetrated on children and ladies of rank, and hundreds of the defenders being crucified.[1]

Tabinshwehti had maintained a cart-track from Pegu to Toungoo; he now maintained one to Prome, said to be much the same as the present alignment. In 1544 the seven *sawbwas* (p. 109) attacked Prome but withdrew on the advance of Tabinshwehti who smashed their war canoes by gunfire, and

[1] See note "Pinto" p. 342.

permanently occupied central Burma as far as the north of Minbu and Myingyan districts. Three years previously he had been crowned at Pegu as king of Lower Burma, and now while halting at Pagan he was crowned as king of Upper Burma.[1] On his return he was crowned at Pegu in 1546 as king of both, using Talaing as well as Burmese rites. Only half his task was done, but the rest was sure, and men again beheld the glory of the ancient ritual; at last, after three centuries of sordid *sawbwas*, there was once more a king in Burma.

In 1546-7 he invaded Arakan. He had engaged a fresh batch of Portuguese under Diogo Soarez de Mello, well armed troops of good quality,[2] and these now accompanied him. The Burmese levies under Bayinnaung marched by the pass from Kyangin in Henzada district, clearing a track as they went; the Talaing levies went by boat round the coast, headed by the king himself and two Portuguese ships, but they suffered severely from weather on the way, the more so as the Talaings were no seamen. Sandoway was already in the king's hands, for its lord had paid homage in return for a promise that he would be given the throne of his nephew the king of Arakan. North of Sandoway the land and water forces united and continued their advance in conjunction, driving in opposition till they camped before Mrohaung. Their only chance of taking a walled town like Mrohaung quickly lay in surprising it when the defences were out of repair. But Arakan happened to have a king who, gauging Tabinshwehti's tendencies, had put his defences in good order (p. 140). The Burmese, unable to make headway, were glad to accept the intercession of the monks; and after the opposing leaders had met and conversed amicably, the invaders returned home.

They returned in haste because Siam, hearing that Tabinshwehti with all his valiant men was away in Arakan, had been unable to resist the temptation of raiding Tavoy. Tabinshwehti summoned the king of Siam to surrender his white elephants and meanwhile he prepared for an expedition[3] in the cold weather 1547-8. He recalled Diogo Soarez de Mello, who had taken leave from Arakan to serve against the

[1] *Phayre* MSS. [2] *Couto* III. i 17-20.
[3] See note "Siamese Chronology" p. 343.

sultan of Achin and now returned with five other captains and 180 men. The Burmese hosts crossed from Martaban to Moulmein on a bridge of boats over which they could ride their ponies at a gallop. His Majesty's elephant was ferried across on a raft, but the other elephants were sent up stream where the fords were shallow; jingals were mounted on many of these elephants. The cannon were kept close to the king, and he moved in great state, surrounded by the choicest elephants, richly attired lords, and 400 Portuguese Guards whose morions and arquebuses were inlaid with gold, for they provided a bodyguard as well as artillery. Little Nandabayin (p. 179) the thirteen-year-old son of Bayinnaung, rode with the armies. Hundreds of workmen went ahead every day to pitch the wooden camp palace,[1] richly painted and gilded; and at each halt there was a *pwe* festival.

The advance was up the Ataran river, through Three Pagodas Pass and down the Meklawng river to Kanburi. Thence they struck at Ayuthia, driving in the Siamese at Yazathein (? near Intaburi), where the king of Siam risked himself in the press, and the queen, rushing up on her elephant to rescue him, was cleft from shoulder to heart by the lord of Prome; her sons advanced and carried off her body.[2]

But the Burmese could not take Ayuthia. The Siamese had cannon made out of the copper which was annually imported from China. The weakest part of the wall was defended by fifty Portuguese who elected one Diogo Pereira as their captain; Tabinshwehti tried to bribe them, but they treated the offer with derision, and one of the Siamese commanders, flinging open the town gate, dared Tabinshwehti to bring the money.

After a month the Burmese withdrew and tried to plunder Kampengpet, a wealthy town; but here again there were Portuguese who used flaming projectiles so that the guns had to be kept in shelter under damp hides. Tabinshwehti, saying the Siamese were devils who, when their own weapons failed, used new ones which had never been known since the beginning of the world, retreated, and it would doubtless have gone hard with him had he not captured the Siamese king's son, brother, and son-in-law in some open fighting. At once

[1] *Stevens* II. 135. [2] *Jones* V. 162.

Siamese envoys came with red and green woollen cloths, *longyis*, and aromatic woods, offering friendly relations in return for the captive princes. Tabinshwehti released not only the princes but also his other prisoners and was thereupon left unmolested during his retreat *via* Raheng.

When conquering the Delta, Tabinshwehti had made no attempt to administer his new subjects through Burmese governors. Any Talaing lord who made timely submission could count on being left in his fief. Consequently from the first he had a large Talaing following. He left the beautiful buildings of the Talaing kings standing when he captured Pegu. Talaings had their full say in his councils, he took care to be crowned with the ritual of a Talaing king, and he gave way to the importunities of his Talaing princesses, letting them dress in their own fashion instead of the Burmese court dress. Finally, hearing an old prophecy that no king with a Burmese hairknot should rule the Talaing land, he bobbed his hair like a Talaing[1] and wore the diadem of a Talaing king.

But on returning from Siam he consorted with a young Portuguese and fell from kingly virtue. The feringhi was an adventurer who had set out from Malacca with seven ships and scores of junks to attack the sultan of Achin; being defeated, he fled with his remaining junks and 300 men to Martaban whose lord sent him under arrest to court. He rose to high favour through his skill in the chase with one of the wonderful new weapons—a fire-arm. The king went hunting with him and in admiration gave him a royal handmaid to wife. The feringhi taught his bride to cook feringhi dishes for the king to eat, and gave him juice of the grape to drink. The juice delighted the king's heart, so that he called the feringhi to where he sat on the throne and drank. Finally the feringhi prepared spirits with honey to sweeten them, and the king drank and lost his wits, respecting not other men's wives,

[1] The Talaings formerly cut their hair all on one pattern. They do not remember what it was but think it was as if a bowl were upturned on the head and the ends evenly trimmed all round the rim. *Dalrymple* I. 99 in a passage dated 1759 says "The Peguers resemble the Malays in their appearance and disposition, though more industrious; they cut their hair round before, and the back-part, from their ears to the crown of their head, is shaved in a semi-circle. The Burmese are darker in complexion than the Peguers."

listening to malicious tales, and sending men to the executioners. Bayinnaung remonstrated with him, saying, "This becometh not a king. It were well to reform"; but he answered "I have made friends with drink. Brother, do thou manage the affairs of state. Bring me no petitions. Leave me to my jollity." Sometimes he attended levees, sometimes he could not. Bayinnaung set the best officers to keep guard over him, and when order after order came to execute innocent men, he saw that no action was taken. Burmese, Shan and Talaing ministers waited on Bayinnaung asking him to take the throne. He answered "Brethren, gratitude and loyalty alike bind us to the king. What ye have said, say it to me alone, tell it not to others. The Lord in His wisdom saith that an evil man, though he live an hundred years, shall not avail against an upright man though he live but a single day. I will advise His Majesty, and if his mind followeth not what I say, then is it for you and me to render him faithful service. Let us hold no more unseemly counsel. Be not anxious but continue in your fiefs [p. 270]. Although, because of sin in a previous existence, the mind of our Sovereign Lord is infirm and he raveth, yet shall the realm not perish if we watch over and defend it." Thereafter he seized the Portuguese favourite, paid him off, set him on a ship, and sent him out of the country.[1]

Tabinshwehti went to live at Pantanaw in Maubin district in the care of Talaing chamberlains, and Bayinnaung went to deal with a rebellion headed by a monk, a bastard of the fallen Talaing dynasty, who, flinging off the robe, assumed the title of Smim Htaw, and occupied Dagon (Rangoon) and Dalla. Bayinnaung was soon chasing him through the Myaungmya and Bassein creeks. But some of the Talaing chamberlains, having sent away their loyal colleagues on a pretext, lured Tabinshwehti from Pantanaw into a jungle saying a white elephant had been traced, and there one evening his sword-bearers cut off his head;[2] they then slew the Burmese attendants, raised their compatriots at Sittaung, drove Bayinnaung's

[1] See note "The young feringhi" p. 343.

[2] Age thirty-five. He is the Tabinshwehti Nat spirit, *Temple* 64.

brother out of Pegu, and set the leading chamberlain, Smim Sawhtut, on the throne.

BAYINNAUNG 1551-81. The fiefs of central Burma all shut their gates and never lifted a finger to help Bayinnaung; his own brothers and kinsmen tried to set up as independent kings in such important charges as Prome and Toungoo itself. There he was, a king without a kingdom, grappling with one Talaing rebel in the west while another sat on his throne in the east, his Burmese people looked on with folded hands, and his own brothers seceded.

At once he sent overseas for Diogo Soarez de Mello and the Portuguese who had rejoined their own people; they came promptly, brushing aside the Talaing rebels who tried to bar the creeks. Bayinnaung was overjoyed,[1] exclaiming "Ah, brother Diogo, brother Diogo, we two, we happy two, I on my elephant and thou on thy horse, could we not conquer the world together?" The levies with him were few but faithful, and he decided to march on Toungoo; it was the family home and there he could raise the Burmese against an opposition which was mainly Talaing and was based on their weariness of serving in the shambles of a Burmese warmonger. Having sworn in the headmen and lords from Dagon to Henzada, he marched up the Pegu river and past the Makaw pagoda at Pale. North of Pegu, Smim Htaw came out with his men, but Bayinnaung, "paying no more heed than a lion does to jackals," swept on his way and stockaded himself successively at Myogyi and Yebokkon near Toungoo.

He was joined by his queen who had escaped from Pegu and came in a palanquin. He sent for the men who had saved her, and some Mahomedans were presented to him; he exclaimed "I asked for men, and you bring me chickens! Go, bring me men." They brought him thirty-nine Portuguese whom the queen identified, and he loaded them with rewards.[2] He then moved to Zeyawaddy thirty miles away. Here he was joined by Shans, Burmans, and even eight Talaing

[1] *Couto* IV. i 136. [2] *Stevens* II. 138, *Couto* IV. i 154.

ministers who had sickened at the new tyranny in Pegu. Smim Sawhtut was killed by a Portuguese bullet[1] in action against Smim Htaw who succeeded him; Talaings from Martaban itself, Smim Htaw's stronghold, came over to Bayinnaung, recognising character when they saw it. Toungoo deserted to him wholesale; he occupied it, forgave his brother, and was crowned.

He occupied Myede in Thayetmyo district where central Burma up to Sagu joined him, and he took Prome, his brother smashing in the town gate on his elephant. He tried to get Ava so as to have still more men at his back before attacking Pegu, but he failed, although its fugitive chief, Mobye Narapati, joined him (p. 109). However, he had now sufficient men for the great venture, including not only Portuguese, Burmans, and Talaings but even some Mone Shan spearmen.

Under the walls of Pegu, just before the hosts met, he poured libation of water from a golden goblet, praying for justice on the right; the sky thundered and flashed with lightning in answer. Smim Htaw fought him in single combat till Bayinnaung, freeing his elephant, drew back and charged, breaking the tusk of his foeman's elephant and driving him off the field followed by all his men. He then sacked Pegu, killing men, women, children, and even animals.[2] Diogo Soarez de Mello, after inducing him to spare the lives of some Portuguese who had fought for the Talaings, was mortally wounded in a brawl with the townsfolk, and then, holding the hand of a friendly lord *smim*, "for he needed a little hope, he confessed his sins and died."

Talaing opposition collapsed with the fall of Pegu. Smim Htaw could get few more followers, but he made a gallant fight, hunted as he was throughout the Delta. Many a jungle has its tradition of his hiding there (p. 120). South of Pyapon town a village bears his name, and south of that again at Myogon, on a pleasant little highland rising out of the rice swamp, amid many a fruit tree, are the remains of a tiny stockade which men say he once occupied. Sometimes he would catch the Burmese boats stranded at low tide in a creek, and wipe them out, sometimes he would surprise an outpost. But as the months passed, the inevitable end drew

[1] *Pinto* 441. [2] *Couto* IV. i 136, *Stevens* II. 136.

nigh. His family fell into the hands of his hunters. He fled alone in a canoe along the coast to Martaban. Once they fell on him during the evening meal, but he escaped with a gash in the neck. At another time they found him asleep in a field, and actually seized him, but he slipped away leaving his clothes in their hands. He hid in the hills round Sittaung, poor and unknown till he took a village girl to wife and told her his secret; she guilelessly told her father who reported to the *talahkwan* (village officers). When he was captured,[1] Bayinnaung had him paraded through the jeering streets and put to a hard death. Thus ended Wareru's lineage.

Having regained the position from which he should have started, Bayinnaung set out on his career of conquest. The size of his armies varied with the area of his kingdom for the time being. At its maximum, when it included Upper Burma, the Shan states, and Siam, it supplied him with a mass levy approaching possibly one hundred thousand.[2] His efforts were on a bigger scale than had hitherto been known in Burma, at least up to the time of Tabinshwehti. The trivial fighting which had dragged on throughout the preceding two and a half centuries now gave place to the mass movements and the knock-out blows of a man who aimed at a decision. No excuses were accepted from the men under him. Long records of faithful service, and the ties of ancient friendship, were to be pleaded in vain by officers who failed; the least they had to fear was the instant deprivation of all their titles and property, and ruthless exile to some fever-stricken spot. As for the rank and file, the severity they suffered, under every determined leader of whom we have a record, was provoked by the fact that so many of the levies were like herds of cattle, and wholesale desertion was a commander's constant dread; the only way of keeping them together and bringing them to action was to use methods of frightfulness.

In 1555 Bayinnaung advanced on Ava. Half the levies went up the Sittang valley to Yamethin and thence eastwards; the other half went by the Irrawaddy in war canoes of many and strange shapes—horse, duck, crocodile, elephant, shark, dragon—led by Bayinnaung on a magnificent barge, shaped

[1] *Stevens* II. 137, *Pinto* 452-9. [2] See "Numerical Note" p. 333.

like a brahminy duck, 134 cubits long. Ava fell at the first blow; her call for aid remained unanswered, as usual, by the other *sawbwas*, who bestirred themselves only after the town had fallen. Bayinnaung had little difficulty in occupying the country up to Bangyi in Monyua district and Myedu in Shwebo district. He returned home after leaving instructions for the cart track from Toungoo to Ava to be kept open.

In three campaigns, 1556-9, he reduced the Shan states Mohnyin, Mogaung, Momeik, Möng Pai, Saga, Lawksawk, Yawnghwe, Hsipaw, Bhamo, Kale, Manipur, and some which are now in Siam—Chiengmai and Linzin (Viengchang). In 1562 he raided the Koshanpye towns up the Taping and Shweli rivers in Yünnan.[1] Later, Hsenwi and Kengtung sent propitiatory homage; he had no authority there but it pleased him to send white umbrellas and the five regalia to Kengtung. The suzerainty of Burma over the Shans dates from this time; the Pagan monarchy had controlled little more than the foot hills; even now, Burmese suzerainty was seldom more than nominal till the second half of the eighteenth century.

It is characteristic that while Bayinnaung was proceeding down the Salween against Chiengmai, his garrison in Mone was murdered and the bridge he had built across the Salween was destroyed by Mone, Yawnghwe, and Lawksawk. Revolts were chronic. In 1562, 1572, 1574-6 he was campaigning against such places as Mohnyin and Mogaung, wearing out his men in pursuits over snow-clad hills in the north. Finally the chiefs submitted, tired of starving in the wilderness. The Mogaung chief was exhibited for a week in fetters at the gates of Pegu; as for some scores of his principal followers, Bayinnaung, saying he was very merciful, refrained from executing them and sent them to be sold as slaves in the Ganges ports.[2]

As was invariably the case, the Burmese no sooner occupied an area than they exacted levies, and the Burmese Shans were at once employed against the Siamese Shans. The chiefs presented daughters to the harem, sent their sons to be brought up in the palace, and paid periodic tribute; Momeik,

[1] See note "Pong and Koshanpye" p. 322.

[2] Doubtless Tamluk and Baleshwar. *Hmannan* III. 47, anachronist as usual, says Calcutta; but Calcutta did not come into existence till a century later.

the most valuable of all, paid rubies; Chiengmai paid elephants, horses, lacquer and silks. Everywhere Bayinnaung deported numbers of the people in order to populate his home land.[1] From Chiengmai he took artisans, especially her famous lacquer workers (p. 119); it is probably these who introduced into Burma the finer sort of lacquerware called *yun*, the name of the Yun or Lao Shan tribes round Chiengmai.[2]

In the 1556 campaign he went by barge as far north as Htigyaing, Katha district, where his land levies crossed to the western bank; his queens and concubines accompanied him, worshipping together at the Shwedagon and the Shwehsandaw at Prome. At the Shwezigon at Pagan he made offerings to as many monks as there were years in his life, and on his return journey in 1557 he set up the great bronze bell, bearing in Pali, Burmese, and Talaing an inscription[3] every line of which breathes imperial pride in his conquests and in the steps he took to promote religion. In the 1557 campaign he did not return home direct, but after reducing Mone went down the Salween to reduce Chiengmai. He promoted religion thus:—

> In Onbaung [Hsipaw], Momeik and the rest of the Shan country when a *sawbwa* died, following heathen doctrine men used to kill his slaves and the dear horses and elephants that he rode, and bury them in the grave with him. His Majesty forbade such evil practices. Moreover, seeing that religion was not firmly established, he built pagodas at Onbaung and Momeik, and dedicated lands to religion, and built monasteries of three stories with ten surrounding monasteries each at Onbaung and Momeik, and invited learned monks to abide there practising religion. The *sawbwas* with all their counsellors and captains listened to the preaching of the law four holy days a month, and learned virtue. His Majesty placed one half the scriptures at Onbaung and the other half at Momeik. (*Hmannan* II. 324. See note "Funeral Sacrifice" p. 343.)

Bayinnaung also discouraged foreign settlers' animal sacrifices, such as the *bakrid*, and abolished the custom,[4]

[1] See note "List of Captives" p. 321.

[2] *JBRS* 1919 Morris "Lacquerware Industry of Burma" and 1920 Kyaw Dun "Lacquerware called Yun."

[3] Unpublished, but will appear in *Epigraphia Birmanica*.

[4] *Hmannan* II. 312, *Wawhayalinatta* 69. See note "Drink" p. 314.

previously in force among the people of the villages round Popa Hill (Pagan, Yuatha, Sale, Pahkannge, Ngathayauk, Tuywindaing, Kyaukpadaung), of slaughtering white animals (buffaloes, kine, goats, pigs, fowls) to the Mahagiri spirit and festooning the shrine with their skulls; hitherto the kings had shared in such offerings, and hereafter they maintained public worship of the Mahagiri spirit, as of all other recognised *nats*, although it involved the use of intoxicants.

The king of Ayuthia, styled Lord of the White Elephants, had recently possessed no fewer than seven; their glory attracted white merchants from the end of the earth and brought Siam unprecedented prosperity; there could be no other cause, for in the days of his predecessors who had far fewer, there was less trade and European merchants had not come. He still had four, and Bayinnaung's soul was stirred to its depths at not having so many himself. He was considering not only his own glory but also the interests of his people: it was essential to their prosperity that he should acquire these elephants. Yet, saying he was a most religious king who abhorred bloodshed, he contented himself with asking for only one, and pointed out that Siam, having presented a white elephant to his predecessor Wareru, was bound by precedent to present one now.[1] Siam sent back the messengers with a refusal. Bayinnaung was deeply shocked but felt he could now fight with a clear conscience. His task was easier than on the last occasion (p. 159); then his brother had only the Delta and central Burma from which to draw levies, whereas now he had also Upper Burma and the Shan states from Mogaung to Chiengmai.

The campaign 1563-4 began with the capture of first Kampengpet and then Sukhotai. The huge host swarmed down on Ayuthia, suffering considerable casualties because of the Siamese and their feringhi gunners, but capturing stockades, war-canoes and three foreign ships. The city yielded quickly in quite unnecessary terror of Bayinnaung's feringhi artillery, which made a fearsome din. The terms were the surrender of the four white elephants, the captivity of the king and some princes as hostages, the presentation of a daughter, the cession

[1] It was not Siam but Chiengmai which had sent the white elephant to Wareru, see *Razadarit Ayedawpon*. See, however, p. 114.

of Tenasserim shipping tolls, and annual tribute of thirty war elephants. Bayinnaung left the Siamese king's son to rule as vassal with a Burmese garrison of 3,000 men. His loot included thirty crude images of men and elephants in bronze (p. 183). He deported thousands of the population[1] roped together in gangs with wooden collars; among them were actors and actresses, and it is probably these who introduced into Burma the songs and dances called Yodaya (Ayuthia). Returning victorious to Pegu,

> Braginoco[2] entered the city in triumph, many wagons going before loaded with idols and inestimable booty. He came at last in a chariot with the conquered queens loaden with jewels at his feet, and drawn by the captive princes and lords; before him marched two thousand elephants richly adorned, and after him his victorious troops. He built a palace as big as an ordinary city. The least part of its beauty was rich painting and gilding; for the roofs of some apartments were covered with plates of solid gold. Some rooms were set with statues of kings and queens of massy gold, set with rich stones, as big as the life. He was carried on a litter of gold upon many men's shoulders, the reverence paid him more like a god than a prince. (*Stevens* III. 118.)

But Siam was not settled by the fall of Ayuthia. Till the end of the reign there were few years in which the royal armies were not campaigning all over the country from the northern Laos downwards. Chiengmai failed to send its levy to the 1563 siege and afterwards gave such trouble that its chief had to be kept at Pegu.[3] In 1567 Pegu was starving, and Linzin (Viengchang) failed to comply with a requisition for rice; indeed she was never really subject, and for many years her elusive chief led Bayinnaung a weary chase through trackless hills where his men were reduced to eating *thekke* grass and died in thousands of starvation and disease. Year after year there was cruel fighting against the Siamese stockades, against their war-canoes and flaming rafts. He usually succeeded in occupying towns, setting his puppet with a Burmese garrison on their little thrones, and dragging away the population, when it had not hidden in the jungle, to work as slaves in Burma if they survived the long march. But

[1] See note "List of Captives" p. 321.
[2] The Portuguese version of Baringyinaungsaw, a variant of Bayinnaung.
[3] He died in captivity and became the Yun Bayin Nat spirit, see *Temple* 65.

more than this he could not do, he could give no settled government to the surviving victims, and some of the chiefs, such as Viengchang, he never caught.

He generously allowed the captive king of Siam, who had become a monk, to return home on pilgrimage; no sooner had he arrived than he flung off the robe and so another siege of Ayuthia became necessary. It lasted ten months, 1568-9. The Burmese built earthworks higher than the walls, in order that the crude Portuguese and Mahomedan cannon might fire into the town, but the siege made no headway. The Burmese losses were so heavy that the men used to take shelter under the piles of their comrades' corpses. The troops sickened of the carnage, and officers were executed right and left for failure. In the town, the old king died, and his son was a fool who accepted the word[1] of the Burmese that they would withdraw if the best Siamese commander were surrendered to them as the cause of the war; the commander was surrendered, but the siege continued. Bayakamani, lord of Syriam, restrained his officers from hounding their men on to the walls, walls which were totally unbreached and could not have been taken even by modern regulars if armed only with swords. For daring to do this he was summoned into the presence. He had been Bayinnaung's comrade from youth up; it was he who fought in the howdah at Bayinnaung's side in the duel with Smim Htaw (p. 163); he was one of the chosen few whose images were deposited along with the king's in the Mahazedi pagoda (p. 172); but all this was nothing—he had dared to use discretion, and he was executed on the spot. His body lay exposed as a warning; his son came and mourned at its side—he was executed for daring to mourn, and his body also was exposed. The family slave, seeing the bodies of his dead masters lying like dogs, covered them with a cloth—he too was executed.[2]

But the town was never taken by storm. Though the besieged were short of food, they held their own until Bayinnaung used treachery, employing one of the hostages yielded by Siam four years previously. This person, Aukbya Setki, entered the town saying he had escaped from his

[1] *Wood.* [2] *Hmannan* II. 437.

Burmese captors. The Siamese gave him high command and one night he opened the gates to the Burmese.

Had Ayuthia not fallen when it did, it would probably not have fallen at all, as the Burmese were suffering acutely in the rains, and soon afterwards a record flood inundated the whole country. Aukbya Setki was rewarded with the offer of a fief in Siam, but having some regard for the wholeness of his skin, he preferred to live elsewhere; he was made lord *binnya* of Dagon (Rangoon) and received the escheated property of officers who had been executed for failure. The king of Ayuthia had to come crawling into Bayinnaung's presence; he was carried off into captivity and fell ill on the way; Bayinnaung ordered the execution of ten doctors who failed to cure him, but in spite of such energy he died.[1]

The former king of Ayuthia, when living at Pegu in captivity, had been reasonably treated. Like the captive chiefs of Ava and Chiengmai, he was even accorded the privilege of living in a double-roofed house painted white. As in other mediæval countries, sumptuary regulations loomed large in the daily life of the people. Probably they were much the same then as they were within living memory. White umbrellas were restricted to the king and the Lord White Elephant alone. The *yuvaraja* (crown prince) and state dignitaries had gold umbrellas, twelve to fifteen feet high, and in number according to their rank. The number of stories to a house, its shape, the style of a corpse's funeral, the size, shape and metal of spittoons, betel-boxes, buttons, anklets, the length, cut and material of clothes, the patterns woven into them, the wearing of rings set with certain stones —these and a hundred such minutiæ were the subject of innumerable regulations.[2] A man's rank or occupation could be told by a glance at his dress.

There is little literature in the reign. Dwe Hla, a royal concubine, was an authoress, and one Yazathara wrote a *paiksonyadu* poem read before His Majesty when the spire was raised on a pagoda. His Majesty's distinguished Talaing officer, the *wungyi* Binnya Dala, wrote the Razadarit Ayedawpon chronicle (p. 115). Nawadegyi, whom the king brought with other deportees from Ava in 1555, had already been taken

[1] *Jones* VI. 268-9. [2] *Shway Yoe* 402.

from Prome to Salin, Sagaing and Ava by the various chiefs who had turned each other out in the preceding decades; for writing a poem on the gates of Pegu city he received his title Nawadegyi from the king; under Nandabayin 1581-99 he accompanied the lords of Chiengmai and Prome in an expedition to crush rebellion at Thaungdut on the Chindwin river, and wrote some verse mentioning the event; he wrote 400 *yadu*, and a song on the Ayuthia princess, sister of Bayinnaung's second son, the prince of Siam.

His Majesty introduced a measure of legal uniformity by summoning distinguished monks and officials from all over his dominions to prescribe an official collection of law books; they prescribed the Wareru *dhammathat* (p. 111) and compiled the Dhammathatkyaw and Kosaungchok.[1] The decisions given in his court were collected in the Hanthawaddy Hsinbyumyashin *pyatton*. He also tried to standardise weights and measures, such as the cubit, tical, and basket throughout the realm (p. 49).

Styling himself the King of Kings, he governed only Pegu and the Talaing country himself, leaving the rest of the realm to vassal kings with palaces at Toungoo, Prome, Ava and Chiengmai. He regarded Chiengmai as the most important, having fifty-seven provinces; these, like the thirty-two provinces of Pegu, were big villages. Chiengmai was a Shan state, not a kingdom, and when he spoke of having twenty-four crowned heads at his command, he was referring to *sawbwas*. Each of the twenty gates of his new city at Pegu was named after the vassal who built it, such as the Prome gate, the Chiengmai gate, the Toungoo gate, the gates of Salin, Dalla, Mohnyin, Tavoy, Hsenwi, Linzin, Tenasserim, Ayuthia, Martaban, Pagan—it was the men of Pagan who had to plant the toddy palms (p. 314) all along the walls and at the street corners.

As a model Buddhist king he distributed copies of the scriptures, fed monks, and built pagodas in Chiengmai, Koshanpye, and other conquered states; at Ayuthia he spent Rs. 300 on pagoda building.[2] Some of these pagodas are still to be seen, and in later ages the Burmese would

[1] *Forchammer* "Jardine Prize" 67.

[2] *Hmannan* II, 376. Commodity prices are not on record, but the real value would be considerable.

point to them as proof of their claim to rule those countries still. He supervised mass ordinations at the Kalyani *thein* (p. 120). Following a royal custom, he would break up his crown and use its jewels to adorn the spire of a pagoda; he did this for the Shwedagon, the Shwemawdaw, the Kyaiktiyo in Thaton district, and many a lesser pagoda. Again, as at the Shwemawdaw, he would build as many surrounding monasteries as there were years in his life at the time, fifty-two; or he would bear the cost of ordaining a similar number of monks. After the 1564 earthquake, which coincided with his queen's death, he repaired the Shwedagon, and added a new spire. His chief foundation was the Mahazedi at Pegu, at which he enshrined a stone *thabeik* (begging bowl) of supernatural origin sent him in 1567 by some Ceylon kinglet, and the tooth (p. 173), with golden images of himself, the royal family, and such of the great officers of state as were in his inner circle.[1] In acting thus he was not only exercising his functions as Head of the Church, but also laying up merit for himself to atone for the bloodshed of his campaigns.

In 1555 he sent rich presents to the Tooth at Kandy in Ceylon and bought land there to keep lights continually burning at the shrine; the craftsmen he sent beautified it, the broom made of his hair, and of his chief Queen's, swept it. In 1560 the Portuguese captured the Tooth and took it to Goa; hearing this, Bayinnaung sent envoys on a Portuguese ship which happened to be in port, offering eight lakhs of rupees, and shiploads of rice, whenever needed, to provision Malacca, in return for the Tooth. The Portuguese viceroy viewed the offer sympathetically; many of his men wished to be put on duty as escort for the Tooth to Pegu, and make money by exhibiting it on the way. Other Buddhist princes made offers. But the matter came to the archbishop's ears; he went to see the viceroy; he preached from the pulpit before the assembled court on Genesis xiv 21 "Da mihi animas, cetera tolle tibi." When the viceroy pointed out that his treasury was low, the archbishop accused him of being a freemason. At this terrible accusation the viceroy wavered. The matter was debated in full council. The priests said the accursed thing must be destroyed, idolatry must be blotted

[1] See note "Tula-dana" p. 328.

out; mere soldiers said, even if the Tooth were destroyed there was nothing to prevent Buddhists inventing a new tooth, calling it genuine, and worshipping that. But the priests were adamant. At Goa in 1561, amid solemn state, while the Burmese envoys gazed in frozen horror, the archbishop placed the Tooth in a mortar, ground it to powder, burnt it in a brazier, and cast the ashes into the river. But the Burmese envoys had scarcely reached home when the Tooth was back in Ceylon. It had slipped through the bottom of the mortar, mounted up into the sky, flown 750 miles to Kandy, and alighted on a lotus there.

Learning from the astrologers that he was destined to wed a Ceylon princess, Bayinnaung in 1574 sent an embassy with monks to demand her. The kinglet of Colombo had no daughter but he sent the daughter of a chamberlain whom he had treated as his own. He had nothing to do with the Temple of the Tooth at Kandy, but his chamberlain showed the envoys and monks, with great mystery under cover of night, a secret shrine before which they prostrated themselves in ecstacy, for it contained a piece of stag's horn which he said was the Tooth. They took the daughter to Bassein where she was received with bands of music and a great procession, and at Pegu she was inducted as a queen. They also reported the matter of the tooth to Bayinnaung who sent rich presents, and in return it was sent on a ship. In 1576 he went to meet it at Bassein in a great procession of magnificent canoes crowded with lords and ladies clad in court dress. He bathed ceremonially, scented himself, and bowed before the shrine. Princes waded into the river and bore it ashore at Pegu walking over the state vestments which the lords took off and spread before them. It was encased in a golden casket studded with the gems of Dammazedi and the kings of old, and of Momeik and of Ayuthia, the vassal kings, and finally it was laid to rest in the Mahazedi pagoda at Pegu. This was the day of days in Bayinnaung's life; his wide conquests, even the white elephants from Siam, faded into insignificance; he said "Heaven is good to me. Anawrahahta could obtain only a replica tooth from Ceylon, Alaungsithu went to China in vain, but I, because of my piety and wisdom, I have been granted this!"

The least he could do was to aid the Colombo kinglet against his foes, the other kinglets. He sent hundreds of his best invulnerables, Burman, Talaing, Siamese, and Shan across the sea to Colombo; there they speared cattle, ripped them open, and ate the raw flesh while the gore ran down their faces, a feat which so terrified the foemen that they submitted to Colombo.[1]

Hearing of the treasures which Bayinnaung had given to him of Colombo, the kinglet of Kandy sent messengers saying he had a genuine daughter and the genuine Tooth. But His Burman Majesty, seeing no reason to reopen the case, would not enter into controversy with such sceptics and dismissed them with thanks.[2]

At the end of his reign he exchanged missions with Bengal. One of these missions claimed to have met Akbar face to face. Akbar was probably the mightiest monarch in Asia, and his palace at Fathpur-Sikri was one of the wonders of the world. The Burmese envoys said they convinced him that their master's timber and gilt palace was equally magnificent; they returned in 1579, completely satisfied at the impression they had made, and the court of Pegu believed that Akbar was preparing to come and take shelter at the Golden Feet of the Lord of the White Elephants.[3] The Moghul records do not so much as mention a Burmese embassy.

Bayinnaung was organising an expedition to overwhelm Arakan, and his levies had actually occupied Sandoway, when he died in 1581 at the age of sixty-six, leaving ninety-seven children. His life was the greatest explosion of human energy ever seen in Burma. From his teens till his death he was constantly in the field, leading every major campaign in person. The failure of other kings who attempted the same conquests is the measure of his ability.

Unlike his successors, who lived in the backwoods, Bayinnaung lived in a seaport and came into contact with men from the outer world. The extent to which overseas traders flocked to the Delta indicates that his regulations were reasonable. European merchants coming from India first sighted Negrais, and saw there, as we see now, the superb Hmawdin

[1] *Hmannan* III. 37. [2] See note "Tooth and Invulnerables" p. 344.
[3] *Hmannan* III. 65-7.

pagoda[1] flashing on the headland, a landmark for a whole day's sail. They went up stream to Bassein and, turning east, passed through the Myaungmya creeks to Pegu. Those creeks were, at least on the main route, crowded with villages almost touching each other throughout the journey, a teeming hive of happy thriving people. There were certain minor exactions, such as the compulsory attendance of merchants to see the white elephants, when tips were exacted all round, and greedy courtiers took heavy toll of all wares; but customs officers, though strict, were not obstructive, and there was free export of commodities such as jewels and rice, a thing subsequently forbidden by the benighted kings of Ava. At Pegu overseas trade was in the hands of eight brokers appointed by the king; their fee was 2 per cent. and their business-like methods and honesty won the esteem of European merchants.

Bassein is scarcely mentioned, the chief ports being on the eastern side, Syriam, Dalla, Martaban[2] and above all Pegu itself where the merchants were allowed to have brick warehouses, by special privilege (p. 360). Dagon (Rangoon) was of no importance save for its great pagoda, surrounded by green fields and shady woodland. But the travellers never tire of describing Pegu—the long moat full of crocodiles, the walls, the watch-towers, the gorgeous palace, the great processions with elephants and palanquins and grandees in shining robes, the shrines filled with images of massy gold and gems, the unending hosts of armed men, and the apparition of the great king himself—

> He sitteth up aloft in a great hall, on a tribunal seat, and lower under him sit all his barons round about, then those that demand audience enter into a great court before the king, and there set them down on the ground forty paces distant from the king's person, and amongst those people there is no difference in matter of audience before the king, but all alike, and there they sit with their supplications in their hands, which are made of long leaves of a tree . . . and with their supplications, they have in their hands a present or gift, according to the weightinesse of their matter. Then come the secretaries down to read these supplications, taking them and reading them

[1] Gasparo Balbi admired it in 1583 (*Hakluyt* X. 150).

[2] *Hamilton* II. 63 says the Burmese conquerors (p. 156) sunk several ships full of stones in the entrance to Martaban so that only small vessels could enter and it did not count as a port in his day, 1727. But in 1568 it was still a port, for it had ninety Portuguese residents (p. 178).

> before the king, and if the king think it good to do to them that favour or justice that they demand, then he commandeth to take the presents out of their hands; but if he think their demand be not just or according to right, he commandeth them away without taking of their gifts or presents. . . . He hath not any army or power by sea, but in the land, for people, dominions, gold, and silver, he far exceeds the power of the Great Turk in treasure and strength. (Year 1569, Cæsar Frederick, a merchant of Venice, *Hakluyt* X. 127, 125.)

These men saw the East in all her glory, such as we no longer see her. We have lost that vision and are the poorer. Yet we have lost it because we have grown richer. Our standards have altered. We no longer accept the pinchbeck and bone which even kings among our forbears were fain to wear as gold and ivory. Our Europe is no longer the little Christendom of Gothic times, living on the scanty produce of grey skies, trembling at every rumour of Saladin or the victorious Turk: she is sovran Europe who holds the East in fee, and the whole round world beside. We have come to know that all that glitters is not gold. These first voyagers did not know it; they came from evil-smelling walled towns, where folk dwelt in kennels and died like flies of epidemics caused by their own insanitation. To men who lived in the cold and changed their clothes but once a year, and went unwashed for months, the sunshine and the clean water, the children splashing all day in the creeks, the girls at the well, were one long delight. Ordure vanished quickly under the tropic sky, and instead of fetid narrow streets, and overhanging houses, they saw the airy spaciousness of Pegu city in its heyday, and wide ways sweeping out of sight towards the four main gates. Men who had wrung a fourfold crop, at best, from the hard northern soil, saw a miracle in rice with its forty-fold out-turn, and in the mango a rare and refreshing fruit. They did not stray inland or far from the capital, these simple sailormen; they saw little but the wealth of a kingdom heaped together on one man, the prince who peacocked it in his palace, and they took such vestures, such jewels, such pomp and circumstance, to be a type of the whole country.[1]

But the splendour was superficial. In spite of its sentimental appeal, the kingship was little loved. Bayinnaung and the princes risked their lives at the head of their men,

[1] See note "The Legend of the East" p. 344.

fighting conspicuously on elephants. Yet what was sport to them was death to the common people. Bayinnaung issued an unctuous edict, proclaimed by beat of drum from the head of an elephant, that no officer was to summon a man between June and September, the months of rice cultivation. But it is hard to see how officers could comply, for he never ceased requisitioning men for wars which frequently continued through the rains. The disorganisation caused by these wars was such that Pegu sometimes starved, as in 1567. Even the fertile Delta cannot grow rice without men to plant it, and they were not there to plant it, having all been dragged away on foreign service. Of those that went, few returned, for if battle casualties were great, the wastage from hunger and dysentery was even greater. Men were sick of being slaughtered. Even if they were not sent to fight, they were herded together and led away in one of the deportations which the kingship found necessary to re-populate ravaged areas.

At least once Bayinnaung had to hurry home from a Siamese campaign to deal with rebellion at his own capital. He had settled in the neighbourhood some twenty thousand captive Shans and Siamese. Talaings made common cause, and led them when they rose in 1564 and burned his city, including the old buildings of Dammazedi and his own magnificent edifices, such as the water pavilion. Worse would have followed had not the captive king of Ava rallied the lords and headed them in driving off the infuriated peasantry. Bayinnaung returned by forced marches from Chiengmai and, arriving near Pegu, saw the smoking ruins of the structures which had been his pride. Without stopping to enter, he marched straight on; in his fury he discarded the trappings of kingship and walked on foot with the men in his jewelled sandals.[1] At Dalla he rounded up the rebels. Numbering several thousand they were penned in huge bamboo cages, to be burnt alive according to immemorial custom. As usual, no provision was made for feeding them while under arrest, but Burmese, Talaing and Shan monks from the capital came out and fed them; nay more, they entreated His Majesty, and finally obtained the lives of them all save seventy ringleaders.

[1] *Hmannan* II. 387.

Bayinnaung made no distinction of race in appointment to office. His best commander was a Talaing, Binnya Dala. As his predecessors had doubtless done for ages, he entered into the *thwethauk* bloodbond (p. 339), a sacramental brotherhood of some round table as it were, with more than a score of his principal officers, and the list includes Talaings. They penetrated his entourage to such an extent that as often as not the word used by European travellers for a court grandee is *semini*, an italianisation of *smim*, the Talaing for lord. Such being his methods, he might have founded a national dynasty and reconciled both races. He failed to do so because he alienated human nature by his murderous wars. The brunt fell on Talaings; hence while at first they had followed him even against claimants of their own race because they believed he could give them settled government, at last the only ones who followed him were office-seekers and hardy spirits desirous of foreign loot.

The grandiloquent language which has been used about him disregards the fact that every other year or so throughout his reign he was hastening somewhere to fight and maintain himself in power. A ruler without an administration, he could not be everywhere at once, and no sooner did he turn his back than the chances were even that a rebellion would break out. Cæsar Frederick, the very man who in a moment of enthusiasm said that Burma possessed a greater power than Turkey, stultifies his own words by relating an incident which he witnessed: In 1568 some Portuguese at Martaban killed five of His Majesty's own runners in a brawl, and the governor could not arrest them because they were supported by all the other Portuguese who, to the number of ninety, marched defiantly through the streets every day with drums beating and colours flying. But any of the Grand Turk's governors in that age would have made short work of ninety Portuguese who resisted arrest.

Bayinnaung's campaigns were the price men had to pay for the unification of Burma. The squabbling chieftains of the preceding period had spilt blood in driblets, continually irritating the sore; he made a deep cut and finished the operation. Thus far he succeeded. Beyond that he failed because he was sterile, like his age—and it was the Age of the Renaissance. He was nothing more than a strong but evanescent personality, and the unity he gave was artificial; within a few years of his death it collapsed, and if it rose again and endured for another century and a half, this was not because he bequeathed a system, but because his immediate successors happened to be men of character, and the listlessness of the people prevented organised opposition.

His son NANDABAYIN 1581-99 choked with laughter on hearing from Gasparo Balbi, a merchant who came to Burma on business, that Venice was a free state without a king; the idea was so unintelligible as to be comic.

Nandabayin's son, the *yuvaraja* (crown prince), was married to his cousin; the pair had a squabble in the course of which blood was drawn from her forehead. She sent the blood-stained handkerchief to her father, viceroy of Ava, who promptly revolted, writing to the viceroys of Prome, Toungoo, and Chiengmai; but they forwarded the letters to the king. Suspecting some court grandees of complicity,

> the King ordained that the morning following they should make an eminent and spacious scaffold, and cause all the grandees to come upon it, and then set fire to it, and burn them all alive. But to show that he did this with justice, he sent another mandate that he should do nothing till he had an olla or letter written with his hand in letters of gold, and in the meantime he commanded him to retain all the prisoners of the grandees' families unto the women great with child, and those in swaddling clothes, and so he brought them all together upon the said scaffold; and the King sent the letter that he should burn them, and the decagini [*thakin* = lords] performed it, and burned them all, so that there was heard nothing but weeping, shriekings, cryings, and sobbings; for there were four thousand in this number which were so burned, great and small, for which execution were public guards placed by the King, and all of the old and new city were forced to assist them; I also went thither and saw it with great compassion and grief, that little children without fault should suffer such martyrdom, and among others there was one of his chief secretaries, who was last put in to be burned, yet was freed by the King's order; but his leg was begun to be burnt, so that he was lame. (Year 1583, Gasparo Balbi, a merchant of Venice, *Hakluyt* X. 160. See "Numerical Note" p. 334.)

Having thus executed justice according to immemorial precedent, the king set out for Ava at the head of his host, riding an elephant whose harness was all gold and jewels, and bearing a Portuguese sword presented to him by the viceroy of Goa. Near Ava he and his rebel uncle, the lord of Ava, fought together on elephants in single combat. The king won, the Ava host collapsed on the spot, and the uncle fled with a following to Kanti on the upper Chindwin where he died while trying to get local support.

There was scarcely a year in which the king did not have to deal with rebellion from Mogaung in the north to Hmawbi in the south, or Moulmein which leagued with the vassal king of Ayuthia. The *yuvaraja* (crown prince) used Talaings for forced labour on his rice land, stored the crop, and made them buy from him alone. The king raised a Noble Guard, the Shwepye Horse, and then killed them. He dragged people from all over the country to populate Pegu. He branded[1] Talaings on the right hand with their name, rank and village; such as were too old for service he sent to Upper Burma, where he sold them in exchange for horses. To evade unending conscription, thousands took holy orders; he appointed bishops to make inquiry and unfrock many. Bassein revolted and the rebels after surrendering were all tortured to death; the surviving population there took to living in the woods where he could not find them.

He could not trust the great Talaing monks, and sent them away to Ava and the Shan states. He instituted a reign of terror among the Talaings, executing them wholesale, and he horrified all by killing the pariah dogs in Pegu town.[2] Talaings in large numbers fled to Arakan and Siam. Indeed it is from this time that their periodic migrations to Siam begin, migrations which lasted down to 1824 and were due to the sustained severity of the Burmese.[3]

[1] *Hakluyt* X. 213. A generation ago, in order to help their claim to Karenni, the Siamese tattooed each adult male on the forearm with their badge (an elephant) and a serial number.

[2] *Hmannan* III. 100.

[3] Talaing exoduses were so frequent that the kings of Siam used to appoint special frontier guards to watch for them, and to maintain granaries along their route. The Talaings addressed the king of Siam as "the Lord of the Golden *Pyathat*, the Righteous King of Ayuthia, the Haven of the Mon people, who on every occasion saved their lives." Martaban was their great rallying place, and

There is no reason to suppose that Nandabayin was not above the average of Burmese kings. The dynasty was not yet effete. From youth upward he had served with the armies and he still led them in person. But he was saddled with an impossible legacy. Bayinnaung could win an empire, but even himself could not have retained it, for the structure was inorganic. The one hope of keeping the country together was to evacuate Siam and retrench in every direction. But neither Bayinnaung nor his energetic son could see it. As there was no administration, the only method by which the king could control remoter areas was by fighting them periodically, a process which used up the only people he could really call his own, the population round the capital. There were not sufficient people left alive to till the soil there, and remoter areas would not send food. In 1596 a plague of field rats destroyed what little crop there was; they were of enormous size, and came from the west in such numbers that the royal retainers, though armed with swords and spears, failed to stop them, and they swarmed on to the city granaries. A terrible famine followed, and it was only one of a series. Large areas in Lower Burma became a desert.

Nandabayin might have held the rest of his kingdom, but it was Ayuthia that ruined him. She was now under the famous king Pra Naret, called the Black Prince because of his swarthy skin. Pra Naret had been ordered to bring a levy against the Ava rebellion, but came late, and finding the king had already reached Ava, proceeded to ravage the country round Pegu city, and returned home with thousands of prisoners from the country population.

By 1593 Nandabayin had made five inroads into Siam; each further reduced his remaining man-power, but none succeeded in taking Ayuthia. He could never put into the field more than a third of the number his father Bayinnaung had led, and a third was too few to surround Ayuthia, so that instead of the besieged it was the besiegers who starved.[1] Of the men who set forth, usually only half returned; and in one

thence the flight was either due east to Raheng, or south-east by Three Pagodas Pass, or south to Tavoy and then east to Kanburi. See *JSS* 1913 Halliday "Immigration of the Mons into Siam."

[1] Probably he could never raise 25,000 men, see "Numerical Note" p. 334.

campaign only a tenth, for the Menam river flooded the country for sixty miles around, and the Siamese streamed out of Ayuthia in war-canoes, spearing the Burmese as they swam. In the 1593 campaign the king's son, the *yuvaraja*, was slain on his elephant in single combat with Pra Naret; the Burmese fled at the sight, and were once more cut to pieces in a long and terrible retreat.[1] After that there were no men left to invade Siam: it is Siam which invades Pegu.

The viceroyships of Chiengmai, Prome, Toungoo, and Ava, and the great fiefs like Nyaungyan in Meiktila district, were held by brothers, sons, and nearest kinsmen. In 1595 the king, besieged in Pegu by the Siamese, summoned them to his aid. After setting out, his son, the prince of Prome, heard that the prince of Toungoo had already taken his levy to Pegu; instead of joining him there, he went off to capture Toungoo town. They were all the same in greater or less degree; none of them rallied to the king. Not only was government despotic, but even the despots could not unite. If the king was not satisfactory, they could have combined to set up somebody who was; but instead of trying to keep the country together, each was out entirely for himself.[2]

The clergy urged that the king must be deposed and that there was no religious objection, provided only that his supplanter placed him on a golden throne to be adored by the people as a divinity. The prince of Toungoo, first cousin to the king, wrote to Arakan proposing a joint attack on the king and a division of the spoil; he chose Arakan because it was furthest and after getting its loot would return home and not be a rival for the throne. The Arakanese shipped a force which occupied Syriam, marched inland, effected a junction with the Toungoo levies, and with them besieged Pegu in 1599. The garrison deserted wholesale. The king's eldest son went

[1] *Stevens* III. 120, *JSS* 1909 Frankfurter "Events in Ayuddhya 686-966," *Jones* VI. 325, *BPP* 1919 XIX Saulière "Jesuits on Pegu" 73, *Hmarnan* III. 97.

[2] It is doubtful how far the concept of a kingdom had penetrated. In the chronicles, every adventurer who becomes independent (e.g. De Brito, p. 185, Gonna-ein, p. 211) is termed a king. At the Annexation of 1885 any pretender who succeeded in levying blackmail for a few miles round, as far as his eye could see, was styled a king . . . two cousins arranged to march against the English by separate routes; one of them cut up a police outpost; instead of joining forces to attack the next headquarters, he perceived that he had annihilated the English, attacked his cousin and overwhelmed him.

over on a promise of good treatment and was promptly executed. The king gave himself up.

Hearing that there was a carcass, the king of Ayuthia came swooping down to see what he could get. Toungoo left the Arakanese to hold Pegu and himself returned home. The Arakanese burnt Pegu and hid themselves in the woods. He of Ayuthia therefore marched on to Toungoo saying "I worship Nandabayin as a god and wish to have his divine presence ever near me. Give him up." He of Toungoo replied "I also worship him as a god and will not give him up." The Siamese then besieged Toungoo; to drain the moat, they cut a channel, called Yodayamyaung, into the Paunglaung river. Meanwhile the Arakanese at Pegu waylaid the Siamese supply columns so that after a month the king of Ayuthia abandoned the siege of Toungoo and returned home, losing prisoners to the Arakanese ambushes near Pegu. But he received the allegiance of the country south of Martaban.

The Arakanese deported 3,000 households of the wretched Pegu folk and returned with a white elephant and a daughter of the fallen king for their royal harem; they also took brazen cannon and the thirty bronze images of Ayuthia (pp. 168, 268); and retaining Syriam they left it in charge of one of their Portuguese mercenaries, Felipe de Brito y Nicote. Mahadammayaza, prince of Toungoo, took away the Ceylon Tooth and stone *thabeik* begging bowl (pp. 172-3), and more than twelve caravan loads of loot, each consisting of 700 elephants and horses.

The fallen king did not live long, being hurriedly murdered one night. Bayinnaung's palace, his radiant buildings decked with the spoil of conquered kings, had gone up in flame during the Arakanese occupation. It was a pitiful ending. The misery in Pegu beggared description: some of it was due to the recent invasions, but much of it was there already, caused by decades of insane fighting abroad and the ruin of agriculture at home. Jesuits were visiting Burma at the time; they write:—

> Yet now there are scarcely found in all that kingdom any men . . . for in late times they have been brought to such misery and want, that they did eat man's flesh and kept public shambles thereof, parents abstained not from their children, and children devoured

their parents. The stronger by force preyed on the weaker, and if any were but skin and bone, yet did they open their entrails to fill their own and sucked out their brains. (Year 1600, Nicholas Pimenta, *Hakluyt* X. 211.)

I also went thither with Philip Brito, and in fifteen days arrived at Syriam, the chief port in Pegu. It is a lamentable spectacle to see the banks of the rivers set with infinite fruit-bearing trees, now overwhelmed with ruins of gilded temples and noble edifices; the ways and fields full of skulls and bones of wretched Peguans, killed or famished or cast into the river, in such numbers that the multitude of carcases prohibits the way and passage of any ship; to omit the burning and massacres by this the cruellest of tyrants that ever breathed (i.e. the king of Arakan. Year 1600, Boves, *Hakluyt* X. 216).

The fall of Pegu is followed by sixteen years of petty states, Ava, Prome, Toungoo, Syriam, Chiengmai, and others even pettier. Some were held by Bayinnaung's sons, notably the lord of Nyaungyan, who held Ava, and dreamed of restoring the monarchy. He spent his life reducing Mogaung, Mohnyin, Bhamo, Mone, and Yawnghwe and actually succeeded in getting China to agree to extradite the fugitive Bhamo *sawbwa*,[1] an act which shows the final abandonment of the Chinese claim to overlordship in Upper Burma. The Chinese themselves admit that after 1628 Burma sent no more "tribute" missions.

The lord of Nyaungyan enclosed three acres near Ava with a wall, naming it Aungdinthazi; here every army on leaving the capital camped for the first day, trod the auspicious earth and made offerings to the *nat* spirits.[2] He held only the country round and above Ava and was actually on the march home from a campaign in Hsenwi when he died in 1605; his body, embalmed and propped up in its jewelled robes on the elephant, was taken home and buried beside his graceful Sandamuni pagoda at Ava.[3] During the funeral obsequies, when his body was half consumed in the fire, his son Anaukpetlun administered the oath of allegiance to all around.

[1] *JASBengal* 1837 Burney "Wars between China and Burma" 125.

[2] *Parlett* 43.

[3] *JBRS* 1915 Enriquez "Capitals of the Alaungpaya dynasty." He had a herald, Sithushwedaung, who wrote *yadu* verse.

ANAUKPETLUN 1605-28 having all Upper Burma and the northern Shans at his back, found little difficulty in conquering the depopulated south. In a few years he had defeated his brothers and kinsmen who divided the states of Burma between them.

When he took Prome in 1607, and the defenders laid down their arms, the vanquished lord sat in solitary state on his throne, awaiting the end. But a little page persisted in standing by him with a sword in each hand, defying all comers. Anaukpetlun took the lad into his service, and he had a great career, dying full of years and honours as the *wungyi* Nandayawta, one of the four ministers of the Hluttaw Council.

In 1610 the king took Toungoo, carrying home to Ava the Ceylon tooth, the stone *thabeik* begging bowl (p. 183), two-thirds of the cattle, and many people, including all who had been deported to Toungoo from Pegu, Prome, and Ava.

Syriam alone remained outside his rule. Felipe de Brito y Nicote, the Portuguese mercenary left behind with fifty of his compatriots by the Arakanese at Syriam in 1600, spent some time in repairing the defences. Arakan, finding him going his own way, sent a flotilla to deal with him. He lay in wait for them at Hainggyi island (Negrais) with four ships,[1] and when they put in there he fell upon them at night and destroyed them, capturing the crown prince of Arakan who headed the expedition. He treated him chivalrously, waiting on him in person, but he exacted a heavy ransom before letting him go.

De Brito had started life as a cabin boy, but nothing succeeds like success, and he now sought official recognition, going to Goa in person. The Viceroy gave him his own niece in marriage, Doña Luisa de Saldaña, born of a Javanese mother; and he sanctioned most of his proceedings; when he did not sanction them, De Brito simply disregarded orders. He returned from Goa with some men and six ships, which were needed, for in his absence the neighbouring princes, Prome and Toungoo, beset Syriam, and Arakan also returned to the attack. For some years after his return these attacks continued. Once his works were burnt to the bare walls, and

[1] *Dinnyawadi Yazawinthit* 210.

on another occasion one of his ships, surrounded by swarms of Arakanese craft, blew herself up sooner than surrender.

But finally he was recognised by all around. His son received as bride the daughter of the lord of Martaban, who though tributary to Ayuthia was practically independent; thus he was allied with the only other important port in Burma. He was now a highly respectable person, the official Portuguese commandant of Syriam, and he built a church; he let his chaplains, two Jesuits,[1] convert the heathen, but cannot have enforced the process as drastically as was usual in Portuguese stations, seeing that he seems to have been liked by the people of the country, for a reason which is easily discernible: he gave them settled government.

His men consisted of a few score Portuguese with a number of Eurasians, negroes, and Malabaris. Most of his energy went in preventing smuggling; that is to say, in order to get his customs tolls, he kept ships cruising to prevent foreign craft from putting in anywhere in Burma save at Syriam. Syriam was already the chief port for the interior and now she became the only one. It made his fortune, but it disgusted the interior which had to pay increased prices on all foreign goods owing to such unprecedented customs efficiency.

Moreover, he did wrong in undertaking a regular campaign of pillaging shrines; thus he removed precious stones from the images, melted down the gold, beat it into leaf, and sold it.[2] He would even melt down the bronze bells[3] of pagodas to save the expense of importing metal for founding cannon. Finally, in 1612 he and the lord of Martaban sacked Toungoo, and having sacked it he proceeded to ally himself with its lord, Natshinnaung, against the king. The king was furious, for Natshinnaung was his cousin and vassal.

> Scarce had he heard the news, when casting on the ground his gown and veil, he vowed to the idol Biay of Degu [? *paya* of Dagon], he would not enter within his gates till this quarrel was revenged. He marched with 120,000 men [p. 334], having put to sea 400 vessels of considerable strength, in which were above 6,000 Moors

[1] See note "The Catholic Mission" p. 345.

[2] *Hmannan* III. 118.

[3] When he removed Dammazedi's great bell (p. 119) from the Shwedagon, it sank in the stream. See *JBRS* 1915 Furnivall "History of Syriam" 53.

of noted valour. . . . All that was without the walls of Syriam he burnt, but met with vigorous opposition at that place, notwithstanding De Brito was quite unprovided, having suffered most of his men to go to India, and being scarce of powder. . . . In this distress he sent a soldier to buy powder at Bengal, and he ran away with the money; and having sent for some to the town of St. Thomas [Madras], they sent him none. . . . For want of powder there was no firing of cannon, they poured boiling pitch and oil upon the enemy. His number of men might suffice, having 100 Portuguese and 3,000 Pegues. De Brito sends out three ships against the fleet, in one of them all the men were slain, the two retired with all theirs wounded. The enemy began to undermine the works, and the besieged laboured much, but to small purpose. After the siege had lasted 34 days, De Brito sent to beg mercy, but was not heard. . . . The King of Arakan whom he had so grievously offended, sent 50 sail to his assistance, which were all taken by the besiegers. The King of Ava gives an assault, and they fought three days without intermission, the end of it was, that 700 of the besieged were slain, one Banna whom De Brito had always honoured having betrayed him, De Brito was taken, carried to the King, and by him ordered to be impaled, and set up in an eminence above the fort, that he might the better look to it, as the King said. He lived two days in that misery. His wife Doña Luisa de Saldaña was kept three days in the river to be cleansed,[1] because the King intended her for himself, but when she was brought into his presence, she turned on him with such scorn and courage that his desire for her beauty was turned to anger and he ordered her leg to be bored and sent her to Ava among the common slaves. . . . She was neither tall nor slender, but had that dash of beauty which is so dangerous in women, especially in the maid servants of Asia and Goa. . . . Francis Mandez and a nephew of his were treated as De Brito. Banna demanding a reward was soon torn to pieces, the King saying, he that betrayed the man who so much honoured him would never be true. Sebastian Rodriguez was cooped up with a yoke about his neck. At first the King designed not to spare any of the inhabitants of that place, but growing calm, he sent many slaves to Ava. Then passing by Martaban he obliged that King to kill his own daughter's husband, because he was De Brito's son, that none of the race might remain. This was the end of that man's avarice, who being naked a few years before, was raised to be worth three millions. . . . The enemy confessed they lost at that siege 30,000

[1] See pp. 9, 19, 173, 222 and cf. Esther ii 12. A queen bathed before her elevation, a king at his coronation, the king of Arakan using Ganges water (*Manrique*, xxxii). In Siam also a ceremonial bath precedes any solemn change in status. Like the priest's *Lavabo*, it is a purificatory rite, unlike the Greek bath, which was a fertility rite (*Fraser* "Magic Art" II. 162). Mediæval knights, and till the seventeenth century the Knights of the Bath, had to bathe at initiation.

> men. . . . Our Viceroy understanding the danger of Syriam, and thinking to relieve it in time, sent thither James de Mendoça Furtado with five galliots . . . he came to Martaban, where in the river he found a fleet of 20 sail, which after a sharp engagement fled, except 4 that were taken with some men, from whom he heard what had happened at Syriam, so that there was no need to go further. (Year 1613, *Stevens'* translation III. 191-4 emended from *Faria y Sousa* III. 238-9.)

The inner works at Syriam were brick, but the outer ones were a stockade, and the final. entry was effected by pulling down three of the posts with ropes and grappling irons after they had been shaken by a mine.[1]

During the siege the defenders used hand-grenades. Natshinnaung was among them; he and De Brito once headed a sortie in person and when they returned, successful but both wounded, blood was streaming over De Brito's legs and boots. The king, wishing to separate the two, sent a letter promising De Brito terms if he would give up Natshinnaung; the bearer of the letter was led blindfold to where they sat together. De Brito—probably he could not read Burmese—handed the letter to Natshinnaung, and after hearing its contents he said to the messenger "Tell your master that we Portuguese keep faith. I have given my word to Natshinnaung and I cannot break it." The king captured a Portuguese galley, cut off the crew's ears, and sent one of the earless men to De Brito saying "Look at this, and think again whether it will profit thee to harbour mine enemy." Natshinnaung said "I am of Burmese race, yet never have I seen man so pitiless. Let me no longer be of his people, make me one of thy people"; and he received baptism from the white priest, De Brito standing sponsor. In happier years he had written verse on the *beinnyin-hnget* (kingfisher); those days were gone, and now, when the town fell, he asked to die with De Brito, saying "He is my brother. I plighted my troth to him and sealed it with the *thwethauk* blood-bond"; he was taken at his word.[2]

De Brito, a sample of the heroic scoundrels who built up Portuguese dominion in the East, was unscrupulous, like the

[1] *Hmannan* III. 174.

[2] *Pawtugi Yazawin* 213-16, *JBRS* 1912 Furnivall "A Forgotten Chronicle." See note "Thwethauk and thissa-ye" p. 339.

princes against whom he was pitted. What the common people thought of him is shown by his nick-name Nga Zinga, meaning, in the patois of the seaports, "good man" (Panjabi *changa* = good). Beyond the fact that he had a good temper, we know little of his character; but a few years ago when people happened to examine a pagoda in Henzada district called Thida, they came across an inscription saying it was built by one Nandabhaya and his sister Supabhadevi, the children of an Arakanese lady, Sawthada of Launggyet, by the feringhi Nga Zinga, king of Syriam.[1]

Anaukpetlun spent a month at Syriam settling affairs. He sent the Portuguese captives into the interior (pp. 208, 349) together with the crews, mostly Mahomedan, of a few ships which were affiliated to De Brito and had returned to port thinking he was still there. Martaban and the country down to Ye in Moulmein district paid homage. He deported the leading families of Ye to live in the palace as hostages, and sent his brother to garrison the town. Its suzerain, the king of Ayuthia, at once drove him out but Anaukpetlun regained the town and tried to take Tenasserim, a wealthier port than Syriam. The Siamese were aided by 40 Portuguese who, desirous of avenging De Brito, put to sea with 70 slaves in four galliots and utterly defeated 500 Burmese craft with a loss of 2,000 men.[2] So in 1614 the king abandoned the siege of Tenasserim. But he retained Tavoy, and successfully interfered among his quarrelling kinsmen at Chiengmai, setting his nominee on its throne in 1615. In anger at the king of Arakan's demand for the cession of some islands on the border, he raided Sandoway, and then in 1616 he grew nervous.

> Fearing his enemies the kings of Siam and Arakan should come to an accommodation with the Portuguese, he sent ambassadors to settle a peace with us [the Portuguese], excusing the killing of De Brito, offering to restore the prisoners he had taken, and to assist us against the king of Arakan, of whose great treasure he desired nothing for

[1] *RSASB* 1915 33. The pagoda was built in the year of his death. As they were old enough to build in 1613, they must have been born about 1590, long before De Brito came to Syriam. Not improbably Sawthada was a handmaiden in the Arakanese palace.

[2] *Stevens* iII. 197.

> himself, but the white elephant. The viceroy accepted the ambassadors' proposals, and sent back with them Martin de Costa Falcam to ratify the agreement. He spent many days in soliciting an hour's audience; at length it was appointed at midnight, and he was led in the dark to a place where they ordered him to speak, for the king heard; he spoke and saw no king nor heard no answer. He signified the desire he had of seeing the king, and was ordered to wait his going abroad. He went out one day upon an elephant, and knowing Falcam waited in the street to see him, never so much as turned his eyes that way . . . so the ambassadors returned to Goa without concluding anything. (Year 1616, *Stevens* III. 255.)

The reason for his behaviour to the Portuguese envoy was that he had ceased to be nervous.

In 1619 he received in full Hluttaw court at Pegu envoys from Bengal, Achin, and the English East India Company in Madras.[1] They were greeted by noblemen in galleys with fifty oars a side, and were housed in accordance with their respective importance, the two Englishmen ranking lowest. The Englishmen came not to open trade but to recover the estate of one of their commercial travellers who, being in Chiengmai when the king captured it in 1615, was, together with his samples, taken away like all foreigners to Pegu, and though reasonably treated, had died. The English envoys spoke through a Portuguese slave of the king's; they found the governor of Syriam "in great state bedeckt, with jewels in his ears with gold rings, with rich stones on his fingers, being a white man and of very good understanding"; but they complained of having continually to give bribes, "for in this place there is nothing to be done or spoken, or any business performed without bribes," and they found it difficult to achieve any results, for although everyone from the king downwards made fair promises, none of these promises were kept.

The Burmese government had scheduled the deceased's estate and had collected some of his debts, but the king objected to returning them, saying that no English ships had ever come to his country, and until they did, and brought trade to his people, he would not give up the estate. Yet finally he gave it up, and sent the two envoys back with a letter written on palm leaf, asking for English ships to come and trade, and with the letter were a ruby ring, two mats, two betel boxes, and other presents.

[1] *Hmannan* III. 108, *Purchas* 1006.

The envoys had been kept waiting six months under strict surveillance, while their money ran out and they were in mortal terror of the king who would not let them go, "for what men soever come into his country, he holds them but as his slaves, neither can any man go out of his country without his leave, for he hath watch both by land and water, and he of himself is a tyrant, and cannot eat before he hath drawn blood from some of his people with death or otherwise."

From about 1627 onwards both the English and Dutch East India Companies had branches in Burma under junior representatives. These branches were closed from time to time, and although profits were occasionally considerable, steady trade was impossible because of the disturbed state of the country. The English were at Syriam, Ava and Bhamo, the Dutch at Syriam, Pegu and Ava. Little trade was done and in 1677 both companies withdrew (p. 203).[1]

Anaukpetlun restored the monarchy and regained control from Tavoy and Chiengmai in the south to Bhamo in the north, including Kenghung and other Shan states which are now in Yünnan. At his death he was thinking of renewing the old adventure against Ayuthia. His methods were as drastic as those of Nandabayin; they were the methods of every energetic Burmese king. His people in delighted terror said he had only to wave his sword and the tide would stop.[2] Yet he had a gentler side; in 1622 he set up at his palace a great bell (p. 145) with an inscription in Burmese and Talaing which says that it was placed under a double roof where the sound could reach his ears and all who had a grievance could strike it and claim his attention. Among his courtiers was Zeyyayandameik (son of Thondaunghmu, p. 125), who had served the lords of Toungoo, writing a song on Natshinnaung (p. 188), and now wrote an adulatory ode on his new master, Natshinnaung's slayer.

After 1613 the king had practically deserted Ava; and it looks as if he intended to retain Pegu as the permanent capital, for in the year of his death he had the remainder of his household brought from Ava to Pegu. Among them

[1] A brick ruin at Old Bhamo, up the Taping river, used to be pointed out as the English factory site. See note "Dutch withdrawal" p. 346.

[2] *Hmannan* III. 193.

were ten ladies of his harem. His son, prince Minredeippa, had a liaison with one of these, the Kengtung *sawbwa's* daughter, and when concealment was no longer possible, the eunuchs told the king. The guilty pair confessed. His Majesty pointed out to the young man that what he had done was high treason and merited roasting alive. Fearing that this would actually happen, the lad collected a party of followers with sticks and knives, entered the king's room at night, and did him to death.[1]

Minredeippa 1628. At once the ministers summoned a general assembly of the court. Early action was necessary, and they took it: they elected the parricide to the throne. Their reasoning was that the king's brothers, his natural successors, were away campaigning in the Shan states—at one time they had gone as far as Kenghung, north-east of Kengtung—and the kingdom would be in turmoil before they could be recalled. Public morality apart, the reasoning was invalid, for young Minredeippa had not the wit to hold a throne, whereas his two uncles were mature men, each in command of an army, and the news reached them easily in nine days. So far from avoiding disorder, the decision of the assembly caused it. The country respected the uncles, for they were men of authority; it knew nothing of Minredeippa, and half a dozen governors took the opportunity to revolt. Deprived of support from Lower Burma, the two uncles had to waste sixteen months reducing the north country. Meanwhile they seized the families of the Upper Burma companies in the palace Guard, making the fact known in Pegu, and thus shaking the allegiance of Minredeippa's guards. He had not the courage to leave his palace and attack them. Town after town fell to them, and when they surrounded Ava, Minredeippa, foreseeing their success, decided to flee to Arakan; but his own followers, in disgust at his cowardice

[1] The king was called Anaukpetlun because he *died on the west side* of the river at Pegu.

and tyranny, seized him and sent a deputation to Ava asking Thalun, one of the uncles, to take the throne. He did so, and immediately on arriving in Pegu executed Minredeippa, sternly rejecting his plea to be allowed to become a monk.

THALUN 1629-48 was crowned with great ceremony at Pegu, surrounded by Burmese, Shan, and Talaing lords. But while he was still in the coronation palace, the men in charge of building his monasteries plotted with Moulmein Talaings and rushed the armoury. A few hundred Kaunghan (p. 347) of the Guard drove them out; they fled to Moulmein, held it in force for some time, and were executed in large numbers. This led to a Talaing exodus into Siam; envoys[1] were sent asking the king of Siam to extradite them, but he refused.

In 1635 the king was again crowned at Ava and moved the palace there. Thereafter it remains the capital. The Delta had lost its advantages now that the idea of attacking Ayuthia was dead, and Pegu ceased to be a seaport when, about 1600, the silting up of the river was complete. The proper site to move to was Syriam, but the court did not realise that the country's future lay on the seacoast (p. 249). The move to Ava signifies the abandonment of Tabinshwehti's dream of a national kingship. The attempted coalescence with the Talaings had failed, and the court relapsed into its tribal homeland, Upper Burma.

The king appointed as *yuvaraja* (crown prince) the brother who had loyally supported him in the march from the Shan states to the throne; but the brother died in 1647. In the same year the king's son Shintalok, abetted by Tavoy men in the household, seduced some of the Guard and drove his father out of the palace. He fled to a neighbouring monastery, and several hundred monks defended him with sticks until his other sons brought up armed men. It was a month before he could retake the palace, as the traitors had the cannon there. He had to improvise cannon out of *ingyin* wood (*Pentacme*

[1] *JSS* 1910 Ravenswaay "Translation of Van Vliet's description of Siam" 33.

suavis). Shintalok tried to fight his way out but was shot dead on his elephant. The defence collapsed and the rebels met their end under the elephants' feet. Elephants who knew their work would toss and worry a man for some time before despatching him, and the kings kept them especially for the purpose.

Hearing of this plot, the raja of Manipur raided Thaungdut on the Chindwin river, and a levy had to be sent there. But the reign was generally peaceful, and the king set himself to stabilise conditions after the terrible wars of his predecessors, which left the country anæmic for a century. The Delta had suffered most, and it is possibly the depopulation of Pegu which made the court return to Upper Burma. The return restored Kyaukse to importance, and Thalun proceeded to reconstruct its canal administration. He went further, overhauling the revenue administration of the whole country, and compiling the Revenue Inquest of 1638, the first in Burmese history (p. 269). How far he originated is uncertain, but if he did no more than restore the rough organisation which had been shattered, he would still be entitled to rank as one of the best kings.[1]

How destructive was the disorder which overwhelmed Burma is shown by the history of the Shwesettaw shrine in Minbu district. It was one of the holiest imaginable, for it contains (*sic*) two of Buddha's footprints. Yet during the sixteenth century, so great was the depopulation caused by the Siamese wars, so little was the intercourse with Arakan over the An Pass, the approaches to which include Shwesettaw, that even this famous spot was entirely forgotten. The king wished it to be found, and in 1638 the famous Taungbila *sayadaw* with several other monks visited the place, succeeded in finding the footprints overgrown with scrub jungle, and restored the shrines.[2]

The Taungbila *sayadaw* received from the king the title Tipitakalankara for his learning; he wrote Wethandayapyo a poetical version of the Vessantara *jataka* story of the Buddha, several Pali works, and Amedawpon, a collection of answers he gave to the king on questions of church and state; leaving the

[1] See note "Thalun's inquest, etc." p. 347.
[2] *Duroiselle* "Notes on the Ancient Geography of Burma" I. 26.

fine monastery built him by the princes, he spent the closing years of his life in solitude on Taungbila Hill near Sagaing. One of his pupils, Mundigotha, also was an author. The king's daughter, Shwehsindu, wrote a number of *yadu* verses, and the king himself kept under his pillow a golden casket containing a *paikson yadu* poem written for him by a monk, Shin Karavika; he admired it so much that he learnt it by heart for it began "May the fourfold power of the king, the god of men, shaded by the white umbrella, increase day by day and . . . ." Another monk, Shin Kumara Kassapa, who dwelt in the Minkyaungdaik at Pahkangyi in Pakokku district, wrote Dhammarasipyo and Dhammayazapyo. Shin Thanhko wrote a poem on the royal elephant, and many songs, including one on prince Minredeippa (p. 192).

These are trivialities, but the work of the minister Kaingsa is of importance. His friend the Taungbila *sayadaw* suggested he should write a law-book. On proceeding to do so he was struck with the fact that the ancient lawgiver Manu is not mentioned in the Buddhist scriptures, which is natural seeing that he is a Hindu myth and has no connection with Buddha. As Manu's personality was unscriptural, Kaingsa discarded him, but as a law-book in his own name would carry no weight and it was necessary to have a halo of tradition, he induced the king to grant him the title of Manu. Then, in the name of Manu (p. 238) he proceeded to write the Manusarashwemin or Maharaja *dhammathat*, the first law-book written in Burmese. It is based on Bayinnaung's compilations (p. 171) and on the preceding Talaing *dhammathats*, but it substitutes Burmese ideas on, for instance, inheritance, for theirs, which were still largely Hindu.[1]

The king's principal foundation is the Yazamanisula (Kaunghmudaw) pagoda at Sagaing, sometimes called the "breast pagoda" owing to a silly ætiological tale; it is of Cingalese pattern. In it he enshrined a golden Buddha image of his own weight,[2] and Bayinnaung's Ceylon tooth and stone *thabeik* begging bowl (p. 185). It is surrounded by a palisade of stone posts. doubtless a descendant of those at the Bhilsa topes in Gwalior and of the forest of taller columns which

[1] *Forchammer* "Jardine Prize" 77.
[2] See note "Tula-dana" p. 328.

surround the dagobas at Anuradhapura in Ceylon; each post is six feet high and eight inches in diameter, with a little cup hollowed out of the side at the top so as to contain oil lights; in former days the pagoda seems to have been gilded,[1] and at night it must have been an imposing sight, with the little lights from 802 posts flickering on the huge golden dome. The slaves dedicated to it were Shan captives from Chiengmai, Anan and Hmaingpun.[2] When seeking an auspicious time for raising the spire, the king was told there was none, the omens showed he would die, and his son would raise the spire. He threatened to burn the soothsayer with all his family if he survived the appointed day, but he did not survive it, and the spire was raised by his son.

PINDALE 1648-61 is called Ngatatdayaka because he built the Ngatatkyi shrine in Sagaing district, containing a very large sitting Buddha image.

When the Ming dynasty 1368-1644 of China was overthrown, Yung-li, last of the Ming race, was pressed down by weight of numbers into Yünnan, fighting gallantly. Here he maintained himself for some years. In his extremity he levied requisitions on Hsenwi and some of the border towns such as Maingmaw[3] which, finding the burden excessive, suddenly exhibited great loyalty to Burma. The king therefore sent levies which took hostages and prevented the exactions from coming further south. Near Têngyüeh in 1658 Yung-li's armies made their last stand for the old cause and were defeated; he sought refuge at Bhamo, asked its *sawbwa* to intercede for him as he wished to take refuge in Ava, and he sent a hundred *viss* of gold (365 lb.) to the king. The king said Yung-li could be sent up if he were properly secured. The *sawbwa* knelt when communicating these orders to Yung-li, for he was an emperor,

[1] There were traces of gilding in 1855, *Yule* "Mission" 65.

[2] *Parlett* 3.

[3] Forty miles E.S.E. of Bhamo town. These frontier states often paid nominal tribute to both sides, cf. *Yule* "Mission" xiii.

and sent him and his family with their 700 disarmed followers by barge to Ava, their horses going overland.

Yung-li paid homage and was allowed to live with his followers at Sagaing, but they were virtually prisoners, and the remnant of the Ming armies, hearing of their plight, tried to rescue them. Infinitely worse was the plague of freebooter armies which had broken out in China during the change of dynasty. These swarmed through the provinces from Ssŭch'uan downwards, but one of their chiefs who had set up as king there was killed and they soon learnt by bitter experience that it did not pay to plunder the Manchus. They looked for easier prey, occupied Mone and Yawnghwe, defeated a Burmese army at Wetwin near Maymyo, and took Taungbalu and Tada-u close to Ava, inflicting severe loss on the Burmese, many of whom were drowned by the weight of their harness when fleeing across the Myitnge river. They plundered the villages, killing men, carrying off women and burning monasteries, while the monks fled in terror to the woods. At length they were driven away from Ava by the help of the feringhi gunners, with the loss of a chief who was killed by a jingal-shot from the walls, and they retired to Mone. Yung-li was pitifully apologetic and explained that all this was done without his authorisation. For the next three years the Chinese continued to build stockades under the walls of Ava, and ravaged Upper Burma from Yawnghwe, occupying Wundwin in Meiktila district. The population took refuge in the western uplands to avoid massacre. The Chinese raided Pagan, drove off every Burmese army and even captured some of the princes.

The king ruled over much the same area as Bayinnaung and had the same resources at his disposal. Bayinnaung would have found a speedy remedy; he would have marched a large force and exacted such reprisals that no Chinaman would have dared show his face across the frontier for a generation. But the king was spiritless and commanded no real following outside his homeland.

The lord of Martaban,[1] indeed, started out with 3,000 men to aid Ava, but the Talaings had no heart in the business and deserted on the march. The punishment for desertion was

[1] *Samuel Smith* 13-16.

burning alive in batches. Their indignant kinsmen rose, fired Martaban, drove the Burmese out, and went off into Siam, 6,000 souls in all, including families and prisoners. The frontier guards reported to the king of Siam who sent lords *smim* to greet them, men of their own race who had long since been settled in Siam. He granted gracious audience to their eleven leaders in the palace at Ayuthia, and allotted them lands.

Taking advantage of a lull in the inroads of the Chinese, the Burmese retaliated by invading Siam, hoping to get if not these Talaings at least substitutes for them. They received no help from their Chiengmai lieges, who, finding Ava powerless, had already made overtures asking Siam to aid them in case of attack from the Chinese freebooters in the Shan states. The Burmese advanced by the Ataran river and Three Pagodas Pass in Moulmein district towards Kanburi stockade. But they never reached it, being severely repulsed, and in their retreat they were ambushed in the passes. Such of them as were not left on the ground ended their days in slavery to the Siamese.

The Talaings had fled into Siam because they well knew they were too weak to stand against Burmese vengeance. Thus, though there is some excuse for the king's failure to get levies from the Delta, there is none for his failure to get its rice which could easily have been brought up stream. He needed that rice, for Kyaukse, the granary of Upper Burma, was in the hands of the Chinese. But he sat with folded hands while they roamed the land at will, the crops could not be sown, the city granaries ran low, and the Guards and palace staff were plunged into mourning by the massacre of their kinsmen in the villages. They could get no food to eat, and finally they found that the royal concubines had cornered what rice there was and were selling it at iniquitous prices. The king exercised no control, and when they appealed to him, he mournfully said he could not help them. They approached his brother Pye who at once marched on the palace. The king in his inner chamber, hearing the drums, sent his eunuchs[1] to see what was toward. They told him, and he ran to hide while the queen with her son aged eight and grandson

[1] Natural defectives. The Burmese do not mutilate.

aged four remained on the couch of state. Pye and his men entered the palace, cutting down some twenty men and women. Pye said "Brother, I wish thee no harm, but these things cannot be. Many a time have the ministers called me, and now I must do as they say." The queen entreated him, saying "Be king but spare our lives. We will end our days in religion. Let the children become monks." But Pye shook his head, saying "When have our family been monks? They will only throw off the robe. Yet will I do you no harm, remembering the oath I sware to our father." He kept them in a royal house, sending them food daily. But after a few weeks the court said "There cannot be two suns in the sky," and he drowned[1] the king, the queen, and their little son and grandson in the Chindwin river. The shrine they had set up north of the town to the Yazapita *nat* spirit was also destroyed, for it had plotted evil.

PYE 1661-72 was troubled in heart over these terrible events and after summoning the monks and listening to the law he said to them "I had no wish to be king, but the ministers and captains insisted that they had no refuge but me. Even as the Lord himself is bound by his clergy, so must I hearken to the voice of my people." The monks did not gainsay him, for he spoke the truth. They represented the public conscience, and every good king strove to win their approval.

He held an investiture, giving his uncle the right to ride in a palanquin and bestowing golden swords, fiefs, titles and privileges on many, including merchants; the most precious title, *Thettawshe*, conferred on one person only, meant "he to whom the king grants long life," for its holder, alone of all men, was exempt from being put to death out of hand. Travellers[2] have often described the dignity of the Burmese court when, through the great hall with its golden pillars, amidst audible silence, while every head, as far as eye could

[1] See note "Royal Drowning" p. 338.

[2] *Wayland* I. 254. The title *Thettawshe* was conferred e.g. in 1659, 1672, 1683 (*Hmannan* III. 269, 294, 306).

see, was bowed to the ground, the king would stride along in solitary grandeur, his vestures stiff with gold and jewels, holding in his hand a gold-sheathed sword. Scenes such as this lingered in the imagination of the people, who felt that far away from their poor little huts, above the dulness of their lives, rose the Golden Palace, enshrining their king amid magnificence such as they had never dreamed of save in a fairy tale. Men live largely by sentiment, and that sentiment was satisfied to the full in the mystery and splendour of the kingship.

King Pye stopped profiteering among the harem women, so that his Guards did not have to go without food for three days at a time as under his predecessor; but otherwise his success was not perceptibly greater. The Siamese, with Martaban, Tavoy and Chiengmai levies in their army, raided Syriam and Pegu, carrying off the population in crowds.[1] The Chinese ravages continued with undiminished intensity. The court suspected Yung-li of complicity and the king decided to summon all his 700 followers to the Tupayon pagoda at Sagaing (p. 100), administer the oath of allegiance, and scatter them in small parties in different villages. They would not go unless the *sawbwa* of Möng Si in north Hsenwi, whom they trusted, was allowed to accompany them. At the pagoda they were surrounded by royal troops and the *sawbwa* was being taken away from them when, suspecting treachery, he seized a sword from one of the Guards and laid about him. The Chinese did likewise. Thereupon musketeers of the Guard mowed them down and the survivors were executed to a man by the king's order. The king sent Yung-li a reassuring message with meat and drink but reproached him for his retinue's conduct, and Yung-li said "They did wrong and were punished. I owe thee my life and ask only to be left in peace."

In time the Chinese freebooters wore themselves out and the iron hand of the Manchu dynasty fell on the remnants. In 1662 the Yünnan viceroy came with 20,000 men and, halting at Aungbinle in Mandalay district, sent a herald summoning the king to surrender Yung-li or take the consequences. This was the pass to which things had come through lack of judgment in admitting Yung-li and lack of manhood in repel-

[1] *Samuel Smith* 22-30.

ling the Chinese. The king called a council; he pointed out that in 1446 the Burmese had surrendered Thonganbwa (p. 99), in 1601 the Chinese had surrendered the Bhamo *sawbwa* (p. 184), and it was therefore in accordance with precedent to surrender Yung-li. The ministers agreed and, disregarding the solemn fact that Yung-li had been admitted to allegiance, they delivered him up to meet his doom.[1]

The king was succeeded by his son NARAWARA 1672-3 who died young. Before the breath was out of his body his sister, some eunuchs and some ministers prevented all communication between the inner and outer palace and proceeded to choose a successor. They went through the list of the dead king's brothers, objecting to one that he drank, to another that he was overbearing, and thus by a process of elimination there remained only a blameless cousin called MINREKYAWDIN 1673-98. Having made him sit on the throne, they announced the king's death and administered the water of allegiance. Two of the princes objected and were immediately led away by the executioners. After that, everyone loyally drank the water. Perhaps the new king was really the best choice; perhaps he was a puppet for those who chose him: they figured in his first honours list.

A fortnight later a kinsman rushed the palace with some companies of the Guard who had not been won over by the clique, but they were all cut down. The Byedaik Privy Council Chamber was red with their blood, and the entrances to the palace roof were choked with their corpses, as some of them tried to take refuge on the roof. The survivors were dealt with according to precedent. Men remembered the horror of those days, and the executions that followed; they told how the palace halls were haunted by the ghosts of the slain.

The reign produced one historical work, the Jatapon, which gives the horoscopes of the kings of Burma and is of great importance because its dates are more reliable than those

[1] See note "Yung-li (Kuei)," p. 352.

of other histories. Every three years or so the garrisons would be relieved in foreign stations, such as Martaban and Chiengmai. Occasionally a petty Shan revolt would be crushed, or a *sawbwa* would abscond to Yünnan which would give him up; the court had a way of appointing its favourite of the native family who had lived at court over the head of the natural heir, and this would cause trouble. A foray would occasionally be made into Ayuthia. In 1695 a minister from Ayuthia deserted with five elephants and a hundred men and took service under the king. Or some of the foreign deportees would revolt, as the Siamese did at Salin in Minbu district in 1680. Sometimes a member of the royal family would have to be drowned. But these are the normal events of any reign.

European trade centred in Siam and Malaya at places such as Mergui (p. 189) which, save under Bayinnaung 1551-81, was in Siamese hands till 1765. The Portuguese ceased to count after 1641 when they were expelled from Malacca by the Dutch, but there is still a colony of their descendants, with high-sounding names they cannot pronounce, round the Catholic church at Mergui. The merchants of Golconda carried the India trade thither; the king of Siam and his minister, Phaulkon, a Greek, wishing to oust them and get the carrying trade for their own ships, employed interlopers, i.e. Englishmen independent of the East India Company. Thus Burneby figures as Governor of Mergui among the seven commissioners appointed by the king of Siam in 1686 to administer the port and province, and Samuel White, another of the commissioners, was Port Officer 1683-7. But the East India Company depended for its security on the king of Golconda and persuaded their principal shareholder, James II., to claim Mergui in 1687. It could have been seized without great ill will on the part of the townsfolk had not some of the English held a banquet aboard a ship in the harbour, getting dead drunk, and firing broadsides at every toast, broadsides which, if you please, were loaded with ball. The townsfolk took reprisals, killing some sixty other English who were ashore.

James II. was also actuated by a desire to forestall Louis XIV. Four companies of French infantry built a fort and garrisoned Mergui during 1688 by arrangement with the king of Siam who played off the European nations against each other. The name French Bay, on the eastern side of King Island, the largest island in the Mergui group, commemorates the fact that it was for a few years about this time the rendezvous of French warships. With the death of the Siamese king and the murder of Phaulkon in 1688, the Siamese ceased to favour the French, and in any case the French before long had no energy to spare for the Farther East.

After 1687 the English continued to trade in Mergui to a certain extent. The Dutch remained predominant; they had the tin monopoly but based their trade on Malacca, and Mergui declined. Sea piracy was everywhere rampant, some of the worst rogues being European renegades, especially Dutchmen. After 1765 Mergui declined still further by passing into the hands of the Burmese whose control spoilt the overland route to Ayuthia.[1]

The French Compagnie des Indes had a branch at Syriam in 1688; its existence, though interrupted at times, lasted nearly a century.[2] The Burmese tried to make the English re-establish the branches which had been closed (p. 191); the go-between was a half-caste Portuguese, and as the English would never trouble to send a proper representative the proposal fell through, although in 1688 the governor of Syriam himself wrote asking them to settle there. A few years later the king received in his gardens at Ava the following, brought by Fleetwood and Sealey who prostrated themselves nine times in the *shikko* position as they approached him:—

> "Letter from the Nathaniel Higginson Esqr etc Governour of Fort St George to the King of Ava.
>
> To his Imperiall Majesty, who blesseth the noble City of Ava, with his Presence, Emperour of Emperours, & excelling the Kings of the East & of the West, in glory & honour. . . .
>
> The fame of so glorious an Emperour, the Lord of Power & Riches, being spread through the whole Earth, all Nations resort to view the splendor of your greatness, &, with your Majesty's Subjects, to partake of the blessings, which God Almighty has bestowed upon your Kingdoms, above all others; your Majesty has

[1] *JBRS* 1917 Furnivall "From China to Peru" and his "Samuel White, Port Officer of Mergui"; *Anderson* "English Intercourse with Siam."

[2] See note "French and Shipbuilding" p. 353.

been pleased to grant especiall favours to the Honorable English Company, whose servant I am; & now send to present before the footstool of your Throne, a few Toys, as an acknowledgment of your Majesty's goodness; which I beg your Majesty to accept, & to vouchsafe an Audience to my Servants, & a gracious Answer to my Petition.

I humbly pray your Majesty's fountain of goodness to continue your wonted favours to the Right Honourable English Company . . . & pray your Majesty to give me leave to send a Factor, next Monsoon, to reside at Syriam. . . .

About 3 Years ago I ordered Bartholomew Rodrigues, Master of a small Sloop, called St Anthony and St Nicholas to go from Acheen to Bengall, laden with divers Commodity's; . . . the said Sloop was fortunately arrived within your Majesty's Kingdoms, & calling there for Wood & Water, your Officers not knowing who she belonged to, had taken care, by your Majesty's Order, for the safe keeping of the Sloop & Cargoe . . . I have now sent this by my Factors, Edward Fleetwood and James Lesly, & humbly pray your Majesty to cause Bartholemew Rodrigues & his People, & that Sloop & Cargo, to be delivered to my said Factors. . . .

Severall Englishmen, who, in former Years, have been in your Majesty's Kingdoms, & have obtained liberty of returning, doe declare the greatness of your Majesty's glory. If there be any now remaining under the misfortune of Captivity, I humbly beg your Majesty wili please to grant their liberty, that they may spread the fame of your Majesty's splendid Greatness, from the rising Sun to the setting Sun.

Adrian Tilbury, a Merchant of this place, was my Servant for many Years, He made a Voyage from hence to Martaban & there dyed; his Widow hath acquainted me, that your Majesty's Governours have according to the usuall Justice of your Majesty's laws, secured his Estate, being a Stranger. I humbly beg your Majesty will be pleased to order the same to be delivered to my Factors, for the use of his Widow & Orphan. . . .

And if your Majesty will grant me leave to build a small Ship, or two, I will send my People the next Year for that purpose.

Your Majesty's most humble
and Devoted Servant
Nat. Higginson.

Dated in Fort St George
the 10th Sept. 1695."

This English version of the letter was the office copy. The issue copy which went to Ava was in Portuguese, because the slaves whom the king kept at Ava as interpreters were half-caste Portuguese.

As Tilbury was an alien dying intestate his estate had

escheated to the crown; the Company did not object, for it was their own custom, and the property would be restored on cause being shown (p. 190). But the rest of the letter, stripped of diplomatic phraseology, constitutes an indictment. Governor Higginson offered to re-open the branch at Syriam, not because he wanted it but because the king of Burma wanted it. The king wanted foreigners to trade in his ports, and since the English would not come he waited till a ship, *St. Anthony and St. Nicholas*, affiliated to them, strayed into his ports, and then seized her in order to attract their attention.

Indeed seafaring men tended to give Burma a wide berth. There were better markets at Malacca, Achin, and Tenasserim, and at these places foreigners received good treatment.. They had reason to doubt the treatment they would get in Burma. No skipper likes paying his crew all the wages due when giving them liberty to go ashore in a foreign port; he likes to retain a balance lest they should desert, and in some navies he is bound by regulation to do so. But the governors of Burmese ports had a way of insisting that crews should be paid in full before landing, and then encouraging them to desert. If a sailor married a woman of the country, the governor would claim him as a Burmese subject, alleging that the husband takes the wife's nationality. A shipmaster could not get his men back, or if he did he had to pay the Burmese officials for each man they returned. It was the king's regular policy to retain every foreigner he could (p. 349). If a ship was driven on to the coast by weather the Burmese government regarded her as a windfall, confiscated her, and enslaved the crew. They argued that under their law anyone who saved another from drowning had the right to possess him as a slave, in the same way a weather-beaten ship owed her life to the port which gave her shelter, therefore the prince of that port had a right to seize her. Nay, if a ship merely touched at a Burmese port for water without being expressly consigned there, she was seized and the crew enslaved on the same reasoning.[1] But here as in so much else the harshness

[1] Year 1755, *Dalrymple* I. 191; year 1781, *Sonnerat* (1806) III. 49; year 1782, *TP* 1890 Cordier "Les Français en Birmanie" 199, 205; year 1808, *Sangermano* 61, The custom continued until the Treaty of Yandabo in 1826, *Crawfurd* II. app. 13.

of the rulers was mitigated by the humanity of the monks: if the distressed mariner wandered into a monastery he was safe, for the monks would bind up his wounds, feed him, clothe him, and send him as if in sanctuary with letters of commendation from monastery to monastery till he could reach Syriam, there to await the chance of some passing ship.[1]

The orders passed by the Burmese court on Governor Higginson's letter were that the restoration of a ship and crew, though contrary to all law and precedent—"it is such as has never yet been granted"—would be conceded as a special case on the understanding that the Company reopened its branch at Syriam; the Company was granted its former site, with dock space, and a rebate of one-third off the customs duties, which were usually 10 per cent. *ad valorem*, exclusive of heavy perquisites. Two years later neither the ship nor the crew had been restored, and Governor Higginson had to send a second mission under Bowyer in 1697 with exactly the same objects.[2] He wanted to export teak, rice, and saltpetre. In practice he was allowed to export teak, but in theory it was prohibited, rice was allowed only in sufficient quantities to feed a crew, and the very idea of allowing the export of saltpetre was so unthinkable that the ministers could not even mention it to His Majesty.

The English factory was established at Syriam in 1709 and lasted till 1743 (p. 213). They imported fire-arms for government, piece-goods, hats and other European wares, areca, and coconuts from the Nicobars; they exported ivory, lac, pepper, cardamum, beeswax, fur, cutch, any amount of raw cotton and silk, together with such jewels, silver, lead, copper, iron, tin and earth-oil as could be got in spite of the prohibition. Moreover, they were allowed to use as much teak as they liked for building ships at Syriam and they built many, the favourite type being brigantines of 40-50 tons.

[1] Year 1727, *Hamilton* II. 62.

[2] Documents relating to the Fleetwood-Sealey and Bowyer missions are at *Dalrymple* II. 337-405. An Armenian at Ava warned Fleetwood not to make presents to the reigning beauty in the palace, as a prince who had recently done so was punished.

SANE 1698-1714, son of his predecessor, built the Manaung pagoda in Sagaing district. In 1707 he sent levies to raid Sandoway. In 1703 deserters from Ayuthia and in 1709 from Viengchang took service at Ava owing to some quarrel with the king of Siam.

The authors of the reign are Yazathuriya, minister of land revenue, and two monks, Shin Zinarama and Shin Aggathamala; the last dwelt at Shwekyetyet and his supporter, the Twinthin minister, would never bring him to the king's notice lest worldly success should spoil him. They wrote verse and commentaries.

TANINGANWE 1714-33, son of his predecessor, built the Lawkamanaung pagoda at Ava. At his accession his uncle, lord of Pagan, rebelled and fled to the hills east of Pegu. In 1721 the first Christian missionaries landed; the king gave them presents for the Pope.[1] In 1724 Mg Kala compiled the Yazawingyi chronicle; it is an important work, based on earlier sources, and similarly large portions of its own text are incorporated *verbatim* in the narrative of the *Hmannan Yazawin*. In 1725 Chiengmai revolted against grinding Burmese taxation and successfully resisted recapture, although the king ordered molten silver to be poured down the throats of officers who had taken bribes from the rebels and failed in their duty.

MAHADAMMAYAZA-DIPATI 1733-52, the son of his predecessor, had a minister, Padethayaza, who had written verse in the two preceding reigns and now proceeded to do so on one of the royal princesses and on the Siamese embassy (p. 214); he accompanied the king to Pegu in 1752 and died at Syriam. In 1736 the Shinhla image (p. 48) at Sagaing

[1] See note "The Catholic Mission" p. 345.

was stolen; His Majesty therefore executed the primate and a Brahman.[1]

Manipur though tributary to Burma under Bayinnaung 1551-81 had gone her own way since his time. In 1647 and 1692 the raja had raided Thaungdut on the Chindwin river, but these were only the ordinary border forays such as Arakan and Siam were always making, and, on the other hand, in 1704 he presented a daughter. But under Gharib Newaz 1714-54 Manipur became a thorn in the side of Upper Burma. The country was famous for its ponies, and in those days every man, however humble his rank, possessed two or three.[2] Polo, played forty a side, was universal and made them all expert horsemen. They now came raiding Upper Burma. They started in 1724 by saying they would present another girl to provide company for the one presented in 1704. But when three hundred lords, ladies and attendants from the Ava court came to escort her at the mouth of the Yu river in the Upper Chindwin district, they were met not by a tame princess but by wild horsemen who carried them all away captive into Manipur. The Burmese sent an expedition in revenge, but it was ambushed in the swamps near Heirok, south-west of Thobal, and losing heavily retreated in haste. In 1735 the Manipuris came to Myedu in Shwebo district and carried off loot, cattle, and a thousand people, mainly descendants of De Brito's Indians (p. 348). In 1737 they killed two-thirds of a royal levy sent to oppose them, including the commander, who was drunk,[3] and swept down to Tabayin in Shwebo district, burning everything they met. In 1738 when the king garrisoned these two places and Mingin in the Upper Chindwin district against them, they simply cantered past, camped at Thalunbyu west of Sagaing, burnt every house and monastery up to the walls of Ava, and stormed the stockade built to protect the Kaunghmudaw pagoda (p. 195). slaughtering the garrison like cattle in a pen and killing the commandant, a minister of the Hluttaw Council; the old door-leaves of the pagoda's eastern gateway show a gash made by the sword of Gharib Newaz when he was forcing an entrance.

[1] *Hmannan* III. 376. See note "Capital Punishment" p. 353.
[2] *Pemberton* 31.
[3] *Hmannan* III. 377. See note "Drink" p. 314.

One reason why the Manipuris raided Burma was that they had just been converted to Hinduism by preachers who said that if they bathed in the Irrawaddy river at Sagaing all blessedness would attend them. Indeed, their chief Brahman insisted on coming to Ava himself in 1744 in order to convert the Golden Palace, but he fell ill and died after staying a month, and his suite of lesser Brahmans then returned home.

The Manipuris raided again in 1740 but in 1741 they sent an envoy with a jacket for the raja's kinswoman who had been presented to the Ava harem in 1704; he also brought complimentary presents for the king, whose orders were that his presents should be sent in at once and then he should be kept waiting a month before being granted an audience or seeing the princess.[1]

In 1749 Gharib Newaz came on his last raid, thinking "If there is an opportunity to fight, I will fight; and if there is not I will present a daughter." On reaching Ava he found the Burmese forces so numerous that they stretched from Shwekyetyet to Londawpauk; moreover, during the night his standard was blown down, a terrible portent; always celebrated for his royal wisdom, he now perceived that this was not an occasion to fight, and instead he presented his twelve-year-old daughter who accompanied him.

The Manipuris were occasionally troubled by Burmese levies, but usually did as they liked. Living in an obscure valley, knowing nothing of the outer world, they thought themselves heroes, able to take their pleasure of Burma when they willed. They did not realise that Burma was several times the size of their country, that they were laying up for themselves a frightful vengeance, and the only reason vengeance never seemed to come was that Burma happened to be under an incapable king.

Mahadammayaza-dipati, king of Burma, angered at his commanders' failure to repel the Manipuris, used to expose them in the sun with a sword on their necks, saying "If a failure like this comes to my golden ears again I will chastise you with my sword." Neither he nor his predecessors since 1648 ever took the field in person. In short, the kingdom was doomed. There is no parallel between Indo-China and developed states where the king's personality matters little, because there is a

[1] *Hmannan* III. 385.

large middle and upper class to galvanise the nation into life. Majestic and complex though the machinery of administration seemed to a simple people, it was ineffective. Character and intelligence were rare, because the instinct of self-preservation drives a despotism to cut off the heads of the tallest lilies in the Tarquin way.

Where society is sound, families possess vitality for centuries, witness such houses as the Cecils and the Lowthers who are now leading their people for the fourth century. But in Burma no reigning family lasted three centuries or retained its vigour for more than three generations. One reason is the large-scale harem system which convention fastened on the monarch. Great kings did not transmit their character but shattered the mould, producing quantity at the expense of quality. The Burmese commoner chose as wife an equal, to be his helpmate; they shared their daily life, its common toil and interest; their children grew up under the care of an equal man, an equal woman, gaining the benefit of a father's as well as a mother's example. But the Burmese king did not choose his wife: he married his half-sisters, and his innumerable lesser wives were not chosen on consideration, to be the noble mothers of children, but were taken on caprice, as distractions. The little prince grew up amid jealousy and intrigue, his mother was often an inferior, and he developed not in the free atmosphere of an equal man and woman, acquiring character from each, but in purely feminine surroundings which his august father seldom entered.

The state to which things had been allowed to drift is indicated by the fact that although fire-arms had been known in Burma since the sixteenth century, the king now had so few that the Manipuris thought he had none.[1] The monarchy was like over-ripe fruit, ready to fall at the first touch, and, as invariably happened at such times, there was a crop of *minlaung* pretenders. Rumours of them were even more plentiful, and dacoity was rampant everywhere. In 1742 a thousand people fled to Arakan, complaining that there was drunkenness in the palace and famine in the villages; and others followed them over the passes in the next decade.[2]

[1] *Pemberton* 39. [2] *Dinnyawadi Yazawinthit* 230-4.

A colony of Gwe Shans[1] at Okpo near Madaya, Mandalay district, disliked the king because he taxed their *kunthibin* areca palms at four annas a tree;[2] the present rate is less than one pie, and four annas in those days was something like four rupees to-day. They set up one of their number, Gonna-ein, as pretender, and Talaing deportees at Madaya joined them. They built a stockade, swept the Burmese out of the locality, went raiding into Shwebo district, and would even venture to attack the retreating Manipuris. On one occasion a number of them were captured by the Burmese, who treated them well, hoping to dissuade them from sending to Pegu for help; they were released, and went away saying they would win over their comrades to pay homage; they returned in strength, found the Burmese holding high festival, and cut them to pieces.

The king had continued to hold the Delta since the sixteenth century. But although he could sometimes rely on raising a levy there, his troops were usually raised in Upper Burma, and it looks as if he had comparatively little to do with Lower Burma, for places there are scarcely mentioned in the recurrent bestowal of fiefs, and the honour lists include few Talaings. The kings kept control of the Irrawaddy highway, of Pegu town, and of Syriam which produced valuable customs revenue, but inland, away from the river banks, Lower Burma was probably left to its own devices. It gave little trouble because the Talaings took generations to recover from the depopulation of the sixteenth century wars. When they did recover, and repeopled the wilderness, trouble began.

It started at Pegu, which the Talaings regarded as divinely appointed to be a royal seat. Burmese taxation there was iniquitous; the very looms were taxed, and women were taxed for suckling their children.[3] Yet the Burmese governor imagined he could become independent among the people he oppressed. Hearing that Ava was beset by the Manipuris, he proclaimed himself king of Pegu in 1740, executed all who refused to drink the water of allegiance, and marched on Syriam. On the march his officers murmured against him, so he arrested

[1] See note "Gwe" p. 354.

[2] Oral tradition. It was an impossible assessment, but the administration was reckless in its arithmetic and also liked to pitch assessments high in order to allow a wide margin for squeezing. See pp. 335, 360.

[3] *Sayadaw Athwa* III. 139.

14

their families, the usual proceeding for preventing desertion, as men hesitate to desert when they know their families will be burned or buried alive. But on this occasion instead of stopping desertion it led to the officers killing him. The king's uncle came from Ava, exterminated the dead man's family and followers according to precedent, and set up a new governor. But as the new governor executed the wrong people wholesale for alleged complicity in the late rebellion, the people killed him, and there was a general Talaing rising. They massacred the Burmese of every age, sex and condition in such places as Martaban and Syriam.

Meanwhile some Gwe Karens[1] outside Pegu town, hearing that a *minlaung* pretender was about to appear, proceeded to identify him in the person of one of their own monks, who, being a son of the former rebel lord of Pagan (p. 207) was of the Ava house, but had been brought up among the Gwe Karens. The Talaing leaders agreed, and he was raised to the throne of Pegu as **Smim Htaw Buddhaketi 1740-7.** The chief of Chiengmai presented him with a daughter, and heaven itself seemed to sanction his elevation, as he had an elephant which, if not white, was at least spotted. His strongest supporter was Binnya Dala who, as Master of the Elephant Stables at Pegu, had helped him to the throne and presented him with a daughter. They soon held Prome and Toungoo towns and all the country to the south, but received little help from Martaban and Tavoy. In 1742 they started raiding annually up the Irrawaddy river as far as Ava. They had the advantage of possessing some fire-arms with a few renegade Dutch and half-caste Portuguese adventurers.[2]

The Burmese usually offered resistance but seldom ventured to carry the war into the Delta because they were liable to be recalled against the Manipuris; they did indeed reoccupy Syriam in 1743, but the Talaings found them all drunk and drove them out with heavy loss.[3] In 1745, when occupying Hsinbyugyun, Minbu district, the Talaings found themselves starving because their supplies failed to come up the river and their ravages had laid waste the surrounding country. Fearing to be harried during their retreat, they wrote to the Burmese,

[1] See note "Gwe" p. 354. [2] *Symes* 5.
[3] *Hmannan* III. 386. See "Drink" p. 314.

who lay at Pagan-Nyaungu, "Your king is related to ours. This warfare is unnatural and bringeth the world to ruin. Let our king and yours speak together as becometh kinsmen, and the land will have peace." The prince commanding the Burmese returned answer "You speak of your pretender at Pegu as kinsman of our king; but a monkey on a tree, though he dress in man's clothes, is not a man." The Talaings then made good their retreat to Pegu.[1]

When sacking Syriam in 1740, the Talaings had respected the property of the East India Company's branch (p. 206), and Smim Htaw Buddhaketi even wrote to the manager pointing out the cruel provocation which had compelled his people to revolt against the Burmese; he gave the English every privilege, but now in 1743, when he again expelled the Burmese, he suspected the English of sympathising with them and burnt the factory to the ground.[2] After that, the mainland was not good enough, and feeling insecure, the Company withdrew to Negrais island at the mouth of the Bassein river. They did indeed keep shipwrights and a branch at Syriam, but their headquarters were in a fortified post constructed in 1753 at Negrais, with moat, glacis and cannon, for in the condition of the country men could not sleep quietly at nights save behind fortified walls. The Burmese could not understand that a seafaring race prefers a base in the sea, and the court saw in the choice of ground clear proof that the English were hatching some plot in a remote fastness (p. 240).

On returning from Europe in 1743 Gallizia, the Catholic bishop, found it impossible to reach Ava in the prevailing anarchy, and instead took his clergy to Pegu where the Talaing king received them well. In 1744 the Ostend Company was expelled from Bankibazar. As the English had just left Syriam, there was a vacancy there, and if the king of Pegu refused facilities it was always possible to bring in the Burmese and claim a settlement in reward for re-instating them. So the Ostend Company fled in six ships to Syriam where the governor in justifiable alarm sent bishop Gallizia aboard to ascertain their intentions. The bishop prevailed upon the commander, Chevalier de Sconenville, with several of his officers, to accompany him to Pegu. There the commander

[1] *Hmannan* III. 386-8. [2] *Dalrymple* I. 101-6.

could get no orders on his application, the court saying that the king was in the country and nothing could be done till his return. Meanwhile the bishop found that the Talaings were arranging to massacre the party; he warned them and they all tried to escape in boats to Syriam. But the banks swarmed with Talaings who killed them, including the bishop and two of his priests. Only four men escaped to reach the ships, which made off.[1]

In the Talaing rising of 1740, the Burmese governors at Martaban and Tavoy tried to raise their districts and march on Pegu; but instead their districts rose against them and slew every Burman within reach. Unable to return to Ava, the two governors, with a combined retinue of 300 souls, fled to Ayuthia where the king of Siam entertained them hospitably. Hearing this, the king of Ava sent grateful acknowledgments in 1744 by envoys bearing presents—gilded lacquer goblets, bowls and dishes, raiment with rich borders, earth-oil, imported piece-goods, a canoe, and robes for a queen. At Ayuthia the envoys would not prostrate themselves before the *thenapati* (commander-in-chief) or the senior ministers, saying that as bearers of royal letters they could not do so until they had first prostrated themselves before the king; and the king of Ayuthia upheld them on the point. In return he sent envoys to Ava with gilded lacquer goblets, dishes and betel-boxes, velvets and silks of dragon pattern, a royal barge, and a letter on gold leaf; the letter was enclosed in caskets of ivory and crystal studded with rubies, wrapped in velvet and tied with gold cord, and it was borne on the back of an elephant. The Siamese envoys came in the cold weather 1745-6 and owing to war conditions they kept to devious routes through the teak forests all the way; on reaching Upper Burma they found the Talaings again in possession at least as far as Hsinbyugyun in Minbu district and fearing for themselves, they spread rumours that they were the advance guard of a Siamese army coming to help Ava. The Talaings therefore retreated to the Delta and the envoys entered Ava. After being kept waiting a necessary time, they were granted audience.[2]

[1] *Bigandet* 15.

[2] *Hmannan* III. 389, *Samuel Smith* 96-8. The majesty of a Burmese king was demeaned by promptitude. The rule at court was to avoid noticing foreign envoys until they had been kept waiting long enough to feel insignificant, see p. 290.

Smim Htaw Buddhaketi was a gentle soul and the people loved him. In spite of his precarious position he spent most of his time hunting elephants in the forest; after all it was necessary to procure a proper white elephant in order to prove himself a proper king. He was such a long time away that his ministers ventured to suggest he should return and see to state affairs. Instead of complying, he had his harem sent to his elephant camp at Sittaung in Thaton district. Moreover, he was an astrologer, and now perceived that his horoscope was bad. Therefore, lest his people should be dragged down with him, he avoided the throne. His lords were compelled to return as the Pegu court threatened to deal with their families according to precedent, but he himself with ten elephants and 300 followers went to Chiengmai. Finding no refuge there, he went to Ayuthia where the king confined him and sent him to China on a junk. But the junk landed him on the west coast, and he went to Yünnan. As Yünnan did not want him, he wandered through the Shan states, nowhere finding a welcome till finally he came to Chiengmai again and was allowed to stay.

Meanwhile the court at Pegu set up as king first a monk, Neko, and then, after a few days, **Binnya Dala 1747-57.** He was crowned with great solemnity, and addressing the assembled court said that Buddha had prophesied greatness for Pegu, Bayinnaung had made her mighty, and now he would restore her greatness. He appointed his younger brother *yuvaraja* (crown prince) and made Talaban *thenapati* (commander-in-chief).[1]

In Upper Burma, the constant raids by the Gwes and Talaings of Madaya-Okpo and by the Pegu levies resulted in the ruin of agriculture. Feeling unsafe, men deserted their fields, and Talaings or dacoits burned whatever little crop was left.

These years are an object lesson in incompetence. The troops did little but run away. Before long the same men were to carry all before them because they had found leaders; those leaders were there now, waiting to be used, but an effete despotism had not the means of selecting them.

In 1750 the king sent an elephant, a golden model of a pagoda, and other homage presents to Yünnan asking for help;

[1] *Sayadaw Athwa* III. 141.

the Yünnan viceroy sent an officer with an armed escort to report on the situation at Ava but he sent no help. Sometimes the Talaings would reach Shwekyetyet north of Ava. Finally at the end of 1751 they occupied Kyaukse, the one place which could have replenished the city's empty granaries.

The king sat in his palace and left everything to his uncle, Toungooyaza, appointing him joint king. Toungooyaza led the field levies against a Talaing force under the *yuvaraja* (crown prince) which came up the Irrawaddy river, but the Talaings drove him in and invested Ava. The defenders grew so weak with hunger that they could hardly lift their weapons. The Talaings were on the point of returning home when they learnt this from deserters, and in April 1752 they forced their way in, sacked the city, and burnt it to the ground. Crowds of captives, including the royal family, were deported to Pegu. Some of the royal princes escaped during the sack and fled to the Shan country; none of them stayed and tried to raise the waiting north. The solitary exception is Toungooyaza; it was he who raided Syriam in 1743 and had commanded against the Manipuris for decades; while being taken down the river to Pegu he escaped in disguise as a fisherman, went to Mogaung and there, trying to collect men, he died within the year, not an able man, but at least a faithful servant.

The Talaings sent out detachments to administer the water of allegiance to all villages. A few weeks later the *yuvaraja* left Talaban with one-third of the forces to garrison Ava, and withdrew with the rest to Pegu as there was some fear that Martaban and Tavoy might bring in the Siamese. But no potential danger from Siam could equal the actual danger from northern Burma. The evacuation, before the Talaings had penetrated the country north of the city, was a capital error. The Ava dynasty was played out, but there was nothing to show that the Burmese people were played out. The *yuvaraja* had ample warning, even if he did not possess the soldier's instinct: a detachment sent to administer the water of allegiance to a village called Moksobomyo was cut to pieces. He was angry, and when handing over to Talaban he said "You will have to make an example of that place, Moksobomyo, or whatever they call it."

217-304

CHAPTER VII

ALAUNGPAYA DYNASTY 1752-1824

CHAPTER VII

ALAUNGPAYA DYNASTY 1752-1824

ALAUNGPAYA 1752-60 was born in 1714 at Shwebo.[1] It was then a village of 300 houses,[2] known as Moksobomyo "town of the hunter chief," and many of his followers were hunters. But he himself belonged to a better class, the landed gentry as it were. For generations his ancestors had been *myothugyis* and rulers. In after times he even claimed descent from Nawrahta, Myaukpet Myinhmu or Commandant of the Northern Cavalry Area, and brother to the Ava chief Mohnyinthado 1427-40. The genealogy[3] is unproved, but the old-established villages of Upper Burma are not like the newly cleared Delta areas where society is positively colonial and men do not know their own pedigree.

The omens which fired his ambition are typical of certain limitations beyond which he never developed. But everyone else had those limitations. What they did not have was his tiger heart. When the Talaings came raiding up to Ava, when the cruel Manipuris cantered past his home, he thought of the kings of old whose blood flowed in his veins. What was the king of Ava now? A dummy on a golden throne, bowed beneath the weight of lofty titles

"Calling a crowned man royal who was no more than a king."

He knew all about that king, the sort who would let himself be led away into captivity like a tame lamb. He heard from his uncle the lord *mingyi* the sort of thing that happened at court. Ava was bound to fall sooner or later; well, the Talaings might take Ava, but they should not take him. He felled toddy trees by the hundred and made them into a stockade round his village, dug a moat, cleared the jungle

[1] *JBRS* 1915 Enriquez "Capitals of the Alaungpaya Dynasty."
[2] *Dalrymple* I. 163.
[3] *Konbaungset* 15, *Alaungpaya Ayedawbon* 6.

outside to form a glacis, and rode out destroying ponds and filling in wells. There was no difficulty, for he was aged thirty-six, the hereditary lord for miles around, and there were scores of good men only waiting for a lead. Forty-six villages joined him, and among them they raised a few muskets.

When Ava fell he was ready. The Talaings sent a small detachment to exact the oath of allegiance. His father made ready to pay homage and to give up half his property, saying "We can do nothing. Fate is against us. Ava has fallen. The Talaing army is too strong. We shall simply be overwhelmed. We may as well give in." "No," said Alaungpaya, "When fighting for your country it matters little whether you are few or many. What does matter is that your comrades have true hearts and strong arms." He went out and met those Talaings in the scrub jungle south of Halin in Shwebo district. They got no homage. Only such as were lucky got away with their lives.

They came back in a large detachment with orders to spare not even infants in the cradle. Alaungpaya built a state hut and sent ten horsemen to conduct them respectfully to it. But they were conducted along a hollow road and in the bushes on each side lay his musket men. The Talaings never reached that hut. A bare half dozen reached Ava alive to tell the tale.

Again they came back, several thousand strong this time, to wipe out Shwebo once and for all; but as they came without cannon the assault failed and they had to undertake a siege. One night Alaungpaya burst out at the head of a general sortie. It was not a defeat but a rout. Word passed along the Burmese pursuers that men had seen Myinbyushin Nat, the spirit Rider of the White Horse, fighting on their side. The Talaings jumped into boats and, without stopping to report at Ava, fled straight home down the river. All their camp and equipment fell into Alaungpaya's hands. His men got clothes, horses, and things which they said were of gold and silver; above all they got scores of muskets, worth their weight in gold in these critical days.

The news spread. There was no need to offer bounties or to press men. They were fighting for the existence of their race; also there would be loot, and they looked forward to the clothes and horses and girls they would take from those dogs of Talaings. Officers and men from the disbanded palace Guard joined him with such arms as they retained. Under the recent kings of Ava the territorial cadres (p. 24) had existed only on paper. But now, from half the villages of Upper Burma lads of spirit came trooping in to take service under the new leader. A dozen legends gathered round his name. Men felt that when he led them they could not fail.

The deficiency of the races of Indo-China in power of combination on a large scale is natural to people whose inherited instincts were formed in a country of great distances and bad communications. But when roused to enthusiasm they have shown considerable capacity for combined action. Among the Burmese the years 1752-7 are a model instance. Alaungpaya was not the only prominent man in Upper Burma. Independent attempts to form centres of resistance had been made at Mogaung in Myitkyina district and Salin in Minbu district. Some of the leaders were men of better birth, who had not to go back nine generations to claim royal blood. There were masterful men with considerable followings, who could have ruined the common cause by insisting on their rights. Not one of them did so, and the hereditary nobles ended by placing the territorial cadres at the disposal of Alaungpaya.[1]

A few of the Upper Burma lords with their Burman, Shan and Kadu retainers, were fighting on the Talaing side. Alaungpaya issued orders that they were to be given quarter; but he burned their villages, and deported their families and herds to Shwebo. The rest took warning and wherever he went men now drank the water of allegiance.

It is difficult to conceive what the Talaing government thought they were doing; they had allowed a formidable situation to develop, which now needed every man they had; yet they sent not a single reinforcement. They merely sent the Toungoo Ngwegunhmu to replace Talaban, who employed Burmese servants, omitted to make men bob their hair in the Talaing fashion, and failed to crush Alaungpaya. The Talaings had northern outposts, operating as far as Wuntho and Kawlin, and the Gwes of Madaya-Okpo joined them. Alaungpaya received many a check but his men fought with the greatest

[1] *JBRS* 1919 Furnivall "An Incident in Burmese history."

spirit, rushing up to stockades and tearing them down with *dahs* and axes. He massacred the Gwes, capturing large numbers of their men and women and driving the rest to take refuge in Hsipaw or with the Talaings.[1]

By October 1752 the Talaings had withdrawn most of their outposts, and in December 1753 he was able to camp under the walls of Ava. The Talaings tried to dislodge him but suffered heavily before his stockade. Deserted by their government, and knowing that as soon as a siege started the Burmese and Shan citizens would rise against them, they evacuated the town silently in the night and retreated to the Delta. Not till next day did the Burmese discover their good fortune. It was such a victory that they did not trouble to pursue. It was enough for them that by January 1754 the whole of Upper Burma was clear of Talaings.

Alaungpaya had been hailed as king from the first and had already built a palace at Shwebo. Ava was a blackened ruin, but he made a formal entry and spent several weeks there in festivities, holding a solemn investiture and worshipping in state at the Shwekyetyet, Yanaungmyin and Shwetaunguchantha pagodas; he worshipped thus wherever he went, strictly enforcing prohibition of intoxicants and cattle slaughter. To secure his rear and subject new areas from which to draw levies, he proceeded in strength up the Irrawaddy, spreading the terror of his name among the wild tribes, and receiving homage or promises of homage from the nearer *sawbwas*. He worshipped at the Thihadaw pagoda on the beautiful island in Shwebo district, and the Zina-Aunggya-Shwebontha pagoda at Tagaung marks the spot where the Momeik *sawbwa* knelt before him. He met the devoted remnant of Toungooyaza's little band (p. 216) and saw that they should not suffer want.

In March 1754 the Talaings did what they should have done two years before, and sent their whole army. It would have been 1751-2 over again; but this time they had to face Alaungpaya instead of an effete dynasty. They drove his sons out of Talokmyo in Myingyan district; the younger son was so overcome with shame that he washed his head in purification (pp. 45, 187). The Talaings besieged Ava; their assaults failed but they carried fire and sword through the

[1] *Dalrymple* I. 165, *Konbaungset* 73.

villages up to Kyaukmyaung in Shwebo district. Finally, Alaungpaya marched down from Shwebo, his son made a sortie from Ava, and the Talaings, finding the rains near and their losses heavy, beat a general retreat in such haste that at Hsinbyugyun in Minbu district they left behind the golden *hti* they had brought to place on the Shwezigon pagoda at Pagan.

Meanwhile the Burmans of the Delta and those whom the Talaings had captured and scattered among the villages, were watching Alaungpaya's fortunes. Parties of them hung together in suspense and disobeyed the Talaing king's order to disperse. Alaungpaya wrote to their leaders promising them the governorship of any districts they could instigate to revolt.[1] In Pegu some thousand Talaings and Burmans plotted to restore the captive Ava king; the *parabaik* lists of their names were betrayed, wholesale executions followed, and the Ava king was drowned with three of his sons.

At this news Alaungpaya swore high vengeance, and the Delta Burmans broke loose, slit the throats of their Talaing *thugyis*, and assembled on the Shwehsandaw pagoda at Prome. Shouting "Shwebotha! Shwebotha!" they rushed into the town. Hearing the Shwebo war-cry the Talaing garrison thought an Upper Burma army was upon them and fled in panic. Alaungpaya bade the victors hold out, and when the Talaing army, retreating from Ava in April 1754, besieged them hard, he came down with all his host. The Talaing besiegers, secure in a great earthwork stockade like jackals in their holes, flung off Alaungpaya's attacks. But waverers met death from his own sword, and in February 1755 the troops, dreading his wrath, forced their way in amid heavy slaughter, capturing many muskets and cannon but very few prisoners: they were in no mood for prisoners. The Talaings retreated wholesale. Alaungpaya entered Prome, returned solemn thanks at the Shwehsandaw pagoda, received the homage of central Burma, and held an investiture, honouring especially the lord of Sale in Myingyan district and the *myothugyi* of Pahkannge in Magwe district who had led the Delta rising.

He occupied Lunhse (Kudut) in Henzada district, naming it Myanaung, "Speedy Victory." Here he built the Shwebontha

[1] *Dalrymple* I. 135.

and other pagodas and held high festival for thirty days and nights, receiving the homage of Toungoo, Henzada, Myaungmya, Bassein and even Sandoway in Arakan. For weeks the jungle lords came bringing elephants, horses, and daughters to the rising king.

In May 1755 he wrested Dagon from the Talaings, called it Rangoon, "End of Strife," and worshipped in state at the Shwedagon pagoda. Finding three small English ships in the port he detained their officers ashore, and sent his men aboard to seize their cannon, small arms and ammunition. They were neutral and he bore them no ill-will but he was in great need of fire-arms. One of the ships, the snow *Arcot*, belonged to the East India Company.[1] Her captain, Jackson, took precedence of the others, and though helpless protested against this incredible breach of international law. He did not realise that the Burmese were not subject to international law; they had not heard of it, for they had no foreign relations: it is doubtful whether they averaged one embassy a year, and that from tribal states. Yet Alaungpaya allowed the protest and took nothing, because he thought it would pay to conciliate Europeans, not because he was afraid—he believed he could beat the French and English just as he beat everyone else.

Jackson had put in to caulk his leaking ship, and he came to Rangoon as the English shipwright had moved there, away from the fighting at Syriam. His ship was so bad and the local labour so incompetent that repairs took five months, during most of which he lay half dying of dysentery. The Burmese, attacked in their stockade at Rangoon, distrusted him for not firing on the Talaings, and threatened him; and the Talaing crown prince at Syriam continually wrote asking him to fire on the Burmese. He was heartily sick of both. He was cut off, without orders, and wondered whether he would ever get out of the place without the assistance of Bourno, the French agent at Syriam, who with three bigger ships was openly siding with the Talaings. Utterly distrusting the Burmese after Alaungpaya's high-handed attempt at seizure, regarding him as a mere usurper who was

[1] Snow, a small brig up to 120 tons, with 4 to 12 cannon, probably nine pounders, and 30 to 50 men. In eastern waters her complement would be lascars save for the captain and perhaps the commander and chief gunner who were white. Jackson's diary is at *Dalrymple* I. 177-200.

bound to fail, and receiving kind messages from his enemy Bourno who chivalrously offered him a doctor, Jackson and his two fellow captains co-operated with the Talaings and French when their ships bombarded Rangoon. The bombardment lasted a week, driving the Burmese from the bank and smashing up their boats, but had no real result because nothing would induce the Talaings to land and face cold steel. Finally Jackson took refuge in Syriam and received kind treatment from the Talaing crown prince who, however, reproached him because the English would not enter into an agreement, refused to give the Talaings stores, and removed the guns of their Syriam factory to Negrais just when the Talaings wanted to use them. While ill in bed, Jackson was struck in the face by a Talaing commander, and finally he got leave to sail away only by surrendering five of his cannon to the Talaings. In the same way the Burmese, on their side, had compelled a Dutch brigantine to fight for them.

Some months previously, Alaungpaya had sent envoys with presents of horses, a ring, 100 *viss* (365 lb.) wax and 100 *viss* ivory, to the Bassein timber depot asking the English to enter into relations: he wanted cannon. The Talaings reoccupied Bassein and demanded the surrender of Burmese envoys but the English factors refused and sent them safely to Negrais where they arranged that Brooke, the chief, should send an envoy to Alaungpaya. Brooke was furious with Jackson's conduct at Syriam and recalled the English there. The envoy, Captain Baker, with a mirror, a twelve pounder cannon, three nine pounders, powder and shot, as presents, arrived at Shwebo in September 1755, and was admitted to the royal presence within a day of arrival:—

> To the palace steps we were conducted by about twenty musketeers headed by a drum. . . . I entered in the midst of a crowd of officers in their court dress, the King's two eldest sons being seated on carpets, one each side the . . . throne where their father sat in state. Having paid my compliments on the knees, bowing the head three times low down, three separate times, he looked at me for some time and at length said "How does your King do?" I answered he was well when we had the last account from Europe. . . . Having paused some time at length says he "Your ships that were at Dagon with Mr. Whitehill,[1] I treated with kindness . . . and

[1] Jackson's colleague. The firing occurred during Baker's journey to Shwebo.

at my leaving . . . to come here to keep our fast, desired him . . . to assist my people, or at least not to join the Peguers against them; which though he promised to observe, yet was the first that fired on them." I answered I was heartily grieved at his being guilty of so rash and imprudent an action and that I was sure His Majesty himself could not be more offended at him than Mr. Brooke would be . . . it was either the force of the Peguers, or the fraud and device of our inveterate enemies the French which had compelled or seduced him to it. "But" says he "had not Mr. Brooke any hand in this, was it not by his counsel?" I gave him all the assurances to the contrary . . . averring that I was sure no other human affair could give him so great uneasiness as the news of this would. He then ordered the letter to be read, to which he gave a calm attention till coming to these words "as you will by this means obtain an alliance and friendship with so great a power as the Honourable East India Company, who can send you such assistance as will support Your Majesty's throne against all future rebellions, domestic feuds and foreign enemies." At which he affected a very hearty laugh (and his officers in attendance like true courtiers joined in the chorus) said "Have I asked? Or do I want any assistance to reduce my enemies to subjection? Let none conceive such an opinion. Have I not extended my conquest three months journey on every quarter without the help of cannon or muskets? Nay, I have with bludgeons only, opposed and defeated these Peguers who destroyed the capital of the kingdom . . . and a month hence I intend to go with a great force to Dagon, where I have an army now lying. . . . I will advance to the walls of Pegu, blockade and starve them out of it, which is the last town I have now to take to complete my conquest, and then I will go in quest of Bourno." Then the secretary proceeding . . . "these gentlemen may be witnesses to Your Majesty's placing your signet to the contract on your part" he again affected the same mirth (and was again joined by his courteous attendance) saying "What madman wrote that? Captain, see this sword! It is now three years since it has been constantly exercised in chastising my enemies, it is indeed almost blunt with use, but it shall be continued . . . till they are utterly dispersed. Don't talk of assistance. I require none. The Peguers I can wipe away as thus" drawing the palm of one hand over the other "See these arms and this thigh" drawing the sleeves of his vesture over his shoulder and tucking the lower part up his crutch . . . "Amongst 1,000 you won't see my match. I myself can crush 100 such as the King of Pegu. . . . With what intention do you come to Negrais?" and without staying for the answer went on again with encomiums on himself . . . and ran on with a narrative of all his actions insomuch that I had not the opportunity to say anything. . . . The 26th at night was told . . . that His Majesty's indisposition had so much increased that he could not grant an audience and therefore desired me to come again in the morning. . . . I went accordingly

> about ten o'clock in the morning on the 27th to the Inner Yondaw . . . whence a messenger informed His Majesty . . . who returned . . . an answer in writing "Do not take it amiss, Captain, that I cannot grant you an interview. My indisposition will not admit of it. I have therefore sent, by my first minister, the Company's letter, and ordered him to give you a horse. Return again with despatch and meet me at Dagon or in the way thither, then the Company shall not want what they would have. I have elephant's teeth, wax, etc., ready for them." This being read . . . the Minister delivered me the King's letter and ordered the horse to be sent to my house. . . . His indisposition was excessive grief. . . . At this time his favourite lay at the point of death and expired about two hours after; she was daughter to a petty prince . . . whom the King had subdued and taken this princess captive. (Baker's report, *Dalrymple* I. 149.)

Thus interrupted by domestic grief, Alaungpaya sent Baker away without the treaty, which did not go through till July 1757. It ceded absolutely and in perpetuity all Negrais and a site at Bassein with permission to fortify, and granted all trade duty free. In return, the English were to send military assistance when paid for, to refrain from assisting the lord of Tavoy (who was making overtures to them) should he fail to submit to Alaungpaya, and to send annual tribute of one twelve pounder cannon and 200 *viss* powder. The treaty was fetched by Ensign Lester at Myanaung in Henzada district whither he had for days accompanied the royal barge.[1] Alaungpaya presented Lester with eighteen oranges, two dozen heads of maize, and five cucumbers, and pointed out that he was a very great king, so great, indeed, that a nine pound ball fired out of a cannon could not injure him, for he was invulnerable. He was immeasurably amused at finding Lester could not *shikko* or kneel for long without getting cramp, and graciously permitted him to sit; pointing to Lester's shoulder knot he asked "What do you wear that for? How much pay do you get a month? Let me feel you," and felt his hand and wrist, saying the English were like women because they were soft and white and did not tattoo. But Lester was meanly treated by everyone else; he was made to give up the boat he had come in,

[1] *Dalrymple* I. 200-26 gives Lester's diary and the text of the treaty. Before the siege of Pegu, when he needed guns badly, Alaungpaya thought of ceding Negrais, Bassein, and a site at Rangoon for 20 cannon and 1,000 muskets down, instead of annual tribute, see *Dalrymple* I. 154.

and was given instead a leaking boat for the return journey; he wrote "Of all mankind which I have seen, the Burman promises the most and performs the least"; and he could not get Alaungpaya's seal affixed to the treaty until, with a shocked protest, he paid one of the princes Rs. 2,000 and another Rs. 1,000, vastly greater sums than now, for rice then sold at twenty baskets a rupee.[1]

The reason why the English envoy in September 1755 had found Alaungpaya at Shwebo was that he sometimes had to return there to settle affairs in the north country. Thus in 1755 he found the Gwe people stirring up trouble with the Shans, and he had also sent an expedition to instil respect into the Manipuris who significantly call this, the first of his dynasty's inroads, "The First Devastation"; the Manipuris found the Burmese on this occasion using fire-arms for the first time, their weapons, like those of the Manipuris, having previously been only swords, spears, bows and arrows.[2] He sent his musketeer captain Minhlaminhkaungkyaw with an imposing escort to visit the Shan states and thus secured the homage of most of them and also recognition from the Yünnan viceroy.

Alaungpaya himself returned with a large force, containing Shan and Chin levies, to Syriam which his men had started to besiege soon after the capture of Rangoon. Rangoon was of no importance in comparison with Syriam, *the* port of Burma. There was much fighting in the Delta not only by land but also between the great war-canoes, driven by sixty oars, which, after using their swivel guns, would ram with terrific effect.[3] Finally the Burmese, burning the villages

[1] See note "Price of Rice" p. 354.

[2] See note "Fire-arms" p. 340.

[3] The men faced aft and rowed on tholepins. The chief sat in the bows, as the stern was derogatory to rank.

"Every town on the river . . . is obliged to furnish a gilt, or common war-boat, and to man and keep it in constant readiness. . . . His Majesty can muster from two to three hundred; they carry from forty to fifty men each, and are, I think, the most respectable part of his force. As they live chiefly by rapine, and are in a state of constant hostility with the rest of the people, they are audacious and prompt to execute any orders, however cruel" (Cox, year 1797, *Snodgrass* 19).

"The famous war-boats are never seen out of the Irrawaddy or Rangoon river, or employed except on special missions or expeditions ordered by the king, or in carrying a royal order to cut off a head or create a governor" (Paper of

A Burmese War Canoe.

Contemporary print, publ. Thos. Clay, Ludgate Hill, on the walls of the Pegu Club, from the original sketch by Captain Marryat, R.N., the sea novelist, who was senior naval officer at Rangoon in 1824.

and killing or deporting the population, closed around Syriam. They invested it tightly, swept away the great Talaing stockade at Dawbon, and cut off communication with Pegu. The garrison commander was the Talaing king's brother Binnyadala.

To irregular troops, unprovided with siege artillery, Syriam was a fearful place. They had nothing but their bare bodies to oppose to the beams and boiling pitch which were hurled down from the wall; even if they succeeded in planting a ladder, the first man to put his hand on the rampart had it chopped off and the ladder was overthrown. To make things worse, there were Frenchmen inside Syriam. The English had long left, and such as were at Rangoon now had orders from Negrais headquarters to assist none but the Burmese, but the French sided with the Talaings, and two French ships of respectable size lay in the river. The Talaing snow and 200 war-canoes could only have held their own against Alaungpaya's flotilla but the French ships' gunfire smashed it to pieces. Though Alaungpaya harried the French with fire-rafts, he could make no progress on the water side. On the land side, his assaults failed with cruel losses among his best officers and men; even later he never had any cannon over 24 pounds calibre, and he could make no impression on a rampart backed by earthwork.

When the siege had lasted a year, starvation began to do its work, and the garrison were reduced to eating roots. Bourno the French agent had a tentative interview with Alaungpaya, and would have deserted to the Burmese had not the Talaings put him under restraint. Finding the defenders faint with hunger and the omens favourable for a certain day, Alaungpaya called for volunteers and selected ninety-three. Among them were the noblest in the land, Guards officers and princes of the blood, and they were known as the Golden Company of Syriam. They fed in the king's presence for

Intelligence from Cox's Bazaar, 20 October 1823, in *BSPC*). This reassured English naval officers, who had asked for information.

In the Franklin Room at the Royal Naval Museum, Greenwich, are two model war-canoes from Rangoon, deposited in mid-Victorian times; neither has a gun-mounting; one has a dragon head and tail, the other is plain, with eyes painted on each side of the bow, and thirty oars a side; the ticket says "Burmese war-boats are all on the same plan, 120 feet in length, from 6 to 7 feet in breadth, and from 3 to 4 feet in depth."

several days, and were given leather helmets and lacquer armour. On the appointed night, in July 1756, the Burmese held a festival with drums and music in their camp at Bogyok. The sound floating over to the Talaing city on the hill induced the watchers to relax their vigilance. The Golden Company found their way over the walls, cut down the guards, and opened the gate to their comrades outside; it was the Wetthattaga, the gate where Nga Than Hlyin in olden days had killed the legendary boar.[1] They poured in, shouting their war-cry "Shwebotha," slaying right and left, and the town was theirs. The Talaing prince Binnyadala rode off with his bare life.

To Alaungpaya's simple men from Upper Burma, Syriam was a veritable Eldorado, and they glutted themselves with mirrors, candlesticks, lamps, chairs, clocks, and suchlike wonders. Alaungpaya made a heap of silver and let the survivors of the Golden Company take away as much as they could carry. Mahomedans and Eurasians were forced to serve in the army; any Europeans he got were generally used as officers. He released the few English he found, and spared such Burmans and Shans as had not been killed out of hand, saying they had opposed him only under Talaing compulsion. He occupied the Catholic mission church and buildings, destroying the town which henceforth is of no importance. Angelo, a Catholic brother, had been killed during the siege while he was tending the wounded. Nerini, the Italian bishop elect, was not a political intriguer, but he doubtless stood in with his French co-religionists, and in any case he had to stay by his native flock in Syriam; Alaungpaya sent for his head. But the soldiers heard of the bishop's virtues, and spared him, killing a half-caste Portuguese priest and trying to palm off his head instead. Alaungpaya was not deceived, and sent them back with positive orders, and this time it was really the white bishop's head that they brought.

Bourno had written to Pondicherry asking for assistance. The French in India, though sore beset, could not afford to lose Syriam, their shipbuilding depot, and they sent three more ships with cannon and munitions. One, *Diligent*, met bad

[1] *JBRS* 1915 Furnivall "The History of Syriam (with translation and notes)"; 1914 his "Notes on the History of Hanthawaddy" reproduced in his "Syriam Gazetteer."

weather and came so late that the news of the fall of Syriam had spread and she returned without entering the port. The others, *Fleury* and *Galathée*, arrived two days after the sack. Alaungpaya made Bourno write asking them to come up the river. The Burman pilot stranded them, and fire-rafts sealed their fate. Bourno and the ships' officers, numbering twelve and including gentlemen of quality, were at once beheaded.[1]

The French were under no obligations to Alaungpaya and as the Talaing state which they were helping was actually in existence, they were entitled to treatment as prisoners of war. But it was customary among the races of Indo-China to give no quarter save to those they carried off into slavery, and beheading was a not unusual fate for officer prisoners. In this case Alaungpaya enforced the rule, hoping to strike terror and to warn the French not to oppose him again. He did not realise that it was the one way to provoke a terrible vengeance, and the only reason vengeance never came was that the French were shortly afterwards defeated in Europe in a country of which neither he nor his successors knew so much as the name, and under the terms of the peace they had to evacuate India.

In *Fleury* and *Galathée* he found thirty-five ship's guns (24 pounders), five field guns, 1,300 muskets, and a large store of ammunition and accoutrements. These were a godsend to him, and it was largely on their account that he gave the crews, over 200 men, their lives: white gunners were too valuable to execute. They were decently treated and given wives; some of them became Captains of the Guard;[2] the rest were a corps d'élite who played no small part in major actions, and when too old to follow the armies they were allowed to retire in the Shwebo villages (pp. 345, 349). There, with a white priest, they ended their days, far from the Breton cliffs and the women who waited in vain for their return.

Thus, until the gunners lost their man-of-war smartness, the

[1] *Sonnerat* (1782) II. 40, (1806) III. 37, *Symes* 18-32.

[2] For instance, the Chevalier Milard, see *Sonnerat* (1782) II. 43, *Bigandet* 21. He was Captain of the Guard and Master of the Ordnance. His Latin and Burmese tombstone at Ngayabya-Ava records that he died in 1778 aged 42 having served His Burman Majesty against Pegu, Ayuthia, Manipur, etc., being Captain of the Feringhis, styled Thiriyazathukyawhtin, lord *myosa* (baron) of Tabe in Sagaing district. Considering their hard life, it is not likely that many of the crews lived to be old.

court had some good artillery. The enemy could tell at once when a gun was laid by one of these Frenchmen. Alaungpaya had indeed already in his possession a number of cannon, mostly taken from the Talaings, but some of them were two hundred years old,[1] and the best of them was the gun used at Prome in 1754. This was a three pounder and it was the pride of the day, because when fired it went off, and when it went off it was the enemy whom it hit, and the enemy whom it hit died; because of these things, it was coated with goldleaf, and men made offerings of spirits to it, reverently perfuming it with scents and wrapping it in fine raiment.[2] Alaungpaya was Head of the Church, but when he came to possess French gunners, he was not responsible for their souls, as they were unbelievers and it was their own concern if they chose to drink damnation. Besides, theologically speaking, he did not countenance their use of intoxicants: he merely permitted the offering of spirits to the Gun Spirit, according to precedent, and the slaves of the Gun Spirit happened to consume the offering.

Alaungpaya enlarged Rangoon, appointing a senior governor, and henceforth it replaced Syriam as the port of Burma. In the open season 1756-7 he advanced on Pegu by land and water, while a second army, mainly of Shan levies, moved towards it from Toungoo. His advance was slow, with grim losses, for the Talaings still had cannon and they were now fighting literally with their backs to the wall. He left pots of poisoned intoxicants[3] where the Talaings would find them, and so killed many until they learnt caution. He piled more than a thousand Talaing heads on a raft and sent it up with the flood tide; the watchers on the city walls saw it float by and read their own doom, while the vultures rose and fell.[4] The defence made desperate stands in forty stockades south of the city, especially near Mokkainggyi, at Kyaikpadaing and Zenyaungbin (Nyaungbin). At Zenyaungbin the Talaings captured many of his jingals and turned them against him; it was a hornet's nest which he captured only by flinging in the Golden Company of Syriam, increased to three hundred;

[1] *Trant* 26. [2] *Konbaungset* 110-12.

[3] *Konbaungset* 198. See note "Drink" p. 314.

[4] *Konbaungset* 212.

undeterred by heavy losses, they pressed on shouting "Shwebotha!" and flung open the gate to their comrades outside.

Finally the Burmese, devastating the country and deporting the population, closed around. The moat turned red in colour; the Talaings watched it with a sinking heart, for this was the fatal sign of 1538 when Tabinshwehti had captured the city. They made sorties. A monastery at Sidi still shows a bell cast by Alaungpaya; he resided there, at the little fort of Zetuwadi, part of which is still in existence though the river bank has eroded; his own camp here was rushed one night by Talaban with a body of picked Talaings who were not driven out till they had inflicted severe losses. But their efforts were vain. The Burmese, aided by their French artillery, and by war-boats which flung off the Talaing fire-rafts, completed their lines round the devoted city.

At length the besieged sent out deputations to intercede with Alaungpaya; prominent in these were their Talaing, Burmese and Shan monks, and Alaungpaya responded in the noblest language. He pointed out that the precedent of Razadarit (p. 88) they quoted was no precedent, for when Razadarit yielded to religious intercession he was fighting on equal terms, whereas he himself was overwhelmingly victorious and could listen to no proposals which did not include complete annexation; but—it is the ambition of every great Buddhist king to be a divine incarnation—he added that he was a divine incarnation, he hoped to become a Buddha, he would promote truth and justice, religion and mercy among all men, and the poor had nothing to fear from him. Finally he gave them two bunches of orchids, saying one was for offering, the other for adornment.

The Talaings breathed more freely. They offered one bunch to the Shwemawdaw pagoda, the other they twined in the tresses of their king's daughter, as for the bride of Alaungpaya. But she was beloved of Talaban, the heart and soul of the defence;[1] he was furious and, finding his advice, to sally forth and die like men, rejected, he collected his family and with some of the best troops broke through the Burmese lines and maintained himself at Sittaung in Thaton district.

[1] *Symes* 34.

The trembling king sent his daughter to Alaungpaya's camp, borne in a gorgeous palanquin, surrounded by a bevy of handmaidens and princes. After kneeling some time in homage, she was conducted into Alaungpaya's harem. There was universal rejoicing and the Talaing crown prince with many of the leaders came over with their families and took Burmese allegiance.

Now was the time for Alaungpaya to fulfil the hopes he had raised and to grant terms however hard; but he did nothing. Under cover of fraternisation, parties of Burmese troops were introduced into the city. The inevitable fracas occurred and the Talaings in disgust shut the gates, renewed the defence, and put their king under restraint as he wished to desert. For them the delay had produced nothing but the desertion of their best men and leaders. After a few weeks they were reduced to eating reptiles. In May 1757, seeing that they were so weak with hunger that an assault was practicable, Alaungpaya said he would spare them from dying of starvation. He pointed cannon with his own hand. The general advance was fixed for moonrise, by which time the stormers were to be in possession of the wall. When the moon rose, they were still under the wall, and Alaungpaya sent word that he was coming to execute the whole detachment; thereupon they swarmed over, cut down the guards, fired the houses, and opened the gate. The Burmese Fury burst headlong in, sparing neither sex nor age nor even the monks. One long wail of horror rose to the deaf skies. Men, women, and children rushed to the twenty gates, flung them open, and tried to escape. Many were crushed to death, some were caught by the guns, others in despair flung themselves from the battlements, many perished in the flames. The roads and gates were choked with dead.[1]

When the sack subsided, Alaungpaya, gleaming aloft on his elephant, with his Guards and Frenchmen, made a state entry in procession through the Mohnyin Gate in the south wall, during a slight drizzle. He returned solemn thanks at the Shwemawdaw pagoda and appointed governors to the newly conquered districts. The captive king, and such of the leaders as had submitted in good time, were reasonably treated. The remnants of

[1] *Konbaungset* 245-6.

the deposed Ava family were sent home, the daughters being taken into Alaungpaya's harem.

> Alaungpaya said to the two Talaing envoys "If as he says your king will really mingle his blood with mine, I will return with all my host to Ava." They told their king and he sent his daughter the lady Megon with an hundred handmaidens and with many attendants and with the ministers Mahagayat and Mahathamun. And Alaungpaya cherished her, yet he withdrew not his army nor kept his promise, but again attacked the town. At midnight on Friday the fifth waning of the moon of Kahson in the year 1119 he captured Pegu. The king Binnyadala, his son Thado Upayaza, his queens, sons, daughters, his chambers of gold and his chambers of silver, Alaungpaya seized them all. Saying "The monks helped the town to resist," he threw more than 3,000 monks to the elephants, the elephants trampled on them, the elephants killed them. Their velvet and satin robes, the officers wore; their cotton robes, men used for pillows, rice-bags, and towels to wipe their feet. They were strewn over the face of the earth, the holy robes; their alms bowls were turned into household pots. The monks who still lived fled east of the Sittang river to the towns of Sittaung, Pan, Shwegyin, Martaban, Labun, Zimme, Yodaya and the Shan towns. The Burmese soldiers seized all the people of the Talaing country, men and women, and sold them some for an hundred pieces, some for fifty, some for twenty-five, some for twenty, some for fifteen pieces. We were sold in the market, we were sold like cattle in the market, and the Burmese soldiers made merry with the price. Sons could not find their mothers, nor mothers their sons, and there was weeping throughout the land. (*Sayadaw Athwa* III. 148.)

He burnt the palace and razed the city wall. He made a desert and called it peace. For the Talaings it was the peace of the grave, and this is the end of them in Burma. Such as were not enslaved sometimes found a refuge in Siam, where they rose to high office and furnished some of the best troops. Such as remained in Burma were prone to rebel, and whenever they dared raise a head it was at once chopped off; they grew fewer and subsided, and their lands relapsed into jungle. Burmese armies on their way to Siam would lighten the tedium of the march by devastating the Pegu country. As time went on, the Burmese of the Delta entered into kindly human relations with the survivors, and some of the governors relented and acted with liberality. But if the racial spirit came to be dead until the British victories of 1824 temporarily revived it, this was not because of any statesmanship on the part of the Burmese government, but simply because there were not sufficient numbers left to keep it alive. Burmese rulers doubtless had their own difficulties, but it is none the less an indelible stain on their administration that the Delta, one of the most fertile areas in Asia, should have been found by the English to be mainly an uncultivated waste, the haunt of the tiger and the elephant.[1]

The Burmese owed their civilisation to the Talaings; it was an older and apparently a gentler civilisation. We know too little to say with confidence why they went under. In Alaungpaya's time their literature was largely destroyed and their language fell into discouragement. Hence we read about them through Burmese spectacles. The Burmese chronicles accuse them of perfidy, and perfidy would account for their defeat; but the instances given do not differ in kind or frequency from those of the Burmese themselves. Probably the ultimate cause of their elimination is that they received no reinforcements by immigration, unlike the Burmese who, lying to the north, were open to a constant trickle of racial invigoration. The proximate cause in 1757 was, firstly, the failure of the Talaing government to subjugate the north immediately after entering Ava and before withdrawing the bulk of the army; secondly, they were divided in their councils, while the Burmese were united under a great leader; thirdly, they had only their own corner of Burma to draw on for men, whereas Alaungpaya's numbers were fed by Shan, Kachin, Chin and Kadu levies.

Alaungpaya was lavish in his praise and rewards. To be named at one of his investitures was the ambition of men's lives. When the brave musketeer captain Minhlaminhkaungkyaw, styled the Mahathenapati, lay dying of his wounds at Syriam, Alaungpaya mourned unaffectedly and honoured him with a funeral under the white umbrella before the whole army. But he was merciless to failure. He judged men largely by the number of heads they could show at the end of a day's fighting.[2] Unsuccessful officers were executed; it was harsh, but every good leader knows the treatment his men require.

He was a guerilla leader of the first quality. His men had

[1] *Symes* 165. and English authors *passim*, e.g. *Crawfurd*, *Laurie*, *Mrs. Judson*.

[2] *Alaungpaya Ayedawbon* 64, *Konbaungset passim*. Cf. *Laurie* "Pegu" 461, 467, and *Crawfurd* II. 40.

not the training or leadership for pitched battles in the open, but excelled in stockade fighting, and in ambushes which showed their individual initiative and cunning to full advantage. They would have made admirable pioneer units, for their woodwork and entrenching were excellent.[1] Outside the Guard not one in twenty had muskets. Men in the levy received rations but no pay, and had to bring their own equipment—*dahs*, bludgeons, and spears which sometimes had an iron head but were more often pointed bamboos. Many came with hammer and nails, for their speciality was stockading, and their best constructions won the respect of English sappers. For greater speed and for ease of provisioning on long marches, their columns broke up into small parties, each finding its own way and reassembling before battle. They were given liberty to maraud and used it impartially on friend and foe alike; and they would carry off women and children and sell them for profit.[2] Each man slung a cooking pot with a fortnight's rice and dried fish at one end of his musket, some powder, a mat and a blanket at the other end, and marched without baggage train of any kind, living on next to nothing;[3] many combined war with trade, carrying a pack of goods as well as their weapons.[4] After 1824, finding themselves outclassed, they became demoralised and devoted their energies to running away. It was quite the most sensible thing to do under the circumstances, but it led to their being regarded as a comic opera army. Yet the first Englishmen to cross swords with them had a different opinion which, though of a later day, assuredly applies to Alaungpaya's own men and is in any case the earliest professional opinion on record:—

> "They fought with a bravery and obstinacy I never witnessed in any troops. . . . They fought desperately, reserving their fire to the last moment and seldom missing their object. . . . Little is known of the march of Mahabandula's force across the mountains of Arakan to the Irrawaddy; a distance, by the shortest route, of upwards of two hundred miles, at a season of the year when none but Burmans could have kept the field for a week, much less have attempted to

[1] *Trant* 125.

[2] *TP* 1891 Cordier "Les Français en Birmanie" 30; *BSPC* 25 September 1812 Canning to Edmonstone; *Yule* "Mission" 250.

[3] Cæsar Frederick, Ralph Fitch (*Hakluyt* X. 125, 189); *Sangermano* 79.

[4] *Cox* 393.

pass the insalubrious jungles and pestilential marshes of Arakan, with rivers, arms of the sea and mountain torrents opposing their progress at every step. . . . The Shans earned with their blood the character of brave men. They fired with the steadiness of veteran troops. Two officers and thirty men of the 41st fell in a moment. . . The Burmese, with spear or musket couched, and their heads lowered to a butting position, blindly charged upon our bayonets; they neither gave nor expected quarter, but continued fighting with the utmost fury long after all hope of success or escape. . . . The gray-headed *sawbwas* of the Shans, in particular, showed a noble example to their men, sword in hand, singly maintaining the unequal conquest, they only sought the death which too many of them found." (Reports of 22 and 25 February 1824 from Col. Bowen to Brigade Major, Dacca, *Wilson* "Documents" 23-4; Mahabandula's march in August 1824, *Snodgrass* 75; action near Prome 1 December 1825, *Havelock* 269; actions near Rangoon 28 May 1824, near Prome 1 December 1825, *Snodgrass* 30, 234.)

About 1750 the Sonta sayadaw, a monk of Hsinbyugyun, Minbu district, compiled the Manu Ring *dhammathat* law-book,[1] which started the fashion of attributing the decisions of Kaingsa Manu (p. 195) to his namesake the ancient sage Manu; it was in Pali verse, and Tejosara in 1755 translated it into Burmese. At Alaungpaya's instance, his minister the soldier Mahasiri-uttamajaya compiled the Manu Kye *dhammathat;* it is not a code but a compilation of existing laws and customs, and of the rulings preserved in previous *dhammathats*, with little arrangement or attempt to explain contradictory passages; it attained an enormous vogue owing to its encyclopædic nature and to its being written in simple Burmese with little Pali. Alaungpaya had several court poets, such as Yanaungbala; and among the great office-bearers Letwethondara, who served at the siege of Pegu, had literary talent (p. 249).

In the cold weather 1758-9 Alaungpaya sent an expedition against the Gwes who were raiding the northern Shan states. He himself invaded Manipur in support of a pretender there. After the murder of Gharib Newaz 1714-54, the Manipur durbar had relapsed into a series of sanguinary plots, and one of the claimants took refuge with Alaungpaya, to whom he presented some princesses. Alaungpaya now proceeded up the Chindwin, devastating the villages of the Kathe (Manipur) Shans on the west bank; he crossed the hills by the Khumbat route, and entered the Manipur valley. The Manipuris say he

[1] *Forchhammer* "Jardine Prize" 92, 96.

was unspeakably cruel; but he was only doing unto them as they had done unto his people (p. 208). At Pulel in the Imole pass they gave him battle.[1] After a stubborn conflict they fled. He entered Imphal, the capital, only to find it empty, for the inhabitants lay hiding in the woods. He halted there for thirteen days, set up a stone inscription, took what loot there was, threw into the river two cannon of a cubit calibre as they were too heavy to move, and returned home, leaving garrisons in permanent stockades at Tamu and Thaungdut. In his capacity as a divine incarnation he promoted religion among the Kathe Shans on his line of march; in his capacity as a king he massacred more than four thousand of his Manipuri prisoners because they stubbornly refused to march away into captivity.[2]

These incursions, lasting down to 1819, ended by depopulating the country and stamping out Manipuri civilisation so completely that we can no longer tell what that civilisation was like.[3] The people were famous for their skill in handicraft, and the Burmese valued them highly, settling them in the capital, in the riverine villages of Sagaing district, and at Amarapura. They served as boatmen and silversmiths; as silkworkers they introduced the *acheik* pattern;[4] they gave the Burmese army its best cavalry (the Cassay Horse), and they supplied the bulk of the court astrologers, who at levees stood robed in white, intoning benedictions, as the king took his seat on the throne.

On arriving home Alaungpaya tried to dam the Mu, and built the Mahananda lake to supply Shwebo town with water. The Mu canals were not successful and the work decayed after his death. He suppressed a Talaing rebellion in Pegu, and seized Whitehill (p. 225) who with his ship had put into Rangoon, but released him on payment of a heavy ransom.

The East India Company had occupied Negrais (p. 213) since 1753 and Alaungpaya had ceded it to them in the treaty of 1757. But their resources were being strained to the uttermost with great events in India, and they withdrew 35

[1] *Pemberton* 40. [2] *Konbaungset* 303. [3] *Hodson* 4, 29, 58.

[4] *Parlett* 4. As late as 1780 the people of Lower Burma had no silk manufacture and contented themselves with cotton, *Sonnerat* (1782) II. 54.

Europeans and 70 Indians, practically the entire staff, in May 1759. In October they sent back a small staff to retain a lien on the island. The governor of Bassein, with Lavine, one of Bourno's men, who was in high favour, and sixty followers, met the new staff on arrival saying they had a letter from the king to show, and the senior Burmese officers messed with the English in the fort. A day later, 6 October 1759, at nine in the morning they were sitting down to breakfast together when the senior guest, the governor of Bassein, gave a sign and some of the 2,000 Burmans concealed in the woods rushed in, killed eight Englishmen and about a hundred Indians, turned the cannon of the fort on the two ships at anchor, and finally withdrew burning the settlement and taking with them all cannon, stores and four English. A midshipman and 64 Indians escaped on board. The ruins are still there.

What had happened was that the Armenians, some of whom held high office at court, were jealous of the English, who outbid them throughout the East. They represented to Alaungpaya that the English were fortifying their stations against him, supplying the Talaings with arms and spoiling his revenue by preventing other traders from coming up the Bassein river. Alaungpaya sent the governor of Rangoon, brother to his queen, to wipe out Negrais. But the governor returned saying there must be some mistake, he had found the English there to be innocuous. Alaungpaya therefore regarded him as a traitor, flogged all his men, sent a second party which actually did the work, and before letting him return to his high office flung him into irons and pegged him out in the sun for some days with three beams across his body so that a year later he was still suffering from the effects. The governor of Bassein subsequently admitted that the English had not intrigued with the Talaings, but had fed a few refugees, just as they fed Burmese refugees, and had made presents of four or five muskets which the Armenians represented to Alaungpaya as 500. The English had not prevented ships coming up the river, because they regarded Alaungpaya as too strong a raja to offend. Under the treaty he had expressly allowed them to erect fortifications.[1]

[1] See note "Negrais Massacre" p. 354.

After the fall of Pegu, envoys from Chiengmai visited Alaungpaya. He told them they must make complete submission. They looked at those blackened ruins and went home; and before long Martaban, Tavoy, Chiengmai, Anan and other states in north-west Siam, sent tribute.

Talaings had taken refuge in Siam; now as ever there were endemic slave raids on the border; and the Siamese had detained the captain of a Burma-owned ship which had been driven under stress of weather into their port of Tenasserim. But the real reason why Alaungpaya now invaded Siam was that he had to work off his energy; moreover, seeing that after his conquest of the Delta he reigned over nothing but ruins, he wished to populate his realm with prisoners obtained in Siam.[1] Early in 1760 he advanced through Martaban and Tavoy.[2] Capturing Tenasserim with the aid of some small ships managed by European captives, he went eastward over the hills to the shore of the Gulf of Siam, turned north, and captured the coast towns, Kuwi, Pran, Nawng Chik, Pechaburi. The Siamese army came out and delayed him still further although he drove them in. Approaching Ayuthia, he burnt some Dutch ships, massacred the defenceless population in crowds regardless of sex or age, and covered the surface of the rivers with their corpses.[3]

Under the walls of Ayuthia he released prominent prisoners with this letter to the king of Siam:—"His Burman Majesty comes as a divine incarnation to spread true religion in your country. Come forth with respect and present him with elephants and a daughter."[4] But the Siamese had among them Talaing refugees who knew the story of Pegu, and they relaxed no effort. Their feringhis and Mahomedans manned the war-boats with cannon in the maze of rivers round the city; the glacis and fords were strewn with caltraps; cannon frowned from the battlements, with thousands of resolute men behind.

[1] *Sonnerat* (1782) II. 41.

[2] Some of his troops must have gone down the Tenasserim river, for tradition says that 530 of his men, with their leader Letyapyanchi, perished in the Shanthondaung (Krantwowai) rapid a day's journey above the Tavoy-Mergui boundary. The name "Rapid of the Three Thousand Shans" is due to a Shan host having been similarly engulfed at some unknown period.

[3] *Samuel Smith* 108. [4] *Konbaungset* 315-8.

Alaungpaya had started much too late in the cold weather. The rains were at hand, when the whole country would be under several feet of water. Half his men were down with dysentery and he himself was far from well.[1] It looked as if the ever victorious army was not going to be victorious. He sent another message telling the Siamese king that he had no wish to dethrone him if only he would submit to religious reform. There was no reply, and Alaungpaya saw that the play was over; he did not hesitate, and within a week of arrival the hosts were in full retreat, abandoning forty guns of three-inch calibre.

He selected the friend of his boyhood, Minhkaungnawrahta, for the signal honour of commanding the rearguard. These were the pick of the army—500 Manipur horse and 6,000 foot, every man of whom had a musket. Minhkaungnawrahta spread them out and it was two days time before the Siamese realised that the main body had left; then they swept out upon him; his men watched the ring closing round them and, fearing to be cut off, begged him to let them fight further back; but he said "Friends, the safety of our Lord the King lies in our keeping. Let us not fight further back, lest the sound of the guns should break his sleep." When they could stand they stood, and when they had to run they ran; they were defeated but never broken, and they withdrew in good order, collecting Alaungpaya's stragglers on the way.

Meanwhile Alaungpaya had gone ahead by forced marches. Perhaps, as he lay in pain jolting along in his litter, he longed for the sights and sounds of home; but he was destined never to see them, for whether he knew it or not the hand of death was upon him. He reached Kinyua, Bilin township, Thaton district, and there at dawn he died.[2]

To his son Hsinbyushin and the other watchers by the bed, it was as if the sky had fallen, but they kept their heads. Heaven alone knew what would happen now; there might be civil war and a struggle for the throne; the men might break if they lost heart, for the Siamese were pressing the rearguard. They kept the death a close secret and sent their swiftest horse-

[1] *Dalrymple* I. 361. [2] 1122 Kahson lazok 12 = Sunday, 11 May 1760.

men to Shwebo so that the crown prince might be the first to know and secure his throne. The body, bound in sheets, was hidden in the curtained litter; and thus in death Alaungpaya still rode with his armies and the daily orders issued in his name.

At Rangoon his death was made public and his body, placed on a state barge, was taken up stream. At Kyaukmyaung landing stage in Shwebo district the whole court came out to meet it, and bore it solemnly in through the Hlaingtha Gate of Shwebo. So he was buried with the ritual[1] of the kings in the palace city which once had been his lowly village, amid the mourning of an entire people. They would never see his like again, the village headman who made himself lord of Burma and received the homage not only of the tribes, but also of French and English captains kneeling to receive his orders in respectful silence. His grave, with an inscription in misspelt English, perhaps by some Negrais captive, is near the Shwebo Deputy Commissioner's court-house; from its shortness you might think him a small man, but he was a fine tall man. The English captain[2] describes him as five feet eleven inches in height, coarse featured, dark complexioned, with a long face and nose, not without an air of majesty. He had reigned only eight years and was under forty-six when he died; but men are remembered by the years they use, not by the years they last.

NAUNGDAWGYI 1760-3. Alaungpaya was succeeded by his eldest son, the crown prince, Naungdawgyi. Kneeling by his father's death-bed, with the eyes of the great commanders upon him, the second son Hsinbyushin could not think unworthy thoughts, and had loyally joined in sending the news to his elder brother. But now that the body had departed, and he rode through the sunshine and fresh air, the Old Adam reasserted itself and he struck for the throne. It was a feeble

[1] Unnecessary stress has been laid on its being the rite for a *setyawade* (universal emperor), as if this had not been used for every nonentity on the throne of Ava for the preceding century.

[2] Captain Baker in *Dalrymple* I. 166-7.

effort, and he soon submitted and was forgiven at the queen mother's intercession.

But the king sent for two of the generals he disliked, and when they came unsuspectingly, he executed them without allowing them to see him. The army was furious. Minhkaungnawrahta, lingering with the rearguard, thought he also might be among the king's dislikes; and now, in the darkness that clouded his mind in the death of his great master, he revolted. Many of the troops who had not yet returned, joined him, for he was the idol of the army; and as nearly all the musketeers had been given him to form the rearguard, he had no difficulty in occupying Ava. Men said he had sent to a scion of the fallen Ava dynasty who was a refugee in Siam, offering to put him on the throne. He can hardly have dreamed of becoming king himself, with six sons born of Alaungpaya's loins against him. The king repeatedly sent monks and old comrades urging him to desist from his folly and offering a free pardon. But he refused them all, saying "What? Surrender with my dear ones that they may suffer the cruel mercies of the king? No, friends, leave me to my fate. I will die like a soldier, I will make these walls my coffin." So with his 12,000 men, the flower of the army, he was tightly besieged in Ava.

While thus besieging him the king stayed at Sagaing, where he granted audience to Captain Alves, the Company's envoy, in September 1760. The Company, fully occupied with winning an empire in India, had no desire for new commitments in Burma, such as the exaction of due amends for the Negrais massacre would involve. But it had to make at least a protest, and to ascertain whether trade relations were still possible. The king gave Alves audience, and having heard his demand for compensation,

> he said he was surprised to think how the Governor of Madras . . . could have the face to demand any satisfaction, which he would not give, for . . . he looked on all that were killed at Negrais, whether guilty or innocent, as born to die there . . . he would never give himself any trouble to enquire farther about the affair. His soldiers were not obliged to know who were guilty or who were not, neither did he expect they would enquire, but in such cases generally killed men, women or child as they pleased. "For instance" says he "As

> soon as ever they get into Ava, I have given them orders to spare nothing that has life, and to burn 'kill and destroy everything in it, though I know that . . . the general and the soldiers are to blame. . . ." I then asked him what crimes the governors of Negrais had committed for which the king his father had been so much offended? He said that Captain Hope, while chief at Negrais, had supplied the Peguers . . . with arms, ammunition, and provisions . . . I answered, if that could be brought to proof, the laws of England would punish him with death if his father had left his punishment to the English. I then asked him what crime the new governor, that arrived the day before, or any of his people, had done, for there was no difference in their punishment. He said "He was born to die there" and laughed "For I suppose you have seen that in this country in the wet season there grows so much long useless grass and weeds in the fields that in the dry season we are forced to burn them to clear the ground. Sometimes it so happens there is some useful herbs among these weeds and grass which, as they cannot be distinguished easily, are burned along with them. So it happened to be the new governor's lot." (Alves' report, *Dalrymple* I. 373.)

Perhaps Alves did not remember many a terrible passage in his own Old Testament scriptures, showing that collective execution is the normal rule in the tribal stage; even good and great men could not see its iniquity until they had developed beyond that stage. The king was no harder on the English than on his own people; having executed justice, he was well disposed towards them and asked them to return although he treated the 1757 treaty as if it did not exist. To Alves, this was a shocking breach of faith, signifying a double dose of original sin; but it was really only unbusinesslike, and signified the inevitable clash between a developed civilisation and a backward community. Having had no international transactions, the Burmese were not acquainted with the nature of treaties.

The king released the half dozen English captives, mostly survivors of the massacre, gave full liberty to trade, and was willing to grant sites anywhere in return for arms and ammunition, and he desired a male and female camel, and a horse and mare each four cubits high, as he wished to breed. But trade was no longer to be duty free, as under the 1757 treaty, and he made one proviso: the headquarters must no longer be at Negrais. Alaungpaya himself had said he would rather they were at Bassein, and the reason the king now gave was that he could not protect Negrais against the French; the real reason was, he had no control over so remote a spot, and wished the English to be on the mainland where he could control them. Although he twitted Alves with being a spy, he was graciously disposed towards him when he came, like every one else, to bring a present and offer congratulations at the Thadingyut festival, and in return he offered him anything he liked for himself; would he like an elephant? There was no love lost between the English and the Dutch, but Alves asked for the release of three Dutch captives, survivors of a station of thirteen whom Alaungpaya had wiped out in Siam; the king said orders to this effect would be drafted at once. When Alves had arrived, the ministers and princes pounced on him, looting his kit and preventing all business until he had paid eight of them a tip of Rs. 300 each; he said he would complain to the king, but was told that the king would laugh, and this was the recognised way in which ministers lived, for they had no salaries. One of the ministers mistranslated the despatches to his own end, and the fraud succeeded until the difference between the two versions slipped out during one of Alves' conversations with the king, who was furious but passed the matter over as he was none too sure of his throne and feared that his officers might desert to Minhkaungnawrahta. The people were sick of perpetual war, and on his way up the river Alves had noticed that the villagers longed for a change, and seemed pleased whenever one of the assaults on Ava failed. Down the river he saw a village in flames, as various high officials were marauding over the country for their own benefit. He was glad to get away from it all to a cleaner atmosphere. He brought back no treaty, but he brought a letter from the king granting the terms promised in the interviews. The English could not return to Negrais, as it was not permitted; they would not go to Bassein, for it was seventy miles from the sea, their base; henceforward they concentrated on Rangoon.

Minhkaungnawrahta had no cannon but the king could not take Ava save by starvation, for light irregulars can do nothing by storm against a fortified town. None the less, as was their wont, they tried to storm it and wasted many lives, among them Lavine the Frenchman who had aided in the Negrais massacre and was now killed leading the stormers. Alves saw some of the poor wretches who had been terribly scalded by the boiling liquids poured down on them when they tried to scale the walls.

At length, his men starving, Minhkaungnawrahta broke out with a band of devoted followers and fled west. More than once the pursuers surrounded him but fell back in awe when he strode through them. In the Shan woodland above Kyaukse, half starving, he was brought down by a musket shot; even then he overpowered the assailant who grappled with him, and had to be finished off with a second shot. Such was the end of Alaungpaya's brother in arms.[1] When the head was laid at his feet, the king mourned, saying "Should ye have slain so great a man?" Like others of his line, Naungdawgyi was doubtless in the habit of uttering the most sublime platitudes—the chronicles are full of it—and he might have acted accordingly; but, on the other hand, he might not. An experienced officer, Minhkaungnawrahta knew what the word of a king was worth in the Golden Palace.

The king's uncle, governor of Toungoo, revolted, was besieged, made submission, and was forgiven in 1762. During the siege Talaban, the great Talaing refugee (p. 233), raided Martaban. An expedition reduced Chiengmai to submission, capturing fugitive Talaing princes and a scion of the fallen Ava house. Talaban had for years maintained himself in the famous caves at Kawgun, Thaton district, and his family were now captured there. Knowing well what their fate would be, he gave himself up and, when brought before the king, claimed their lives in return for his own; struck by his chivalry, the king released them all and took Talaban into his service.[2]

Naungdawgyi's principal poet was Seindakyawthu 1736-71, a skilful rimester, nephew to the Twinthintaikwun (p. 268). He was a native of Maungdaung village in Alon, Monyua district, and in his teens had served under Toungooyaza (p. 216). He wrote poems on weddings in the royal family, etc., and on the invasion of Siam describing how all the kings of the earth bow down before Alaungpaya; but his chief works are the Kawiletkanathatpon and Awwadatupyo.[3]

[1] *Konbaungset* 324-40.

[2] *Konbaungset* 350, *Symes* 38. For the Kawgun caves, see *IA* 1892 Taw Sein Ko "Notes on an archeological tour through Ramannadesa" and 1893 Temple "Notes on antiquities in Ramannadesa."

[3] *JBRS* 1918 Ba Han "Seindakyawthu: man and poet."

The king died while engaged on works of merit. He built two pagodas on the Mahananda lake near Shwebo, and sent offerings to Shwesettaw in Minbu district. He was aged twenty-nine, left seven children, was succeeded by his brother.

HSINBYUSHIN 1763-76 himself raided Manipur in December 1764, carrying away its people into captivity, for he wished to increase the population of the new capital, Ava, into which he moved in April 1765. The gates of restored Ava were named after conquered states, some of them being —on the east side, Chiengmai, Martaban, Mogaung; on the south, Kaingma, Hanthawaddy, Myede, Onbaung (Hsipaw); on the west, Gandalarit, Sandapuri (Viengchang, Linzin), Kenghung; on the north, Tenasserim, Yodaya (Siam). The various wards were, according to precedent, allotted on racial lines; thus the Indian traders lived in one, the Chinese in another, Christians in another, and in others were the Siamese and Manipur captives; such captives were often a source of suspicion, as in 1774 when the leading families of the Manipur colony were extirpated for alleged plotting. The wall, sixteen feet high, backed by earthwork, was of indifferent quality, but adequate to the only style of warfare it would have to meet. As was usual in Burmese capitals, the palace was an inner city, with its own moat, wall, and a massive teak stockade outside.[1]

The transfer to Ava was a wise step so far as it went, for it placed the king in direct communication along the Myitnge river with the Kyaukse granary, and it was on the great river, whereas Shwebo was landlocked. But the step did not go far enough. From the day that Vasco da Gama opened the sea route in 1498, the centre of gravity had shifted to the Delta. The kings from Bayinnaung 1551-81 to Anaukpetlun 1605-28 acted as if they realised this, making Pegu their headquarters. But none of their successors realised it, and their failure to do so sealed the fate of the monarchy. Rangoon might have let a little fresh air from the outer world into the court. To

[1] *Konbaungset* 377, *Crawfurd* II. 1, *JBRS* 1915 Enriquez "Capitals of the Alaungpaya dynasty."

the Burmese, the Delta was a foreign country, and they did not feel safe among the Talaings. Hence there was some excuse for the earlier kings. But there was none for the Alaungpaya dynasty, which exterminated the Talaings; the remnant continued to rebel for some time, but these rebellions were crushed with ease, and need not have occurred had the kings, instead of wasting their energy on wars in Siam and Assam, used half of it in giving the Delta a good administration. As they would not move to the Delta, the atmosphere of their palace was that of the Upper Burma villages among which it lay. Their ideas remained in the nineteenth century what they had been in the ninth. To build pagodas, to collect daughters from tributary chiefs, to sally forth on slave raids, to make wars for white elephants—these conceptions had had their day, and a monarchy which failed to get beyond them was doomed. It is probably more than coincidence that Siam, which had its capital in a seaport, developed a more enlightened government than the Burmese kingship, and is independent to-day.

The king sent to Benares for Brahmans. Nine came, and they were frequently consulted on matters of state. With their help the Maungdaung *sayadaw* translated into Burmese numerous Sanskrit works on grammar, medicine, astrology, erotic lore, etc., known as the Vyakarana.[1] In 1771 an official, Manu Wannana Kyawhtin, compiled the Manusarashwemin *dhammathat* based on older law-books; also, with the aid of Taungdwin *sayadaw* and other learned monks he compiled the Manu Vannana law-book in Pali and Burmese stanzas, the monks helping him to polish the Pali. The king had a concubine, Ma Htwe, who was a poetess, and he himself took an interest in letters; Letwethondara (pp. 238, 269), a secretary to the Hluttaw Council, whom he had exiled to Meza hill, Katha district, in 1763, earned his recall two months later by writing the well-known Mezataungche poem bewailing his grief and loneliness. The third verse describes the Nyaung-ye festival he saw in exile among the wooded hills:—

> At the Nyaung-ye festival
> Meza people, all devout,
> Duly fall in prayer and pour
> Water to the banyan-tree.

[1] *Forchammer* "Jardine Prize" 104.

From the valley, see, the shrine
Rises even to the sky.
Meza! thy pagoda old
Of the Golden Cave is there,
Fair to look on evermore.
Dimly glimmering o'er the mount,
Dusky floor to shadowy head,
Steady hang night's vapours yet;
Soon, as a billowing net, are stirred,
Surging fretful as a flood,
Huddle upward, tower, and crowd;
Then in cloudy streamers free
Stretched across the sea of dawn,
Darkling wreathe the heights around
Lost and drowned. The ravelled mist,
Shredded now by twisting winds,
Patters—listen!—to the ground;
Drip—drop—the sound is loud
Like the rounded clear refrain
Of the rain, though none there be.
See! the chariot of the sun
Peeps o'er Mount Yugandhara,
Stooping under vapours wan.
Numbed, the noon I fondly wait,
Counting on my fingers chill
Hours and minutes, till the rays
Spreading fill the world with warmth.

The main armies spent 1764-7 against Siam. The Burmese claim rested on Bayinnaung's conquest in 1564. It was a false claim, for they had never administered the country. Bayinnaung had merely held it to tribute for twenty years, and the claim had lapsed ever since. Starting from Kengtung with 20,000 men, mostly Shans, Thihapate slowly fought his way down from Chiengmai through Viengchang (Linzin), while another army of the same size under Mahanawrahta fought its way south-east from Tavoy to Pechaburi. The Tavoy people had revolted, massacring all Burmans and making overtures to Siam; they now had bitter cause to repent.

To delay Mahanawrahta, the Siamese pressed an English merchant ship into their service; her broadsides did great execution in the Burmese stockades near Nontaburi, thirty miles from the mouth of the Menam; but as soon as she could, she flung off the Siamese and returned to sea. Thihapate had to storm town after town, and found the villages stockaded against him. When roused, the men fought with spirit, vying among themselves as to who should first mount the wall. They died like flies from preventible disease, and suffered ghastly wounds for which they got no thanks from the king, as the loss of a limb, even in honourable service, disqualified a man from entering the palace: His Majesty's sight must not be sullied by reality.[1] They kept the field all the year round, a rare thing for Burmese levies, spending the rains in the towns they had won. At Chiengmai they had to resort to mining, with movable shelters under the wall; finally they captured part of the wall with its guns and turned them all night down into the terror-stricken population who sent their monks to surrender in the morning. The prettiest girls and choicest loot were sent to the king at Ava.

Gradually they swept over the whole country, burning the towns and making the chiefs drink the water of allegiance. Such of the population as had not stampeded eastwards ran a risk of having to contribute to the heads which the Burmese hacked off and piled up in great heaps under the walls of the towns they besieged, in order to terrify the defenders.[2] They were sometimes besieged themselves, for the Ayuthia armies came out and pressed them hard, striving to prevent their effecting a junction.

But finally the two commanders joined hands under the walls of Ayuthia. Mahanawrahta fixed his headquarters there at a pagoda built by Bayinnaung. In spite of wastage their hosts were as numerous as ever, as they had exacted contingents from the states which they had conquered, and according to Burmese custom their prisoners were made to fight for them. They were to spend fourteen months before Ayuthia. The rains came and flooded them out: they stood their ground. Their commanders died of hardship: they did not lose heart. Imperial armies from China invaded Upper Burma: they were not recalled. During the first open season they could not get near the walls because of the numerous stockades outside the city. Sometimes the whole plain was alive with swarms of Siamese working under the supervision of grandees who were carried about in sedan chairs. Both sides used bamboo matting

[1] *Crawfurd* I. 439. [2] *Konbaungset* 381.

between two uprights containing earth for temporary defence while they constructed permanent works. The Siamese had foreign adventurers fighting for them, one of their outworks containing four hundred Chinamen. When the rains began to lay the whole country several feet under water, the commanders urged Mahanawrahta to withdraw but he refused and Thihapate supported him. The men stayed on knolls of rising ground or built dykes to keep out the water. The Siamese seeing them scattered in isolated groups attacked them in boats. In one of these attacks a Siamese leader while waving his sword and hurling defiance in the bows of his boat, was brought down by a musket shot and fell into the water, and the whole flotilla fled. Ayuthia prided itself on its great guns, some of them thirty feet long with a 30 *viss* (100 lb.) ball. One of these burst with an overcharge but the shot killed several men on two Burmese boats. The Burmese had war-boats in plenty, constructed by their lieges up the rivers, and so they were able to prevent provisions entering the city. When the dry season returned they reconstructed their earthworks. Some of these were higher than the walls, and the cannon were also mounted aloft on pagodas so as to fire down into the palace. Often the palace guns ceased fire because the king yielded to the entreaties of his harem who were terrified at the noise.[1] The city starved. Shan states tributary to Siam sent an army which came down from the north and tried to raise the siege; they were swept away. The king and princes tried to cut their way out and escape; they were driven back. They asked what they had done to merit these horrors and were curtly told they were rebels and traitors and deserved all they were going to get. The commander-in-chief Mahanawrahta died, and by royal decree was buried with extraordinary honours; he deserved them. Thihapate had to finish the siege alone. The end was now near. In the palace chapels, where women knelt in prayer throughout the night, the holy images were seen to weep. At four in the afternoon, 28 March 1767, the French guns opened for the last time. The wall had been mined; by sunset the breach was practicable and the stormers effected an entry. The slaughter was indiscriminate. The king's body was identified next day near the west gate by his

[1] Siamese palace tradition.

brother whom the Burmese found in chains and released.[1] The houses, the monasteries, the temples, the great palace itself, went up in flame; the walls were razed to the ground; the city was never restored as a capital. The princes, the harem, the clergy, foreigners including a French Catholic bishop,[2] and thousands of the population were carried away into captivity, so that many a private could boast of four slaves. Such of the guns as were too big to move were burst or thrown into the rivers.[3] There was gold, silver and jewels in abundance, for the royal treasure was immense. This is the secret of these continual Burmese attacks on Ayuthia: it was at once a thriving seaport and a king's palace, one of the wealthiest cities in Indo-China, so that its treasures were a standing temptation to the Burmese hordes.

The Lao and Shan levies were allowed to return home, probably because the long absence was rendering them unreliable and many of them were prisoners serving under compulsion. But there was no rest for the weary Burmans. If Ayuthia had not fallen when it did, the siege would have had to be abandoned, as royal despatches now came urgently recalling the armies to take their place in the line against the Chinese whose attacks on Ava looked like breaking through; for the years 1765-9 saw a series of murderous Chinese invasions.[4]

Some of the *sawbwas* on the Yünnan border now ceased paying tribute to Burma, which therefore marched against them; one fled to Yünnan, and the Kengtung *sawbwa* made a foray there at the instigation of the Gwe (p. 222) in the course of their wanderings. Moreover the Chinese were dissatisfied with the treatment their merchants received in Burma. At Bhamo a Chinese caravaneer, angry at delay in getting sanction to build a bridge, insulted the Burmese governor who therefore arrested him; and when released he found that the Burmese officers had looted his caravan. At Kengtung a Chinaman was killed in a dispute

[1] *Konbaungset* 417.

[2] He was called Brigot and arrived opportunely in Burma as Percoto, the bishop elect there, was looking for a consecrator. Subsequently the Burmese let Brigot return, *Bigandet* 19-21. See also note "List of Captives" p. 321.

[3] Four of the light guns taken here are now in the Madras Museum, with Burmese inscriptions recording the date and hour of their capture, *RSASB* 1917. 21.

[4] See note "Chinese War 1765-9" p. 355.

about payment; the Burmese resident offered blood-money and even talked of executing the slayer, but would not hand him over, and the Chinese would take nothing less. Such instances were trivial and could have been adjusted had the two governments been in communication with each other; but they had no embassy system.

The Chinese invaded Burma in great strength with the active or passive co-operation of Hsenwi, Bhamo, Mogaung and Kengtung. The fighting was in the triangle Mogaung, Kenghung on the Mekong river, and down the Myitnge valley to within three marches of Ava. The Chinese had bases at Bhamo and Lashio and their line of advance was usually down the Shweli and Myitnge valleys. But the principal theatre was in Bhamo district where Balamindin won fame by his great defence of Kaungton, twelve miles to the east of which, at Shwenyaungbin, the Chinese also had a gigantic stockade, "as big as a city."

The Burmese had better war-canoes than the Chinese, they received invaluable help from their captive French gunners, and they won most of the dozen major actions which were spread over four campaigns; but the suspense was terrible; as soon as one Chinese army was driven back, another come on in greater numbers than ever. The earth quaked, rending the national shrines; to placate the unseen powers, the king flung thousands of gold and silver images into the Shwezigon at Pagan and the Shwedagon.

The Chinese proved useless as soldiers, but the Manchu contingents were good troops who with ladders, axes, hooks and ropes, would rush up to the stockades against a withering fire, while boiling lead poured down on them and their bodies were crushed by great beams[1] of which the lashings were cut as soon as the stormers were underneath. The Chinese ought to have won, although their casualties from disease were heavy; but whereas the Burmese commanders worked together hand in hand, the Chinese lacked co-ordination, and threw away the advantage of superior numbers by allowing themselves to be overwhelmed

[1] This was so all over Indo-China. The Assamese prided themselves on their stockades and the Siamese boasted that when their stormers were sufficiently numerous they could receive the falling beams on their spears and toss them off; but the beams were often whole teak trees, see *Samuel Smith* 36, *Snodgrass* 66. Until superseded by the stone keep, the stockade was normal in Europe—the Bayeux tapestry shews the Normans erecting one at Hastings.

in detail. The best of their generals, Mingjui, son-in-law to the Emperor, who had won distinction in Turkestan, fought his way from Lashio, smashing a Burmese army and driving it past the Gokteik gorge to Singaung, three marches from Ava. The court in panic urged the king to flee but he scornfully refused saying he and his brother princes, the sons of Alaungpaya, would face the Chinese single handed if necessary. Mingjui's colleagues failed to support him, Burmese armies in his rear cut off his supplies, his men were starving, and he had to retreat, beset by overwhelming odds. The slaughter was such that the Burmese could hardly grip their swords as the hilts were slippery with enemy blood. Mingjui fought in the rearguard till he saw his men were safe and then, obeying the tradition of the Manchu officer corps, he cut off his plaited hair, sent it as a token to his Emperor, and hanged himself on a tree; his servant hid his body with leaves lest the Burmese should desecrate it according to their wont. The following is from Chinese records:—

> The Burmese had a device of pretending to negotiate and then suddenly appearing with a new army. . . . They had no regular army; in times of danger Shan levies were called out. There was however at Ava a standing force of 10,000 men called the "Invincibles." In actual fighting the Shan levies were placed in front and the "Invincibles" occupied the rear. Cavalry were posted on either flank to close in upon the enemy. If victory appeared doubtful the army rapidly entrenched itself under cover of a heavy fire from artillery and small arms. When the smoke cleared away the stockade was complete, and the men inside were ready to defend it. These were the invariable tactics of the Burmese. . . .
>
> When Mingjui began his retreat from Burma the enemy's ranks were continually reinforced from all sides, whereas he had no supports or reserve. They could procure supplies anywhere, whereas we had no system of supply. They had cannon mounted on elephants, while we had only small arms and these decreased from day to day. In action the noise of their cannon and musketry was as ten myriad fireworks exploding at once, rendering speech inaudible. . . . Mingjui each morning rose early and directed the operations in person with the fighting and retreating columns alternately. He often came into camp at nightfall not having drunk a drop of water all day. Grain had long been finished, and sliced beef was the only provision; of this he took his share with men in the ranks. He looked kindly to the wants of his commanders who suffered much from exhaustion, hunger and wounds; and he refused to abandon his sick and wounded men, ordering them to be carried by the local

levies. Thus it was that no man, however much he suffered, had a word of blame for the General.

Mingjui died, not because he could not have saved himself, but because he was returning without having carried out the instructions of his master. It is true that the Emperor had ordered the return of the force, but these orders never reached Mingjui. Encompassed daily with growing difficulties he would say to his officers "The enemy are aware that we are in extremity, but for the sake of our country we must fight on, that they may know that its orders are clear and irrevocable and that its servants fulfil them to the death. No reinforcements are coming but we must do our utmost, that the enemy may be impressed by our determination and that the work may be rendered easier for those who come after us." This was a far-sighted patriotic resolve, not the decision of a desperate man. . . . The people of Yünnan and the troops who had accompanied him never spoke of Mingjui without tears, for his hold upon their affections was not less than that of famous commanders of olden time. His death was unfortunate too for another reason, because the events which immediately followed the battle in which he fell could not be properly reported to the Emperor or made known to the people at large. . . .

Kaungton was on the Irrawaddy and the enemy held both banks of the river. We took up a position close to their eastern camp, which they had built on an eminence, their lines reaching to the river. It was 2 *li* [1 *li* = 631 yards] in circuit, constructed of large trees deeply sunk in the ground; outside were three trenches, and beyond was a stockade of trees laid horizontally, their branches being pointed and directed outwards. This was the usual clever contrivance of the Burmese when defending important positions. Our first step was to raise a mound from which we cannonaded the fort. This was unsuccessful, for the breaches made in the timber were promptly repaired by the Burmese and the stockade remained intact. Next we tried with long thongs of raw hide to pull down the posts of the stockade, but the thongs broke. A similar attempt was then made by night with canes several hundred yards long which we procured in the jungle. Two or three thousand men took part in this attack which however did not succeed, as the enemy cut the canes with their *dahs*. Fuhêng then ordered the stockade to be burnt. A large body of our men with torches advanced under cover of shields specially constructed to ward off fire from the fort. The three trenches were crossed and the leading party reached the stockade, when a river fog rose at 2 a.m. and lasted till 8 a.m. This so damped the wood that it could not be ignited, and the wind also being in the wrong direction the attempt was abandoned. Finally, mines were laid and and exploded; part of the stockade was lifted bodily by the shock and the enemy were thrown into the greatest alarm, but the posts still remained upright. This happened three times, and the explanation was that the stockade being built on rising ground our excavations were too level and our mines were exploded at too great a depth below the surface. (*Warry.*)

The Chinese never succeeded in taking the Kaungton stockade, and at length in the fourth year, 1769, after losing, from first to last, 20,000 men and a quantity of arms and ammunition which went to equip fresh Burmese levies, they were themselves driven out of their great stockade at Shwenyaungbin and their generals asked for terms. The Burmese staff were averse to granting terms, saying that the Chinese were surrounded like cattle in a pen, they were starving and in a few days they could be wiped out to a man. Luckily Mahathihathura, the commander-in-chief, saw that the loss of a few armies would merely stiffen the resolution of the Chinese government. He sent back the messenger with a conciliatory reply. At Kaungton, in a seven-roofed hut, fourteen Burmese and thirteen Chinese officers drew up a written agreement whereby the Chinese were allowed to withdraw, trade was to be restored, and, to prevent misunderstanding, decennial missions were to pass between the two sovereigns. The Chinese burnt their boats and melted down their cannon; and then, while the Burmese stood to arms and looked down, their columns marched sullenly away up the Taping valley, to perish by thousands of hunger in the passes.

When he heard that the Chinese had been allowed to depart, the king was angry; he thought they should all have been killed. So the armies, afraid to return home, went off to Manipur in January 1770. Under a good raja, Manipur was recovering from the last devastation, and the commanders scented a fresh harvest of slaves and cattle with which to appease the king.[1] The men of Manipur fought gallantly but were overwhelmed in a three days' battle near Langthabal. The raja fled to Assam. The Burmese raised their own nominee to the throne and returned, taking with them such of the population as were not hiding in the woods. The king's anger had subsided, and as after all they had won victories and preserved his throne, he was merciful; he sent Mahathihathura a woman's dress to wear, and exiled him and the commanders to the Shan states; he would not allow them to see him, and he also exiled the ministers who dared to speak on their behalf. Their wives, including the sister of his queen, were exposed in the sun at the western gate of the palace, with

[1] *Pemberton* 43.

the Chinese presents of silk on their heads, a public mock for three days.

By granting honourable terms the Burmese gave the Chinese Emperor a loophole to withdraw from a costly adventure; and although pride prevented him from acknowledging the treaty, his silence gave consent, and soon the caravans of 400 oxen or 2,000 ponies started coming down from Yünnan as of old, and the Burmese were once more able to find a market for their cotton.[1] Burma remained in possession of Koshanpye, the nine Shan towns above Bhamo. The Chinese prisoners taken in the war, numbering 2,500, were settled in the capital as gardeners and craftsmen, and were given Burmese wives. But the material was as nothing to the moral gain. Their other victories were over states on their own level such as Siam; this was won over an empire. Alaungpaya's crusade against the Talaings was stained with treachery: the great siege of Ayuthia 1766-7 was a magnificent dacoity; but in the Chinese war the Burmese were waging a righteous war of defence against the invader.

The victory, coming as it did on top of a generation of continuous warfare which might well have exhausted the race, shows that the exploits of Alaungpaya were no mere flash in the pan but were broad-based on the energy of the race as a whole. His tradition was not only maintained, it was eclipsed. The chronicles for the period are verbose and pompous, but it is impossible to read them without being struck with their fierce pride. The Burmese knew that to the north lay a big country called China; to the east, Shans of various sorts, some of whom had a kingdom called Siam; to the west, a place called India and, further west still, a country of white people, which some people said was an island. All these countries, except China, were uncivilised and not worth studying. The white people called themselves various

[1] For Koshanpye, see note "Pong and Koshanpye" p. 322.

The imports from China were silks and raw silk, velvet for state robes, Chinese-Shan tea, gold, hams, copper, steel, liquor, mercury for vermilion lacquer, and large quantities of needles and thread. The exports to China were cotton above all, edible birds' nests, salt, ivory, horn, amber and a little lacquer ware and precious stones (the mines, so far as they were worked, were worked by Chinese lessees). The total trade was, see p. 359, inconsiderable. See *Wayland* I. 132, *Crawfurd* II. appendix, *Parker* "Précis."

names such as Portuguese, Dutch, French, and English, but they were all much the same just as the various Shans were much the same; and in any case they were not a numerous race and were usually crushed with ease. The Indians were more important but even they could not count for much, judging by the way the Manipuris had been wiped out. The Siamese and Chinese, on the other hand, were really great powers, but they had been defeated. Thus the whole world was accounted for; and the Burmese felt equal to anything. They had some justification for their pride. They had no commissariat, and on the march they perished of under-feeding and disease. They were the ordinary little people you can see in any village to-day, led by their *myothugyis*, who ranked as lords. Yet their spirit carried their bare feet from Bhamo to Bangkok, they fought and died by hundreds and thousands, leaving their bones to bleach from Junkceylon to the banks of the Brahmaputra. They had bought those lands with their blood. Doubtless it was a small world, but it was the only world they knew, and the Burmese minister could say with truth to his English suitor "You do not realise. We have never yet met the race that can withstand us."[1]

In 1773 the Talaing levies who had been mustered against Siam mutinied. The Burmese commanders and guards had to run for their lives, first to Martaban and then to Rangoon. The mutineers failed to take the Rangoon stockade but fired the town and burnt several foreign ships which were building on the stocks. They treated foreigners decently, but some French shipmasters who were in port would have nothing to do with them and lay in hiding with their wives; one of the wives was granddaughter to Phaulkon (p. 203), another was a bride fresh from Pondicherry. A week later the Burmese brought up reinforcements, used a Dutch ship and retook the town with the aid of her gunfire; they then robbed her of all guns and munitions and sent her to sea where she foundered a few days later. The mutineers made off, collected their families, and migrated to Siam, three thousand in number. But the general population could not flee, and from them the Burmese exacted vengeance, massacring both sexes. They dragged the French from hiding, distributed the wives among

[1] *Gouger* 104.

the officers, selling one of them for Rs. 400,[1] and made them look on while their husbands were bound hand and foot and thrown into the river. One, a man of great strength, burst his bonds and swam ashore. When he reappeared as if from the dead, the Burmese regarded him as supernatural and did him no more harm.[2]

In 1774 the king made a royal progress down the river to Rangoon in splendid barges with the queens, the court, and the captive Talaing princes in his train, holding high festival at every halt and worshipping at the pagodas on the way, especially the Shwezigon at Pagan and the Shwehsandaw at Prome. His camp at Prome was on a sandbank by the mouth of the Nawin stream, and when returning he placed a new spire on the pagoda which crowns the Po-u-daung hill near Prome.[3] He came to Rangoon to impress the Talaings in two ways. Firstly, he raised the Shwedagon pagoda to its present height, 327 feet (p. 117), gilding it with his own weight[4] in gold and erecting a golden spire studded with gems to replace the one thrown down during the 1769 earthquake (p. 254); secondly he executed the captive king of Pegu with his brother the crown prince, and son. They had been prisoners seventeen years without opportunity of doing harm, but considerations such as the recent mutiny sealed their fate.

The king's prayers were for victory on his arms. The situation in Siam was serious. His supremacy there began to collapse almost before the ruins of Ayuthia had ceased to smoulder. When the Burmese hosts were sweeping down upon Ayuthia in 1765, there was a governor of a northern province who would not drink the water of allegiance. He was the son of a Chinese father and a Siamese mother and his name was Paya Tak.[5] He collected a few hundred determined men like himself and withdrew to the hills. The Burmese tried to dislodge him but he flung them back each time. He went east and gained Cambodia, vastly increasing his resources. The men of Siam,

[1] An enormous price, as a Siamese girl slave cost only Rs. 5, *Crawfurd* I. 424.

[2] *Sonnerat* (1806) III. 64-5, *TP* 1891 Cordier "Les Français en Birmanie" 31-2, *Konbaungset* 504.

[3] *IA* 1893 Taw Sein Ko "Preliminary study of the Po-u-daung inscription."

[4] Twelve stone three. See note "Tuladana" p. 328.

[5] *Pallegoix* II. 94-8.

sick of oppression, rose and called on him to lead them, for their lawful princes were in captivity. In 1768 he wiped out several Burmese garrisons, reoccupied Ayuthia, and founded the present capital, Bangkok. He was now king but his palace never saw him, as he lived in the field. The Burmese sent expeditions. He harried them in ambushes, cut them off, starved them out. He and his people were united in a just cause. Whether the Burmese could in any case have held Siam for long is doubtful, but whatever chances they had were ruined by the disunion which now became the curse of their armies in the field: the spoilers fell out over their prey. Captains like Mahathihathura, the hero of the Chinese war, and Thihapate, the conqueror of Ayuthia, continued to win occasional victories, but they could achieve nothing permanent in the face of rampant insubordination. If a commander disapproved the plan of campaign, he showed his disapproval by simply withdrawing his levies and marching off elsewhere. Some of them were executed; but the harm had been done. By 1775 the Burmese had been driven across the frontier, and even in Chiengmai they were ill at ease, when the king died; he was aged thirty-nine, left forty-one children, and was succeeded by his twenty-year-old son.

SINGU 1776-82 at once finished the Siamese escapade by withdrawing the armies. His only wars were in Manipur. The rightful raja who fled from the Burmese in 1770 made four attempts to oust their nominee between 1775 and 1782; his base was in Cachar and they drove him back each time but after 1782 left him in possession, perhaps because the country was now so thoroughly devastated that nothing more could be wrung out of it.[1] In the first two years, for which Singu was not responsible, the army was absent continuously, losing 20,000 men, partly by fever, and gaining barren victories in Cachar and Jaintia. These states had to present daughters and pay tribute of a tree with the earth still clinging to its roots in token that the king had seizin of the land, and

[1] *Pemberton* 43.

henceforth he claimed these countries.[1] His suzerainty was only nominal.

The people liked Singu because he stopped these everlasting wars, which made everyone miserable and led to migrations. Thus, the Yaw folk fled from their original home to the remote Mu valley in Katha district in order to get out of the king's reach.[2] If a town was depopulated by rebellion or by the wastage of its levy during foreign service, a few hundred households would be transferred to it from another charge, sometimes a week's journey distant, whether they wanted to go or not.[3]

The people did not know that Singu was seldom sober; all they knew was that he left them alone, and they were deeply grateful. He built many pagodas, for he spent much of his time in prayer; he was an angler too, and had an eye for scenery, to judge from some of his favourite haunts, where the gleam of a golden spire is reflected in the green depths of the stream below. His chief queen had a talent for verse, and the tutor of his youth was the poet Nga Hpyaw, author of *Paleiksa-egyin*, who now received the title Minyeyaza. Sleep, prayer, fishing, the laughter of the palace ladies in some sequestered woodland—it was all very pleasant, far pleasanter than the hard life of the soldier in foreign fields.

Of course there were the occasional cares of office. He executed his younger brother, his uncle the Amyin prince, fourth son of Alaungpaya, and with them several ministers with their dependants in the usual way, for alleged treason. Some princesses, his sisters, died in like manner, especially when he was angry as well as drunk. He deposed his queen, and sent her back to her father Mahathihathura who, on arriving from Siam, was deprived of all his offices; later he drowned her too.

Had he been a man of ordinary character, such acts would doubtless have been accepted as being in accordance with custom. But the court could not respect a man who was often unconscious for hours and was surrounded by ministers and swordbearers most of whom followed his example.[4] His habit of making pilgrimages with only a small court, leaving the

[1] *Symes* 80. [2] *Clayton* 9. [3] *Dalrymple* I. 390.
[4] *Konbaungset* 530. See note "Drink" p. 314.

palace vacant for weeks at a time, and returning in slipshod fashion at any hour of night, gave conspirators their opportunity. While he was absent at Thihadaw pagoda on the Irrawaddy island in Shwebo district, a party came to the palace at midnight. With them was a puppet of eighteen, Maung Maung, lord of Paungga in Sagaing district, dressed up so as to resemble the king his cousin. The Guard passed them in, thinking it was the king; some, who realised their mistake and resisted, were cut down. When day broke, part of the Guard continued to resist and having cannon held their own until their Armenian captain was speared, whereupon they fled. Mahathihathura returned from retirement and took command of the Guard in Maung Maung's behalf.

When the news reached king Singu, his followers fled and he thought of taking refuge in Manipur but his mother, the queen dowager, indignantly insisted on his playing the man. He went alone at dawn to the palace gate, and when challenged by the Guard answered "It is I, Singu, lawful lord of the palace." They fell back respectfully, and he entered the courtyard. There he saw a minister, father to one of the queens he had murdered. He made for him exclaiming "Traitor, I am come to take possession of my right." The minister seized a sword and cut him down.[1] At least he died royally.

Maung Maung was miserable. He had spent most of his life in a monastery, and now that he was put in possession of the palace, he tried to induce his seniors to take the crown, recalling them from the villages in which they had been made to live for the sake of his predecessor's safety.[2] He gave them precedence and pressed them each in turn to relieve him of the kingship. They all suspected some deep device, and refused. But soon they saw there was no need to fear him, and after seven days on his unhappy throne he was executed by one who had many faults but was not a puppet.

This was Bodawpaya, the senior of Alaungpaya's surviving sons. Alaungpaya had expressed the wish that he should be succeeded by his sons in turn, and Hsinbyushin had disregarded

[1] *Symes* 95.

[2] *Sangermano* 53. They were the three surviving sons of Alaungpaya, see *IA* 1892 Temple "The Order of Succession in the Alompra Dynasty."

that wish by nominating his own son Singu. Half the palace plots which were the bane of Burma proceeded from the lack of any clear law of succession. The king nominated whom he liked, sometimes a son, sometimes a brother, his choice being subject to only one restriction—that the nominee be born of a queen, not of a concubine.

BODAWPAYA 1782-1819 at once enforced the Massacre of the Kinsmen (p. 338), making a clean sweep of his rivals, with their followers, servants, and children. Singu's queens and his lesser ladies had laughed their little day in forest glades; they now laughed no more, for they were burnt alive, every one, holding their babes in their arms.

He rewarded his followers generously, especially Mahathihathura. But a few months later he found his brother plotting against him, and among the faction was none other than Mahathihathura himself. The shock to the king's faith was such that never again, to the end of his life, did he put his trust in mortal man, no not even his nearest kin; and from that time onward he changed his room and his bed daily.[1] All the faction, with their families and attendants, were exterminated; and thus the old general, who had so often led his countrymen to victory and had won the greatest of their wars, died the death of a traitor.

At the end of the year a *minlaung* pretender, Nga Myat Pon, with two hundred wretchedly armed followers scaled the palace wall by night, seized the cannon and turned them on the palace, firing blank as they could find no ball.[2] When day dawned and it was seen how few they were, they were overpowered and cruelly executed. Nga Myat Pon claimed to be a prince of the deposed Ava dynasty who to avoid captivity among the Talaings had fled to the Shans and Red Karens. He was really a native of Möng Küng in the Southern Shan States, and many of his followers were from Möng Pai

[1] *Sangermano* 53. Bodawpaya's changing his room does not appear to have been a palace custom, as it was at Pataliputra (Strabo xv 55).

[2] *Konbaungset* 551-5, *Sangermano* 54, *Parlett* 44.

and Yawnghwe. They had plighted their troth with the *thwethauk* blood bond at Aungzigon pagoda south of Pinya; their plans were matured and their ladders made at Paungga, Sagaing district, some of whose people hated the king, as was natural in the fief of the slain seven-days king. They were now dealt with according to precedent—the whole population, down to infants and monks, was burnt alive, the fruit-trees cut down, the crops ploughed up, the village burnt and left to relapse into jungle. Many officers and men who had failed to detect the conspiracy, or to prevent the escalade, or had helped under compulsion to fire the blank rounds, were executed. Bodawpaya built, on the site of the humble house he had occupied as a junior prince at Sagaing, the Aungmyelawka (Eindawya) pagoda, dedicating as slaves such people from the Paungga locality as had escaped burning, for he was a most religious king.[1] After the English annexation they returned to their villages.

A year after coming to the throne, Bodawpaya moved the capital, causing hardship not only to the citizens but also to the country at large which had to pay heavy contributions in money and labour. Such hardship was justifiable in 1765 when the move had been from Shwebo, a bad site, to Ava, a good site; but now the move was to Amarapura, an indifferent site six miles away, and it was undertaken for astrological reasons.[2]

One evening in September 1783 three hundred Talaings from the Bassein province, armed with swords and bamboo spears, suddenly rowed up to Rangoon at sunset, rushed into the town, killed everyone they met, cut the governor's throat, burnt his offices, and seized the armoury containing 200 muskets with ammunition.[3] The townsfolk ran up to see what the fire was, and fifty were at once cut down. Many of the rest, with all the officials, ran off into the woods, thinking the Talaings more numerous than they really were. The Talaings shut the gates, patrolled the streets, killed all who would not drink the water

[1] *Konbaungset* 784.

[2] *Sangermano* 56, *Gouger* 25, *Crawfurd* I. 147. Sangermano put the city population at 200,000; *Crawfurd* II. 9 put Ava at 50,000 in 1826; Mandalay was 65,000 under Mindon, *Fytche* I. 252, 218,000 in 1886 (old office files), and 138,000 in 1922. See p. 139, note "Shifting Capitals" p. 356.

[3] Rangoon was a stockade until 1841 (illustrated at p. 304). See *JBRS* 1912 Saya Thein "Rangoon in 1852" and 1920 Fraser "Old Rangoon."

of allegiance, and made everyone stay indoors. They maintained good order and prevented theft; they presented the Portuguese and Armenians to their *minlaung* pretender, a young man dressed in shining raiment, and compelled them to assist; they got no help from the European ships and were too few to compel it. Two days later the Burmese in the woods assembled a levy and sent three hundred men who pretended to side with the Talaings and stood under the gates asking to be admitted and promising to drink the water of allegiance. The Talaings let them in and administered the great oath. The Burmese then stormed the north gate, leaving four hundred casualties on the ground, drove the Talaings to the centre of the town, and were there checked, for they had no muskets. But one hundred and fifty of their men, led by a Siamese, breaking down the west gate with axes, ran up with some muskets, the three hundred men who had sworn allegiance suddenly threw off the mask, and the Talaings were overpowered, hunted out from the houses, and killed. The Burmese seized the ammunition of some European ships lying in the port, and compelled one hundred and fifty Europeans and Eurasians to serve; they put them in charge of armed parties and left the most important points, such as the city gates, in their keeping. Next day Talaing reinforcements arrived. The first canoe, arriving singly, was sunk by a cannon shot and as her crew, numbering sixty, swam ashore, they were cut down. One hundred and twenty men, coming up in two more canoes, were quietly allowed to land and were then suddenly set upon and killed. The leading prisoners were cross-examined, and after confessing the full extent of their plans they were beheaded.[1] The shore was littered with Talaing corpses, a feast for dogs and vultures, and the river was bloodstained for a whole day. In the next few days scores of Talaing canoes appeared but guessed there had been a miscarriage and returned without landing. Subsequently twenty-two canoes flying red flags brought a great governor, Master of the Royal She-elephants, who levied a heavy fine on the townsfolk for their failure to prevent the Talaing entry. But before he had left, an even greater governor, Lord of the East Gate of the Palace, arrived

[1] A readiness to confess is still noticeable in the less sophisticated parts of the country. Beheading with the *dah* was invariably an instantaneous death, and Burmese rulers did not grant it to those who failed to confess.

with orders to hold an inquiry; he put the Master of the Royal She-elephants into irons, saying he had no authority to levy fines for his own benefit, and returned to the capital taking with him all officials; some at least cannot have been responsible for the initial surprise, and had subsequently shown great courage and determination, but they also were led away in fetters.[1]

An Arakanese, lord Hari, came asking Bodawpaya to take over his distracted country (p. 149), alleging that everyone would welcome so noble a ruler. Bodawpaya feared the Mahamuni image which overshadowed Arakan with its protecting power. He sent spies to report. Two of them were qualified in witchcraft; disguised as monks, they worshipped at the Mahamuni shrine and performed magical rites to neutralise the power of the image. At the end of 1784 upwards of 30,000 men under the crown prince invaded Arakan in four divisions. The first went by the pass from Pa-aing, Minbu district, the second by the pass from Padaung, Prome district, the third by the pass from Kyangin, Henzada district, the fourth with the guns went by boat round Negrais. They united on the west coast, swept the Arakanese royal army out of Ramree Island, and camped along the Dalet river north-west of An, receiving the homage of the surrounding country. Subsequent fighting took place through the creeks and islands, and the Arakanese came out to offer resistance both on land and sea; but they were outnumbered three to one and never succeeded in seriously checking the Burmese who occupied the capital Mrohaung without difficulty, inflicting wanton cruelties on the population,[2] leaving them tied to stakes at low-water mark, or burying them up to the chin in fields which they then proceeded to harrow.[3] The king of Arakan had been advised by his council to make submission and present a daughter, but he refused to go down to history as having disgraced his country and he himself led the army. After his defeat he fled by boat with his harem but was overtaken and brought back a prisoner to his own capital. The Burmese constituted Arakan a province under a governor at Mrohaung with a garrison of several thousand men, having Sandoway, Ramree and Cheduba

[1] See note "Administrative Conditions" p. 357.
[2] *Symes* 110.
[3] Arakanese family tradition.

as sub-provinces. They then returned in February 1785 with the royal family and 20,000 inhabitants; it was these prisoners who introduced [1] inoculation against small-pox, already practised in Arakan, into Burma. The captive king was given reasonable treatment in the capital till his death a year later, after which his kinsmen were suffered to sink into obscurity and want.

Among the spoil was a cannon thirty feet long, and the thirty bronze images of Ayuthia (p. 183); six survive at the Arakan pagoda, Mandalay. This pagoda was built to enshrine the Mahamuni image which was now brought from near Mrohaung, being the greatest of all the spoil; Bodawpaya himself went forth to meet and greet it on its way. Through the long colonnades leading to the pagoda,[2] there used to come daily from the Burmese palace, so long as a king reigned there, sumptuous offerings borne in stately procession, marshalled by a minister and shaded by the white umbrella. Nowhere, even at the Shwedagon or Shwesettaw, is the devotional atmosphere more intense. On its first arrival 125 captive Arakanese families were dedicated as slaves to the image, and the number was subsequently increased.

In the long gallery are 600 inscriptions, collected by Bodawpaya, not for archæological reasons but because he thought the clergy were getting more rent than was their due. He therefore instituted a close scrutiny of the inscriptions in which pious dedications were recorded, causing copies to be made and to be deposited here.[3] Unfortunately the copies are frequently inaccurate, and many original inscriptions were broken or thrown away on the road by cartmen groaning under forced labour, especially when they were pagoda slaves wishing to destroy the evidence of their bondage. None the less, the collection is a veritable mine for the archæologist, and luckily it was from the first entrusted to the care of the Twinthintaikwun 1726-92, a monk who turned layman before the fall of Ava in 1752. He was respected for sane speech and integrity, and Alaungpaya made him tutor to Bodawpaya. On becoming king, Bodawpaya appointed him *Kyiwun*, "Commissioner of the Granaries," and gave him many titles with a jewelled staff.

[1] *Sangermano* 136. [2] See note "Mahamuni" p. 313.

[3] Talaing plaques of circ. 1059 at the Shwehsandaw, Prome, are in round character, but it was usually reserved for palm leaf until this reign, when the use of marble for inscriptions became fashionable and led to the disuse of square character.

He wrote prose and verse—for instance, Wethandayapyo, Zanekapyo, 66 *jatakas*, and the great Yazawinthit history, a task for which he was especially qualified by his knowledge of the inscriptions in his care. He died full of years and honours at Mingun while the king was building the pagoda (p. 275), on which the old man had written some courtly stanzas.

Quite a number of other courtiers dabbled in literature, and the king encouraged it. Nga Aung Hpyo wrote verse on Kyanzittha and on the China tooth (p. 279) and compiled a *thamaing* history of Halin, the ancient Pyu site in Shwebo district. Nawadenge, *thugyi* of Yuawe in Sadaung, Sagaing district, wrote court verse on the royal family and a *mawgun* on the Meiktila lake when the king was superintending repairs there in 1796; he received high offices and titles together with a jewelled staff and the privilege of driving up to the very gates of the palace. In 1785 U Awbatha, a monk, wrote a fine prose version of the Mahajanaka *jataka* story of Buddha; he wrote it at Minbu in his monastery, the pond of which still survives under the east side of the Deputy Commissioner's court. One of the judges in Bodawpaya's court was Letwethondara who, born in 1727, lived until just before the First Anglo-Burmese War; he had been one of the secretaries to the Hluttaw Council before the fall of Ava, and the Alaungpaya dynasty continued to employ him, just as the English government continued to employ his descendants; his best-known work was the poem written in exile (p. 249) but he wrote several other works, such as court verse on the 1767 conquest of Siam, the coronation of Bodawpaya, the conquest of Arakan in 1785, the Mingun pagoda, and a rimed law-book, the Winisaya-pakathani *dhammathat*.[1]

The king's scrutiny of inscriptions was only part of a general revenue inquest undertaken in 1784 and again in 1803. It was based on the depositions of village headmen all over the country, detailing the boundaries of their jurisdiction, the type of produce, the kind and amount of revenue, and the population in each—the total population was barely two million (p. 333). There is no reason to doubt that the figures were roughly accurate and gave the central government a much better idea

[1] *JBRS* 1916 Saya Thein "Letwethondara: judge and poet," 1917 Po Byu "A study of Letwethondara's poem written during his exile."

of the country's resources than it had ever had since 1638, when king Thalun had held a similar inquest (p. 194). But, like the English Doomsday Book of 1086, it was popularly regarded as the instrument of fresh exactions.[1] At the 1784 inquest His Majesty decreed that legal claims should not lapse with a change of king or dynasty. The kings often issued such decrees and they were as often disregarded. Burma possessed the germ of many an institution, crude no doubt but scarcely cruder than those in feudal lands; yet whereas feudal lands retained and developed them, Burma could not develop, because every change of dynasty, nay even a change of king, cancelled existing rights, rendering continuity impossible.[2]

The conquest of Arakan, a thinly populated strip of country which had been still further weakened by civil war, convinced Bodawpaya that he was destined to be a world conqueror. He talked of annexing China and India.[3] As a preliminary he set forth to annex Siam in 1785-6. He took the field in person, thus giving his armies the immense advantage of unity of command, which was seldom attainable by an ordinary commander; Shan chiefs, being royalty, took orders from the crown alone.[4] The plan of campaign was excellent, overwhelming the country from four points simultaneously. One army with Shan levies was to sweep down from Chiengmai, another would advance up the Ataran river and through Three Pagodas Pass in Moulmein district, the third from Tavoy would prevent the provinces in the Malay Peninsula from sending assistance to the Siamese king, the fourth was to occupy the important trading island of Junkceylon south of Mergui district and so prevent fire-arms reaching Siam.

Unfortunately things did not go according to plan. Paya Tak was dead but his spirit lived on in his comrade-in-arms, the founder of the present Siamese dynasty. The Chiengmai army indeed met with some success but everywhere else the Burmese

[1] Masses of the record for both 1784 and 1803 survive on palmleaf and *parabaik* in the Bernard Free Library, Rangoon. For specimens, see *JBRS* 1912 Furnivall "Matriarchy in Burma" and 1916, 1918, 1919 "Some historical documents." These specimens mention the regulation whereby foreign ships arriving at Rangoon had to land their cannon and rudder; a similar regulation existed in Japan.

[2] *Forchammer* "Jardine Prize" 91.

[3] *Sangermano* 58.

[4] *Gouger* 269.

were checkmated. The fourth army in war-boats with eleven ships,[1] managed by half-caste Portuguese who were seamen of a sort, coasted down to Junkceylon, landed and built stockades round its northern city Chalang; the governor had just died, so his widow the lady Chan,[2] and her young sister, took command, themselves leading their men in the field with such effect that the Burmese withdrew in a month. The third army from Tavoy occupied Ligor and was then wiped out. The leading divisions of Bodawpaya's own army met with much the same fate before they had advanced far beyond Three Pagodas Pass. The men were hampered by their absurd cannon, old ship guns mounted on cumbrous carriages; they might have been some use if the men behind them had known their work, but the generation of French gunners had now passed away. Abandoning these, his elephants and stores, and leaving his men to their fate, Bodawpaya ran for his life to Rangoon where he said prayers at the Shwedagon pagoda and was comforted by his queens.[3] The invasion collapsed and he reconsidered his decision to annex China and India.

He kept his throne for thirty-seven years because he was a masterful man who never hesitated to punish. But this campaign discloses the extent of his ability. He persisted in taking the field with a huge army which had no transport, as he issued orders without allowing time for arrangements to be made. Of course he blamed others, threatening to burn the whole staff, and actually carrying out the threat to a certain extent. The staff thought he could have won even yet had he persevered, for his numbers were overwhelming; instead, he himself set the example of a shameful flight.

For the next decade he continued to send armies against Siam, partly in self-defence, partly in the hope of recovering the southernmost Shans who of course went over to the conqueror. Indeed, fighting continued intermittently throughout most of the reign. In 1803 the Siamese ravaged as far as Kenghung and carried away the Kengtung population wholesale to Chiengmai; many of these went by collusion, hoping

[1] *Symes* II, 123.

[2] *JSS* 1905 Gerini "Historical retrospect of Junkceylon island" 60.

[3] He also built the Letkattaung pagoda at Launglon, in Tavoy district, during this campaign.

for better treatment from the Siamese than they received from the Burmese.[1] In 1814 the Talaings of Martaban rebelled and fled in large numbers to Siam; Siamese princes of the blood were sent to greet them and make arrangements along their route. In 1809-11 Bodawpaya's forces four times raided the Siamese coast villages south of the Isthmus of Kra and landed on Junkceylon; here they sometimes captured a town and carried off the population but sometimes were themselves captured and carried off into Siam in numbers, the officers being executed. But there were no big operations, he never regained Chiengmai, and it was probably well for him that the Siamese government was comparatively unaggressive.

The ravages of his dynasty had reduced parts of Siam to a desert[2] which seventy years later had not yet recovered its population.[3] There was many an old score for the Siamese to repay, and they made extensive slave raids into Tenasserim, which continued for some months after the English occupation in 1824. The Burmese retained Tavoy and Mergui; after the 1760 conquest (p. 241), when the Siamese had either been killed or had run away, these areas had been repopulated by batches of people sent down from Burma; but they were too few to keep out Siamese raiders, and when they failed, they paid homage to Siam, fearing Bodawpaya's vengeance. Some of his garrison commanders were devoted men, and on those who were not he would pass orders "Execute them in such fashion that all who even hear of it will shudder."[4]

The drain on Upper as well as Lower Burma was such that the framework of society cracked, and bands of brigands infested the entire realm; to crown all, the rains failed for several seasons in succession; probably 1812 saw the climax of the years 1807-16 which are still remembered in many a northern village as a time of terror and starvation. When the condition of the people was reported to Bodawpaya, he said "We must hold the people down by oppression so that they may not dare to think of rebellion."[5]

The largest number of men in any one of these 1809-11 campaigns was on paper 80,000 and in reality 36,000, of whom

[1] *GUB* II. i. 407. [2] *Aymonier* III. 790.
[3] *Anderson* "English intercourse with Siam" 8, 395-6.
[4] *Konbaungset* 648. [5] *Sangermano* 81.

8,000 died of hunger and disease before striking a blow, since no arrangements had been made for supply. When embarked, hundreds of them were tied hand and leg, like so many cattle, lest they should desert.[1] Their line of march from Upper Burma resembled that of a hostile army, leaving devastated villages in its trail. As a Myede levy of 1,500 men was slow in coming up, the commander-in-chief sent a detachment to punish them; the detachment met the unsuspecting levy on the road, cut down a hundred, seized four to five hundred before they could run, bound them hand and foot and left them lying at low water in a creek where the tide came in and drowned them. Men deserted wholesale and, unable to return to their villages where they would have been punished, roamed in bodies over the country, living by dacoity. What the army did at Tavoy is not on record, but for months after, the town was one long silence, for years the fields around were white with human bones, and, prominent among the five lakhs of gold and silver loot, was a quantity of bangles, chains, and other ornaments of the kind worn by women and children. The king was delighted at such prowess on the part of his favourite commander until he requested permission to delay his return and spend the rains in Tavoy as he was tired with his exertions and overcome with grief at the death of a concubine there. The request aroused the king's suspicions, for he prided himself on his penetrating intellect. Indeed, the courtiers said His Majesty possessed *deippa sekku nyan*, the supernatural faculty of perceiving what is going on at the other side of the world. This faculty now enabled him to perceive the real reason why the commander was delaying to return: he was plotting rebellion. Therefore he sent orders "Roast him at a slow fire, taking particular care that none of his bones should be broken or dislocated, which might tend to shorten his sufferings." Even the commander's service rivals, who were to carry out this order, hesitated, for they admitted that he was entirely innocent; and meanwhile he succeeded in capturing a small white elephant in the jungle. Amid the universal rejoicings which followed, he received a free pardon.[2]

Indeed there was no sin so scarlet but the finding of a white elephant would purge it whiter than snow. The chronicles

[1] *Crawfurd* II. 159.

[2] *BSPC* despatch 25 September 1812 Canning to Edmonstone.

scarcely deign to mention English missions or the causes leading up to the catastrophic war of 1824, but they are full of this sacred quadruped. Like the king, he was a living sacrament and together they shared some mysterious divinity. It had ever been thus, and when the Buddha became incarnate of the lady Maya, the annunciation took the form of a white elephant. Red, black, and spotted elephants were all valued, but the white elephant was in a class by himself. Of course he was only technically white, and it needed a trained eye to diagnose him; whoever did so and captured him, was ennobled. Bringing him from the jungles to the palace was a triumphal procession. It might be an arduous task, for he sometimes resisted his worshippers and destroyed the crops; but the royal aesthete, with a commendable disregard of earthly dross, would exclaim "What signifies the destruction of ten thousand baskets of rice compared with the possession of a white elephant?" At every halt on his way, a gorgeous pavilion would be erected, and crowds flocked to kneel and adore. Arrived at the capital, he was given a separate court of his own, with minister and secretary, and fiefs for his support. If the revenue from these fiefs was diminished, the king would write him an apologetic letter in his own royal hand, explaining the circumstances. A Guards detachment was on duty at his palace, the king himself made offerings and paid him reverence, he was bathed every day in scented water, all his vessels were of pure gold, dancers danced to him, and palace singers sang him to sleep. No milk save human milk was good enough for him, and every morning twenty nursing mothers waited on him in a row. His trappings were of finest silk, bosses of solid gold studded with rubies and emeralds hung all over his body, his tusks and his feet were ringed with gold, and his forehead bore a gold plate recording his voluminous Pali titles. He alone, with the king, was entitled to the white umbrella. If he sickened, the king might sicken; if he died, the king might die—nay, the whole country might come to ruin; therefore his death caused universal consternation and plunged the land into mourning; if a male, he was buried with the ritual of a king, if a female, with the ritual of a queen. He might live sixty years in his palace, unless he died prematurely of eating too many sweets from the hands of his adorers.[1]

[1] See note "White elephant" p. 361.

Bodawpaya repaired the embankments of the Nanda, Aungbinle and Maungmagan lakes in Mandalay district, and of the Meiktila lake. The last involved forced labour by levies dragged from the Shan states, Arakan, and the Talaing country. He first came to Meiktila in 1785, staying at the Nandawgon hillock near the present courthouse. During his stay he cast his eye on the daughter of the *myothugyi* Nga Kyu who, unwilling to give her up, said she was a leper. The king built a three storied monastery, Nga Kyu a two storied one. The king scented the falsehood and perceived that the building of the rival monastery was high treason; with that punning allusiveness which struck the courtiers as so exquisite, he murmured the adage ကျူပင်ခုတ်ကျူငုတ်မှမကျန်စေနှင့်။ "Cut down the *kyu* [reed], let not the stump remain." Thereupon Nga Kyu, his daughter, and the whole family were exterminated in the most correct manner. Their broad acres, requiring 1,000 baskets of seed, with their 51 serfs, escheated to the crown, according to the law whereby the king seized the property of people he condemned in person—wealth was not always an enviable possession.[1]

Occasionally he executed Burmese heretics,[2] and he built pagodas by the dozen, the largest being the Mingun pagoda in Sagaing district. This was to stagger humanity by its vastness. He himself frequently superintended the work 1790-7, camping on an island in the river and taking great pride in the leaden image-vaults which were his own idea. Thagyamin, the King of the Spirits, aided in the construction of these, sending angels to forward the work during the night; doubtless the miracle was as genuine as those which occur previously in the chronicles, but an observer[3] who was not gifted with the eye of faith noted that the angels must have used artificial light, for melted wax, such as mortals use for candles, lay all over the slabs. The king enshrined many treasures beyond price, also bits of coloured glass, and a genuine soda-water machine. The *chinthe* gryphon images were 95 feet high, their eyeballs were 13 feet in circumference, and the

[1] *Gibson* 51. Cf. *Cox* 342.
[2] *Sangermano* 89.
[3] *Cox* 108.

height of the pagoda was to be 500 feet. But when it reached a third of this height, a prophecy arose, "The pagoda is finished and the great country ruined!" Now there had been precisely the same prophecy in 1274 when Narathihapate built the Mingalazedi pagoda (p. 63) and, lo! the Chinese overthrew the kingdom. Bodawpaya therefore abandoned the construction. The great bell, weighing 80 tons, is the second largest in the world, and the pagoda enjoys the distinction of being the biggest heap of shoddy in existence.

During his stay at Mingun he was struck with a revelation that he was god; he opened his golden mouth and announced amid impressive silence that he was Arimittiya, the coming Buddha. But there are limits to the power of the most portentous potentate: the clergy were adamant in their opposition. The royal hermit pined for the luxury of his palace and the society of his ladies; before long the beatific vision faded and he came down to earth again.[1]

Indeed scepticism seized him for a time. It is human to doubt, and still more human to be jealous of the clergy, who received more homage than befitted subjects. He directed that their title Pongyi, "The Great Glory," should cease, for he alone was glorious. He thought them too numerous, caused inquiry to be made, found them lazy and ignorant, and issued orders that stricter examination should be made into the attainments of heads of monasteries. His orders were carried out in so far as the confiscation of certain church lands was concerned, but for the rest, the crown prince saw that nothing so alarming as a real change was made. His Majesty had been shocked at the primate's inability to solve his metaphysical conundrums, and began to think there must be something wrong with Buddhism. He heard that Mahomedans would die rather than eat pork; if that were true, there must be some reality in their faith and it might be worth adopting. He summoned the *maulvis* of Amarapura to the palace where pork was laid before them and they were commanded to eat. They looked at the pork, they looked at the king, they thought

[1] *Sangermano* 61, cf. pp. 182, 241 above. Paya Tak (p. 260) was being worshipped as a Buddha when he was assassinated, and "Buddha that is to be" sometimes occurs in the style of the Siamese royal house. There are living Buddhas in Tibet.

of the executioner's sword outside, and—they ate the pork. So evidently there was nothing in Mahomedanism and His Majesty continued to build pagodas. Sometimes he would break out into eccentricities and queer superstitions, but they were checked by his natural shrewdness.[1]

In 1785 he had two new golden heads of the Mahagiri Nat spirits made for the shrine at Popa Hill (p. 16), and in 1812 he replaced them with larger heads, weighing 2½ lb.[2]

Cingalese religious missions had for some time past gone to Siam, thinking that religion was purest there; but in 1802 and 1812 they came to Burma. The 1802 mission was of some importance. Kirti Siri Raja Singha, king of Ceylon 1748-78, had introduced a system whereby ordination was restricted to the agricultural caste; the lower castes were indignant and some of their novices came to Burma where Bodawpaya gave them audience and, amid a scene of great magnificence, himself presented them to the primate for ordination; they returned to Ceylon taking with them some Burmese monks and a letter from the Burmese primate to the Cingalese primate. The Burmese monks were five in number, a full chapter, and on their arrival they proceeded to make further ordinations so that in Ceylon to-day their successors are known as the Amarapura school, which protests against caste distinctions in the order and is separate from the older body, known as the Siam school.[3]

In 1810 the king sent lords and Brahmans to Buddhagaya in Bengal.[4] They went by the An Pass to Arakan and thence through Chittagong, bearing rich offerings with which they worshipped the Holy Tree after sprinkling it with scented water. They brought back detailed drawings and plans of the tree, together with little models of the pagoda, images, some of the sacred earth, and two shoots from off the Tree. The images were kept in a chapel in the palace, and the shoots, planted in the sacred earth, were kept in two jewelled pots on the north-west of the Pahtodawgyi pagoda which the king was building at Amarapura.

[1] *Sangermano* 92, *Cox* 230, *Gouger* 96-100, *Crawfurd* I. 399.

[2] *GUB* I. ii 21.

[3] *Hardy* 327; *Tennent* 224, 246; despatch of 4 March 1812 from Governor-General to Court of Directors, para 29 (*PP* 17).

[4] *Konbaungset* 749-54.

In 1813 Judson, with the saintly and heroic lady who was his wife, arrived in Burma where, with small beginnings, they founded the great American Baptist Mission. They came by accident, for they had left America intending to work in India, but they were at once ejected from India by the British Government which then discouraged missionaries on the ground that they would stir up religious strife and expose government to the charge of favouring its own creed. Although the king when granting the Judsons audience contemptuously flung their tracts to the ground, he passed no order against them; although they met with petty opposition from the monks, they met with nothing but protection from successive governors of Rangoon and with the most charming courtesy from the governors' wives; and when, some years later, they underwent what may fairly be called martyrdom, it was for political not for religious motives.[1]

Bodawpaya punished with death the drinking of intoxicants, the smoking of opium, and the killing of any large animal, as an ox, or buffalo; and when he was in a really devout mood he would make drinkers drink boiling lead.[2] In the provinces governors contented themselves with decapitation, but it was inflicted even for selling liquor, and sex was no exemption. The clergy would sometimes intervene, and their robes, flung over a criminal when he was kneeling under the executioner's uplifted sword, were so absolute a reprieve that government usually took steps to prevent their attendance; a person thus pardoned, for this or worse offences, became the monk's slave and had to dress in white, take vows, and serve the monastery.[3]

Diplomatic intercourse with China resulted from the peace terms of 1769. It was the first time the Burmese made a serious effort to maintain regular foreign relations, and the results were wholly to the good, smoothing out the friction that was always arising on the disorderly frontier. China sent missions

[1] *Wayland.* The king who granted them audience was Bagyidaw, *Mrs. Judson* 231.

[2] *Sangermano* 68, *Gouger* 278. See note "Drink" p. 314.

[3] *TP* 1891 Cordier "Les Français en Birmanie" 13. The monks would even attack the ministers of justice with sticks, *Sangermano* 97. In 1837 their threats so enraged a judge that he forthwith executed, for petty theft, two boys whom he had all along intended to reprieve, *McLeod and Richardson* 129.

to Burma in 1787, 1790, 1795, 1796, 1822; and Burma to China in 1782, 1787, 1792, 1823. As a result of the 1787 embassies the Chinese extradited a fugitive Bhamo *sawbwa*, and the two countries began to release some of the surviving prisoners of the war. In 1790 the Burmese restored some Chinamen they had captured in Siam. In his 1796 embassy the Emperor announced his abdication, asking Burma to recognise his son. In their 1792 embassy the Burmese sent patents of nobility with the usual gold phylacteries to various Chinese dignitaries, and an enormously long Pali title for the Emperor; their envoys came back with a great seal bearing Chinese characters and shaped like a camel; the king hesitated to accept it lest he should thereby admit investiture from China, but its value—three *viss* (10 lb.) of solid gold—decided him to retain it, while carefully omitting the fact from his chronicles. Some of his letters were studiously curt, but the Emperor none the less persisted in regarding him as a vassal. In many cases the Chinese embassies were provincial not imperial, but sometimes they were magnificent cavalcades of 400 horsemen, headed by Guards officers. Three of the Burmese embassies actually reached Pekin after a five months' journey and came home with a detailed itinerary and a glowing account of how gracious the Emperor had been, how he had insisted on hearing a Burmese band, how he had feasted them day and night with theatres, what a wonderful city it was, how they had been carried round in sedan chairs to see the sights, what dresses the mandarins wore, etc., etc. The monarchs exchanged devotional images before which they had themselves worshipped. The king would send the Emperor elephants, ivory by the hundredweight, English piecegoods and carpets, ivory helmets studded with rubies and sapphires, Pagan lacquer boxes, jewelled rings and peacock tails. The Emperor would send the king fans, dwarf gardens, horses, tea sets, fur jackets lined with yellow silk, and *lo* mules which the Burmese believed to be prolific. But the best of all was the 1790 Chinese mission which brought a Buddha tooth and three ladies for the royal harem. The acquisition of the tooth showed Bodawpaya that he was a greater king than Anawrahta 1044-77 who had failed to obtain the tooth from China. And as for the ladies, were they not princesses of the Imperial House of China? Was not the Emperor his vassal and did he not admit it by sending tribute of his own granddaughters? He failed to realise that they were ordinary Yünnanese girls.[1]

Before returning with his army from Arakan, the crown prince had made all headmen take out appointment orders under the Burmese seal, and had scattered outposts throughout the land; thus there were 300 men in Sandoway, 500 at Ramree and a few thousand at Mrohaung.[2] But from the very first year, 1785, there had been continual disorder; it was no unusual thing for a Burman outpost to have to run for their lives; terrible reprisals were exacted but the trouble continued.

The Arakanese had every excuse; they were rebelling not against government but against tyranny.[3] They would be called in to the various garrison headquarters on the pretext of disarming them, and when they arrived the Burmese would round them up and massacre them. Quite apart from revenue exactions—even infants were not exempt from poll-tax—there were continual exactions of human cattle. Sometimes three hundred youths would be packed off to wait in the palace at Amarapura, having tattoed on their arms the fact that they were sent in lieu of revenue. Sometimes men would be called up in crowds across the passes to pay homage to the Lord White Elephant. 3,000 were requisitioned to work on the Meiktila lake reconstruction, and none returned. 6,000 were dragged away in 1790 to serve against Chiengmai, where they died of disease in numbers.

When, in 1797, the Burmese came demanding 2,000 more to make bricks and work on the Mingun pagoda, village after village beat the war-drum and the people rose wholesale; their principal leader was Nga Chin Pyan (Kingberring), lord *myosa* of Sindin in Akyab district, who up to this time had served the Burmese. Year in, year out, the fighting never ceased, while thousands fled to Chittagong in British territory where taxation

[1] See note "Chinese embassies" p. 362. The tooth, enclosed in five little metal pagodas, fitting one inside the other, was enshrined in the Mingun pagoda (p. 275).

[2] The occupation led to the An Pass from Minbu district being put into repair. In 1816 seven hundred men were employed upon it and every traveller was required, in lieu of toll, to carry tools and do some repairs during his journey. (*GUB* II. i. s.v. "Aeng").

[3] *Nga Me; Dinnyawadi Yazawinthit* 253, 260; *San Shwe Bu.*

was reasonable and a man could go to bed at night without wondering whether his throat would be cut in the morning by order of some official. Arakan had never been populous, and now it became a desert; the towns were deserted and overgrown with jungle, and there was nothing to be seen but "utter desolation . . . morass, pestilence and death."[1]

Among the refugees were fierce spirits who used British territory as a base for fresh attacks on the Burmese. The handful of British officers at Chittagong and their native subordinates, unacquainted with the Magh language, could not keep in touch with their plans or movements, and the Bengali police were not equal to the control of men so much more energetic than themselves.[2] The frontier was wild jungle with little population; in such places even modern government finds difficulty in exercising control, and under eighteenth-century conditions half a dozen raids could be hatched before the Chittagong magistrate knew anything about it.

But the Burmese never gave him a chance to know anything about it. In 1794 one of their governors marched 5,000 men across the frontier, the Naaf river, and stockaded himself well inside British territory, neither knowing nor caring that this in itself was a *casus belli;* the king's orders were that he was not to return without three fugitive Arakanese lords. A battalion of white troops, with sepoys and artillery, was at once despatched from Calcutta and camped against the Burmese stockade. The Burman governor at first bluffed, but finally called on the English major-general explaining that he must have the three fugitives as they were dacoits with a long record of crime and he would never evacuate British territory until he had them. However, he consented to withdraw on receiving assurances that full inquiry would be made; soon after his withdrawal, the three fugitives were classed as dacoits and handed over to him, and the incident closed.[3] The three men were as much patriots as dacoits; on the way to Amarapura one of them slipped his leg-irons and escaped at Hsinbyugyun, Minbu district; the other two, brought before the king's minister,

[1] Paper of intelligence from Cox's Bazaar dated 20 October 1823, in *BSPC.*
[2] *Robertson* 19.
[3] *Symes* 120.

defied him to his face and dared him to do his worst; he did it, and one of them, Nga Po Lon, the lord of Ramree, spent sixty hours in dying.[1]

In 1798 a horde of terrified Arakanese poured into Chittagong as a result of Nga Chin Pyan's unsuccessful revolt; Cox's Bazaar, a sub-divisional headquarters, is populated mainly by their descendants, and takes its name from Lieutenant Cox who was sent to supervise them and prevent a food shortage. A Burmese force failed to recover them but stockaded itself miles inside the English frontier, and drove off a police battalion with considerable loss. The king sent an envoy to Calcutta telling the Viceroy to deliver up his ungrateful "slaves" (i.e. subjects) who had dared to run away from his beneficent rule. The Viceroy replied that this could not be done but they would be prevented from making raids. The king thereupon threatened immediate war but nothing happened; to him the refusal to surrender rebels was an act of plain hostility. But for centuries it has been the boast of Anglo-Saxon governments that, while they will surrender criminal refugees, they will never surrender political refugees even to their best ally. In the present case it was increasingly evident that most of the fugitives were not even political refugees but simply harmless people fleeing from death; as the years went by there came to be some 50,000 of them—it was little short of a racial migration.[2]

In 1811, however, the Burmese had just cause of complaint as Nga Chin Pyan, after taking refuge in Chittagong, again broke out in Burmese territory. He made several raids, each time returning into difficult hill country inside British territory; once he overran the whole of Arakan, wiping out the Burmese garrisons save at Mrohaung. After this the English washed their hands of him; he had abused their hospitality and they now captured his principal officers, deported them to Dacca, set on his head a price of Rs. 5,000 (equivalent to half a lakh nowadays), harried him with their troops, and invited Burmese

[1] *Dinnyawadi Yazawinthit* 259.

[2] *Passim*, e.g. para. 3 of despatch dated 9 March 1812 from Governor-General to Court of Directors (*PP* 26); incidentally para. 11 attributes an infraction of territory to the Burmese troops having no pay or food and being driven to forage across the frontier; but they were also burning villages.

armies to cross the frontier and hunt him down; but although he was thus prevented from doing more harm, he was still at large when, to everybody's relief, he died in 1815. For seventeen years he had led his people gallantly, the most famous of all the insurgents; but he never had a chance, because he could rely on the other leaders for nothing save to fail him, out of jealousy, at the critical moment. The facilities given by the English should have sufficed to show their good faith, and possibly some of the Burmese officers who met them understood this; but the court did not, and merely saw in these facilities proof that the English were trembling in their shoes before the dazzling glory and power of the Golden Throne.

Manipur relapsed into civil war and Marjit Singh, one of the princes, brought in the Burmese who invaded the country in 1812-13 and, after heavy fighting in which some of the commanders were killed, set him on the throne and were rewarded with the cession of the Kabaw valley.

The Ahom Shan kingdom of Assam, with capital at Rangpur in Sibsagar district, extended along the Brahmaputra river from Goalpara in the west to Sadiya in the east. It was in a state of dissolution and in 1805, at the request of some rebels, the Burmese twice marched into the country but were bribed and withdrew. Later a governor, who had plotted against one of the best ministers who ever ruled Assam, fled to Calcutta; there he failed to get English assistance but fell in with a Burmese envoy who listened to his tale and took him to Amarapura. Bodawpaya gave him audience and in 1816 sent 8,000 men to Jorhat in Sibsagar district; on the way they picked up Manipur and Hukong levies so that they were 16,000 strong when they entered Assam, overcame resistance, and reinstated the governor; they then withdrew taking a large subsidy, fifty elephants, sacred things such as Ganges water, and also a girl whom they accepted as a daughter of the Ahom raja for Bodawpaya's harem.[1]

In 1795 the English began to send embassies to Burma.

[1] *Gait* 218-23, *Konbaungset* 781. She had, allotted for her support, some of the 500 Assamese who settled near Bhamo under the brother of a Burmese nominee to the throne of Assam; this colony still exists, its numbers having been fed by compatriots bought in Bhamo market from Chin slave raiders. There are Burmese villages in Lakhimpur and Sibsagar districts, Assam, founded by prisoners taken in the 1824 evacuation; their people are great brewers and smugglers of country spirit, wear Burmese dress, and are visited by monks who come from Burma via the Hukong valley.

Previously they had sent none, for envoys such as Baker (p. 225) were mere concession seekers. The immediate cause of these embassies was the expansion of Burma in Arakan, but the ultimate cause was the world situation. England was at death grips with France. Two generations of naval warfare so depleted her oak forests that access to teak forests became increasingly important. Rangoon was one of the shipbuilding centres of the East, and many of the merchant ships which provisioned England during the struggle, though built in Calcutta, were built of Burma teak.[1] Suffren, the greatest of French admirals, after holding the eastern seas from 1781 to 1784, told his government that Burma was the country through which the English might be attacked with most advantage.[2] His government never occupied Burma because they were too fully occupied elsewhere, and not having command of the seas they could not regain their lost empire in the East; but they wished to do so, and might succeed in doing so; they had wrested the command of the seas from England in 1779, for a short time only it is true, but that short time had sufficed for America to win her independence; what had happened before might happen again, and the English took steps to counteract even the feeblest French efforts in the East. Thus, they hunted down the French privateers which occasionally used the Burmese ports and sold muskets to the king;[3] and they intercepted the correspondence which passed between Indian kings and the French Republic.

Burma knew nothing of international affairs save through bazaar rumour and through the tales, usually anti-English propaganda, of Armenian and Mahomedan merchants who knew little of the French but thought that anything was preferable to the East India Company's monopoly. Burma never succeeded in getting into real communication with the French, but she sent embassies to Indian kings with a view to making a combined attack on the English. Thus in 1813 the king talked of making a pilgrimage to Buddhagaya and Benares attended by 40,000 men; and in 1807, '08, '13, '17, '20, '23 he sent to northern India missions consisting of lords and

[1] See note "French and shipbuilding" p. 353. [2] *Bayfield* x.
[3] *Bayfield* xxiii, xxviii; *Cox* 145; *Crawfurd* I. 162.

Brahmans who went as far as Delhi and Lahore if not even to Peshawar and elsewhere; they collected sacred books, relics, and Hindustani girls whom they presented to the king as daughters presented in homage by Indian rajas. When the English, who had at first given them facilities for pilgrimage, found that the pilgrims were communicating with kings such as the Mahratta Confederacy, they stopped them and sent them back.[1] In any case they usually came a year or so late, after their intended allies had been crushed.

The English missions from 1795 onwards, being political and no longer commercial, were on a superior scale, with imperial officers, sepoy escorts, and rich presents. The first was that of Captain Symes in 1795; he was sent to secure the release of British subjects from exactions other than legal port dues, to ask that ships suffering from stress of weather be given the treatment usual among civilised nations instead of being confiscated (p. 205), to open up diplomatic relations, and to secure the establishment of an English political agent at Rangoon. He secured all these by a paper which he imagined to be a treaty, but the king regarded it as a mere grant and failed to observe its terms. Symes was permitted to look at the king on his throne but was not granted audience; and he gained permission to go to Amarapura only by threatening to withdraw with the presents which the king was desirous of receiving. The shortness of his stay rendered his impressions superficial. A pachyderm, he saw everything *couleur de rose*, overestimating the population by 400 per cent. and the sanity of the court by considerably more. If his account had been only a travel book, this would not have mattered; but it was an official report, and seriously misled his government.

His successor, the Rangoon political agent Captain Cox, was sent in 1797 to ask that a Burmese embassy might go to Calcutta. The king kept him waiting nine months, partly on a sandbank at the Mingun pagoda construction camp, but granted audience and actually spoke to him with his own golden lips. The mission was a complete failure, none of its objects being achieved, and Cox brought back such an amazing account, so utterly at variance with Symes', that the Government of India thought he must be ill and overwrought, or perhaps he had

[1] *Bayfield* xxxvi-vii; *PP* 87, 106.

made some mistake; they wrote to the king saying they regretted that the envoy had failed to give satisfaction, and that they proposed sending another officer who would prove more satisfactory.

The next envoy, in 1802, was the redoubtable Symes himself; but he was treated in exactly the same way as Cox, being put off from day to day for three months, half of which he was made to live on an island where corpses were burnt and criminals were executed; he did not write a book this time.

The last missions were those of Captain Canning in 1803, '09 and '11. At royal audiences, the king pointedly talked about His Britannic Majesty only, avoiding reference to the Viceroy; it was beneath his dignity to mention a viceroy. A prince-minister said[1] to Canning "You see how difficult you make it for us by coming from a viceroy only. His Majesty is longing to enter into the closest alliance, but how can he do so unless proposals come from your king himself? Look at all the years you have wasted by failing to realise this little technicality. I hear you are at war with the French. Now just think, if only you had come from your king himself, the whole business could have gone through at once and we would have done everything to help you. Indeed I would probably have led the army myself, and I would have conquered France for you by now"—this was a few months after Wagram.

It was natural that Bodawpaya should disregard the Viceroy and insist on dealing only with His Britannic Majesty as king to king, for had he been told that His Britannic Majesty heard of him, if at all, only as one among other rajas in the Farther East, he would not have believed it. And as the years went by, and still the English sent no ambassador from their king, there grew up at court a mass of silent resentment. The only kind of viceroy the king of Burma knew was his own provincial governors; indeed, he usually referred to the Viceroy of India as *Bengalamyosa*. No doubt the viceregal governor of Rangoon was one viceroy and the Viceroy of India was another; but quite apart from the fact that the Rangoon viceroy was officially styled *nga kyun*, "my slave," and was sometimes treated as such, being sent to the palace in chains and pegged out in the

[1] Year 1810, *Bayfield* xxx.

sun, he ruled over little more than a district, and he possessed no sovereign powers such as the power of making peace and war. The Viceroy of India possessed these powers and was treated as an equal by mightier monarchs with longer pedigrees than the king of Burma.

On his third deputation, Canning refused to leave Rangoon and attend court unless reasonable conditions were assured. The king therefore ordered the governor of Rangoon to send him up in fetters; but the governor's staff could not keep a secret and Canning escaped out of the governor's reach on to his ship, the Company's light cruiser *Malabar* (54 guns). The very officers who had tried to catch him now came alongside and, nothing ashamed, asked to be shown over her; so the gangway sentries passed them and they swarmed over her white decks chattering with delight at the compact power of the first warship they had ever seen.

Living in a seaport, the governor was less afflicted with parochialism than the court, and apologised to Canning for the way he had to behave under orders, adding "Our king is absolute. His commands must be unreservedly obeyed and he disregards the forms and usages of all nations. Indeed, Captain, between ourselves, I sometimes wonder whether His Majesty is quite right in the head, for they say in the Palace he does things which entirely indicate a disordered mind."[1]

In despair at Canning's escape, the governor said "I wish you would let my men fire a few shots at you—no offence intended, of course, but you see I really must be able to convince His Majesty that I made a desperate effort to capture you!" When the news that Canning had sailed away reached the king, he ordered the governor to be sent up in chains, and the collective wisdom of the Hluttaw Council was exercised in selecting an appropriate method of execution. On the whole, they inclined to the view that the best method was to crucify him on a raft in seven fathoms of water at the mouth of the Rangoon river so that his body might float to Bengal and show the Viceroy the result of disobedience to royal orders. But while the Hluttaw was debating the question, a courtier distracted the king's attention with some fine new presents and at last so

[1] *BSPC* despatch 25 September 1812 Canning to Edmonstone.

pacified him that instead of executing the governor he transferred him to Dalla.[1]

After this the Viceroy sent no more embassies and, whenever he wished to address the king, wrote a letter to the viceregal governor of Rangoon. To be appreciated, these embassies 1795-1811 must be studied in detail. A great bone of contention was the shoe question. English officers never made any difficulty about taking off their shoes in the palace and kneeling in the king's presence; even in 1826 when the court was beaten to the dust, Havelock and his officers from the victorious army bowed thrice of their own accord when the opening gates revealed the palace, took off their shoes at the foot of the great stairs, and of course addressed the king on their knees though they neither took off their shoes nor knelt to their own king.[2] But before 1826 the court was not content; it wished envoys to run barefoot and bareheaded in the sun along the roads, grovelling at every corner of the walls, at every spire. They would keep an envoy waiting two months and then ostentatiously admit within a few days of arrival what they called a French embassy, consisting of an American who had escaped from Calcutta jail, and two half-castes, all three dragged off a French merchant ship by some minister and compelled to dress up and appear at court as if they were French ambassadors, while all the time they were astonished out of their minds and were trying to avoid the farce which they feared might have serious consequences.[3] A minister would invite an envoy on to his house, swearing he loved him as a brother, begging him on no account to remove his shoes, but when he came that night, dressed in full regimentals, he would be kept waiting two hours in the hall amid a crowd of village petitioners and would have to return without seeing his host; or a minister would pass him several times and deliberately look away so as not to see him. The king would ask for some rupees and a coining machine from Calcutta, as he was thinking of introducing a coinage into his dominions; when the rupees arrived, containing 17 per cent. alloy for hardness' sake as is usual, the king returned the gift saying he could allow only pure silver to circulate in his dominions; and then he proceeded

[1] *BSPC* despatch 5 February 1813 Canning to Adam.

[2] *Havelock* 350. See p. 336 below.

[3] Year 1802, *Bayfield* xxiv.

From Capt. Cox's Journal, 1797.

to pay English claims in silver which was 25 per cent. or 40 per cent. alloy. One day they would tell the envoy that they were going to present him with two elephants, the next that he must buy his own boats for departure. He would learn that the king was himself about to accompany him to Rangoon and instal him as resident; the next moment, he was near being arrested as a hostage for the surrender of the Arakanese refugees, or was asked to drink the water of allegiance as he might be plotting against His Majesty. The king would go into raptures over the presents such as an English coach, or beg for the envoy's own hat, and put it on saying delightedly "See! This is a high proof of the envoy's regard for me. He could not do more for his own king!" and when his son the prince asked for it he would say "No, no! The hat is not for you, it is for me alone." The envoy would be invited, as a great delicacy, to see an exhibition of fireworks in which scores of deserters were to be burnt in the wheels. Sometimes he would be ignored for weeks; then suddenly half a dozen great personages would call on him with the utmost affability asking him to get the Viceroy to obtain a Buddha tooth from Ceylon; or perhaps they had discovered that he had some more presents to give them. One day they would tell him that he must pay large bribes to get an audience, the next that the king was longing to see him, the third that they wondered he was still here, why had he not left long ago? One day it would be announced that an army was about to march against England; another, the whole population of Rangoon, headed by the governor, would stampede into the woods because a pilot schooner with despatches for the envoy had appeared in the river, carrying two tiny cannon without ammunition. In the morning men would set about arresting the envoy; in the evening, the governor of Rangoon would send an urgent message asking him to come and stand beside him and show his face to calm the town which was on the verge of revolt —this, from a viceregal governor in his own headquarters surrounded by his guards. A governor would ask the envoy to come and receive the bullion paid by the king in settlement of some shipping dispute; and when he came, the governor would say "There it is, you may have it, but you must not take it away." An envoy wrote:—

> Surely, never had poor diplomatic wight such a strange crew to deal with as has fallen to my lot, ignorant of the first principles of government, policy, or politeness, and their words, actions, and sentiments, continually at variance; detesting, backbiting, and undermining each other, yet occasionally combining to perplex me. . . . A man had great need of patience in dealing with these people, who are the most ignorant, presuming, and rapacious set of beings that I ever met with. (*Cox* 182, 236.)

The English envoys had no special cause for complaint, as, although it is doubtful whether the whole of this etiquette was prescribed for Burmans at court, there is evidence to show that it was commonly prescribed for foreign envoys in order to impress them with a due sense of the king's unique majesty (pp. 57, 64, 98, 190, 191, 209, 214).

The letters addressed at this period by Burmese governors to the English magistracy are filled with an unconcealed fury. The Burmese lived in a land which was geographically isolated. Nobody from other lands came to them, except a few shipmen and some tribal immigrants; nor did they themselves visit other lands, for their population was so small that it could not fill even their own country. They lived in a world of their own.

With such governments as they knew, Yünnan and Siam, there had been mutual extradition of fugitive rebels. The land on the frontiers was largely uninhabited. If a rebel ran away the Burmese chased him to the hills. It mattered little whether those hills were in Burma or not, and if the pursuers occasionally met some chief he either grovelled before them or they burnt his village and cut off his head. It had been ever thus. But now, when the pursuers went to Chittagong, they found an unprecedented phenomenon: a regular administration with outposts, *dak* runners, offices, records, and white men at the back of it all. There were never more than two or three white men actually to be seen, but with them were hundreds of disciplined sepoys, every one of whom had a musket and knew how to use it. It was very difficult to understand these people. If a rebel ran away into their territory and the Burmese chased him there, a white man would appear and say there was no thoroughfare; if they pointed out that they were after a rebel, he would say he was sorry, but they must not catch the rebel here; if they asked him to catch the rebel for them, he would say no, it was not the custom of his government to deliver up a fugitive; if they said it was the king's order, he would say that was nothing to him, the king was not his king. It was insufferable: who were these English to pay no attention to the King of Kings, the Arbiter of Existence, the Master of the Earth and Water and all that therein is? Besides, if one did not produce the rebel's head, what would happen to one's own head? Save that the Burman's letter is less furious than some, the following is typical of the correspondence which passed between Burma and the Government of India for a generation:—

Translation of a letter from the Raja of Ramree to the Governor-General. Received 8 *June* 1818.—I, Nameo Sura, Governor of (Yamawoody) Ramree, placing my head under the royal feet, resembling the golden lily, and bowing to the commands of the most illustrious sovereign of the universe, king of great and exalted virtue, lord of white elephants, called Saddan, strict observer of the divine laws, who fulfils the ten precepts, and performs all the good works commanded by former virtuous kings, who assists and protects all living beings, whether near or remote, and possesses miraculous and invincible arms, etc. etc. address and inform the Governor-General of Bengal, that our mighty monarch is distinguished throughout the vast world, for his unexampled piety and justice. He has a hundred sons, a thousand grandsons, and one great grand son, whom he nourishes in his arms, and who is inexpressibly esteemed and beloved, as a rarity of as great a magnitude as the white elephant is superior to ten other various species of rare elephants; the acquisition of this royal infant, is considered as an offering made to the king, by the angel of heaven himself. The power, good luck, and inestimable reputation of our great sovereign is universally known, and he is duly recognised by all foreign kings. Those who come to him for the purpose of paying due homage and respect, are invariably taught the principles of religion, and the system of good government. Our master, in fact, protects all living beings.

From Keopugan Lengen Peyagee, and the nine cities of Shyan, situated to the eastward, king Woody [Utibwa of China pp. 30, 280], sent three of his esteemed daughters, as offerings to the golden soles of the royal feet of our gracious sovereign, and thereby established a happy friendship between the two kingdoms, which intercourse has been attended with incalculable advantages. . . .

Those who do not minutely and scrupulously observe the laws of good government, and exercise oppression and injustice, incur the marked displeasure of our sovereign; who in similar cases, invariably sends armies under generals to capture their provinces but not to plunder them, and subsequently restore them to the monarch entitled to its inheritance.

Our sovereign is an admirer of justice, and a strict observer of the laws, and usages, as they existed in ancient times, and strongly disapproves everything unjust and unreasonable. Ramoo, Chittagong, Moorshedabad, and Dacca, are countries which do not belong to the English, they are provinces, distant from the Arracanese capital, but were originally subject to the government of Arracan, and now belong to our sovereign. Neither the English Company nor their nation observe the ancient laws strictly, they ought not to have levied revenues, tributes, etc. from these provinces, nor have disposed of such funds at their discretion. The Governor-General, representing the English Company, should surrender these dominions, and pay the collection realised therefrom to our sovereign. If this is refused, I shall represent it to His Majesty. Generals with powerful forces will be dispatched, both by sea and land, and I shall myself come for the purpose of storming, capturing and destroying the whole of the English possessions, which I shall afterwards offer to my sovereign; but I send this letter, in the first place, to make the demand from the Governor-General.

Letter from the Governor-General of India to His Excellency the Viceroy of Pegu etc. dated 22 June 1818.—A letter having been addressed to me by the Raja of Ramree containing a demand for the cession of certain provinces belonging to the British Government, I deem it incumbent on me, in consideration of the friendship subsisting between His Burmese Majesty and the British Government, to transmit to you a copy of that extraordinary document.

If that letter be written by order of the King of Ava, I must lament that persons utterly incompetent to form a just notion of the state of the British power in India, have ventured to practise on the judgment of so dignified a sovereign. Any hopes those individuals may have held out to His Majesty that the British Government would be embarrassed by contests in other quarters are altogether vain, and this Government must be indifferent to attack, further than as it would regard with concern the waste of lives in an unmeaning quarrel.

My respect for His Majesty, however, induces me rather to adopt the belief, that the Raja of Ramree has, for some unworthy purpose of his own, assumed the tone of insolence and menace exhibited in his letter, without authority from the King, and that a procedure so calculated to produce dissension between two friendly states will experience His Majesty's just displeasure.

If I could suppose that letter to have been dictated by the King of Ava, the British Government would be justified in considering war as already declared, and in, consequently, destroying the trade of His Majesty's empire. Even in this supposition, however, the British Government would have no disposition to take up the matter captiously, but, trusting that the wisdom of the King of Ava would enable him to see the folly of the counsellors who would plunge him into a calamitous war and that His Majesty would thence refrain from entailing ruin on the commerce of his dominions, the British Government would forbear (unless forced by actual hostilities) from any procedure which can interrupt those existing relations so beneficial to both countries. (*Wilson* "Documents" 5.)

The king never disavowed the governor of Ramree's letter; indeed he never condescended to answer the Viceroy at all. The only reason why he did not at once carry out the threat in the letter, and invade Bengal, was that he now heard of the defeat of the Mahratta Confederacy with whom he had hoped to co-operate against the English.[1]

He claimed Bengal far beyond Calcutta because he was successor to the rajas of Arakan who at various times in the middle ages had ruled Ramu and Chittagong and sometimes raided Dacca and Murshidabad. He failed to note that long since then the Moghuls had included those places in their empire, and that the English as legatees of the Great Moghul had been in charge of their daily administration since 1760. He had no claim, and was estopped from raising one because during his occupation of Arakan, now thirty-three years old, he had frequently acknowledged possession by applying to the English for extradition of the Arakanese fugitives. The Burmese thought that to have raided a country centuries ago, gives a claim to it now; raiding was their conception of conquest. But, as the Chinese had pointed out to them in 1769, such reasoning would justify the Chinese in claiming Burma down to Tarokmaw below Prome because they had marched there in 1287.[2]

Bodawpaya died in the thirty-eighth year of his reign and the seventy-fifth of his age, leaving 122 children and 208 grandchildren. With the possible exception of Bayinnaung 1551-81 he was the most powerful monarch who ever ruled Burma, and the chronicles regard him as one of the best. With characteristic shrewdness he decided the succession long in advance, appointing his eldest son crown prince.

[1] Despatch dated 17 March 1820 from Governor-General to Court of Directors (*PP* 120).

[2] *Konbaungset* 467.

One of his brothers had thereupon remarked that this was not in accordance with their father Alaungpaya's behest whereby the brothers were to succeed in order of seniority, and Bodawpaya himself owed his succession to this behest; this remark helped to bring its maker to the executioners. But the crown prince, although he lived to do service such as the conquest of Arakan, died in 1808 leaving a son. Bodawpaya lost no time in nominating that son; consequently the court had a decade in which to regard the matter as settled, and the heir succeeded without difficulty.

BAGYIDAW 1819-37 was thirty-five years of age at his succession. He was graceful and dignified in public; in private he had charming manners and was most approachable. He took exercise daily, riding an elephant or pick-a-back on a favourite whom he bridled with a kerchief in the mouth; and he delighted in the magnificent regattas which were such a feature under the kings. His queen was of low origin and had sold fish in the bazaar; of her brother, the power behind the throne, the less said the better. The chief counsellors in foreign affairs were men such as a half-caste Portuguese who nowadays would not be accepted for a clerkship but was regarded as an authority because he had actually travelled as far as Calcutta. The king's exceptional kindness made him so revered and beloved that there was no rebellion throughout all the disasters of his reign, which would have overthrown any other king. He had the receding forehead of his family and could not fix his attention on a subject for more than ten minutes. When annoyed he had a way of stepping off his throne into an inner chamber; everyone knew what to expect and prepared for flight; in a moment he would return with a spear—princes, ministers, generals, courtiers would go tumbling over one another down the palace stairs, while he came after them hurling the spear into their midst. If he returned from an excursion by land and not, as expected, by the waterside where they were awaiting him, three *wungyis*, all the *wundauks*, and all the *atwinwuns* would be clapped into three pair fetters and spend the night in the common jail. The spire of his new palace at Ava was overthrown by a thunderstorm; he could not punish the thunder so he punished the architect, who was immediately led away to execution, the king impatiently exclaiming "Is he dead?" "Is he dead?" every few minutes; in the evening his merciful heart made him send a reprieve, but when it arrived the architect's head was no longer on its shoulders. He was most unfortunate to reign at a period when publicity was increasing.[1]

At his coronation he announced his benevolent intentions, remitted central taxation for three years, and held a great investiture. Two of his uncles fell from power and one of them, the prince of Toungoo, was executed with all his family and followers according to the correct procedure; the king ordered that the other, the prince of Prome, should be spared, but the queen thought otherwise, and he died of a sudden complaint.[2] What they had done is uncertain, but under the kings, especially at times of succession, suspicion and guilt were synonymous—at least they met the same fate—and quite possibly the two uncles had contemplated rebelling as their only chance of safety.

Like every other king, Bagyidaw performed the sacramental ploughing of the fields in June each year, wearing his crown, riding the Lord White Elephant from the palace to the field, and using a gilded harrow drawn by milk-white oxen which were harnessed in gold trappings studded with rubies and diamonds.[3]

The capital (p. 265) was moved back to Ava and in 1823 the king took possession of his new palace with a ceremonial procession of great beauty, in which all the great office-bearers and vassal chiefs wore their robes of state, and only the king and queen, walking hand in hand, were clad in the simple dress of householders.[4] These changes of capital had become a habit with the dynasty. The ancient transfers between Prome, Pagan, Ava, Toungoo, and Pegu were justified on the ground of some

[1] *Crawfurd passim, Gouger* 34, 71, 73.
[2] *Trant* 80, *Gouger* 100.
[3] See note "Lehtunmingala" p. 362.
[4] *Wayland* I. 336, *Gouger* 25, *Crawfurd* I. 147.

pressing need; but after 1765, in the Age of Prose and Reason, the transfers took place on purely astrological grounds.

Nga Min, the royal bard, wrote a eulogy for the state entry into the palace and received as a reward Rs. 400 with a barge; he enjoyed the salt revenue of Hainggyi island (Negrais). Nga Chein, the author of Woharalinatta-dipani, was a senior herald in this reign. Nga Sa, son of a cavalry commandant of Mauktet, Monyua district, was private secretary to Bagyidaw both as crown prince and as king; in 1819 he commanded the Manipur expedition and in 1824 he was Mahabandula's second in command against the English in Arakan; later he was made a minister of the Hluttaw Council and administrator of crown lands; he wrote the Shwebonnidan and in youth he translated the Enaungzat from Siamese into Burmese and wrote a drama on it with songs.

When in 1813 the Burmese had set Marjit Singh on the throne of Manipur (p. 283), his rival brothers fled to Cachar.[1] He and his lords, having lived at the Burmese court, introduced luxurious habits and affected a degree of splendour in their dress and cavalcades which contrasted greatly with the natural simplicity of Manipur; but they were bloodthirsty tyrants, tolerated by the people only from fear of the Burmese. They had to be rebuked for cutting timber in the Kabaw valley and for building a gilded palace which the Burmese allowed to no king but their own; and Marjit Singh, in spite of all he owed to Bagyidaw who when a prince had always spoken in his favour, disloyally failed to appear at Bagyidaw's coronation. The Burmese therefore again overran Manipur in 1819 and stayed in the country but were seldom safe outside their stockades; they suffered ghastly ambushes, and could get nothing to eat because their own devastations had made the land a desert. Marjit Singh with thousands of his people fled to his brothers in Cachar, became reconciled to them, and proceeded to persecute that country also. They then re-entered Manipur in overwhelming strength and nearly took the Burmese stockade at Imphal, but the garrison made a magnificent defence until reinforcements arrived, whereupon the Manipuris made off

[1] *Konbaungset* 850-71, *Pemberton* 45, *Gait* 252, *Naga Hills and Manipur Gazetteer* 17.

to Cachar. There the rival Manipuri princes again fell out, this time over a polo pony; one of them applied to the English for help, and so did the rightful raja of Cachar. In 1762, angry at the Negrais massacre, the English had made a treaty with the Manipuris against the Burmese but had done nothing in fulfilment; even now they refused both applications, saying they could not interfere in internal affairs. The rightful raja of Cachar thereupon brought in the Burmese but this was in 1824 when the English, seeing that it was no longer possible to stand aloof, had already declared Cachar to be a protected state and sent a force which neutralised the Burmese advance beyond Manipur.

The rebel governor whom the Burmese in 1816 had helped to return to Assam (p. 283) was soon murdered as he deserved and the raja, Chandrakant, was deposed. So the Burmese in 1819 again overran the hapless land and reinstated the raja; but as they killed people and passed orders without even the pretence of consulting him, he and many lords fled in terror across the English frontier; the English refused the Burmese demands for their extradition. These demands were in studiously provocative terms, for the Burmese felt they had taken the measure of the English, having defeated not only the dismal detachments recruited in Chittagong (p. 282), but also the Assamese, whom the raja dressed and drilled after the Company's model. In 1821 they entered English territory (which extended up the Brahmaputra river to Goalpara), because Chandrakant was using it as a base for his counter attacks with considerable success; he had in his service Bruce, a country-born adventurer with 300 muskets procured in Calcutta, and he raised 2,000 men, mostly Sikhs and Hindustanis, in British territory. He evaded English magistrates by bribing their native subordinates not to report his actions, and in any case the English soon ceased to care, for the Burmese atrocities in Assam gave them moral justification and they were beginning to see that peaceful methods were wasted; they were but acceding to the self-determination of a people begging to be rescued from hell on earth.

Hitherto it has been difficult to say what the wars which had been depopulating Indo-China from time immemorial meant to the non-combatant population; but at this time it is easy, for the country comes under observation by a trained staff. Consider this deposition:—

> I am a native of the village of Udarbund, in the country of Cachar. I have been a prisoner of war in Ava. I was seized at my native village, about twenty months ago, by a party of Burmese, belonging to the army. . . . About six thousand persons, including men, women, and children, were seized about the same time. We were all taken away from Cachar. We were treated with great rigour; we were chained two and two, got very little food, were made to carry heavy loads on the march. Women, with infants at the breast, and who on this account, could not carry loads, had the infants snatched from them, their heads chopped off before them, and their bodies thrown into the rivers. I have witnessed murders of this description twelve or thirteen times myself. Old and sick persons, who could not carry burdens, were often killed by the Burman soldiers; and their loads, which consisted of plunder, were divided among the other prisoners. (Deposition of Mahomed Ruffy, recorded in June 1826, *Crawfurd* I. 423.)

Thirty thousand souls were carried away from Assam alone.[1] To cow the people they were flayed alived, burnt in oil, or driven in crowds into the village prayer-houses which were set on fire;[2] women, old as well as young, were outraged with every circumstance of barbarity;[3] sometimes bamboo cages would be constructed to burn men, women and infants two hundred or so at a time; and the more imaginative among the Burmese braves would add variations, such as cutting pieces off the bodies of their lingering victims under whose eyes they would eat the raw flesh.[4] Such being their energy, it is hardly surprising that the Burmese should, during the seven years of their intervention in Assam, have reduced the population by more than half, that some valleys are still suffering from this depopulation, and that in many a village to-day men speak with a shudder of *Mānar Upadrab*, "the oppressions of the Burmese."

These oppressions were committed out of set policy, and the Burmese prided themselves on it, saying that though at

[1] *Gait* 284. [2] *Gait* 277.

[3] *Gait* 227, *Nowgong Gazetteer* 39.

[4] *Butler* 248. Cf. pp. 37, 94, 174 above. This practice of eating prisoners alive was continued in 1887 by Ya Nyun, the Burmese king's trusty and well-beloved Myingaung (Cavalry Commandant) of Welaung, Myingyan district, as men still living remember.

home they were a mild people, when invading foreign countries they deliberately gave way to all their passions, plundering and murdering without control so that foreigners should learn not to provoke them.[1]

Naturally atrocities diminished after the Burmese had been some time in a country and conditions became more settled; but there was no knowing when they might not recur. Thus, for sixty years the Burmese would march into Manipur whenever the mood seized them, round up several thousand hapless people, and re-enact the same terrible scenes as before. Two generations after Alaungpaya had swept away the Talaing kingdom, seven Talaing villagers were fishing in a canoe on the Panhlaing river thirty miles above Rangoon when a Burmese war-canoe came by, bearing royal despatches; she swept along under sixty oars, and her commander's gold umbrella flashed in the sun; his eye fell on the seven men in the canoe and he ordered them aboard; they had done no harm, but the Burmese were out to break the spirit of the Talaings; therefore those seven men were made to kneel at the head of the boat, stretching their necks over the water, and without more ado, in cold blood, the heads of six of them were struck off.[2] Such things were so liable to happen that Talaing housewives habitually kept a store of rice which had been boiled and then dried in the sun, so as to have a supply of portable cooked food in case they had to flee at a moment's notice.[3]

The most favoured tributaries were the Shans. All that the Burmese did was to keep them down with a garrison and leave them well alone, provided they paid tribute. Yet even the Shans, who spoke with liking and respect of their Chinese overlords, had not a good word to say for their Burmese overlords.[4] Travellers noted that the Burmese Shans were shabbier and had poorer houses than the Siamese Shans, and seemed to have all the heart taken out of them by the crushing revenue which the Burmese exacted; yet they got nothing in return, and the Burmese did not protect them from the cruel Karen slave raids which were the terror of their lives. Even well-intentioned chiefs would be driven to practise extortion in

[1] *Crawfurd* I. 422. [2] *Gouger* 310. [3] Talaing family tradition.
[4] *JASBengal* 1837 MacLeod "Journal of an Expedition to Kiang Hung" 998; *McLeod and Richardson* 71, 82, 118-9.

order to recoup the bribes they had to pay at court to secure investiture. They were sometimes sent flying at each other's throats, for the Burmese fostered feuds and would promise a pretender the succession if he could oust the reigning *sawbwa*. The chroniclers regard such methods as statesmanship, and delight to relate the wise minister's parable of the man who sets two wild animals fighting until they are exhausted, and then captures both.

The Assamese campaigns, waged amid strange races and magnificent scenery, powerfully affected the imagination of the Burmese as they swarmed through the passes or floated for hundred of miles down the Brahmaputra river on rafts. They marched with the tread of conquerors, and the earth seemed to tremble under their feet. The succession of victories confirmed the opinion they had of themselves, and whetted their appetite for further conquest. Among the commanders who thus won fame was Mahabandula,[1] a handsome man of fine presence, born about 1780 at Ngapayin in Monyua district, where he subsequently became governor of Alon. As a youth he had waited long at court until in despair he committed a violent assault on a minister; thereupon king Bodawpaya, perceiving that he had a valiant soul, had employed him as a soldier. It was sometimes impossible to get a word out of him, for he would remain lost in silent contemplation of his own glory. His reputation puzzled the only trained soldiers he ever met, for although they respected him as a resolute man they found his judgment to be nothing out of the ordinary. Like Alaungpaya, he owed his fame largely to the fact that his opponents were obscure tribes. He obtained his results by using methods known to every energetic Burmese commander. Thus, a fault in even a senior officer would be visited with the penalty of being sawn in two; some commanders did not always inflict such punishment very intelligently, as when a scout reported that the enemy were advancing, and was at once

[1] *Gouger* 107, *Crawfurd* I. 14 and II. app. 100. *Snodgrass* 176, *Trant* 140, *Wilson* "Documents" 102 and "Introductory sketch" 66, *Robertson* 24, *JBRS* 1915 Stewart "Ex Libris Bandulae."

BURMA IN 1824

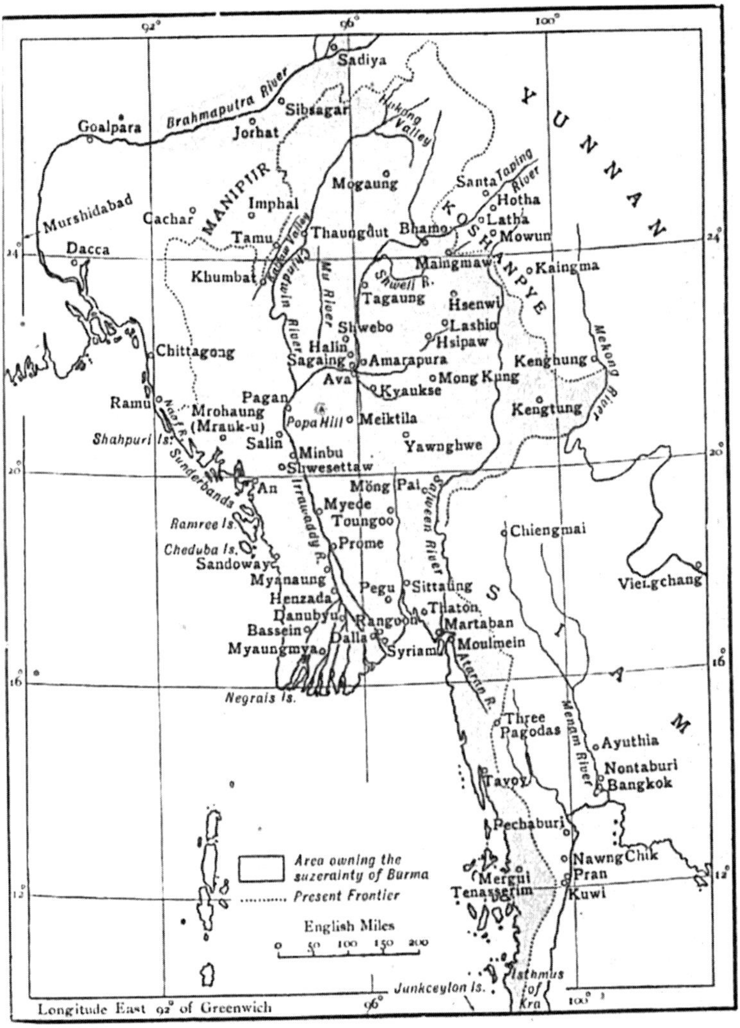

Emery Walker Ltd. sc.

Longmans, Green, & Co. London, New York, Toronto, Bombay, Calcutta & Madras.

executed for bringing sad news, and the execution was hardly over before the enemy made hand-to-hand contact. But his followers adored Mahabandula; he was pre-eminent in stratagems of a type which was devastating against enemies of his own class, and in the management of Burmese levies, no light task, he evinced real talent. He was just, self-sacrificing, honest to an unusual degree, and, unlike the court, he was willing to learn by experience. He learnt to disregard the astrologers whose humbug guided armies in the field. When he found an enemy who treated his wounded well instead of mutilating them in the way which he had believed to be universal he promptly ordered his men to do likewise. And when, all too late, he realised that there were more things on earth than he had dreamed of, he evinced a grave courtesy and an unflinching resolution, in contrast to his colleagues who vented their panic-stricken fury on all around and ran for their lives. He was an imperialist of the most aggressive type, yet it is unjust to regard him as responsible for the war of 1824; he did indeed force it on, but in advocating it he was merely the mouthpiece of the entire people.

Burmese frontier guards sometimes fired on British subjects proceeding in their canoes down the Naaf estuary, the frontier between Arakan and English territory. The villagers were frightened and could not go about their business. After February 1823 therefore the English stationed an outpost on Shahpuri Island (Shinmapyugyun) at the southern extremity of Tek Naaf police station in Chittagong district.[1] The people's fears were allayed and things went on in the ordinary quiet way for months, till suddenly at midnight 23-4 September 1823 a thousand Burmese soldiers swarmed onto the island in boats with flaming torches. The outpost consisted of a dozen nameless sepoys under a jemadar; there was nobody to whom they could apply for orders, but they knew their duty and did it quickly. After finishing them off, the Burmese (no longer a full thousand, for there were now gaps in their ranks) burnt the outpost stockade to the ground and garrisoned the island.

When the papers, including a survivor's statement, were laid before the Viceroy, he repressed his first impulse and wrote personally to the king of Burma asking him to reflect

[1] *Wilson* "Documents" 14-18; *Crawfurd* II. app. 122.

on what the consequences of this sort of thing must inevitably be, and offering him the loophole of disavowal. The king did not deign to reply. Shahpuri Island had been under the Collector of Chittagong for generations, it was in his old files and had regularly been included in the revenue settlements. Yet even now the Government of India, with all their experience of human weakness and folly, hesitated to believe that the king really meant war; as late as 24 November 1823 the Adjutant General, discussing troop movements, wrote that it would be necessary to strengthen the frontier guards, but that there was no need actually to anticipate a campaign.[1]

For twenty-nine years the Burmese had habitually crossed the frontier at will, occasionally murdering and enslaving British subjects, destroying lakhs' worth of property, holding the Company's elephant hunters to ransom, claiming the surrender of crowds of panic-stricken refugees, and seeking to drive their slave-gangs[2] home through British territory. Letter after letter from the Viceroy remained deliberately unanswered, and his envoys had been subjected to vulgarities of a type associated with the scullery. Every few years some extraordinary person, smiling all over with satisfaction at himself, would prance up to British officers and hand them a letter full of white elephants, golden feet, etc., commanding the Viceroy of India to make haste and *shihko* (prostrate himself) before the throne of Amarapura and beg pardon for his sins or it would be worse for him. Successive Viceroys had gone out of their way to make allowances for the mentality of the Burmese court, but every act of consideration had been interpreted as cringing. These things had ceased to be comic and even the Government of India now began to see that, as the unfortunate Cox had told them twenty-six years previously, there was only one way to bring this people to its senses. But it mattered little whether the Government of India saw it or not, for the decision was taken out of their hands: the king of Burma had slipped the leash, and his exultant armies were now speeding across the frontier with orders to finish the English once and for all.

[1] *Wilson* "Documents" 21.

[2] Para. 31 of despatch dated 10 September 1824 from Governor-General to Court of Directors (*PP* 129).

The king had not taken this drastic step without profound consideration. In the year of grace 1823, midway between the French Revolution and the electric telegraph, his considered judgment was as follows.[1] He was partial to Europeans, but they had repaid him ill: these English had the impertinence to possess a larger territory than his and to refuse him homage; his dignified silences, the exquisitely delicate hints of his ministers, the stern warnings of his generals, had all failed; he had spared them too often and it was now time to teach them a lesson. War was expensive but the loot of Calcutta would compensate him for that; the muskets and cannon captured from the English would come in very useful for his projected conquest of Siam; and as for the wastage in man-power, this would be made good by the myriads of prisoners his great generals would bring home. No doubt the English were quite good soldiers in their way, but they had won their reputation at the expense of black Hindus: they would find things very different when they met real Burmans. The Chins, the Singphos, the Manipuris, the Assamese, etc., etc., all the nations of the earth, had gone down before his men. Who were the English to fare any better? Everyone knew that one Burman was worth four Englishmen; the English knew it themselves, for they were evidently afraid to fight—had they not given way on every occasion since he first had dealings with them twenty-nine years ago? Mahabandula had pointed out that the English were mere merchants and such indifferent soldiers that it was unnecessary to send proper Burmese troops, and Assamese levies would suffice to conquer Bengal. Mahabandula was a man of his word; the English might have some good commanders, but it was not likely that any of them could equal the genius of Mahabandula; for in war bravery is not enough, high strategy also is necessary; there are many, many stratagems, and Mahabandula was master of them all. The English evidently knew nothing about high strategy, for they did not understand entrenching and used to march about in red coats, exposing their whole bodies and giving notice of their onset by beating drums; doubtless that was their way of doing things, and they had some reason of their own for it; it might do well enough against mere Hindus, but Burma was

[1] *Crawfurd* II. app. *passim*.

different from India, and if they tried that sort of thing in Burma they would all be ambushed[1] and blown to pieces and their heads would be taken in thousands. Some fool said that the English had 200,000 trained sepoys[2] and would bring an army by sea from Calcutta to Rangoon; had anyone ever heard such nonsense? There could not be 200,000 troops in the whole world put together, and as for transporting an army from Calcutta, why, the place was at the other end of the world. If the English ever did land a few men in Rangoon, they would certainly never get out again, and he would take such steps that even old women would not be disturbed in cooking their rice.[3] The main theatre would be in the north-west, where his armies would take Calcutta, march to England,[4] and establish his son as viceroy of all the English countries. But even at this dread hour the royal heart was merciful, for the hosts were enjoined to spare the life of the English Viceroy; and the royal taste was exquisite, for the chains in which he was to be brought back were coated with gold.[5]

It was not the king who led the people but the people who led the king into war. For long he had been a moderating influence, hesitating to accept the advice of his commanders, who thirsted for fresh victories. The war was popular not only with the princes and the army but also with all classes: the Burmese people willed the war.[6] Their armies crossed the frontier in January 1824; when challenged, they announced that hostilities had begun, and they followed up the announcement by drawing English blood.[7] The Viceroy of India merely recognised existing conditions when, 5 March 1824, he notified a state of war. A few weeks later, English transports drew alongside the Rangoon stockade.

[1] *Gouger* 104.

[2] *Crawfurd* II. app. 97. It did not take a tenth of this number of effectives to dispose of Burma.

[3] *Snodgrass* 25.

[4] *Wilson* "Documents" 19.

[5] *Snodgrass* 277, *Trant* 75.

[6] See note "Popular feeling" p. 363.

[7] Four English officers and 155 sepoys killed and wounded at Dudpatli—Col. Bowen's report dated 22 February 1824 to Brigade Major, Dacca. The Burmese had fired the first shot on 18 January, at Bikrampur inside our Cachar frontier (*Wilson* "Documents" 23).

RANGOON IN 1824.

From an engraving by William Daniell, 1832, on the walls of the Maymyo Club. The only letterpress on it is "Rangoon from the Anchorage. | Drawn on the spot by Capt. Kershaw, 13th Light Infantry," one of H.M.'s regiments at Rangoon in 1824.

APPENDIX

APPENDIX

Inscriptions the Touchstone.[1]—The Pali inscriptions at Prome, and the Pyu inscriptions, resemble the Kadamba script used in the fifth to sixth century in north Canara near Goa; the Talaing inscription at Lopburi in Siam resembles the Pallava script used in these centuries (Dhammapala's age) at Conjeveram. See *RSASB* 1919 20, Blagden "Pyu inscriptions" in *Epigraphia Indica* XII and *JBRS* 1917, and Tun Nyein "Maunggun gold plates" in *Epigraphia Indica* V.

Such inscriptions contain texts indicating an advanced knowledge of Buddhist scripture; but this does not show the widespread existence of Buddhist civilisation any more than the presence in Burma of eighteenth century Latin inscriptions shows the establishment of Christian civilisation under Alaungpaya.

Writing reached Upper Burma even later. Although its dry climate is so favourable to preservation, the earliest inscriptions so far found there (except perhaps a Pyu fragment at Halin) are in tenth century north Indian script. The earliest in Burmese is dated 1058 (*Inscriptions* 1913 1); the script is a copy of the Talaing, and the crude and variable spelling indicates that the scribes were trying their hand on a new medium; Talaing inscriptions of the same period are more advanced in both spelling and style. There seems to have been a Sanskrit canon at Pagan before the eleventh century, but its possessors probably kept the art of writing to themselves.

The absence of earlier inscriptions largely invalidates the native accounts of Burmese history before the reign of Anawrahta 1044-77. These accounts are as follows:—

Abhiraza with his Sakya clansmen came from Kapilavastu in India, founding Tagaung 850 B.C. and Kyaukpadaung in Arakan 825 B.C. Tagaung was overthrown by the Chinese about 600 B.C., and its people then founded Old Pagan; they went further south also, founding in 443 B.C. Prome, a glorious city which, under the great king Duttapaung 443-373 B.C. contained a splendid court and 3,000 Buddhist monks. Meanwhile Buddha himself had visited Legaing and Shwesettaw (in Minbu district), as is borne out by the existence of Kyaungdawya pagoda, and of his two footprints, each three cubits long, at Shwesettaw; on his way back he passed by Prome—witness the Po-u-daung pagoda there, and look at the very hill where he stopped, Tankyidaung (to be distinguished from its namesake opposite Pagan). In his lifetime, his disciples had founded

[1] See p. 4.

the Shwedagon and Shwemawdaw pagodas. Later, under Asoka 272-32 B.C., two missionaries, Soṇa and Uttara, were sent from the Council of Patna and evangelised Thaton where they had 60,000 converts. Prome being overthrown in A.D. 95 through dissension among the tribes, its people migrated, founded Pagan in 105, dropped their separate tribal names, and henceforth are all known as Burmans; their king Pyusawti 168-243 inflicted a sanguinary defeat on the Chinese. In 403 the great apostle Buddhaghosa brought the scriptures from Ceylon to Thaton, whence copies immediately spread to Pagan, Arakan, and the Shans.

Buddha's coming to Burma is on a level with Joseph of Arimathea's planting the Glastonbury Thorn. The Shwesettaw legend is not even original; it comes from the commentary on the Samyutta Nikaya, and the Sanskrit Divyavadana; it refers to the Konkan, and not to Burma, see *Duroiselle* "Notes on the ancient geography of Burma." Other incidents told as historical in the chronicles and thamaings are copies of foreign originals. The Shwedagon legend is found in the Mahavastu, and when first told it has no reference to Burma. The legend of Alaungdaw Kathapa is found in the Sanskrit canon Mula-Sarvastadina as preserved in the Chinese translation. The Tagaung princess Beda is simply the Padmavati and Nalini of the Mahavastu, a Mahayanist work in corrupt Sanskrit; her parthenogenesis from a doe in a hermit's mingeing place is found in Pali Jatakas 523 (Alambusa) and 526 (Nalinika), in the Ramayana, in Chinese jataka collections, in the No plays of Japan, and in one of the Tun-huang tapestries (Stein Collection, British Museum no. 12).

Chinese records make no mention of any direct dealings with Burma before the thirteenth century, still less do they mention a victorious campaign crushing Tagaung about 600 B.C. On the other hand, the Nanchao (Yünnan) chief Kolofêng subjugated the Pyu and the tribes of the upper Irrawaddy shortly after A.D. 754. Perhaps this is the Chinese invasion of 600 B.C., antedated as usual to give Pagan a hoary antiquity. Kolofêng also defeated the Chinese and others; the Nanchao armies used to include levies from subject tribes. Probably Pyusawti furnished a contingent to his overlord Kolofêng and when he returned home his share of the fighting would not lose in the telling: this may be the original of Pyusawti's victory over the Chinese. His name is Chinese Shan. *Saw* is the same word as *saw* in *sawbwa*, as *chao* the Nanchao for king; *ti* is the Chinese for king (*Taw Sein Ko* "Burmese Sketches" 20). Pyusawti is therefore the Chinese Shan for "Pyu prince"; it is also the Nanchao name for a legendary son of Asoka who, the Nanchao possibly thought, was a Pyu (*BEFEO* 1904 Pelliot "Deux itinéraires"). Whereas the stories of other early princes are copied from Indian sources, Pyusawti's story is from Shan sources. He was born of a dragon's egg; it is a common folk-lore motive in Indo-China; the Shans and Palaungs have similar legends, see *Cochrane* I. 58.

There is no *a priori* difficulty in Asoka's sending Sona and Uttara to Thaton which lay so near on a good sea route, but he does not claim to have sent them; their mission is not mentioned till seven hundred years later, in the Ceylon chronicle Mahavamsa, compiled in the early sixth century Christian era. It is not mentioned in Rock Edicts II., V., XIII., where Asoka 272-32 B.C. catalogues his missions, including missions which he must have known were fruitless, to persons like Ptolemy of Egypt and Antigonus of Macedonia (*Epigraphia Indica* II. Bühler "Asoka's Rock Edicts,"); yet we are to believe that he omitted a mission to Thaton which produced sixty thousand converts If the mission ever went to Thaton, it can have had little result. No trace of Asokan script has been found in Burma. See *IA* 1905 Vincen. Smith "Asoka's alleged mission to Pegu."

There is a considerable literature in the name of Buddhaghosa, and doubtless he existed as a person and wrote some of it, but the accounts of him vary so enormously that this is all we can say; see *IA* 1890 Foulkes "Buddhaghosa." The Kalyani Inscriptions (p. 120) do not mention him. If he brought the scriptures to Thaton in 403 and a few years later they reached Pagan, Pagan in 1057 would not have had to fight Thaton to get them (p. 27).

The glorious king Duttapaung is possibly a composite figure embodying memories of the Pyu dynasty at Prome. Blagden suspects that Duttapaung is not a proper name but a title (*RSASB* 1912 11); the Pyu for *His Majesty* tdạ̥̊ ḅḁ̊ is practically the same word as Duttapaung; indeed (though this counts for little) Duttapaung happens to be used as a title at *Thatonmyo Shwezayan Thamaing* 19, 56.

The elimination of Prome as the Pyu capital in A.D. 95 is inconsistent with the existence there of Pyu rulers' inscriptions dating from apparently the seventh and eighth centuries. The records of the Chinese Tang dynasty 618-905, the Chinese travellers I-ching 671-95 and Hsüan-chuang 629-45, and the Chinese geographer Chia-tan 785-805, point to Prome as the Pyu capital. They do not mention Pagan, and it was not of sufficient importance to be founded as a town till 849 (*Hmannan* I. 223).

Ancient sites.[1]—The principal are, among the Talaings—Thaton, Twante, Rangoon, and Pegu which was an offshoot from Thaton formed some time after the sixth century; among the Arakanese—Sandoway, Vesali; among tribes which seem to have been half Shan, half Pyu—Tagaung; among the Pyu—Prome, Halin (in Shwebo district), Nyaunglun (in Yamethin district), Peikthano (in Magwe district), and Powundaung (in Monyua district). See *ARASI* 1909-10 Taw Sein Ko "Excavations at Hmawza," 1911-12 Duroiselle "Excavations at Hmawza," 1914-15 Duroiselle "Rock-cut temples of Powundaung"; *RSASB* 1905 7 Taw Sein Ko's visit to Halin; *JBRS* 1917 Stewart "Excavation and exploration at Pegu"; *Forchammer* "Notes on early history and geography" and "Arakan"; *IA* 1892 Taw Sein Ko "Archæological tour through Ramannadesa" and 1893 Temple "Notes on antiquities in Ramannadesa." Legends are found in *GUB*, e.g. II. i. 115 and II. ii. 92. See also *JBRS* 1911 May Oung "Prome and the Pyus" and 1916 Taw Sein Ko "Derivation of the word Prome."

[1] See p. 7.

Führer's inscription.[1]—The idea that the remains at Tagaung are of great antiquity rests largely on Führer's statement in 1894 that he found at Tagaung a stone slab dated A.D. 416 with a Sanskrit inscription telling how Tagaung was founded by immigrant princes from Hastinapura (Old Delhi). His statement is quoted verbatim in *GUB* I. ii. 193 (similar "inscriptions" are mentioned at 186), is accepted in *Gerini* 471, 746, and has passed into popular works, e.g. *Scott O'Connor* 208. Unfortunately this precious slab has never been produced, and in view of Führer's service record its production is essential.

Eastern shipping.[2]—Although English officers in 1750 noted that Talaings were capable of making good seamen (*Dalrymple* I. 130), the Burmese never had any shipping (*Hobson-Jobson* s.v. "Burma") because they had no seamen (*Hakluyt* X. 159), and the Portuguese noted the worthlessness of their coasting craft (*Couto* III. i. 20).

The sea voyages of the Hinduised Malays of Sumatra who, about the time of Christ, colonised Madagascar and East Africa, have not yet been worked out. For Roman trading settlements in southern India, see *Vincent Smith* "Early History of India." Roman shipping never went beyond Ceylon and disappeared in the fifth century. From the first to the ninth century, Chinese junks went as far as the Persian Gulf; thereafter they seldom went west of Malacca. From the eighth century till the arrival of the Portuguese in the fifteenth, Arab seamen practically monopolised the carrying trade from Egypt and Madagascar to China. See *Radhakumud Mookerji*, *Yule* "Cathay," *Beazley*, *Chau Ju-kua*, *TP* 1914 and 1915 Rockhill "Notes on the trade of China with the coast of the Indian Ocean during the fifteenth century," Mayers "Chinese explorations of the Indian Ocean during the fifteenth century" in *China Review* III., *Hunter* I. ch. i.

Golden Land.[3]—The name would be intelligible if, as is quite possible, Burmese pagodas were gilded in those days. Burma is not a noticeable source of precious metals and there is nothing to show that she ever was. The gold output even in the record years 1914, 1915, was under four thousand ounces, as against the world output of twenty-two million ounces; the producing districts are Myitkyina and to a negligible extent Salween, Shwebo, Katha, Upper Chindwin. The record silver output in Burma, that of 1918, was under two million ounces, all from Bawdwin, as against the world output of two hundred million. Temple half thinks Ἀργύρη (Silver Land), Ptolemy's name for Arakan, to be a corruption of Arkang, the Indian pronunciation of Rahkaing (Arakan); mediæval travellers do not mention silver in Arakan and the name may be due to desire for symmetry—if there is a golden land, there must also be a silver one. Both names may be based on mere travellers' tales. However, since the Middle Ages the annual gold output of the world has grown one hundred times, and the total stock has grown one hundred and sixty times; so perhaps the precious metals of Burma, which hardly attract attention now, were really noticeable for ancient times. Yünnan certainly had plentiful

[1] See p. 9. [2] See pp. 9, 57. [3] See p. 9.

silver, and also seems to have had gold; in mediæval times it used to be said of any very wealthy person in southern China that he must be from Yünnan. Similarly gold was found, over the Siamese border at the ancient city of U Thong, which means "the golden"; and in the Malay state of Pahang are the remains of immense gold mines on a scale which has no counterpart in southern Asia. Pahang may have been the original of Ptolemy's Golden Land, though he places it distinctly in Lower Burma. Gold-washing on the Sittang cannot have been sufficiently productive to create the name. Since it is to Sumatra that the name Suvannabhumi is applied *par excellence* (*JBRS* 1923 153), one cannot help wondering whether Thaton was not colonised from Sumatra and took its mother's name. See *Coedès*, *JSS* 1916 Prince Damrong "Siamese history prior to the founding of Ayuddhya," *IA* 1894 Taw Sein Ko "Some remarks on the Kalyani inscriptions," *Gerini*, *Hobson-Jobson* s.v. "Arakan."

Teak.[1]—Yet the export of teak from India, probably the Malabar coast, existed from ancient times, at least as a luxury article; it was used by Nebuchadnezzar 604-562 B.C., and teak beams, still undecayed, exist in the great palace of the Sassanid kings at Seleucia or Ctesiphon, dating from the middle of the sixth century. The first European mention of Burma teak seems to be in 1597 when the king of Portugal told his viceroy at Goa not to let the Turks export it from Pegu. See 353, *Hobson-Jobson* s.v. "Teak," *Radhakumud Mookerji* 85-7.

Ancient coastline.[2]—Hsüan-chuang 629-45 heard of Prome as near a sea harbour; but there is no evidence to support the tradition that she was actually on the sea until the volcano Popa Hill burst into eruption and Lower Burma heaved above the waves. South of Prome the great stretches of alluvial land were doubtless under water, but not the high land, of which there is plenty; there is nothing to show that there has been any volcanic upheaval on the Burma mainland in human times. The occurrence of bracken and other plants of temperate regions on the summit of Popa Hill suggests that the close of the Glacial Age found its surface in a fit stage to support vegetation—i.e. it can hardly have been violently active in human times. See *RSASB* 1910 13, *JASBengal* 1862 Blandford "Account of a visit to Puppa-doung."

At Payagyi, north of Pegu town, at Ayetthima (Taikkala) in Thaton district, and at Thaton town, bolts, cables, and other parts of foreign ships have been unearthed. Rocks on the hills near Shwegyin show traces of sea-erosion. See *Stewart* "Pegu Gazetteer" 4, 32; *Furnivall* "Syriam Gazetteer" 12; *Forchammer* "Notes on the early history and geography of British Burma (II.)." For some early traditions, see *Shwemawdaw Thamaing*, *Shwe Naw*.

By the time of Anawrahta 1044-77 much of the Delta had long been mainland. When he overthrew Thaton 1057 she was doubtless ceasing to be a seaport. Pegu continued to be a seaport till about 1600 but the Sittang river was silting up in 1569 when the Venetian Cæsar Frederick

[1] See p. 10. [2] See p. 11.

(*Hakluyt* X. 119) describes the violent tide which ships had to catch in order to shoot up the narrow channel to the town. The decline of Pegu town after 1600 is due to its being no longer accessible to merchant ships. The remains of Portuguese docks at Syriam show that even within the last three centuries much land has been reclaimed.

Pyu physiognomy.[1]—The people called Pyu in the chronicles, the people who lorded it at Prome, the people called P'iao by the Chinese, and the people who wrote the Pyu inscriptions, may have been distinct peoples. Villagers call these inscriptions "Pyu writing," but they tend to give the name Pyu to any writing they do not understand. All authorities agree provisionally to assume that these peoples are one and the same, but we really know next to nothing of the Pyu, and it does not look as if we ever shall. One is therefore inclined to be sceptical when one reads Mr Taw Sein Ko's categorical statement at *RSASB* 1919 38, that the fresco he reproduces from Kyanzittha's Onhmin, Pagan, depicts a Pyu lady. She is a type commonly found in the frescoes of Talaing pagodas at Pagan, there is nothing to show her nationality, and other observers do not think it is Pyu. He proceeds to say that the Pyus had an "aquiline nose, small mouth, pointed chin and well-developed jaw." But nobody has ever seen a Pyu, they have been extinct six centuries, and if, as is generally held, they were a Tibeto-Burman tribe, their features would be the reverse of aquiline.

Nanchao (p. 15)—the Chinese called it *nan* = south + *chao* = prince. Nanchao represents the southernmost limit in the direction of Burma reached by Chinese cultural influence, and so far as her people could write at all, they wrote in Chinese script. Their Buddhism is of a type which comes from Tibet and China, not from the south; thus, in 777 they built a monastery to Kuan Yin the Mahayanist madonna (*Sainson* 47).

Nanchao		*Pagan*
Hsi-nu-lo 649-74.		Pyusawti 167-242.
Lo-shêng 674-712.		Timinyi 242-99.
Shêng-lo-pi 712-28.		Yimminpaik 299-324
P'i-lo-ko 728-48.		Paikthili 324-44.
Ko-lo-fêng 748-78.		Thinlikyaung 344-87.
Fêng-ch'ieh-i, died young.		Kyaungdurit 387-412
I-mou-hsün 778-808.		
Hsün-ko-ch'üan 808-9.		
Ch'üan-lung-shêng 809-16	brothers.	
Ch'üan-li 816-24		
Ch'üan-fêng-yu 824-59		
Shih-lung 859-77.		
Lung-shun 877-97.		
Shun-hua-chên 897-902.		

[1] See p. 11.

BEFEO 1904 Pelliot "Deux itinéraires" 165 notes the similarity between Nanchao and Pagan royal nomenclature whereby the last syllable of the father's name forms the first of the son's. Above are the fourteen chiefs of the Mêng dynasty 649-902 of Nanchao, with their dates, which are well substantiated by Chinese records, and the six chiefs of Pagan with the Hmannan dates which are unsubstantiated; the identity of system indicates a common origin, probably community of race.

Mahamuni.[1]—The shrine, usually at Dinnyawadi, 22 miles north of Mrohaung, in Akyab district, was possibly the oldest in Burma, and certainly contained the oldest image [The Arakanese assign it to the reign of one Sandathuriya 146-98, if not to Buddha's lifetime. But early Buddhists, like early Christians, never made an image of their Master; they did not start doing so till the rise of Græco-Buddhist sculpture at Gandhara in the first century.] See *Forchammer* "Mahamuni pagoda," *JBRS* 1912 Chan Htwan Oung "The Mahamuni Shrine" and 1916 San Shwe Bu "The Story of Mahamuni."

The manner by which the image was taken in 1785 to Mandalay (p. 268) has been made the subject of unnecessary mystery, as if there were any difficulty in transporting even larger masses by forced labour. Some writers think there is a conflict of evidence between *Symes* 109 who says it was brought by water, and *Crawfurd* I. 476 who says "it was transported by the difficult route of Padaung, taken to pieces." Neither is a primary authority, and in any case *Symes* is superficial. *Konbaungset* 581-3 describes how it was taken by sea to Taungup in Sandoway district, by land over the pass to Padaung in Prome district, and by river to the capital; and in final corroboration we have the evidence of an officer who accompanied Trant over the An Pass in 1826. He writes (*IA* 1897 Temple "An unpublished document relating to the First Burmese War") that when marching through An town he was told "the head was taken off and the body divided above the navel. Three rafts were then constructed on which these different parts were floated down the Sunderbands to Sandoway; thence it was transported in the same way to Tongo Koung at the foot of the hills, where it remained till a road was formed to Padaung just below Prome. When the road was made, the three parts were placed on sledges and dragged by manual labour over the mountains to the . . . Irrawaddy."

Ari.[2]—The Thayapu pagoda, built in the eleventh century, at Lethkok in Myingyan district, contains frescoes showing Ari in black robes. The *locus classicus* is *ARASI* 1915-16 Duroiselle "The Ari of Burma and Tantric Buddhism." Mr. Taw Sein Ko at *RSASB* 1909 9 says an inscription records their existence in 1468 at Kyauksauk in Myingyan district; doubtless they existed then and even later, but the inscription, at *Inscriptions* 1903 181, does not mention them.

For the *droit de seigneur* of king and priest in so many parts of the world, see *Westermarck* I. ch. v. Its existence among certain types of Brahman is what one might expect, but its existence among Buddhist clergy

[1] See pp. 17, 137. [2] See pp. 17, 95.

is surprising, and is of course very rare; in Indo-China the only instances beside the Ari seem to be among the Hkamti Shans even now, and in the thirteenth century among some of the clergy in Siam, the Laos, and Cambodia where the Chinese observer calls it the *chentan*. Tradition says that the Popa *myothugyi* exercised it till three generations ago.

Long after the Ari had ceased to exercise the right, the Burmese *cum uxorem ducunt, nouam nuptam ad tempus primae noctis alio uiro tradunt, qui eam uitiet, hanc ad rem peregrinos ex occidente maximi faciunt, interdum etiam fit ut pater ipse suae filiae uim attulerit, antequam eam nouo marito in manus dederit.* This is first mentioned (*Badger* 203) by Ludovico de Varthema about 1505 at Tenasserim, but *Anderson* "English intercourse with Siam" 26 shows he was never there, so that this entry by itself proves nothing. But it does not stand by itself. *Linschoten* I. 99, writing in 1592, refers to the custom at Pegu, and *Schouten* I. 254 refers to it in Arakan in the seventeenth century, Richard (*Pinkerton* IX. 760) in the eighteenth, adding that Dutch sailors were paid for the service; cf. *TP* 1891 Cordier "Les Français en Birmanie" 27, written by 1786. The custom is quite obsolete and forgotten.

Another curious Burmese custom, whether connected with the Ari or not, is *in mulierum gratiam ad membrum uirile tintinabula aurea uel argenta appensa gestant ut sonum reddant dum per ciuitatem deambulant.* This [quite distinct from the ring worn by Chins, Karalingis, Zulus, and Romans (Pliny, Nat. Hist. XXXIII. 54) as an aid to continence] is mentioned at Ava by Nicolo di Conti about 1435 (*Badger*); at Pegu in 1511 by Ruy Nunez d'Acunha (*Hakluyt* X. 29), in 1586 by Fitch (*Hakluyt* X. 196), in 1592 (*Linschoten* I. 99), and somewhat later by *Stevens* I. 228, and in Arakan about 1724 by *Valentyn* V. i. 136. One hears vaguely of shot being used in the same way *ad lubidinem* in Indian towns nowadays. Possibly, too, the noise of the bells was intended to scare away evil spirits, for in northern India cowry shells are thus hung on little boys to ward off the evil eye, and little girls wear anklets of tinkling bells partly to scare away evil spirits. The custom is no longer remembered in Burma, but perhaps some cognate idea underlies the imbedding of solid metal pellets under the skin of arms and chest by dacoits as a charm against wounds.

Drink.—In addition to these instances above (pp. 17, 60, 80, 95, 110, 122, 123, 160, 167, 171, 201, 208, 210, 212, 222, 232, 262, 278, 283, 340), there are the following:—

From the first the kings of Pagan took part in the annual Mahagiri sacrifice (p. 167), which was also a drinking feast (*Wawhayalinatta* 69). At Martaban in 1281 Aleimma and Wareru plotted to make each other drunk and then let loose assassins (*Razadarit Ayedawpon*). In 1336 money was smuggled into the Sagaing palace in pots of liquor (*Hmannan* I. 396). Cæsar Frederick, year 1567 (*Hakluyt* X. 115), says the chief product of Mergui is nyper wine made from the *dani* palm (Nipa fructicans, Wumb.); *Linschoten* I. 103, writing in 1592, says it is exported from Tenasserim in great Pegu jars to India where women drink it secretly and gossip. Gasparo Balbi, year 1583 (*Hakluyt* X. 153), says the Delta folk live in boats covered with straw and drink hot waters made from rice, strong as our aquavitae. Cæsar Frederick, year 1567, and Fitch, year 1586 (*Hakluyt* X. 128, 191), mention opium from Mecca and Cambay as one of the principal imports into Burma. The Maung Minbyu Nat spirit is a prince who died of opium, being the son of Bayinnaung 1551-81; the Minye Aungdin Nat spirit is a prince who died of drink, being the son of king Anaukpetlun 1605-28 (*Temple* 37). *Manrique* xxi, xxix, year 1630, found locally made wine on sale in Mrohaung bazaar, and mentions Arakanese officers getting drunk on rice liquor given them by a monk. *Manucci* IV. 210, writing in 1701-05, speaks of the Burmese governor's drinking feasts at the annual Shwedagon festival, where a law officer once got so drunk that for a bet he was fired into the air at the tail of a giant rocket, and his charred body was found next morning far away in the jungle. In 1797 the young nobles at the Amarapura palace were passionately addicted to liquor and intoxicating drugs, employing secret agents to obtain them at any price, though the penalty was death (*Cox* 250). In 1824 the royal bodyguard drank on the sly everything they could get (*Gouger* 138, 141). Officers of the victorious army in 1825 found that the Burmese commanders who dined with them drank very sparingly in public, out of respect for the king's orders, but the lower classes were so excessively fond of liquor of any description that, death penalty or no death penalty, they drank everything they could get, and had plenty of toddy and fermented rice (*Snodgrass* 223, *Trant* 229); we often found Burmese soldiers under the influence of opium, and the captured stockades contained opium balls in large quantities (*Trant* 128). In 1826 opium and liquor were staple imports; imports were subject to 10 per cent. customs duty, but inside the country there was no excise duty, for Government did not recognise the existence of intoxicants, and governors who received money for permitting their use were acting unofficially (*Crawford* II. 180, 182, and app. 78). The Hsenwi *sawbwa* in 1837 had learnt to get intoxicated on drink and opium in the Ava palace (*McLeod and Richardson* 126). The first English administrators of Pegu in 1853 found intoxicants used to excess, toddy being drunk from the palmtrees that grew everywhere, and opium being sold in quantities by Chinamen—see old office files and *Perkins* 91.

Prohibition does not appear to have developed until the time of Bayinnaung 1551-81. Down to the last generation or two, travellers never describe the people of Burma as either sober or drunken, but seem to have regarded them as much the same as other people.

Cucumber King.[1]—See *BEFEO* 1905 Huber "Le jardinier régicide qui devint roi." There are at least three other versions—an exact parallel in the Burmese fairy tale book "Princess Thudhammasari," and two variants in Cambodian history, one in the eighth and the other in the fourteenth century. The present king of Cambodia claims descent from the gardener and proves it by showing, in his palace at Pnom Penh, the very spear and sword with which his ancestor slew the royal trespasser.

[1] See p. 19.

The Burmese and Cambodian chroniclers, wishing to have a history in the remote past, made up for the absence of material by drawing on folk-lore. The underlying idea is that in the Priest of the Golden Bough, see *Frazer* "Magic Art and the Evolution of Kings" I. 2.

Vesali in the Indian Land.[1]—*Hmannan* I. 234 calls it "Vesali in Missimataik," which is the Middle Country, Buddha's homeland. Hence *Phayre* "History" 22 surmises that Vesali is Basarh village, north-east of Patna. The distance of Basarh presents no great difficulty, for there was an overland route in use (pp. 9, 17). Nor does the difference of language, for the kings took women into their harems regardless of the fact that they had not a word in common (pp. 280, 283). The caste difficulty however remains, and it is less likely that Anawrahta really sent so far afield than that his late chronicler thinks it fitting for his hero to have a queen from the Holy Land.

Assam was called Vesali. There was also a Vesali town in Akyab district, and *Do We* expressly admits that its lord presented his daughter Hti Hlaing Pru to Anawrahta when he was invading Arakan, *RSASB* 1918 13; it does not follow that it was this princess, among the many presented to Anawrahta, who was Kyanzittha's mother, but, if she was, there was enough Indian blood in Arakan to give her son Kyanzittha his un-Burmese features.

The story of Kyanzittha with its accretions is a fairy tale; his mother Panchakalyani shares the glamour, and it is improbable that her identity will ever be settled. The weight of feeling seems to be against Kyanzittha being the son of Anawrahta. The following is mostly from MS. authorities —Dammazedi-ahtokpatti, "Did not Kyanzittha, though only a commoner, become king?"; Scindakyawthubwehkan, "Sawlu was of the blood royal, Kyanzittha was not"; *Hmannan* I. 277, "The wise said 'With this child [Sawlu] the royal blood shall end'"; Yazawunthazalini, "Kyanzittha's paternity is unascertainable." In his inscriptions, Kyanzittha claims to be of dragon race. Twinthin, Mg Kala, Ishugumawgun, Yazawunthazalini, all make him the son of a dragon.

Massacre of the Innocents.[2]—This story, in *Hmannan* I. 235, closely following Mg Kala's chronicle (p. 207), bears the stamp of an ætiological myth, invented to account for the name Kyanzittha. The Palaungs know it, but only as part of the Kyanzittha legend, which has passed over to them.

In Herodotos V. 92 the ruling clan at Corinth, hearing that the infant Cypselus will prove formidable to them, send to slay him; he smiles in his cradle and the slayers relent. The story is not parallel, as there is no attempt to kill other children. The following are real parallels.

In St. Matthew II., the number of children slain by Herod is not stated, but tradition makes the number very large, e.g. the Greek Liturgy says 14,000.

In the Ceylon chronicle Mahavamsa IX. and X., the royal uncles,

[1] See p. 23. [2] See p. 24.

hearing that Pandukabhaya, who afterwards became king of Ceylon, 377-307 B.C., would be born and overthrow them, twice killed his companions, hoping to kill him—once when he was seven and again when he was twelve.

In *Wilson* "Vishnu Purana" 498, 504, 558 king Kansa, hearing that his sister shall bear a child, Krishna, to slay him, kills her children one after another as soon as they are born, but she manages to preserve Krishna; hearing that he has escaped, Kansa orders "Let active search be made for whatever young children there may be on earth, and let every boy in whom there are signs of unusual vigour be slain without remorse"; but still Krishna escapes and finally slays Kansa.

The raja of Manipur, warned by prophecy that he would be slain by his son, has all boy babies in his harem killed at birth. But the mother of Gharib Newaz 1714-54 (p. 208) smuggles him away into a village where he is brought up by Naga tribesmen. Later, the raja has his suspicions aroused and orders all the children in that village to stand on a bridge and watch boats racing beneath; he had caused the bridge to be sawn through, so the children fell into the water and were drowned. But the guardians of Gharib Newaz had been warned, so he escaped, grew up, entered his father the raja's service, accidentally killed him while they were hunting together, and then, the truth coming out, succeeded to the throne (*Hodson* 79).

Such stories recall customs whereby chiefs killed all boy babies born in the harem to wives other than the head wife. One version of the Gharib Newaz story specifically says this was the custom in Manipur until he abrogated it to celebrate his escape, and paid the penalty by being murdered by one of his own bastards. Indeed conquerors sometimes safeguarded themselves by extirpating the boy babies of subject tribes; Pharoah passed such a decree against the Israelites (Exodus I. 8-28).

But Kyanzittha's must be regarded as a case of literary influence, unless his story can be pushed back much further than 1724, when Mg Kala was written. St. Matthew dates from the second century, the Puranas from the fourth; Mahavamsa was not written till the early sixth and so may conceivably have been influenced by the Christian story, for Christianity was already old at Madras by then. There were Catholics (p. 189) at the Burmese court long before Mg Kala was written; the court Brahmans were of course soaked in the Puranas. The Burmese chroniclers probably heard the Christ and Krishna stories; they certainly knew the story of Pandukabhaya, for Mahavamsa was one of their greatest classics.

Byatta [1] was shipwrecked at Thaton with an elder brother Byatwi; the Zingyaik pagoda there is ascribed to the royal chaplain who adopted them. They proceeded to roast and eat the corpse of a magician, which made them each as strong as a full grown male elephant. The chief of Thaton grew afraid of such powerful servants and tried to get rid of them. Byatta escaped to Pagan but his elder brother was killed and the chief of Thaton buried different parts of his body with magical rites at places

[1] See pp. 24, 27, 30.

round the city so as to make it impregnable. When Anawrahta dug them up and flung them into the sea, the water shot up as high as a palm tree, *Hmannan* I. 246-50.

The idea that it is possible to partake of a man's nature by eating his flesh underlies the cannibalism of the South Sea Islands and is sublimated in the Eucharist—

Et antiquum documentum
Novo cedat ritui.

The notorious bandit Twet Ngalu had been a monk and a magician and was elaborately tattooed; when he was killed in 1888, nothing would satisfy the nearest Shan chief but to dig up the body and boil it down into a concoction which he persisted in wanting to share with the English Chief Commissioner so that they both might become invincible. Burmese and Shan legends are full of stories about eating corpses to obtain magical powers such as flying. Similarly in 1907 Saya I, a Burmese wizard doctor, was convicted at Hanthawaddy Sessions for a shocking act of murder and cannibalism—*mulierem grauidam occidit, puerumque utero exsecuit coxit, deuorauit;* and while I was at Bassein in 1914 a Burman was tried and convicted for disinterring a corpse in the town cemetery, apparently with the same object.

The burial of Byatwi's body round Thaton walls is based on the same reasoning as the *myosade* (p. 320). In the Norse Saga, Ragnar Lodbrog's son, dying in Northumbria, was buried at his own wish where his realm was most exposed to attack, nor could William the Conquerer 1066-87 penetrate the frontier until he had dug up the body and burnt it to ashes. A century ago the Burma-China frontier was fixed at Kenglaw between Kengtung and Kenghung by burying two men alive, one facing north the other facing south; in British times two images of Buddha, placed back to back, were substituted. Perhaps Anawrahta's magical images of men left "in the Indian land of Bengal" were set there with a similar idea, although they were musicians, not armed men, and his frontier did not extend as far (*Hmannan* I. 272). See *Encycl. Relig. and Ethics* s.vv. "Burma" and "Foundation, Foundation-Rites."

Burmese Irrigation.[1]—Population in Kyaukse was maintained by fresh batches of prisoners of war. In early times the method of keeping them there was to make them responsible for the upkeep of a pagoda and bind them to attend two festivals a year. After the first quarter of the seventeenth century the method was to allot prisoners of war to a unit of the army, at the same time giving them land in Kyaukse. To be a canal tenant was not serfdom but an honour (p. 347).

The area irrigated was rather more than 100,000 acres at the end of native rule. It was administered directly under the Crown by two governors, one for the Zawgyi and one for the Panlaung. At each weir was a *sebin* village whose inhabitants had to keep constant watch on the weir and were exempt from all other duties and from *thathameda* (household tax); they formed a hereditary profession and were employed on

[1] See pp. 25, 58.

construction of weirs, repair of breaches, etc. Some are still employed. This system of *sebin* villages was peculiar to Kyaukse among irrigated districts.

Until within living memory revenue was usually in kind and was sometimes farmed. For two years running, 1869-70, the king required twenty lakhs (two million bushels) of paddy, much of which was stored as a famine precaution. In 1883 the revenue was farmed for Rs. 400,000 and in 1885 for Rs. 500,000, the real value of which was more than the present settlement Rs. 800,000; indeed it was crushing, see *Stewart* "Kyaukse Settlement Report" ch. V.

The grain boats went down the Zawgyi to the Myitnge river, then into Irrawaddy, and so to wherever the capital was. The chronicles usually refer to the canal area by the name Yehlwengahkayaing, "the Five Sluices." The principal additions after Anawrahta's time were Kyaukse weir by king Narapatisithu 1173-1210, Thindwe by Athinhkaya the Shan chief of Myinsaing in 1300, Zidaw by Minkyiswasawke chief of Ava 1368-1401, Ngakyi by Mobye Narapati chief of Ava 1546-52, Pinda and Htongyi by king Mindon 1853-78. It looks as if the Pagan dynasty diverted the Zawgyi river; it now flows north but there are traces of an old bed as if it originally ran west from the great Yehlwe. The canal system is fathered on Anawrahta, but doubtless he found works already in existence.

Other Burmese irrigation works, with the acreage nominally irrigated in Burmese times, are as follows. Save at Kyaukse and in Meiktila lake they were rarely in full working order.

Meiktila district: Meiktila lake, 15,000, dating from an unknown period, as Anawrahta only repaired it. Nyaungyan-Minhla lakes, 18,000, reconstructed by king Mindon 1853-78.

Yamethin district: Kyaukse lake, 5,000, apparently prehistoric. Yamethin lake or Kyinikan, 5,000.

Mandalay district: Shwetachaung canal 20,000. Shwelaung canal, 20,000, constructed by Mindon and abandoned five years later. Nanda and Maungmagan lakes by king Alaungsithu 1112-67; Aungbinle and Tamokso lakes by his son Minshinzaw, all four now extinct.

Shwebo district: the Mu canals, the most ambitious and least successful of all, dating from king Narapatisithu 1173-1210. If successful they could have commanded 300,000 acres but it is doubtful if they ever supplied 30,000. Alaungpaya 1752-60 repaired them and constructed the Mahananda lake to supply Shwebo with water.

Minbu district: Man 15,000 and Salin 20,000. The origin of these canals is prehistoric and they originated with the people, not with the king.

The Burmese worked without scientific formulae, relying on trial and error. It was a most expensive method, and it would have been impossible but for the large reserves of forced labour which the king could command. Maintenance was terribly burdensome as construction relied largely on palm trees and jungle wood which did not last three years, and owing to defective methods serious breaches were the rule. If a construction failed, it was tried again two or three times, and if it still failed it was abandoned on the ground that the gods were against it. Thus, the Mon system in Minbu district always failed; when the English built it a decade ago many men refused to apply for land, saying that king Narapatisithu 1173-1210 himself had failed there, Thagyamin, the King of the Spirits, was clearly against the project, it could never succeed, it was flying in the face of providence, etc. etc. Yet after these deductions are made, the fact remains that Burmese irrigation works are a monument to the skill and energy of the race. The best stonework is good, and the alignment is extraordinarily fine. The cultivator has a good eye for levels; he has seen the land under rain year by year, and can tell to a nicety which way water will run off. English irrigation officers have seldom been able to better the main alignment of any Burmese canal system. They have straightened channels and cut off bends which were unavoidable to builders who did not use falls, but they have not bettered the sites as a whole, and they now admit that the Burmese site of the Mu canal would have given a better alignment than the one now utilised. See *Stuart* "Old Burmese irrigation works," *JBRS* 1921 Stewart "Burmese irrigation: a sidelight on Burmese history."

Myosade[1] is the Burmese name for a human victim buried alive under the foundations of a great building in order to provide a guardian spirit. The idea occurs in one form or another all the world over (see *Encycl. of Religion and Ethics* s.vv. "Bridge" and "Foundation, Foundation-Rites"). Thus, Hiel laid the foundation of Jericho in his firstborn and set up the gates thereof in his youngest son (1 Kings XVI 34). Men were buried under the round towers of prehistoric Ireland. In the Merlin legend, Vortigern, the fifth century British tribal chief, needs the life-blood of a boy to secure the foundations of his new castle. The custom passed over into Christian times, for in 563 when St. Columba built Iona, St. Oran offered himself and was buried at the foundation; later, human lives were spared and substitutes were used. When the keep of the Tower of London was built in 1078, the mortar was tempered with the blood of beasts.

In backward countries the full custom survived. In seventeenth-century Japan it was an honourable act for a slave to offer himself as a foundation; he would lie down in the trench and the great stones were then lowered. In 1634 the king of Siam renewed seventeen gates of Ayuthia, two victims were required for each of the two posts of each gate, and sixty-eight pregnant women were therefore chosen; but owing to peculiar omens an exception was made and only four actually suffered (*JSS* 1910 Ravenswaay "Translation of Van Vliet's description of Siam" 19). In the Balkans the instinct for human victims survives but is inhibited by modern government. In Turkey in 1865 two soldiers had to be prevented from burying children in the foundations of a blockhouse.

These recent instances, in countries not less civilised, render less surprising the survival of the custom in Burma at a late date. Although tradition says the custom was observed at the foundation of every city,

[1] See pp. 25, 41.

the chronicles seldom mention it. The chroniclers may have taken it for granted, and being monks they would tend to slur over a pagan survival. The Manu Kye *dhammathat* lawbook (p. 238 above) rules that no debt can be demanded when human victims are being buried at the corners of the capital. *Razadarit Ayedawpon*, recording the foundation of Martaban in 1287, says that a pregnant woman was crushed under the gate post at the correct astrological moment. An eye-witness told Dr. Mason that when Tavoy was rebuilt after 1751, a criminal was put in the post hole of each gate (*Mason* 106). *Hmannan* III. 303 records without comment the burying of *myosade* in the Wunbe In palace at Ava in 1676; had the custom been obsolete and revolting in 1829, when the compilers wrote, they would have added a word of palliation—and there are no grounds for supposing Burmese civilisation in their day to be any different from what it had been in 1676. The memory is still vivid in backward areas—in 1917 the *myosa* of Möng Küng, Southern Shan States, tried a villager for murdering a monastery servant; the villager pleaded that he had been driven to it as the monastery servant had threatened to have him offered to the Bridge Spirit.

King Mindon 1853-78 was a truthful old gentleman but he had a way of considering himself entitled to deny a thing merely because he had shut his eyes to it. He used to say that he never had a man executed; it is true that he hated the death sentence, but he used to say "Take him away. Let me never see his face again," and everyone knew what followed those words. He told the Chief Commissioner of British Burma that the *myosade* custom had not been followed at the foundation of Mandalay in 1857 (*Fytche* I. 251). But he used to offer fruit and flowers in the palace to a *myosade* spirit (*GUB* I. ii. 35). Dr. Bastian, who was at Mandalay in 1860, wrote "The king was opposed to the gruesome ceremony, but the ministers saw that it was carried out in accordance with ancient custom" (*Bastian* II. 91). The conscience of decent people hated the rite, but it does not follow that it was not carried out without the king's express sanction, in hole and corner fashion at night.

List of Captives.[1]—When discussing the antiquity of some particular craft, the pundits often appeal to *Hmannan* I. 251 which gives a detailed list of the various types of craftsmen carried away from Thaton by Anawrahta. Unfortunately this list has the air of meticulous exactitude which one associates with complete fiction, and it bears a family resemblance to similar lists which the chroniclers cannot resist introducing whenever a capital is enslaved—e.g. Chiengmai 1558 (*Hmannan* II. 339), Ayuthia 1563 (*Hmannan* II. 376), Pegu 1757 (*Konbaungset* 261), Ayuthia 1767 (*Konbaungset* 420). The Thaton list, in *Hmannan* compiled in 1829, can have no validity *per se* for what happened in 1057; and its value can be gauged from the fact that it includes makers of cannon and muskets among the craftsmen carried off by Anawrahta. See note "Firearms" p. 340.

[1] See pp. 28, 166, 168, 235, 253, 268.

Cholas in the Delta.[1]—*Forchammer* "Jardine Prize" 22 thinks that Anawrahta's objective may have been the Tamil colonies rather then the Talaings, and *Stewart* "Pegu Gazetteer" 21 writes as if Anawrahta foresaw a Chola invasion of Burm. and forestalled it by conquering the Delta. But the nineteenth century revealed how little the Burmese knew about neighbouring countries even under Bodawpaya, a more powerful monarch than Anawrahta. Nor is there anything to show that the Cholas ever contemplated invading even Lower Burma, let alone the interior; they found all the field they wanted in Malaya, Java and Sumatra. The theory rests on the obsolete surmise that Kidaram, one of the Chola conquests, is identical with Pegu; Mr Taw Sein Ko, after accepting this identification, continues, categorically, with reference to two stone posts at Pegu, about which there is no record, "Rajendra Chola I . . . in order to commemorate his conquest . . . erected these Pillars of Victory, in accordance with a well-known Indian custom" (*RSASE* 1907 19, 1910 14, 1919 24). But *BEFEO* 1918 Cœdès "Le royaume de Çrivijaya" shows conclusively that Kidaram is Kedah in the Malay states. Had there been a Chola ruler in the Delta, the Burmese chronicles would surely mention him as vanquished in Anawrahta's 1057 campaign or Kyanzittha's expedition.

There remains the undoubted presence of a Chola "prince" in Burma (p. 42). But he may not have been a prince—cf. Alaungpaya's "embassy from the king of London town, England," and Bodawpaya's Chinese "princesses" (pp. 280, 291, 362). There is nothing to show that he was ruling anywhere in Burma; he may have been passing through on some mission further east.

Pong and Koshanpye.[2]—*Dalrymple* II. 477-82 gives a note dated 1763 on a hilly country, apparently south-east of Assam and north-west of Burma, called Poong. The map at the end of *Trant*, published 1827, shows Bong as an area at 96° east, 26° north. *Pemberton* 108-46 shortly before 1835 visited Manipur and found there a Shan MS., which his interpreters translated into Manipuri, giving the history of a mighty kingdom, which stretched between latitudes 27° and 22° north and was called Pong.

Ever since then people have wondered what the kingdom of Pong was, and have inclined to regard it as an ancient Shan empire. *Parker* "Burma, relations with China" 23 identifies it as part of Nanchao (Yünnan). *GUB* I. i. 190 follows him. *BEFEO* 1904 Pelliot "Deux itinéraires" 160 shows that the identification is inadmissible; see also *Hodson* 114. Pemberton says the Burmese called it not Pong but Mogaung.

The empire is simply the state of Mogaung; Pong is the same word as Maw, and the people were the Maw Shans. At one time or another they wandered across quite an extensive area between the Brahmaputra and Salween rivers, but they did not occupy it all simultaneously, still less did they organise a kingdom. They extended sometimes along the Shweli river, sometimes over Mogaung and Mohnyin, sometimes over the upper Chindwin river and into Manipur. It is impossible to say in which of these areas they were when they paid homage to Anawrahta and gave him

[1] See pp. 28, 42.
[2] See pp. 31, 165, 171, 258, 291.

a princess. In the Hmannan account of the fourteenth and fifteenth centuries they centre at Mogaung and Mohnyin, sometimes a single state, sometimes a joint state, sometimes two states. Its subject states, i.e. villages, in 1442 are enumerated at *Tun Nyein* 38.

Another fabulous empire is Koshanpye. Kawsampi, the classical name of an area in the Holy Land of Upper India, became one of the resounding titles of major Shan states (*Cochrane* I. 46, 67, and *GUB* I. i. 189). Burmese officials in the Shan states could not resist the similarity between Kawsampi and *ko shan pye*, "nine Shan countries," especially as the number nine is so popular—witness the nine *hkayaing* in Kyaukse, the ninety-nine *sawbwas*, and the year 999 beloved of village antiquaries. *Yule* "Mission" 292 enumerates the Koshanpye or Kopyedaung—the towns of Kaingma, Maingmaw, Mowun, Latha, Hotha, Santa, and Mona, Mainglyin, Sigwin; the first six are shown on the map in his end flap. They lay north and east of Bhamo in what is now Yünnan. They were raided by Bayinnaung in 1562 (*Hmannan* II. 357) though the Chinese (*Parker* "Burma, relations with China" 69) give the chief Burmese raid as being in 1583; from this time Bhamo and the Koshanpye begin to fall under Burmese influence (p. 165) and in 1769 that influence became paramount (p. 258). After 1594 the Chinese maintained eight "Frontier Gates" or "Iron Gates" across the main routes; their position varied somewhat at times; the brick arches of three are still visible slightly east of the Myitkyina frontier, one of them with an opening above, for the purpose, say the Kachins, of spearing the war elephants of the Burmese; no iron door-leaves are traceable.

The Guards.[1]—Anawrahta must have had some sort of *ahmudan* or permanent troops on duty in the palace, such as can be seen in the Shan states to-day, but the first specific mention of a palace guard is *Hmannan* I. 323 which says Narapatisithu 1173-1210 formed "two companies inner and outer, and they kept watch in ranks one behind the other, for he knew with what ease he had slain his brother Naratheinhka." The Guard formed the nucleus round which the mass levy assembled in war time; it was the standing army. Under great kings it was naturally bigger than usual. *Hmannan* II. 258 gives a glowing description of how Bayinnaung 1551-81 marched to war surrounded by his Guards in golden helmets and splendid dresses, and doubtless it was a great sight although the gold was gilt, and order was conspicuous by its absence, for even in the nineteenth century, when they had some hireling European instructors, the Guards were not strong at drill; but when *Hmannan* II. 299 goes on to say that Bayinnaung had a guard of 40,000 marching round him, the number must be reduced by just one figure—a decimal—for the reasons given in "Numerical Note" p. 333. The energetic Alaungpaya dynasty was at least as powerful as Bayinnaung and its Guard was only a few thousand. *Symes* 318 who saw them in 1795 says there were always 700 on duty in the palace and not more than 2,000 all told in the city. *Havelock* 353 who saw them in the palace in 1826 says their full strength was 4,000—5,000

[1] See pp. 31, 57.

and they were "habited in the war jackets of dark glazed cloth so familiar to the English." *Gouger* 106 who lived in the capital and saw the army march out rejoicing against the English says "each man was attired in a comfortable campaigning jacket of black cloth, thickly wadded and quilted with cotton"—doubtless the same thing as is to be seen in the Shan states to-day, and not improbably it was used by Bayinnaung's men against the cold of the field.

The Guard was divided into four *win*, each of which resided in barracks outside the palace, one at each point of the compass. The commander of each was a *winhmu*, a very great personage. The men were selected for trustworthiness and many of them were gentry (pp. 180, 347).

Married his father's queen,[1] a frequent occurrence among the kings of Indo-China. Kachins marry their stepmothers. In the same way Oidipous married his mother, and Anglo-Saxon kings of England married their stepmothers as a matter of course; as late as the eleventh century Knut married the elderly widow of Aelthred whom he had ousted. The reason was throughout the same: to marry the dowager strengthened a claimant's title. She was the queen bee, the great mother of the tribe. Sometimes she could sting, as in the case of the lady Shin Bo-me, of noble birth, who was queen to the following five chiefs of Ava in succession :—

1. Minhkaung 1401-22.
2. His son Thihathu 1422-6 whom she caused to be slain because he favoured another queen. As the court would not crown the slayer, and set up the slain king's nine-year-old son,
3. Minhlange 1426, she poisoned him and then set up her lover,
4. Kalekyetaungnyo 1426 who was driven out by
5. Mohnyinthado 1427-40 who finally mastered her, p. 97.

Burmese kings habitually married their half-sisters. The king's eldest daughter was kept unmarried in a *tabindaing-ein* (one post house) until he died; then she married his successor, *Shway Yoe* 442, 448; so, in Pali Jataka no. 454 (Ghata), princess Devagabbha is kept in a single round-tower, like Danae, because the Brahmans prophecy that a son born of her will overthrow the dynasty. Commoners among the Veddahs of Ceylon, many African tribes, and even the civilised Egyptians under the Ptolemies and the Romans, married their sisters. Royalty did so among the Incas of Peru, the Pharaohs and Ptolemies of Egypt, some of the ancient Persians (e.g. Kambuses), some tribes in Africa and the Dutch East Indies, and the Siamese until the present king objected. Zeus married Hera, Osiris Isis, and Abraham his sister Sarah (Genesis XX. 12 and cf. 2 Samuel XIII. 13). *Hmannan* II. 313 and III. 155 gives a reason—"From of old kings have always married their sisters so that the blood royal may be pure." Methold, writing in 1619 of Arakan, says "The king marrieth constantly his own sister, and giveth for reason the first men's practice in the infancy of the world, affirming that no religion can deny that Adam's sons married Adam's daughters" (*Purchas* 1005).

See *Frazer* "The Magic Art" II. 283, his "Adonis Attis Osiris" I.

[1] See pp. 34, 38, 80, 81, 97, 104, 112.

316, *Westermarck* II. 90, *Yule* "Mission" 86, *JBRS* 1911 Furnivall "Matriarchal vestiges in Burma."

Coronation and Palace.[1]—The ritual was Brahmanical not Buddhist, and it was in use all over the Hindu world. In the full Hindu ceremony there was an unction with oil; in Buddhist countries this and certain other features were dropped and the sacring lay in a baptism with water. Several vernacular MS. accounts of the Burmese rite exist and all are in substantial agreement. *First*, the king went in procession to the coronation pavilions of which there might be three, four or five; he was accompanied by the royal white horse and the white elephant, as was decreed from time immemorial and is mentioned in the Mahabharata; *second*, he seats himself on the throne; *third*, Brahmans hand him the five regalia (white umbrella, yaktail fan, crown, sword, sandals); *fourth*, eight noble maidens administer the holy water, solemnly adjuring him in set words to rule justly; *fifth*, the Brahmans raise the white umbrella above his head; *sixth*, the Brahmans in their turn administer the holy water and adjure him; *seventh*, the merchants do likewise; *eighth*, the king says aloud the words ascribed to Buddha at birth, "I am foremost in all the world! I am the most excellent in all the world! I am peerless in all the world!"; *ninth*, he makes invocation by pouring water from a golden ewer; *tenth*, he meditates on the Three Jewels. There was no oath. An Arakanese coronation is described in *JBRS* 1917 San Shwe Bu "Coronation of king Datharaja A.D. 1153-65." A modern collection of royal paraphernalia is described at *IA* 1902 Temple "Notes on a collection of regalia of the kings of the Alompra dynasty."

As with the coronation, so with the palace city: there were few changes, for royalty is essentially conservative. Save that the Brahmanical details were probably further elaborated after the conquest of Manipur in the eighteenth century, the most recent coronation probably differed little from Kyanzittha's, and Mandalay, built in 1857, differs little from Pagan, save in being larger. The Burmese kingship, with its teak palace, claims to derive from north India; and the ancient palaces of north India in their turn owed much to Persia. Twenty-two centuries ago, when north India was Buddhist, even the greatest temples and the most gorgeous palaces were of wood; we catch glimpses of them in the writings of Greek and Chinese travellers—the palace at Patna with its halls of gilded pillars, the temple at Peshawar four hundred feet high, with thirteen timber storeys and glittering spire, enshrining the Buddha relics that now rest at Mandalay. The use of timber as building material seems to result in a style of its own, for the wooden churches of Norway are strangely reminiscent of Burmese monasteries and the temples of Nepal. It may well be that in the Mandalay palace to-day we behold the ghost of a vanished architecture, of Asoka's ancestral halls and Solomon's House of the Forest of Lebanon. See *ARASI* 1912-13 Spooner "Excavations at Pataliputra," *Fergusson* I. 51 and II. 369. *Epigraphia Birmanica* III i 1-68 gives the dedication ritual of an eleventh century Burmese palace.

[1] See p. 38.

Primate.[1]—A primate did not crown the king, for he was not a priest, and the coronation was Brahmanical. Indeed, the word primate is a misnomer because Burmese Buddhism has nothing which anyone acquainted with Historic Christianity would recognise as a hierarchy; he would regard Burmese clergy not so much as a church as an aggregation of individual ascetics. None the less, the king's chaplain had great power; his appointment is mentioned and his name is clear from the time of Anawrahta onward, save under the Shan chiefs of Ava in the fifteenth-sixteenth century.

Indeed we know that under the Alaungpaya dynasty he had, either as an individual *thathanabaing* or as a commission of eight, definite powers, appointing *gainggyok* as it were bishops throughout the realm, and having jurisdiction in cases under *Vinaya*, the rule governing the clergy, disputes about monasteries, gardens attached thereto, etc. He recommended learned monks for appointment as *sayadaw*, conducted the annual Patamabyan examination in scripture, and saw to monastic education. He was assisted by two departments appointed and paid by the king—the Wutmyewun (commissioner of ecclesiastical lands) and the Mahadanwun (ecclesiastical censor). The Wutmyewun saw to the maintenance of pagodas, pagoda slaves, monasteries, and church lands, and under a king like Bodawpaya (p. 276) he would see that those lands were not too extensive. The Mahadanwun with eight secretaries prepared, at the beginning of each Lent, a list of clergy throughout the realm according to districts, with their age, years of ordination, etc., and submitted it to the primate, under whose guidance he saw to the disciplining of disorderly clerics: they were made to wear a white robe, i.e. were unfrocked, and were then handed over to the secular arm. It is therefore permissible to style the *thathanabaing* primate. Doubtless some such organisation existed long before the Alaungpaya dynasty. The king in his own interests must always have made some effort to control the clergy, and defective as the organisation may have been, it really served to lessen the scandal of scamps putting on the yellow robe at option.

Pateikkaya and Macchagiri.[2]—*Phayre* "History" 38 takes Pateikkaya as part of Bengal; *Tun Nyein* 4, followed by *Gerini* 740, as Chittagong; Mr N. K. Bhattasali at *RSASB* 1923. 32 as a ruined site in Patikkara *pargana*, Tippera district. An inscription of the Pagan period (*Inscriptions* 1897 I. 296) places it west of Pagan. *Hmannan* I. 284 makes it the south-west frontier of the Pagan kingdom. But Arakanese records, e.g. *Do We*, seem to use the word as the name of a king "Pateikkaya king of Marawa." The location of Marawa is equally conjectural. *Do We*, in a variant of the Lady of Pateikkaya story (pp. 49-51 above), says she was captured by a king of Pagan while travelling at Thingadaung pass in the Yomadaung, i.e. in a hill country. *San Shwe Bu* thinks Thingadaung pass is north of Mount Victoria and Marawa to be Mawyin, the Kabaw valley; if so, Pateikkaya is near south Manipur.

Inscriptions 1897 I. 296, describing Anawrahta's borders, calls

[1] See p. 38. [2] See pp. 39, 49, 61.

Macchagiri "the tract crossing over to Pateikkaya." *Hmannan* I. 348-50 describing Yazathinkyan's campaign (p. 62 above) says the Macchagiri ruler took position on Thet hill and awaited Yazathinkyan's onset. Thet town is Thayetmyo, for *Dinnyawaa Yazawinthit* 126-7 describes how the Arakanese captured Minshinsaw, lord of Thet town, in 1333, and *Hmannan* I. 409 describing the same event calls him lord of Thayetmyo. Thet hill is thus some hill country west of Thayetmyo. An inscription (*Inscriptions* 1897 II. 836) dated 1096 shows that Macchagiri is in Arakan. It is unnecessary to suppose that it stretched as far as the sea-coast just because *Hmannan* I. 350 says Yazathinkyan died on reaching Dalla during the journey home; the details of the period are vague, and he may have been settling some Delta revolt when he was taken ill at Dalla.

Thambula.[1]—U-hsaukpan means an artificial flower of silver or gold used as a hair ornament. Other queens held the title—one a queen of Sawlu, one of Alaungsithu, and one of Narapatisithu (see *Hmannan*). Its Pali equivalent, *Vatamsaka*, forms part of the title given to Thambula in the Myazedi inscription, *Trilokavatamsaka* "Adornment of the Three Worlds," as who should say Rosa Mundi.

The story of her son is from *Hmannan* I. 269-86. In Pali Jataka no. 7 (Katthahari), Brahmadatta, king of Benares, while roaming in his pleasaunce for fruit and flowers found a girl singing merrily as she picked up sticks. He gave her his ring, saying "If thy child be a girl, spend this ring on her nurture; but if it be a boy, bring ring and child to me." When her son could walk, she took him to the palace gate and was summoned to the presence. The king took the boy in his arms, acknowledged him heir, and made the mother queen consort. See also Pali Jataka no. 487 (Uddalaka).

In the Mahabharata, king Dushyakanta while hunting in the forest met Sakuntala, the ward of a hermit, and left her a ring. Later she came to his palace with her son Bharata; he acknowledged Bharata heir to the throne and made her chief queen. The same story forms the subject of Kalidasa's drama "The Lost Ring," written in the third century.

Ancestor Worship.[2]—Much of religion originates in the worship of the dead. In Burma it is clearest among wild tribes such as the Hpon, Miaotzu and Lisaw; but most of the Thirty-Seven Nats are deified heroes—e.g. king Tabinshwehti 1531-50. As part of the system of government it occurs in Melanesia, China and Japan, and formerly among the Romans and all Teutonic races—e.g. the ancestral images at Rome, and the early English kings who were all descended from the god Woden. In China the imperial ancestors were worshipped with tablets and not, as in Burma, with images. See *Hmannan* I. 305, *Ridgeway* 233, *Encycl. Religion and Ethics* s.vv. "Ancestor worship," "Communion with the dead," "Images and idols."

When the Alaungpaya dynasty fell in 1885 there were in the palace a set of images and a book of odes to be chanted before them according

[1] See p. 40. [2] See p. 46.

to a prescribed ritual. The images were of solid gold, each stamped with its weight and with the name of the personage represented. The number is variously stated at 13 to 17, and the height varied from six inches to two feet. Only the Alaungpaya dynasty was represented. The rule was to make an image of a king at his death, if he died on the throne, and of a queen if she died while her husband was on the throne, but not of a king who died after deposition or of a queen who survived her husband; the sword, spear, betel-box, etc. used by the dead personage was preserved along with his image. They were kept in the palace treasury and were produced in the Zetawunzaung (Hall of the Ancestors) thrice a year, on the eve of the three great Homage Days (New Year, beginning of Lent, end of Lent), for the king and queen to reverence before themselves receiving reverence from the court and vassals. Eleven images came into the hands of the English Prize Court, which sent them to the Superintendent, Governor's Estates, Bengal, and as there was nobody to take any interest in them they were ultimately melted down.

Cingalese raid 1180.[1]—As the Burmese chronicles do not mention these events, there is no check on the Cingalese version, Mahavamsa LXXVI. 10-75, and it may be accepted as substantially correct. Mahavamsa says that the envoys were imprisoned in Malaya or the hill country —the meaning is ambiguous, see *RSASB* 1920 19. It goes on to say that the invaders fought many fierce battles, slaying thousands: like furious elephants they destroyed groves of coconut trees, they devastated half the kingdom, killed the king of Burma, and rode in triumph round his city on his white elephant proclaiming the supreme authority of their own king, till the Burmese all trembled and begged pardon, sending yearly tribute of elephants. In the same way the Burmese chronicles describe mighty wars causing all the kings of the earth to tremble before the might, majesty, dominion and power of the king of Burma. Mahavamsa does not explain how a few little mediæval ships could transport enough men to ravage half Burma and fight many fierce battles. The invasion was of course a raid, and probably over before news of it reached Pagan. The mention of an export trade in elephants to Ceylon is curious seeing that Ceylon had plenty of elephants in her own jungles.

Tula-dana.[2]—Hindu rajas practised the rite, and Moghul Emperors, even the orthodox Aurangzib, followed them. The Great Moghul was weighed every birthday twelve times over, once against each of twelve commodities such as gold, quicksilver and silk down to grain and salt, and he gave away as many cattle as there were years in his life. To this day the raja of Travancore passes through a golden cow which is then broken up and distributed to Brahmans, and the cow must be of his own weight. The underlying idea is that under the symbol of the image the donor gives himself up, body and soul, to good works. See *Crooke* I. 206, III. 194.

[1] See p. 57. [2] See pp. 57, 63, 114, 119, 166, 172, 195, 260.

The Whitlow.[1]—This version is from *Hmannan* I. 322. In the Ramayana, king Dasaratha, wounded in battle, is sleeplessly nursed by his second queen Kaikeyi; in response to her importunities he appoints her son heir over the head of the first queen's son. A Bengali version says he had an eruption on his finger, and Kaikeyi sucked it.

In *Zinattapakathani-kyan* 261, a life of Buddha with jataka tales, king Okkakarit has a whitlow on his finger; a lesser queen sucks and swallows it and in response to her importunities he makes her son heir over the head of senior sons. The episode is popular with Burmese actors and is often to be seen on the village stage under varying names.

Hluttaw and kingship.[2]—For the Hluttaw, see *Pagan Yazawinthit*, *Hmannan* I. 333, *Konbaungset* 1641, *Shwebonnidan* 55, *Symes*, *Yule* "Mission," *Fytche* I. 239, *Nisbet* I. 176, *Shway Yoe* 506, *GUB* I. ii. 156 and 469, *Taw Sein Ko* "Selections from records of the Hluttaw." What it was in earlier times we do not know, but it was probably much the same as under the Alaungpaya dynasty 1752-1885. It was then distinct from the *atwinwuns* (His Majesty's personal secretaries), being the supreme court of the realm in all causes, executive and judicial, for they were not divided; it was composed of the principal ministers, presided over by a senior prince, sometimes the *yuvaraja* (crown prince); they could require His Majesty's personal attendance and an empty throne was always ready in the council chamber. He was expected not to override their collective decisions. Furthermore, following the practice of every business establishment, the king did not ordinarily recall an order he disliked, once it had issued; instead, he reprimanded the ministers or removed them if they continued to pass unsuitable orders without reference. Thus, save under an energetic king, the Hluttaw Council was the real ruler of the country. But it never acquired the independence and security of even a tsardom's cabinet, and being appointed not from below but from above, consisting entirely of the king's nominees, it could not develop even the germ of a responsible constitution. To the end of native rule, the Hluttaw was liable without a moment's notice to be flung into jail for a night or two, while its office remained closed, merely because the king was displeased for some trivial reason (*Cox* 311, *Crawfurd* I. 303, 497).

The largest unit the Burmese could systematise was the village community. Beyond that they failed to build, and so the higher structure of central government inevitably fell into the form of despotism, which is anarchy, the negation of system. They did not indeed regard the king as a law unto himself, and he was not absolute in the sense in which the *turannos* was absolute. The Ten Moral Precepts for Princes to which he was expected to conform might be nothing more than pious platitudes, but he really was bound by immemorial custom and religious awe. Of legislation, as western states understand it, there was none. The king never issued a command which jurists would recognise as a law. The rules which regulated the daily life of the people were derived not from legislation but from anonymous custom, and these rules were administered by the village

[1] See p. 58. [2] See p. 59.

elders nor did the king consider himself empowered to alter them. Still, he took his seat unconditionally, for there were no charters, no coronation oaths such as every feudal king took. The coronation ceremony did indeed prescribe ritual forms exhorting the king to rule justly, but these were pious exhortations, not binding oaths. No doubt he usually strove to win the respect of those around him, and to conciliate public opinion so far as it existed or could reach his ears. Ancient legends, in Burma as in most other countries, even the most savage, tell how the first king on earth, Mahathamada, was an elective king; and in historic times there are on record several occasions when the court chose a king (pp. 36, 61, 81, 108, 117, 161, 192, 198). Such incidents, however, emanate from no constitutional requirement but from the fact, recognised in the most despotically governed countries, that the ultimate source of authority all the world over is the people. Throughout Burmese history there was no check on her king save his own conscience and the fear of rebellion.

The Temples and their Builders.[1]—The religious buildings at Pagan are copiously illustrated in *Scott O'Connor* and are described in *Yule* "Mission," *Fergusson*, Luce "The greater temples of Pagan," in *JBRS* 1918; and Sinclair "Monasteries of Pagan," Luce "The smaller temples of Pagan," Mg Mya "Monasteries of Pagan, a review" in *JBRS* 1920. Sinclair thinks that the flame-like ornamentation of Burmese architecture derives from the leaves of the palm trees whose stems were presumably the medium in which the Burmese originally worked. But similar ornamentation exists on the roofs of timber churches in Norway, where palm trees do not exist; it seems to be the natural concomitant of timber architecture. So far as the pattern was consciously intended in Indo-China to represent anything, it represented, as Mg Mya points out, a dragon, for the earliest examples, dating from the eighth century and found elsewhere in Indo-China, deliberately portray a dragon.

The radiating arch, at that time rare in India and unknown in Further India, is common in the temples of Pagan. Mr Taw Sein Ko at *PSASB* 1917 33 says that it was introduced from China, as it was unknown in India before the Mahomedan conquest in the twelfth century. But there is nothing to show that China had any perceptible influence on Burmese architecture. Mr Taw Sein Ko does not mention the standard authorities—*Cunningham and Beglar* 186-7 and plate XVII., *Vincent Smith* "History of fine art in India and Ceylon" 13 footnote, *Havell* "Indian architecture" 53-6 and his "Ancient and mediæval architecture of India" 3, 100—which show that the arch was well known in India long before the twelfth century and before the temples of Pagan were built. Presumably it came to Pagan from India, for everything points to Burmese temples being built by Indian architects. Temples of similar type, though without the arch, are found in Sumatra where Hindus of Madras had their great colonies. The Ananda temple was built in 1090 on an Indian model (*Hmannan* I. 288); in the same way English officers in 1826 found the king employing a Madras architect (*Crawfurd* I. 279).

[1] See p. 59.

The visitor to Pagan is first struck by the extreme solidity of the temples which are mountains of brickwork with scarcely an opening. The cathedrals of the West were built round the ritual of the Mass. Their architects had to produce halls which would not only be stable but also would possess the maximum of interior visibility. The cathedral was too vast, the worshippers too multitudinous, for any but a few to hear the words of the great incantation. Hence the high altar had to be visible from every part of the building, so that men could at least see the elevation of the Host. In their struggle to achieve this, the Masonic Guilds developed intellectual powers which still move us to admiration when we realise the structural difficulties they had to face. But Burmese Buddism has no priest, no sacrifice, no ritual; hence the architect is under no obligation to give us any interiors at all; in the ordinary pagoda he has none, and such as he gives us at Pagan are acts of grace.

None of the temples at Pagan took more than a few years to build, and some were finished in six months. The Gothic cathedrals took generations, and the hand that laid the first stone had fallen to dust before the spire was raised. The temples of Pagan were each designed by an architect or a small group which imposed its will on mere executants. The Gothic cathedrals are anonymous; they were built not by great heroes of art but by guilds of craftsmen; each member was free to use his imagination and to impress his personality on his own little gargoyle or window-tracery. No one individual knew all that others were doing, but each laboured in his place; even the architect had only a rough idea of what the building would be. The master who drew the first outline passed away, and with him died his concept; other leaders grew up, laboured, and died each in his turn. Yet the completed work has unity, for it expressed the collective spirit of the age. The Gothic cathedrals are the work of the seething democracy of the mediæval cities. The temples of Pagan symbolise the might of a great despotism, and they were built by the forced labour of villagers torn in thousands from their husbandry.

Yet though they grumbled the people would not have had it otherwise. The dynasty appealed to their imagination, and the age they lived in was an age of religious enthusiasm. Consider this inscription :—

> "In the month Wazo 541 B.E. [A.D. 1179] Abinandathu, a court official, regilded the Tainggyut pagoda, set a golden spire on it, built a new offering-platform nearby, regilded the statues of [the chief Disciples] Sariputto and Moggalano . . . and fed and clothed many monks. Then he offered himself, his wife, and his two sons as slaves to the pagoda. Also he offered Nga Kyan Gaung, Nga Kywin, Nga Letkana, Nga Swa, Nga Lu Nge, making nine slaves in all. Moreover he offered five acres of rice-fields called Tanaunggyi in order that their produce might be used for rice-offering at the pagoda. By virtue of this my meritorious deed, may I and my pastors, masters, friends and kinsmen, escape the miseries of life in this world and the next, and at last attain Nirvana, and may I become a Buddha." (Inscription from the porch of the Tainggyut temple, now in the Museum, Pagan, *Inscriptions* 1892 139.)

There is nothing to show that this self-offering was involuntary. At a period when a lord could outcaste himself for religion's sake, it is not surprising to find a whole people swarming forth to build pagodas, so that their ruins at Pagan to-day are spread over sixteen square miles and number nearly a thousand. Indeed it is hard to look at the detail there without being driven to the conclusion that this was a labour of love. There are whole furlongs of wall as at the Dammayan temple, in which the outer bricks, without cement, are joined so finely that scarce a knife blade can be inserted.

Moreover, it is incorrect to regard the government as an undiluted despotism. It was that, and nothing more, at the capital and its environs. But the king's arm was never very long or strong. What with great distances, tropical heat and rain, and the entire absence of roads, he had in practice to leave the greater part of his realm to its own devices. Far away in the quiet countryside dwelt the mass of the people, a homely folk who were ruled by their elders and headmen. They had their songs and gladness, their household cares and village fêtes, they neither knew nor cared what happened at court. The bigger headmen were not so very different from lords of the manor in mediæval England with its communal fields. In villages near the capital, where they intrigued at the palace and had the royal power to back them, local magnates could treat their subjects as they liked. But in the remoter regions, they had to mete out reasonable justice to folk among whom they were born and lived and died. The village in Burma had indeed no assembly of the freemen such as existed among the Anglo-Saxon tribes, nor did it send representatives to some Witenagemot or king's council; yet, as in many another mediæval country, it was to a very real degree a democracy, and the elders of the common people had a say in public matters.

The latent instinct for freedom comes out in their choice of popular heroes. It is not the great kings but the humble victims of their tyranny, who are enthroned in the affections of the people. Anawrahta is the greatest figure in the story of their kings; none worship at his shrine, yet they offer flowers daily to the Shan girl he did to death at the Kyaukse weirs. The king of Tagaung is forgotten, but Nga Tin De, and the sister who flung aside her state to die with him, are remembered.

The fact that a large proportion of the population were slaves is not incompatible with this. Slavery has been the normal lot of the mass of humanity throughout the historic period, and Burma is one of the countries where the institution was comparatively mild. Setting aside officials and men of birth, most of the people were probably serfs; it was only on crown slaves and pagoda outcastes that slavery pressed hard. Even pagoda outcastes could be happy enough when, as in the case of the greater pagodas, they were sufficiently numerous to form large villages of their own; they were usually prisoners of war. Consider these two inscriptions:—

"On Friday the 8th waxing of the month Thadingyut 560 B.E. [A.D. 1198] when placing the finial, king Narapatisithu gave away a thousand robes for monks, a thousand slaves of whom five hundred were Burmese and five hundred were Indian, five hundred acres and five hundred cattle." (Ink inscription on the wall of the Dammayazika pagoda, Pagan, *Inscriptions* 1900 330.)

"In 656 B.E. [A.D. 1294] when dedicating a *pyathat* the minister Indapissiya dedicated four hundred Indian slaves, of whom one hundred were men and three hundred were women." (*Inscriptions* 1892 123.)

Indians were usually captured in Arakan and the north-west. There are a number of such inscriptions; they indicate the presence of numerous foreign captives who, as often as not, instead of being dedicated to pagodas, were employed as servants and became merged in the general population; and they help to explode the modern idea that the Burmese were once a pure race but are now losing their identity beneath a flood of alien immigration. Not only had the Burmese received colonists from India in olden times, but ever since, right through the middle ages, they have been mingling with foreign races; and so far from losing their identity, it is they who have absorbed the immigrants and caused them to lose their identity (p. 121).

Numerical Note.[1]—Experience, culminating in the Great War, shows that even an organised state is lucky to get 10 per cent of its population under arms. *Crawfurd* II. ch. vii shows by several cross-checks that in 1824 the population of Burma with its tributaries was under four million. He is confirmed by the registers of Bodawpaya's 1784 Revenue Inquest which, revised for 1826, show the population, excluding the "wild tribes," to be 1,831,467 (*JASBengal* 1835 180); to this may be added some 170,000, the population of Arakan and Tenasserim (*Fytche* II. 288), which in 1826 had passed into British possession, so that the total would be 2,001,467; hence including the tributaries it may conceivably have approached three million or a dozen to the square mile, nearly a quarter of the population in 1923. It is notorious that under mediæval conditions population tends to be stationary; thus the population of England remained at 2½ million from William the Conqueror to Elizabeth. The figure for Burma after the Shan influx of the thirteenth and succeeding centuries may therefore be left at nearly three million.

Until 1785 Bayinnaung was the only king to hold the whole area or its equivalent. Ten per cent gives him a mass levy of 300,000; but so high a figure is improbable: he had no transport and could not have fed them. At Ngasaunggyan in 1277 the Burmese had 60,000, says Marco Polo (*Yule* "Book of Ser Marco Polo" II. 99), between 40,000 and 60,000 says the Chinese official despatch (*BEFEO* 1909 Huber "Fin de la dynastie de Pagan" 667); both these are doubtless eye-estimates and err on the side of generosity as the Chinese would not wish to diminish their glory in defeating superior numbers. Captain Baker in 1755 spent weeks in observation and says that Alaungpaya's levies in Upper and Lower Burma put together could not exceed 50,000 men though the Burmese put it at more than twice that (*Dalrymple* I. 166). *Sonnerat*

[1] See pp. 63, 82, 164, 179, 181.

(1782) II. 41 says Alaungpaya's army which invaded Siam in 1759 was 40,000. Mahabandula never had more than 60,000, a number which was spoken of with bated breath as the largest army ever raised in Burma (*Snodgrass* 94). These independent estimates by trained officers show that even under the Alaungpaya dynasty, which had greater driving power than any of its predecessors save perhaps Bayinnaung, the country could not put more than 60,000 into the field.

A cross check gives a similar figure for Bayinnaung. *Hmannan* III. 87-8 says that in 1586-7 his son Nandabayin besieged Ayuthia with 250,000 men but could not surround it and supplies kept going in. That is to say, he cannot have had over 25,000, which would be ample to seal it against any supplies. Now if Nandabayin's 250,000 be really under 25,000, Bayinnaung's 700,000 will be really 70,000.

Hmannan II. 422 gives various estimates of the number of men Bayinnaung led into Siam 1568-9, varying up to a million. Cæsar Frederick (*Hakluyt* X. 111) says he saw 500,000 march under his own eyes, and Ralph Fitch (*Hakluyt* X. 189) says he was there when 300,000 left Pegu. These estimates are obviously bazaar rumour. In the same way, the million armies mentioned in Burma by the Portuguese chroniclers are swashbucklers' yarns. The danger of judging by the eye is shown by Gasparo Balbi (p. 179 above); he says he saw 4,000 burnt alive; but *Hmannan* III. 78 says "more than 30 ministers" were burnt; according to custom their families and followers would burn with them, and as they were great personages with, say, 15 dependents each, the total would be about 450; it was a terrible sight, that flaming shrieking mass, and the spectators said "Poor things, hundreds and thousands of them."

Take the following analysis of typical Burmese statements. *Hmannan* frequently describes how, in the mediæval period, the Burmese armies invading the Pegu state or fighting the Shan *sawbwas* would consist of over a hundred thousand men, and the other side would have a similar number; yet at the end of a day's heroic fighting the casualties number 200 dead; possibly the number of dead is correctly stated, and the levies on each side may have numbered several thousand. *Hmannan* I. 293 says the Ceylon king gave Alaungsithu 1112-67 a ship holding 800,000 people. *Hmannan* I. 357-8 says that at Ngasaunggyan 1277 six million Chinese overwhelmed 400,000 Burmans (p. 65 above), but the Chinese had only 12,000 and *Hmannan* does not explain why, if Narathihapate had 36,000,000 soldiers as stated in his Mingalazedi inscription (p. 63 above) which was well known to the compilers, he used only 400,000 when he was fighting for his existence. The Burmese boast (*Tun Nyein* 146) that in 1300 they gloriously defeated 120,000 Chinese; but they did not defeat them, they bribed them to withdraw (p. 77 above), and the Chinese were exactly one-tenth of this number, being 12,000 men, see the Chinese official sanction (*BEFEO* 1909 Huber "Fin de la dynastie de Pagan" 676).

Hmannan II. 187 says that in 1492 when the Talaings with 100 elephants and 160,000 men were besieging the Toungoo Burmans in

Dwayawadi, they were routed by Minkyinyo marching out of the south gate with 30 elephants and 10,000 men and Sithukyawhtin marching out of the west gate with 80 elephants and 10,000 men; *Hmannan* does not explain what enabled 20,000 men to defeat eight times their number of troops who were of much the same quality as themselves and were undemoralised by any defeat; nor how a small town could contain, in addition to its own inhabitants, 110 elephants and 20,000 fighting men (to say nothing of such followers as even a Burmese army must have had) who were not trained compact infantry but straggling irregulars; nor how 110 ponderous elephants and 20,000 men could file out of two narrow gates in the face of 160,000 troops waiting outside to catch them. *Hmannan* II. 204 says that just before the fight at Naung-yo 1538, Bayinnaung, wishing to ascertain the enemy's number, sent a soldier up a tree to look at them. The soldier climbed the tree and said "There are over 200 elephants, over 800 horses, and some 80,000 men"; as if 80,000 irregulars scattered about in jungle camps could even be seen simultaneously. *Hmannan* II. 210-5 says Bayinnaung besieged Martaban in 1541 with 180,000 men yet could not prevent supplies from entering the city; in other words, he had not sufficient men to surround it adequately; but even 18,000 could surround it tightly with the greatest ease. *Hmannan* II. 227 says that in 1543 Tabinshwehti was besieging Prome with over 180,000 men; that it was a small town with few supplies and many useless mouths inside, such as old women and young persons; yet that in spite of a complete blockade, when at the end of five months a relieving army of Arakanese approached, it was still holding out; obviously therefore, on considerations of food alone, the garrison could not have exceeded a few thousand and could easily have been contained by the tiniest fraction of the 180,000 besiegers who were still practically intact; and the bulk of the 180,000 could have left the siege without any anxiety, to deal with the Arakanese; yet *Hmannan* proceeds to reduce its own figures to absurdity by describing a long council of war held by the officers of the besieging army to decide whether they could afford to detach a force against the Arakanese. *Hmannan* II. 332 asks us to believe that Bayinnaung, whose ability it never tires of extolling, found it necessary to use 400,000 men to beat a few petty chiefs —Mone, Yawnghwe, Lawksawk, Naungmun, Saga. *Hmannan* III. 84-5 says that the Burmese army which attacked Siam in 1586 was 120,000; but it gives details which total 180,000; a mere 33 per cent difference, a trifle of 60,000 is nothing to the chroniclers.

The inscription on Anaukpetlun's bell (p. 191) says its weight is 8254 *viss*, whereas the actual weight is approximately 825 *viss*. In an engagement in 1824 where they repulsed the English so that, remaining in possession of the ground and of the enemy bodies left there, they were in the best possible position to estimate the casualties, the Burmese reported having killed and wounded 1,000 English, when the muster rolls showed the total killed and wounded to be 106 (*Trant* 97-8). The Burmese resident *sitke* in the Shan states said the Shan contingent was 91,000 although English officers who fought against it knew that it was about 8,000 (*McLeod and Richardson* 129).

The Shoe Question.[1]—*Hmannan* I. 357 says the Chinese ambassadors in 1273 were rude, but does not say in what way. Burney, writing in 1830, records the Burmese court tradition that their rudeness was appearing in the presence of King Narathihapate with their shoes on (*Yule* "Mission" 79). *Cox* 13, writing in 1796, notes that although no Burman would ever dream of going up to the Shwedagon with his shoes on, he saw Europeans and native Christians doing so as a matter of course and nobody interfered with them. But whenever the Burmese were annoyed, for instance, when feeling ran high before the outbreak of the First Anglo-Burmese War 1824-6, they expressed much dissatisfaction with Judson for not removing his shoes at the Shwehsandaw pagoda, Prome (*Crawfurd* I. 63).

Ngasaunggyan 1277.[2]—Marco Polo catches the spirit of it all, but his details need modification. Narathihapate never took the field in person. Nasr-uddin, the provincial governor, was not present, but he took part in the great drive down to Kaungsin after the battle. The battle was not at the plain of Vochang (Yungch'ang), seventy miles N.E. of the actual site, but at a plain in the Taping valley near Kanngai, in the Yungch'ang prefecture. The Burmese never got beyond the Kanngai area. Ngasaunggyan may be a corruption of Nangsung, the old name for Nantien near Kanngai. There is now a Ngasaunggyan near Bhamo and it may have been stockaded during the subsequent fighting, but it is not the scene of the great battle.

As the Burmese account makes the enemy nearly all horse, and they relied on arrows, it looks as if Marco Polo is right in saying that the 12,000 were Tartars, for the Tartars were the finest of cavalry, and their famous weapon was the bow, discharged while they were riding full gallop. The Burmese elephants wore a sort of armour, and slung to their sides were hollow bamboos containing scores of lances for the men in the howdahs to use. As for the capacity of howdahs, Nicolo di Conti about 1435 mentions howdahs carrying eight to ten men (p. 98 above), Cæsar Frederick in 1568 mentions four men (*Hakluyt* X. 124).

It is nowhere said that Pagan was sacked, and the Tartars probably did less architectural damage than Narathihapate as they had orders to respect religious buildings. But it is not improbable that, having lost 7,000 comrades, they acted up to their name, "The Scourge of God," so far as the population was concerned, and the terror which is patent in the Burmese account must have some basis. The second sack, by wild Shans in 1299, was doubtless worse. Perhaps it is the ease with which Pagan was conquered that lies at the root of Marco Polo's yarn about Kubla Khan telling his gleemen and jugglers to go and take Burma.

Because the Chinese failed badly in 1765-9, complaining of the heat and an impossible climate (p. 356), it has been doubted whether they really reached Pagan in 1287. But in 1287 they were first class Tartar troops in the flush of their great tradition and although they grumbled at the heat they did not make it an excuse. Not only does Marco Polo describe Pagan with the most faithful touches, not only does the official Chinese despatch claim to have occupied it and to have sent out detach-

[1] See pp. 64, 288. [2] See p. 67.

ments all over the country, but also the standard Burmese account admits that the Chinese occupied Pagan and reached Tarokmaw. Scepticism is therefore gratuitous.

The Burmese account is bad. It telescopes several years and works everything up into the dramatic climax of one battle, Ngasaunggyan, where it says Anantapyissi the commander was slain, whereas he was alive eight years later. But it is not so wrong as it looks in saying that the slaying of the ambassadors provoked the war, for when Thihathu murdered his father he also murdered, amongst others, the latest Chinese envoys. Hence the Burmese murdered envoys twice, the first time in 1273, four years before any fighting, and the second in 1287 immediately before the great catastrophe. The Burmese account says, the exact opposite of the truth, that they were overwhelmed by numbers, having *sic* only 400,000 men against more than 6,000,000 Chinese—as to these figures, see p. 333; its dates are wrong by several years, and the Chinese dates are shown to be right by Burmese inscriptions, e.g. one by Anantapyissi's own daughter at *Inscriptions* 1900 227.

See *Hmannan* I. 357-64, *Parker* "Précis" and "Burma Relations with China" 28-37, *Yule* "Book of Ser Marco Polo" II. 98-114, *Macgowan* 433-40, *RSASB* 1917 36, *Cordier* "Histoire de la Chine" II. 304-10 and above all *BEFEO* 1909 Huber "Fin de la dynastie de Pagan" which gives a Chinese account.

Chinese Inscription.[1]—These considerations cast considerable doubt on Mr Taw Sein Ko's idea that China played an important part in moulding Burmese civilisation. Since, in the one period when we know that she had influence in Burma, civilisation retrogressed and Chinese influence left no mark, what reason is there to imagine that she did anything in earlier periods when it cannot be shown that she had any influence at all?

There is a stone, found near the Sarabha gate at Pagan and now in the museum there. No history mentions it, nor is there anything to show who set it up, and when. It is inscribed in Pyu on one side and in Chinese on the other. Neither is decipherable, but Mr Taw Sein Ko (*RSASB* 1916 20 and 1917 25) says that it commemorates the Tartar conquest of Pagan, and was set up at the time, and the Pyu text is a translation of the Chinese text. The Chinese text was still legible in 1905, and it is a pity there was nobody in Burma to read it then.

Mr Taw Sein Ko in *IA* 1906 "Chinese words in the Burmese language" says "for practical purposes it may be accepted that Buddhism was introduced from China into Burma during the fourth century after Christ . . . [Apparently] at Tagaung, Prome and Pagan, in the early centuries of the Christian era, Chinese missionaries taught Buddhism in Chinese side by side with Indian missionaries who taught it in Sanskrit, but Chinese political influence being in the ascendant, Chinese monks were in greater favour and their teaching made the greater headway . . . [and] became predominant." That being so, there should be a number of ancient Chinese inscriptions in Burma: there is only one, this one. There should

[1] See p. 73.

also be some trace of Chinese influence on the vernacular alphabets: there is none. In Yünnan, where the Chinese had influence, the alphabet, from the Nanchao 766 inscription onwards, is Chinese. There are some thousands of vernacular inscriptions in Burma, and every one of them is in a script which is admittedly of Indian origin.

In his "Chinese words in the Burmese language," an article repeated in five different places, Mr Taw Sein Ko says the chief words in Burmese religious terminology are of Chinese origin; but some of his words are Sanskrit, there is nothing to show that they came through China, and in the case of others the equation is doubtful. *JBRS* 1915 and '16 Blagden "Some alleged Chinese words in Burmese" points this out, and Huber at *BEFEO* 1909 585 dismisses the idea in a line.

Massacre of the Kinsmen.—Instances or quasi instances are at pp. 75, 80, 117, 120, 145, 201, 264. The best known—Thibaw's massacre of between seventy and eighty of his brothers and other near kinsmen at Mandalay in 1878—probably differed from its forerunners neither in extent nor horror but only in taking place in the full light of modern publicity; the court notified it to the English as "a purging of the realm according to custom," and men who were in touch with the palace tell me that Thibaw and his ministers seem to have been genuinely surprised at the horror with which the announcement was received. Defective though Burmese records may be, there can be little doubt that such massacres recurred from time immemorial, that they took place at the option of government when a new king felt insecure, that they were justified by the inherent weakness of the central government, and that the conscience of the race permitted them with the pang of regret which a dog fancier feels at drowning a litter.

The acts of Abimelech in slaying his seventy brothers (Judges IX 1-5), of Baasha in extirpating the house of Jeroboam (1 Kings XV 29) and of Jehu in slaying the seventy sons of Ahab (2 Kings X 1-11) may have been the acts of usurpers. But the following instances, among races which

bear, like the Turk,
No brother near the throne,

show the existence of a customary law and even a rite.—When a king of Benin came to the throne, he used to command his brothers to hang themselves, and then he buried them with great pomp; and in Uganda when a young king came of age, all his brothers were burnt, except two or three who were preserved to maintain the succession (*Fraser* "Taboo and the perils of the soul" 243). Mr. F. W. H. Migeod, who visited Ngala in March 1922 and saw one of the skeletons in the wall, tells me that in Ngala, ten miles south of Lake Chad, at each accession, if the new king were not himself the eldest brother, the court took his elder brothers and buried them alive in the wall of the palace. See p. 316, and the article here below.

Royal drowning.[1]—Drowning in a velvet sack was one of the privileges of royalty not only in Burma but also elsewhere in Indo-China. Thus in

[1] See pp. 77, 95, 102, 199, 202, 223

Siam royal victims were tied in sacks of finest velvet so that they might not be polluted by the touch of common hands, and they were then dropped into the Menam river, having sometimes first been clubbed to death by great bars of aromatic wood (*Samuel Smith passim*, *Pallegoix* I. 271, *Anderson* "English intercourse with Siam" 370). In Tonkin commoners were beheaded but royalties were strangled. The Tartar Khans would kill each other to get the throne, but they scrupulously avoided bloodshed: thus, Kubla Khan 1259-94 executed his uncle Nayan by wrapping him in a carpet and tossing him to and fro till he expired. The prejudice against shedding royal blood extends to Africa, where in Ashanti royalties are drowned, in Dahomey drowned or strangled, in Benin hanged, in Madagascar burnt alive, in Uganda burnt alive or starved (*Frazer* "Taboo and the perils of the soul" 242). In Burma, not only kings but even their bones were drowned. Thus at Amarapura the tombs of Bodawpaya 1782-1819 and Bagyidaw 1819-37 are cenotaphs, marking the cremation site, and their bones after burning were placed in a velvet bag and thrown into the Irrawaddy as in the case of Kyawswa 1287-98.

Smim Payan.[1]—*Hmannan* II. 30-9 says that in 1415 the Mawke Mawdon brothers were aided by a Chinese host in investing Ava and withdrew because their champion was defeated by the Burmese champion, a captive Talaing. *Hmannan* II. 116-20 says that in 1476 the Burmese, having captured a Talaing sent by Dammazedi to Yünnan, used him as a champion against the Chinese who were again investing Ava. The stories are a perfect doublet, even to such details as the Talaing's name (Smim Payan), his equipment, and the colour of his horse. There was no Chinese siege of Ava in 1415, still less was there a Chinese inroad in 1476. Possibly on the second occasion the Burmese waylaid Dammazedi's envoy (p. 199 above).

Thwethauk and Thissa-ye.[2]—Two men contract brotherhood by *thwethauk* drinking blood together, i.e. each makes an incision in his arm and the other drinks the blood, so that they twain become one flesh; or the blood may be obtained by killing an animal and be drunk in water or spirits. The resultant relationship is recognised in the *dhammathat* law books. In Burma and Siam the rite is now common only among the wilder tribes, see *Forchammer* "Jardine Prize" 16, *IA* 1891 Taw Sein Ko "Thwethauk." It was at one time or another used all over the world and still survives among tribes in e.g. Africa. Artificial brotherhood in mediæval Europe was usually contracted by some ceremony such as the exchange of weapons, an idea which underlies the wapentake. But the actual drinking of blood is mentioned by Greek and Latin authors as being practised among some of the surrounding barbarians, and to this day it occurs among the southern Slavs in one of the many ceremonies for artificial brotherhood sanctioned by the Eastern Church. See *Encycl. Religion and Ethics* s.v. "Brotherhood (artificial)".

[1] See p. 87. [2] See pp. 106, 178, 188.

Thissa-ye, the Water of Allegiance, was drunk in Burma as in the surrounding localities, e.g. Siam; thus the Siamese chronicles mention its being drunk to the king at his coronation, see *Samuel Smith* 1. Every office holder in Burma drank it on assuming charge. Some of the wild *sawbwas* were called in to drink it before the *sitke* resident once a year. The commonest form was for an animal to be sacrificed to the *nat* spirits and its blood to be mingled with intoxicants in water which was then stirred with the point of spears, swords and, in later times, muskets; the blood in the water bound together all the drinkers, including the king's representative, and the spears, etc., typified the violent death which would befall those who broke the oath. But sometimes, as among Shan-Chinese on the border, the oath would be written out, the paper burnt, the ashes mixed with water, and the whole was then handed round and drunk. See *Cox* 236, *JASBengal* 1837 Hannay "Route from Ava to Assam" 275, *Fytche* II. 111.

Fire-arms.[1]—*Hmannan* I. 251 mentions gunsmiths as taken from Thaton to Pagan by Anawrahta in 1057. *Pagan Yazawinthit* mentions "cannon, jingals, bombs, muskets" as being used at the battle of Pyedawthagyun 1084. *Razadarit Ayedawpon* says that when Tarabya was plotting against Wareru in 1287 he went to Pegu and collected feringhi musketeers; and that Binnya U found difficulty in besieging Martaban about 1360 because of musketeers on the walls. *Hmannan* I. 427 mentions foreign musketeers in the fighting between Burmese and Talaings in 1387; and II. 59 mentions whole regiments of feringhi artillery and musketeers fighting for the Talaings against the Burmese at the siege of Bassein in 1418.

A certain amount of evidence (e.g. *TP* 1902 Schlegel "On the invention of fire-arms in China prior to the arrival of Europeans") exists in support of the popular view that fire-arms were used in China for some centuries before the beginning of wholesale European intercourse, but it is by no means an established view. They were certainly not used anywhere else in the East. It is generally accepted that in Indian warfare they were first used by Babar at Panipat in 1526, being introduced from Turkey and Europe. In 1506 the Cingalese had never dreamt of them, and fled at the mere noise of the Portuguese guns (*Whiteway* 37). Now Burma was in regular communication with Ceylon, and had fire-arms been known in Burma prior to 1506 they would have been known in Ceylon, especially as the Burmese chronicles clearly indicate that the gunners were shipmen from abroad. References before this time are obviously anachronisms, like the references to feringhis, who did not frequent the East till after 1498. It is possible that Mahomedan shipmen, when hired to fight, used in Burma on a few occasions towards the end of the fifteenth century something that could be distinguished as a fire-arm. But, although it is unlikely that fire-arms had got so far inland at that time, the earliest mention that is at all probable is that of Shwenankyawshin's being killed at Ava by a jingal shot in 1527 (*Hmannan* II. 147); and the first extensive use of fire-arms that can

[1] See pp. 106, 155.

be accepted without question is at Martaban in 1541 when the Portuguese were present. Thereafter till the time of Alaungpaya 1752-60 fire-arms were used by the foreign mercenaries or captives of the Guard, i.e. feringhis and a few Mahomedans. The Manipuris (*Pemberton* 39) noted that the first time their Burmese opponents used fire-arms was in 1755, i.e. Alaungpaya had then introduced fire-arms among his Burmans; under his incompetent predecessors even the feringhis of the Guard had apparently decayed. After his time they were regularly used by the Burmans of the Guard as well as the feringhis, and were also served out to selected portions of the levy on mobilisation. Early in the nineteenth century the palace arsenal had up to 35,000 muskets, but they were mostly rejects from French and English arsenals, and the powder was so bad that it would not have been passed in the armies of Indian princes (*Phayre* "History" 258, *Snodgrass*, *Havelock*, *Trant*, *Crawfurd*, *passim*). The artillery was always a joke but, though the levy never learnt how to take care of their muskets and had to find out to use them, use them they did, and with surprising effect. As for the first line troops under good commanders in the Burman heyday, every enemy opinion on record is that their musketry was of a formidable description; see pp. 237-8 and also compare the Chinese opinion at p. 255 with the English report of the Ramu disaster 17 May 1824 where the Burmese brought their saps up to within twelve paces and poured in such a fire that our bugles could not be heard and the signals miscarried (*Wilson* "Documents" 41).

Pegu merchants abroad.[1]—They are mentioned in foreign ports during the sixteenth century. Thus Albuquerque at the siege of Malacca in 1510 used "300 men belonging to the merchants of Pegu" (*Stevens* I. 181). In 1511 the administration of foreigners in Malacca was in the hands of commissioners, one for each race, and among the races enumerated are "the people of Pegu" (*Hobson-Jobson* s.v. "Kling"). *Linschoten* I. 100, writing in 1592, after residing in Goa, says he bases his extraordinarily accurate information about Burma, which he never saw, "not only by the daily trafficking of the Portuguese out of India thither, but also by the Peguans themselves, whereof many dwell in India, some of them being Christians." But these observers, like Nitikin (p. 121 above), were interested in the business community, which was largely foreign, and when they talk of Peguans they possibly mean Burmanised Indians and, as Linschoten's remark about Christians indicates, Armenians from Pegu; some of them may have been born of intermarriage with the people of Pegu. But the people themselves were not maritime traders, for Barbosa in 1516 says little information can be obtained about Burma "because it has no shipping" (*Hobson-Jobson* s.v. "Burma").

For the trade of this period, see *Hakluyt X. passim*, *Anderson* "English intercourse with Siam," *Linschoten*, *Badger*, *Stevens*. Good articles on the trade routes are *JBRS* 1917 Furnivall "From China to Peru" and "Samuel White." Pegu jars are first mentioned in 1350, by a

[1] See p. 122.

Mahomedan trader in India, see *Hobson-Jobson* s.v. "Martaban"; *Linschoten* I. 268 says they were used to carry water on ships throughout the East. For *ganza*, see *Hobson-Jobson* s.v.

Tabinshwehti and Bayinnaung.[1]—*Hmannan* II. 172-92 gives the history of Toungoo with Minkyinyo's family tree. When his son was born in 1517 there were such prophecies about him that Minkyinyo had gold umbrellas erected over his cradle, hence the name Tabinshwehti. *Hmannan* II. 197-8 says Tabinshwehti was the re-incarnation of a prince who, put to death by his father Dammazedi 1472-92, king of Pegu, prayed the same prayer as Bawlawkyantaw (p. 114 above).

Hmannan II. 279-80 gives a family tree for Bayinnaung showing him to derive from Thihathu 1312-24, the Shan Brother (p. 76). But Mr Taw Sein Ko at *RSASB* 1910 21 records the tradition which makes him the son of a toddy climber from Ngathayauk in Pagan township. The low standard of education, the lack of documentation, and the absence of primogeniture, render it improbable that any but a few Burmans retain for long a correct knowledge of their ancestry, and the family trees sported by men after they attain greatness must be suspect. On the other hand, the fact that Bayinnaung's father was a toddy climber no more precludes the possibility of his having royal ancestors than it precluded his becoming vassal king of Toungoo when his son rose to greatness.

Pinto[2] is not so much a liar as an inveterate rhetorician. Like a true Portuguese of his age, he makes no effort to understand the customs and religion of the races with which he mixed. Just as other Portuguese writers in India said that the cow was an animal which the Mahomedans worshipped with abominable rites as the repository of their souls (*Whiteway*), so Pinto says that the despairing lord of Martaban proposed to offer human sacrifice to the God of Battles, some of his princesses had white skins and auburn hair, he had a temple to the God of Thunder, and he and his family prayed prayers the words of which might have come out of the breviary.

His statement that the lord of Prome was at once cruelly executed with his wife is improbable, because *Hmannan* II. 148, 292 and III. 70, 119 shows that they were kept in captivity till 1553 when the husband was executed and the wife passed into the harem of Bayinnaung, who named her Sandadevi; by Bayinnaung she had a daughter Minhkinsaw whose son by the lord of Toungoo was Natshinnaung (p. 188). On the other hand, Pinto is doubtless right in saying that the lord of Martaban was executed, as the chronicle is ominously silent about him. Nor is there any reason to doubt the pitiful atrocities which he describes, for they accord only too well with what we know, on overwhelming evidence, to have been Burmese custom in the eighteenth and nineteenth centuries.

Cogan's translation of Pinto is thoroughly bad; not only does it mangle the sense and take serious liberties with proper names but also it miscopies dates so badly that it is useless for purposes of chronological comparison.

[1] See pp. 125, 153. [2] See p. 157.

Siamese chronology.[1]—The dates of the Burmese invasions hitherto given in books on Siam differ by decades from those in the Burmese chronicles, which I have followed. The Siamese archives were wiped out in 1767 when the Burmese destroyed Ayuthia. Chronicles compiled after that event were naturally inaccurate for the preceding period. Hluang Prasöt, however, in 1907 found a chronicle written in 1680 and based on earlier material; it is more accurate as to dates than most others and it is translated into English at *JSS* 1909 Frankfurter "Events in Ayuthia 686-966." Prince Damrong, in his notes to king Mongkut's "History of Siam" published in Siamese by the Vajirañāṇa National Library, Bangkok, 1914, shows that hitherto the chronology of the annals has been based on the supposition that king Mahachakrapadhi reigned from 1529. The annalists knew that the first Burmese invasion was in his first regnal year, so they assigned it to 1530. But Hluang Prasöt shows him to have reigned from 1547, and hence the first Burmese invasion was in 1547-8, the date given by the Burmese chronicles. Prince Damrong and other leading Siamese authorities now accept the Burmese chronology for these years, which is also in the main confirmed by the Portuguese writers and the European travellers in *Hakluyt*, to say nothing of Burmese inscriptions.

The young feringhi.[2]—There is no Portuguese version that I can trace. I have given the Burmese account, *Hmannan* II. 268-70, which says that he was nephew to the lord of Peissarit who sent him to attack Achin from Malacca. Peissarit is unidentified; the nearest names are Pedir, Pacem and Patani, all in Portuguese hands at this time. *Phayre* "History" 101 says the feringhi was nephew to Diogo Soarez de Mello but does not give the process whereby he comes to this conclusion. I have not found a nephew of his mentioned as being in Burma; he himself put into the coast of Pegu for a time under stress of weather in 1545, but he was not interned and went away again (*Couto* III. i. 16), and after serving Tabinshwehti against Arakan in 1546 (III. i 21) he serves the Portuguese against the sultan of Achin, but he is not beaten, he gloriously defeats the sultan, (III i. 348 and ii. 118), and after helping Bayinnaung to invade Siam and to sack Pegu in 1551 he dies there (IV. i. 136). Couto mentions some half dozen Portuguese captains in Burma by name, and Diogo Soarez de Mello had a son there, but none of them fit in with the *Hmannan* story, which may well be mistaken.

Funeral sacrifice.[3]—The numbers could be considerable; thus, 10 elephants, 100 horses, and 100 each of men and women were slaughtered at the grave of a major *sawbwa*. The Ahom Shan kings of Assam continued the custom at least as late as the seventeenth century, and would even bury one of the slaves alive to look after the lamp in the tomb (*Gait* 121). Until the English compelled them to abandon slave-holding, the White Karens and the Danaws buried slaves alive with their masters; a small hole was left in the grave through which they could breathe, and food was supplied to them for seven days; if they could then rise

[1] See p. 158. [2] See p. 161. [3] See p. 166.

unaided they became free. The same train of thought underlies the *myosade* (p. 320) and the head-hunting of the Wild Wa to-day, who hunt especially before sowing time so as to ensure the presence of a new ghost to look after the fields (*GUB* I. i. 498). In Karen villages pigs are the property of the women and know their mistress's voice; when a woman dies, her pigs are killed so that they may accompany her. In Karenni in 1908, when the *myosa* of Kyebogyi was buried, the people wished to bury his pony with him, but were dissuaded by the Assistant Political Officer. Funeral sacrifice is of course universal. Thus Achilles, after sacrificing four horses and two dogs on the funeral pyre of Patroklos, crowns the ceremony by slaying twelve Trojans (Iliad XXIII. 175). Around their dead king the Scythians would bury one of his concubines, his cupbearer, cook, groom, lacquey, messenger and horses lest he should lack servants in the hereafter (Herodotus IV. 71). Viking barrows in Norway dating from the eleventh century contain the skeletons not only of the chief but also of the followers who were buried with him. In the Norse Saga, the Viking chief, sick unto death, is carried aboard his favourite ship, his best warriors clamorously man her, she is set on fire, the sails are hoisted, she blows out to sea, and thus they all die together rejoicing. See *Encycl. Religion and Ethics* s.vv. "Burma," "Death and the disposal of the dead," "Human sacrifice."

Tooth and Invulnerables.[1]—The dates 1574 and 1576 of the daughter and the tooth are just a decade later in the Burmese version, *Hmannan* III. 8, 33-5, than in the Portuguese versions. See *Stevens* II. 207-9, 251-2 (where Faria y Sousa tells a naughty story about the tooth), *Linschoten* I. 293, and above all *Gerson da Cunha* whose memoir gives a complete history of the Kandy Tooth down to the present day.

These Invulnerables, mentioned at *Hmannan* III. 37, are not peculiar to Burma. Siam also had them. *Samuel Smith* 17-30 mentions them as being sent with Phaulkon's embassy to France, where *sic* the Guards of Louis XIV. fired at them but could not injure them, and as taking part in the 1661 raid into Burma (p. 200) where they rendered themselves invisible and, though heavily outnumbered, so terrified the Burmese by their invulnerability that they won easily. *Trant*, *Havelock* and *Snodgrass* describe the show the Burmese Invulnerables made in 1824-6 when they were frequently found to be doped with opium, but not so heavily that they could not run quite fast. They survive to-day in the form of dacoits with magical tattooing and with pieces of metal buried under the skin as charms against wounds (p. 314).

The Legend of the East[2] faded on examination. *Bernier* 55, 225, 229, writing in 1670, pointed out the prevailing destitution and ignorance in India; and he, like *Manucci* II. 441, writing in 1700, was of opinion that 30,000 white troops would suffice to sweep the Moghul Empire off the face of the earth. As for Burma, take the following. (Sir Thomas Herbert was the cavalier who attended Charles I. to the scaffold. Hamilton was a ship-owner who spent a lifetime in the East.)

[1] See p. 174. [2] See p. 176.

"I might tell you of the vanitie of the king of Burma, in his loading himself with glittering gems, his head, ears, arms, hands, legs and feet resembling a bespangled firmament; such as may amaze a good sense, yea, dazzle a good eye, and force some men to judge him infinitely rich; but I behold him otherwise and judge him poor and miserable." (Year 1629. *Herbert* 322.)

"As King of the twenty-four white Somereroes, I believe few Kings will much care to dispute that glorious Title with him, for those Somereroes are only common China Umbrellaes, covered over with thin Chormondel Beteellaes, and their Canes lackt and gilded, and because his own Subjects dare not use any such Umbrellaes, he wisely lays his imperial Commands on all other Kings to forbear wearing of them when they go abroad . . . Tho' the Palace is very large, yet the Buildings are but mean, and the City tho' great and populous, is only built of Bambow Canes, thatcht with Straw or Reeds, and the Floors of Teak Plank, or split Bambows, because if Treason or other capital Crimes be detected, the Criminals may have no Place of Shelter, for if they do not appear on the first Summons, Fire will fetch them out of their combustible Habitations." (Year 1727. *Hamilton* II. 45, 47).

The Catholic Mission.[1]—Bonfer, a French Franciscan who was chaplain to the seaport Portuguese in 1554-7, also "spent years in learning the Pegues' language and mysteries that he might preach among them, but was forced to give over, desiring rather (as did S. Anthony) to preach among pigs than such a swinish generation." The first church was built by De Brito's Jesuit chaplains at Syriam, who did some mission work there and doubtless accompanied the Portuguese captives of 1613 into the interior. After that there were no white clergy, but there were always two resident chaplains, one for the feringhi community at Syriam, the other for the descendants of the Christian captives at court and in the Shwebo villages; both chaplains were Goanese, under the bishop of Mylapur (Madras); they knew no Burmese, and spoke pigeon Portuguese, and their morals were on a level with their intelligence.

The first missionaries were Genoud and Joret, of the Missions Etrangères de Paris; serving in the Siam mission, they tended Talaing and Burmese captives, whose kinsmen invited them to Burma; they arrived at Syriam in 1689 and founded a little hospital, but were denounced by the monks, taken to court, stripped and exposed to mosquitoes, sewn up in sacks and drowned near Ava in 1693. Nothing further happened till 1721 when Calchi, a Barnabite, and Vittoni, a secular, both Italians, landed and came to court; the fury of the Portuguese priests knew no bounds; they delated the two Italians to the king as spies, and when Calchi lay dying alone they refused him the last sacraments. None the less the king granted facilities and henceforward there was, almost without intermission, at least one resident priest in the country, under, till 1829, the control of Italian Barnabites. The Burmese government, though

[1] See pp. 186, 207, 231.

tolerant as regards religion, was suspicious of wandering strangers, and would not allow them to go into the interior; hence, they had to confine their efforts to Syriam and its successor Rangoon, to the capital, and to the Shwebo villages where, since 1770, the church has been at Monhla. The first bishop, Gallizia, consecrated in 1742, met a tragic end (p. 213). He had only three priests, often there were fewer, and there were never more than half-a-dozen until the English occupation, by opening up freedom of travel, made missionary work possible. Nerini (p. 230) expanded a small Burmese vocabulary left by Calchi, and their work is the basis of subsequent dictionaries. Nerini also founded a girls' orphanage at Syriam, and built Syriam church in 1750, the first brick church in Burma, using Coromandel labour because the local labour was incompetent. The first book printed in Burmese was a little grammar by Carpani, a missionary on leave in Italy; the dies were cut at the Propaganda in Rome, the resultant book being the quaint "Alphabetum Barmanorum seu Bomanorum Regni Avœ finitarumque regionum, Romæ MDCCLXXVI. Typis Sacrœ Congreg. de Propaganda Fide. Prœ sidum adprobatione" (Bodleian—8° z. 126 BS, British Museum—68. a. 29). The first Burman to visit Europe was Maung Saw, a monk; he became a Catholic and went to Rome in 1784 with Montegazza who died as bishop in 1794 at the capital Amarapura—his tombstone is still to be seen. Sangermano, who wrote "The Burmese Empire," the first general account of the country, served at Rangoon 1783-1806, founding St. John's church and school there.

The mission records show a terribly high death rate; it was lower than that of lay Europeans, with their less abstemious habits, but in the eighteenth century men did not wear sun helmets or understand how to live in the tropics. The flock consisted mainly of the *bayingyi* villages in the Shwebo area, with 2,000 souls including wives and children, but there were some converts in Rangoon, bringing the gross total to perhaps 5,000 in 1800. The jurisdiction of the Portuguese clergy in India is racial rather than territorial and until shortly after 1800 they continued to exist at Tatkale in Rangoon side by side with the Italian mission, having a congregation of a few hundred Indians and half-caste Portuguese.

It was an Armenian who supplied funds for the building of Syriam church. The Rangoon Armenian Church Kalendar shows that Armenians first came to Burma in 1612 and that they dwelt in Syriam; their first tombstone is dated 1725.

See *Purchas* 507, *Herbert* 318, *Launay* II. 274 and 332, *Annales de la Propagation* 1864 49, *Hamilton* II. 63, *Bigandet*.

Dutch withdrawal.[1]—*Dalrymple* I. 98 infers Dutch possession of Negrais from the existence of a tombstone there recording the burial of a Dutch colonel in 1608; but their papers mention no settlement there. He goes on to say that during some dispute with the Burmese they threatened to bring in the Chinese, whereupon the Burmese expelled them and all other Europeans; he gives no reference, and the statement is doubtful. The Dutch were engrossed elsewhere, they held the prize of all Asia in

[1] See p. 191.

the Spice Islands, and profitable trade could not go through in Burma with any regularity. The decision of the Council at Batavia in 1676 to abandon Pegu says nothing of a quarrel or an expulsion order, and four years later they were still winding up their affairs at Pegu (India Office, Mackenzie Collection of MSS., Private no. 40, p, 59; *Dagh Register* 1680). As for the English, who withdrew about the same time, Governor Higginson, year 1695, in his secret instructions to envoy Fleetwood (p. 203 above) explicitly says that the East India Company had withdrawn its branches from Burma, "the trade proving unprofitable."

Thalun's Inquest, etc.[1]—As institutions which survived till yesterday, such as some of the land tenures in Kyaukse, are ascribed to Thalun, and so much of his work links up with other matters, this seems the place for a note on general conditions.

None of the record of the 1638 inquest has been found, but probably it resembles that of king Bodawpaya (p. 269), and some references to what he did survive. Thus at Syriam he ordained, in addition to the port customs, twelve kinds of revenue—a toll of gold, a toll of silver, a toll of rope, a toll of each of the two kinds of cane, a toll of wood oil, a toll of madder, a toll of rice, a toll of powder, a toll of chillies, a toll of salt, and a toll of salt fish.

Instead of dedicating prisoners of war as slaves to pagodas, Thalun found a new use for them: he settled them as tenants at Kyaukse where their families supplied labour for the canals and they themselves served as soldiers (p. 318). Indeed some of these canal tenants were not prisoners. Thus Linzin (Viengchang) youths of good family volunteered, probably under pressure, for service under their suzerain, the king of Burma; the Linzin Foot Guards were a crack regiment with land in the canal area, one *thwethauksu* (platoon) being settled at Thindaing and one at Thanyua; they also formed a war-canoe corps.

Thalun settled Chiengmai and Kaunghan (? Kenghung) Shans along the Mu and Chindwin rivers in three corps (Yun-kaunghan, Win-kaunghan, Tat-kaunghan); many of these were not pure Shans but descendants of the Burmese left at Chiengmai by Bayinnaung 1551-81. Bayinnaung himself had settled his Mohnyin and Mogaung prisoners in Shwebo district where they finally occupied the Pyinzala-ngamyo area in the Kanbalu subdivision (Nyaungbin, Yuatha, Hngetpyaw, Nagasin, Pintha) serving as hereditary *daing-asu* (shield men) and *le-asu* (archers). The men in such units entered into *thwethauk* brotherhood (p. 339) with each other, and *thwethauksu* (a body of men who have drunk each other's blood) was the name for a platoon. Nwetame near Kyabin in Minbu district was peopled, probably at this period, by Shan prisoners from Chiengmai who introduced the local irrigation system and served as *Yun-ahmudan* (Chiengmai troops).[2] Now, as later, the kings brought men from all over the Shan states and from distant parts like Tavoy to serve in the plains or at court, usually as soldiers; it supplied government with men, it Burmanised the Shans, and these outlying states would have rebelled even more frequently than they

[1] See p. 194. [2] *Parsons* 2.

did had not many of their sons, from chief to commoner, been hostages in the king's hands. It was the same with all subject races: villages with such names as Shanzu, Talaingzu, where captive Shans, Siamese, and Talaings were settled, occur all over Upper Burma. It is probably the prisoners taken in the 1629 rebellion who supplied the Talaing settlements at Shwebontha, Zigon, Ngabe, Sulegon and Pyinka island in Sagaing district, consisting of *hsin-ahmudan* (keepers and catchers of elephants) a dangerous service for which they volunteered to avoid being dedicated to the Shwepaunglaung pagoda at Kyaukyit (p. 96). Other parts of the Talaing elephant corps were scattered over Mankyo and Aukkyaung near Sagu, Magyibya, and Sinkya near Salin, and Thalundin near Paunglin, in Minbu district; Myinshisse near Sale in Myingyan district; Hngetpyawdaw near Yesagyo, Sincheya and Pandawyua near Pahkangyi, in Pakokku district; and at Sindaw near Ma-u, Thitsein, Sadon, and Ngakon in the Monyua district.[1]

In Myingyan district are Talaing colonies, claiming originally from prisoners taken at Thaton in 1057 and during the attacks made on the Delta by the chief of Ava, Minhkaung 1401-22; they were settled according to their craft, on which the court had first claim—for instance, Shwega, the village of the shield makers; Sinhka, the village of the howdah makers; Kabyu, Kamye, Kani where saddles were made, white for commoners, black for junior officials, red for senior officials; Thintabaw, Thintaya, the villages of hairdressers; Pontha, the village of musicians.[2]

Mahomedans were captured among the defenders of Pegu in 1539 and 1599, and they were taken in Arakan, during raids such as those of Tabinshwehti on Mrohaung in 1547 and of Sane's officers on Sandoway in 1707; these, and De Brito's Mahomedan followers captured at the fall of Syriam in 1613 or in the stray ships which arrived just after, were settled at Myedu in Shwebo district, Pinya and Kanlu in Sagaing, Yindaw in Yamethin, and Leppan in Kyaukse, receiving land in lieu of pay for their services as hereditary musketeers of the Guard.[3]

The Portuguese captured at Syriam in 1613 numbered perhaps 400 including Eurasians, women, and children. They were kept for a time at Payeinma[4] in Sagaing district, and then were scattered among villages between the Chindwin and Mu rivers. There they were given land, a Catholic priest attended them, and they formed a Christian community which has retained its identity to this day, with the name *bayingyi* (feringhi). Intermarrying with the people, they lost their distinctive features and many relapsed from Catholicism, being known as *kalapyet* (lapsed foreigners); but, on the other hand, their numbers were occasionally swelled, as stray Europeans who fell into the king's hands were sent

[1] *Parlett* 4. [2] *Carey* 2.

[3] *Parlett* 4, *Grahame* 13-8, *JBRS* 1915 Furnivall "History of Syriam" 53.

[4] *Bigandet* 71 says he saw, about 1867, bricks there of what once had been their church. They themselves say they came to Burma in 999 B.B. (A.D. 1637) but 999 is a mere jingle. He gives two lists, similar to mine, compiled by the Burmese military authorities in 1777 and by himself in 1867. In his lists the *bayingyis* are scattered in smaller packets over more villages.

there, a notable acquisition being the French crews captured in 1757 (p. 231). From 1613 onward they formed the musketeers and gunners of the Guard. Even to-day some of them are to be found with beards and with blue or green eyes from Dutch or northern French ancestors. Their present numbers and localities are

	Mandalay town	500
Sagaing district		
	Nabet	300
	Chaungu	400
Shwebo district		
	Monhla	483
	Ye-u	120
	Chanthayua	600

The treatment of the Portuguese prisoners seems brutal. But it was the custom of the Burmese to deport prisoners, unless indeed they massacred them out of hand. They were acting in accordance with the common custom of antiquity, of which the Babylonian Captivity is a well-known example. From the beginning of their history to the end, the Burmese regarded slaves as one of the chief spoils of war, and habitually settled them all over the country. In Indo-China generally, wars were glorified slave raids. In 1855 the Red Karens were still carrying off Burmans and Shans, whom they bartered for cattle,[1] the Siamese raided Tenasserim until the British occupation in 1825 (p. 272), the Arakanese raided the Burmese border villages and for centuries their slave ships were the terror of Bengal and Assam (p. 143). The Burmese raided their neighbours in the same way, deporting whole cities—Thaton, Ayuthia, and Mrohaung. The Chins say they tattoo the faces of their women because the Burmese were always carrying off the pretty ones. Captives suffered on the march (p. 298), but once they had been brought into Burma, they were often decently treated. The king had first choice, and those he selected were dedicated to pagodas or settled in the villages; but often the troops were allowed to keep a prisoner or two each for themselves, the officers getting more, according to rank; they were either used as servants, or sold in the market, usually for a very low price because they were liable to abscond; thus about 1800 a Siamese woman captive sold for a bottle of intoxicants.[2] Slaves allotted to private soldiers were often treated as members of the family, for the common liability to oppression aroused mutual sympathy, and no man knew when he too might become a slave either at the caprice of government or for failure to pay his revenue (p. 359).[3]

Ruling a poor and thinly populated country, the king of Burma regarded captives as a form of wealth, just as a planter would like to have a gang of labourers who worked for nothing. The same desire for population explains the king's habit of seizing mariners (p. 205),

[1] *Yule* "Mission" 297. [2] *Crawfurd* I. 424.

[3] *Sangermano* 126, *TP* 1891 Cordier "Les Français en Birmanie" 393, *Crawfurd* II. 133, *Bayfield* xxv, Fortnightly Review 1897 Parker "The Burmo-Chinese frontier and the Kakhyen tribes."

and the custom whereby any foreigner temporarily residing in the country was not merely allowed but was publicly encouraged[1] to take a wife for the period of his stay; he had to pay her off before leaving, and never under any circumstances could he take her or his female children out of the country, though he might, on payment of a heavy tax, get sanction to take his male children. Every ship on arrival was carefully searched for women, and if, on leaving, it contained one woman more than it did on arrival, that ship was confiscated and the crew enslaved: women could breed subjects for the king, and therefore they were not allowed to emigrate.

Just as the king would not allow the export of his live-stock in the form of human beings, so he would not allow the export of his dead-stock in the form of the country's natural products—e.g. rubies, teak, rice (p. 357). A man who goes to trade in a country can take payment only in two ways—either in precious metal or in goods. In Burma it was difficult to take it in goods, because almost every local product worth having was prohibited from export. But if payment was taken in gold or silver, there was the same difficulty: under the king's order the money could not be taken away lest the country should be impoverished. The result might be that the merchant made arrangements to spend it in the country, for instance by building a ship, thus benefiting local labour, which is just what the king intended; but the result might also be that he took good care not to come to Burma again, which is just the opposite of what the king intended. There were a number of countries in the vicinity of which the king had never heard; there were literally scores of ports where money could be used to better advantage because the rajas were less obstructive. In practice even the rulers of Ava did not enforce their prohibitions to the letter. There was not only smuggling, but also there were various exceptions made on application, and there were demi-official evasions. But the prohibitions were never relaxed in the case of the precious metals,[2] and the circumvention of the others was sufficiently cumbrous to prevent Syriam and its successor Rangoon from ever thriving.

These ideas resembled, in essence, those underlying the Mercantile Theory, and there was much to be said for some of them at the time. Take the prohibition on the export of rice. There was no regular surplus for export, because a self-contained population whose numbers are stationary grows only enough for its own support. Government was never stable and at any moment the king in his palace was liable to be cut off by rebellion from Kyaukse and the Delta, the main sources of his supply. He habitually brought large quantities of rice from such

[1] Year 1592 (*Linschoten* I. 98), year 1727 (*Hamilton* II. 51-3), year 1782 (*TP* 1890 Cordier "Les Français en Birmanie" 190 and 1891 25), year 1795 (*Symes* 329). Foreign settlers felt the restriction against taking their children away, but even in the 1826 treaty the English could not get the restriction removed (*Crawfurd* II. app. 14).

[2] Even in the 1826 treaty the English could not get the prohibition removed from precious metals, *Crawfurd* I. 210 and II. app. 14. See also *Gouger* 60-7, *Sangermano* 176.

places and stored it in the palace against a possibility of siege, and down the Irrawaddy river there were grain depots, as at Myanaung and Bassein, where food was supposed to be, and sometimes was, stored for dispatch to hungry districts.[1] The king lived, to an extent hardly realisable to-day, in continual dread of famine in the capital, and famines are constantly mentioned in the chronicles.

The organisation of society was tribal.[2] Down to the English annexation, the Sit-thu Prince, or Slave-King, i.e. the headman of Nyaung-u West village near Pagan, who is descended from Manuha chief of Thaton (p. 28), controlled and assessed not only his own village but also eighty families in Pakokku, over ten in both Magwe and Myingyan, and over twenty in both Sale and Minbu, all being Talaings and slaves. Society was honeycombed with class distinctions. Before men "went mad and cast aside their hereditary dignities" a member of the cavalry levy would not eat with a *lamaing* (crown serf) or even sit on the same level. The rules of inheritance varied in different classes. Probably these class distinctions originated in race, commoners tending to be the conquered mass, e.g. Chins and all manner of imported captives, the official classes tending to be the conquerors, i.e. the Burmese themselves—that is one reason why the Burmese are a proud race. People were subordinate not so much to the local headman as to the overseer of their order or tribe, though both offices were frequently combined in the person of the *myothugyi* who was the overseer for the servile classes in his area. Thus Daungbo in Myingyan district contained villagers who when called up served in the cavalry, spearmen and shieldmen respectively; instead of paying revenue to the headman, they paid it to the head of their class. Similarly the privileges of each order were independent of area. A man might live in one village and be entitled to work land in another ten miles away because that land was allotted to his class. If he migrated, he was liable for taxes not to his new village but to his old overseer so long as the latter could trace him. This applies not only to military units, but also to the rest of the population, which was regimented, as in feudal countries. The regimentation was complex and obstructive, and governmental control was facilitated by the unusually high standard of literacy—"it is a kingdom governed by the pen, for not a single person can go from one village into another without a paper or writing."[3] The various classes were clans, with rights accruing from a certain office which it was their hereditary duty to fill; marriage outside the clan entailed loss of status, and the king could degrade a man from one clan to another, for instance from the *sadawchet-asu*, fish-cooks, to the *hsindaing-asu*, elephant scavengers. Society was tribal not territorial, an organisation not of local communities but of occupational guilds. This comes out even in its pageantry: when the Lord Governor of Rangoon kept the Feast of Thadingyut and went in

[1] *Symes* 233, *JBRS* 1915 Furnivall "History of Syriam" 143.

[2] *Carey* 2, *Furnivall* "Myingyan Settlement" 8, 13; *JBRS* 1914 Furnivall "Notes on the history of Hanthawaddy" and 1915 his "History of Syriam"; *Forchammer* "Jardine Prize" 7.

[3] Year 1700, *Manucci* I. 373.

solemn procession to the Shwedagon, with his staff, his musketeers, his spearmen, his boats' crews and all his lieges, the salt boilers had to carry the silver candlesticks. When the English annexed Lower Burma they found authority vested not in the head of each village but in the head of each class—the head over the Karens of each township, the head over its fishermen, the heads over its brokers, its palm-juice drawers, its garden cultivators, its field cultivators, its elephants, its buffaloes, its horses. Early Deputy Commissioners found it hard to make *taikthugyis* realise that their jurisdiction was territorial not personal, and that they were responsible for all residents in their tract. Revenue was sometimes levied on the area a man worked, the unit being the area a pair of buffaloes could plough, but often this was totally disregarded [1] and a man paid a poll tax in his capacity as betel grower, fruit gardener, wood oil tapper, fisherman, salt boiler and so forth. Karens paid revenue not as residents or cultivators but as Karens, a heavy poll tax, and were exempted from military service although they might be requisitioned [2] on emergency to suppress rebellion. Revenue was paid in kind; thus a township in Henzada district paid 10 per cent. of its rice crop, and Tharrawaddy paid 100 *viss* (365 lb.) each of honey and beeswax and 100 mats. Elephant's tusks were a common medium. Syriam paid fish, coconut, plantains, royal tribute of betel from the Dalla gardens, and sugar of which vast quantities were consumed by the elephants. But revenue was also paid in service. For instance, Syriam had to maintain three war-boats, and to keep watch against raiders from Arakan; indeed every big riverside village, such as Shwehle in Minbu district and the Bangyi area in Monyua district, maintained war-canoes for the levy, and races between them were magnificent spectacles, the local lords taking their smartest boats to court and showing them off at the king's regattas.

Yung-li (Kuei) [3] was strangled with a bowstring in the market-place of Yünnan Fu and was buried there, aged 38. His heir aged 14 met with a like fate. A little son is buried at a small monastery on an island opposite Shwegu in Bhamo district. His women were taken to Pekin and received good treatment in captivity. The heir was called Constantine, the empress Anne, the dowagers Helen and Mary and the able eunuch Achilles, for the whole family had become Catholic, with a Jesuit confessor who gave them these names to invoke the tradition of the Byzantine house. Yung-li himself, though Christianised, was not baptized because he could not forsake his wives. When Sankuei, viceroy of Yünnan, marched into Burma to seize him, Yung-li sent him a letter asking for pity and reminding him of past favours. Sankuei owed his career to the Ming dynasty, but that did not prevent him from hunting Yung-li down like vermin. See *Hmannan* III. 261-82; *Warry; Parker* "Précis" and "Letters from a Chinese empress and a Chinese eunuch to the Pope in the Year 1650" in Contemporary Review 1912; *Père d'Orléans;*

[1] *British Burma Gazetteer* I. 439, 450.
[2] *TP* 1891 Cordier "Les Français en Birmanie" 395.
[3] See p. 201.

Du Halde I. 487, *Macgowan* 526, *Cordier* "Histoire de la Chine" III. 240-4; *Anderson* "Expedition to western Yünnan" 19-20.

French and Shipbuilding.[1]—In 1769 the French obtained greater privileges than the English, such as the right to fly their flag at Rangoon, but the branch soon after died out with the waning of French interests in the Far East. In the eighteenth century their shipwrights were probably the best in Europe, and it is from them that the Delta received its first lessons in shipbuilding. Dupleix 1720-54 liked Syriam because it was out of the way of the English; he regarded it as his chief shipbuilding centre, because labour and material were cheap, and many of the ships he sent to trade in the Red Sea and Manilla were built there; *Diligent* and the ill-fated *Fleury* (p. 231) were built there in 1755. The Talaings and Burmese were slow and wasted timber because they did not know the use of the saw, but in other respects they were excellent carpenters. Although Malabar and Surat teak was preferred, Burma teak was known in India from the sixteenth century. It was the finest wood imaginable for shipbuilding because it resisted sea water and did not splinter under gunfire, a principal cause of casualties in the sea fights of the eighteenth century. Rangoon, which succeeded Syriam in 1755, was a minor centre in comparison with Calcutta and the great Parsee yards at Bombay, but none the less it supported a shipbuilding industry under French, English and Armenian contractors, numbering perhaps half a dozen. Their ships tended to be weak in the keel because of scamped construction, but they could be built up to 1,000 tons, and the cost was only two-thirds of that at Calcutta. Most were built for Mahomedan and Armenian merchants, but they were resold, and some of the longest found their way into the battle squadrons of the English East India Company. The English invaders in 1824 found on the stocks two unfinished frigates of 300 tons each, built by a shipwright called Turner for the Imam of Muscat. The industry was killed by the invention of iron ships. See *Sonnerat* (1782) II. 43-53 and (1806) III. 40-3, *Symes* 217 and 457-60, *Cordier* "La France en Chine" I. xlviii and "Historique abrégé" 6, *TP* 1891 Cordier "Les Français en Birmanie" 39, *Havelock* 49, *Trant* 26.

Capital punishment[2] is contrary to Buddhist ethics. A criminal may die by the judge's order, yet he dies not because of his crime, but because he is doomed by his evil deeds in a previous existence to have his head chopped off in five or ten subsequent existences; for his present crime he will suffer in some future existence under the process of *karma*, the indissoluble nexus of cause and effect. As *karma* acts as judge, there is no need for an earthly judge to do more than protect without punishing, and a ruler who takes upon him to pass sentence of death will himself in future existences suffer the misery resulting from manslaughter. Therefore Burmese rulers devoutly refrained from passing sentence of death. But they said "Let him travel by the usual road," and they

[1] See pp. 203, 284. [2] See p. 208.

said it very often—*Crawfurd* II. 52, 148, written in 1826, records that in the Rangoon area, with a population of 18,000, there were twenty-five to thirty executions a year, which would give the present Rangoon, with its 340,000 inhabitants, no fewer than 519 executions a year, against the actual 2. See p. 358.

Gwe.[1]—Two colonies are mentioned, one at Awaing village near Pegu, consisting of Gwe Karens (*Hmannan* III. 383), and another at Okpo in Mandalay district (*Hmannan* III. 393). The former are doubtless the Sêm Kwe of the Siamese chronicles, a boorish folk 3,000 strong who, speaking a language distinct from Talaing, follow the exile Smim Htaw Buddhaketi to Ayuthia (*Wood*). The latter are called simply Gwe in *Hmannan*, but *Konbaungset* 71 calls them Gwe Lawa, Lawa meaning Wa; *Scott* "Burma, a handbook" 181 thinks them Shans from Möng Kwi. The kings had frequently deported Shans, among other races, and settled them in the plains (pp. 166, 347 above). *Parker* "Burma, relations with China" 75 mentions a Chinese belief that they were descended from the retinue of the fugitive emperor Kuei; but the mere similarity of names means nothing, and the retinue, consisting of only 600-700 people, was practically exterminated (p. 200).

Price of Rice.[2]—Three of these baskets went to an English ship's rice bay, which Professor H. Dodwell tells me was at Madras in 1782, 150-60 lb., so the basket was evidently much the same as the present Burmese paddy basket of 46 lb. In 1759 the price was fifteen baskets to the rupee (*Dalrymple* I. 110). In 1795 the price at the capital, Amarapura, was 1½ baskets (each of 16 *viss* = 58 lb.) a rupee, at Rangoon and Martaban 4 to 5 baskets (*Symes* 326). In 1813, during the famine years, the price at Amarapura was Rs. 5 a basket (*BSPC* despatch 5 February 1813 Canning to Adam). At the outbreak of war in 1824 the Rangoon price was 4 baskets a rupee but during the war it was 1 basket (*Alexander* 21). Old men in the Henzada island can remember paddy selling at 10 baskets a rupee.

Negrais Massacre.[3]—Alves' reports are at *Dalrymple* I. 343-98. The Burmese account, *Konbaungset* 144-7, overlooking the fact that this was in 1759, four years after Pegu had been razed and the struggle was over, adds that Talaing prisoners said they were receiving cannon from the English heretics. The king, in the letter sent by Alves (*Dalrymple* I. 394) says he is sure the governor of Madras would never have allowed help to be given to the Talaings, and Negrais must have been acting without orders; the king had no conception of the Company's organisation or the control it had over its staff. Things were no longer as in 1755 when ships at Rangoon, having no orders either way, could fire on the Burmese and receive no more than an angry reprimand; after 1755 the Company declared its policy towards Alaungpaya, in 1757 it signed a treaty with him, and its officers had orders accordingly. The king also believed (*Dalrymple* I. 374) that

[1] See pp. 211, 212. [2] See p. 228. [3] See p. 240.

Negrais was in contract with the Talaings to buy half their loot; but the English, though capable of buying anything and asking no questions as to its origin, were out for teak and so forth, not the sort of stuff Talaings looted.

The Burmese account makes no attempt to conceal Alaungpaya's personal insistence on the whole operation, or the manner in which it was carried out at a friendly meeting, doubtless regarding it all as high strategy. It is also characteristic that when he had a real grievance, a *casus belli*, in the firing of the ships at Rangoon in 1755, Alaungpaya failed to send a mission demanding immediate disavowal and reparation; yet four years later, when even the grievance that existed in his mind could have been settled by departmental adjustment, he broke out into wholesale murder. His entourage included men such as the governor of Bassein, who made lamentations to Alves, saying he merely looked on at the massacre, and, instead of saying frankly he took a share of the loot, went out of his way to deny that he took any; when Alves found one of the captives' clothes in his possession, he mumbled "I was only taking care of it for him" (*Dalrymple* I. 358).

Grave doubts are raised as to the accuracy of Burmese chronicles for earlier periods when even such recent events as these are so inaccurately recorded. Thus *Konbaungset* 141 *et seqq.* puts Lester's embassy to Myanaung in April 1755 or at Rangoon in May 1756, whereas it was really in July 1757; the Negrais massacre in May 1755, whereas it was actually 6 October 1759; Alves' embassy in August 1755, though it did not take place till five years later in the next reign, September 1760. It insists that an embassy came from the king of London town, England, as well as from the Company, mentions many embassies that did not occur, omits the firing of the ships at Rangoon, and the execution of the French officers at Syriam, though it mentions the capture of *kala* ships and crews; and says that the white gunners at the siege of Pegu made shells (an impossibility in the East), that they included 200 English marine artillerymen, and that Alaungpaya had 5,000 white troops. But there had never been a fraction of that number in Burma, and he cannot have had more than 300, mostly the captive French crews. When Alves was allowed to claim all the English and Dutch in Burma, the two together amounted to only nine.

Chinese War 1765-9.[1]—See *Konbaungset* 425-92, *Symes* 69, *Crawfurd* II. 284, *JASBengal* 1837 Burney "Some account of the wars between Burma and China," *McLeod* 60, *Macgowan* 548, *Cordier* "Histoire générale de la Chine" III. 353, *Warry*, *Parker* "Précis" and "Burma, relations with China" 83-94.

The account I have given of the traders' disputes does not put the Burmese in the wrong; it is the Burmese account. The notes which the Emperor recorded on the file show that his designs were imperialistic: he intended to annex Burma and set his nominee on the throne.

The Chinese were severely handicapped by lack of topographical

[1] See p. 253.

information. One of their armies spent two months wandering blindly through Mogaung and Mohnyin when it was urgently needed elsewhere. The Chinese generals studied the records of their 1277 invasion but found them useless as the place names had changed, *BEFEO* 1909 Huber "Fin de la dynastie de Pagan" 669. The Emperor wrote "The Burmese cannot meet even our wretched Chinese troops in the open, let alone our splendid Manchus, but know their strength in stockade fighting and in an impossible climate." One Chinese account calls the Burmese "Blackbellies," referring to their tattooed bodies.

Symes 69 says the Chinese came with 50,000 men; even that number must have been a severe test for their lines of communication, and the Chinese official records show that 41,000 was the maximum used in any one year. The Burmese account characteristically says the Chinese numbered half a million, *Konbaungset* 456; see note "Numerical Note" p. 333.

What seem to be the graves of the Manchu generals can be seen at Maingtin near Pyaunggaung (Sakantha) railway station east of Maymyo, see *RSASB* 1918 22. The Emperor was furious on finding that poor Mingjui had after all lost only 15 per cent. of his men and could easily have won with a little timely support.

The written terms say nothing about boundaries; nor do they include the surrender of *sawbwas* by the Chinese, and of prisoners, especially by the Burmese, two items orally agreed to but not fulfilled in spite of subsequent bickering. With their 1787 embassy, however, the Burmese sent back a few of the surviving senior prisoners, and apparently some more in later years when the Chinese had released all Burmese prisoners. The reason why China won so easily in 1287 is that the Pagan kingdom was less powerful than the developed kingdom of Burma; the fierce young Alaungpaya dynasty in 1769 had a much larger area from which to draw levies.

Shifting Capitals.[1]—Each Turkish sultan was supposed to build a new palace. The Mikados of Japan used regularly to do so. In Africa, a Baganda king's first duty is to choose the site for a new capital (*Roscoe* 200). In India, Ahmad Shah 1422-35, having suffered from illness at Kulbarga, perceived that the site was unlucky and moved his capital sixty miles to Bidar; and in 1569 Akbar, having lost two children at Agra, decided that it was inauspicious and moved his capital twenty-three miles to Fathpur-Sikri (*Vincent Smith* "Oxford History of India" 278, 351). Prejudice against repairing an old house accounts for the many ruined houses one sees in Indian towns. The underlying belief may be that places, like persons, have only a limited share of luck allotted to them, and it becomes exhausted after a time. Such reasoning would appeal to an agricultural people like the Burmese who are familar with shifting cultivation, a system of exhaustion followed by fallow.

Administrative conditions.[2]—This vivid account of the Talaing outbreak at Rangoon in 1783 is, needless to say, from foreign sources—it

[1] See p. 265. [2] See p. 267.

is the account of a French naval officer (*TP* 1891 Cordier "Les Français en Birmanie" 32-9). Indeed it is only now, in the latter half of the eighteenth century, when the outer world comes into closer contact with Burma, that we begin to get some idea of what general conditions were like. The following is culled from the actual words of men belonging to six nationalities, differing widely in class and mental outlook, so that their consensus is significant.

The people were sober, industrious,[1] kindly and intelligent; yet, owing partly to egregious misgovernment, neither their agriculture nor their craftsmanship was at a level with their intelligence; they could not make the simplest things but left them either to be made by foreign craftsmen such as Manipuri captives or to be imported from India.[2] The land was mainly unoccupied waste, for wholesale executions, anarchic wars, and the consequent famines, kept the population down to an absurd figure, two million (p. 333); luckily this scantiness of population caused a high rate of wages and thus acted as some check on the tyranny of the government.[3] The mines were undeveloped because the king had no idea of how to develop them and yet insisted on keeping them for himself, wishing his people to have nothing beyond the bare necessities of life.[4]

Rangoon, which should have been a thriving port, was a half-stagnant town of 10,000 inhabitants[5] with at most a dozen brick houses[6]; few foreign merchants save broken men would reside there, because government was extortionate and obstructive. Thus in 1812 its governor made a Mahomedan merchant pay twenty thousand rupees for daring to say that his rival, the late governor, might return.[7] Bodawpaya heard that other countries became rich by means of companies. He did not know what a joint-stock company was and took no steps to find out. He thought it was a monopoly and he proceeded to sell every kind of trade, even vegetables in the bazaar of his capital, to monopolists, regardless of the hardship inflicted on the people by profiteers.[8] Little business could be done, because everything was tied up in royal orders. Teak should have been a thriving business, yet so little was exported that the monopoly sold for only three lakhs; and it was about the only thing men could export, for there were no finished articles and the export of most raw materials was prohibited.[9] Thus, the silk imported overland from China might not be sold out of the country, lest sufficient should not remain for the clothing of the population; rice, frequently produced to such excess that the combined efforts of men and cattle could not consume it, might not be exported lest the people should starve; gold, silver, money and jewels might not be exported lest the country should be impoverished, and ponies could not be exported lest no horses should be left. It is therefore hardly surprising

[1] *Sonnerat* (1806) III. 63, *TP* 1891 "Les Français en Birmanie" 4.

[2] *Crawfurd* II. vi. [3] *Crawfurd* II. 239 and vii.

[4] *Sonnerat* (1806) III. 58, *TP* 1891 "Les Français en Birmanie" 4, *Sangermano* 81.

[5] *Crawfurd* II. 52. [6] *Havelock* 34.

[7] *BSPC* despatch 5 February 1813 Canning to Adam.

[8] *BSPC* 25 September 1812 Canning to Edmonstone. *Gouger* 60-7.

that trade was negligible, and one of the reasons why the Emperor of China abandoned the 1765-9 war was, as he minuted on the file, that Burma did little trade, it was mostly seaborne, and what went overland was so negligible that she was not worth the expense of further campaigns.[1]

If the people sometimes had the reputation of being cruel and treacherous, this applied mainly to the vile race of officials who battened on them and corrupted their natural good qualities.[2] For although by nature they tended to be free and manly, the government was as complete a despotism as can well be conceived,[3] and the customs of the court were slavish to a degree rare even in Asiatic courts.[4] Yet in spite of its severity, government was exceptionally inefficient, responsibility being shifted from one person to another so that even a royal order sometimes failed to command attention five miles from the palace.[5]

Criminal administration was severe. Witnesses were liable to be tortured in open court under instructions from the presiding judge.[6] A thief was branded on each cheek and with the word "Thief" on his chest, for the first offence; for the second, his hands were cut off, and for the third, he lost his head; if the amount stolen was Rs. 800 or upwards, he was beheaded for the first offence.[7] For aggravated offences there was a variety of punishments. Disembowelling, impaling, burying alive, throwing to tigers, breaking every bone in a man's body and leaving him to linger sometimes for a week[8]—these were some of the methods in the provinces; at the capital the executioners were, of course, more ingenious.

But these punishments pressed only on the poor. Except treason and sacrilege there was hardly an offence the consequences of which could not be evaded by those who could afford it. Thus, a man was tied to the stake and the marksman fired at him four times without result; at each shot there was a peal of laughter from the crowd; after the fourth shot he was declared invulnerable, pardoned, and employed in a confidential capacity by the governor; he had paid a large amount.[9] A favourite way of dealing with dacoits was to paint bull's eyes on their bodies, tie them to a tree, and practice marksmanship on them.[10]

In spite of the appalling frequency of capital punishment (p. 354), crime was rampant, and folk could seldom sleep easily in their beds. In Rangoon, an important charge always under a picked governor, there were nightly robberies, sometimes by gangs of twenty, and the governor would send a senior officer with 300 men to track them down.[11] You could not travel up the Irrawaddy, the great highway of the country, without guns.

[1] *Parker* "Précis." [2] *Snodgrass* 204, 208. [3] *Crawfurd* II. 136.
[4] *Bayfield* liv; *Sonnerat* (1782) II. 47, (1806) III. 20.
[5] *Crawfurd* II. 157. [6] *Gouger* 161.
[7] *Symes* 307, *Sonnerat* (1806) III. 22, *TP* 1891 "Les Français en Birmanie" 45.
[8] *Crawfurd* II. 50 and 147-8, *Mrs Judson* 33, *Trant* 276.
[9] *Crawfurd* II. 150. [10] *Mrs Judson* 86, *Gouger* 101.
[11] *Mrs Judson* 30; cf. *Dalrymple* I. 387 and despatch dated 4 March 1812 from Governor-General to Court of Directors (*PP* 16).

Even a governor on the way to court would be murdered in spite of his escort of fifty men.[1] The civil law also was severe; not only was a defaulting debtor liable to enslavement, but also his wife and daughters were seized by the creditor and made to earn money in a brothel.[2] A woman who owed Rs. 25 or upwards and failed to pay became her creditor's slave but the debt was cancelled if she bore him a child.[3]

The kingship boasted of its wealth and made a great display of generosity in feeding envoys with rice, which cost nothing. It bought some arms and ammunition for the Guard but otherwise had few expenses, as each locality paid for its own administration and maintained its own levy in war-time.[4] The king's principal expenditure was on trinkets and golden vessels bestowed on public officers at their elevation to various grades of nobility, on gilding the palace, and on offerings to pagodas.[5] The chronicles describe images buried in pagodas as being of gold; but competent observers[6] who saw them being enshrined described them as trumpery shams and such as have come to light are seldom valuable.

The golden court was largely tinsel. Its revenue did not exceed a few lakhs, perhaps only two,[7] against the present eight hundred. But the people did not get off so lightly: two lakhs was the amount that reached the king, not the amount collected. In a not untypical instance, out of Rs. 27,000 collected, only Rs. 15,000 reached the treasury, the balance Rs. 12,000 sticking to the hands of the collectors.[8] Revenue was much heavier than now. It was usually paid in kind. The assessment was impossible, often Rs. 100 a household[9] in an age when rice sold at 24 *viss* (88 lb.) for a rupee;[10] in addition there were heavy personal services. Of course the full assessment was not collected save on some special emergency; but what was collected sufficed to crush people and leave them looking shabby.[11] Revenue defaulters for Rs. 30 and upwards were sold into slavery, but as they were then exempt from further taxation, men occasionally preferred to be sold and be free from further trouble.[12]

The king's two lakhs came only from the subject states and from such parts of Burma as were directly under his administration. The rest, probably the greater part[13] of Burma, was appropriated to public services (e.g. the Lord White Elephant, the war-boats, the elephants) or to the local lords; these local lords were usually the governors, but sometimes they were non-resident favourites in whose case the title *myosa* "eater of the township" is a sadly literal description of their energies.

The tribute from subject states consisted of fine cloths, shoes, goblets, tinsel flowers, gilt candles,[14] with a weight of precious metal which varied

[1] *Mrs Judson* 222.
[2] *Symes* 217.
[3] *Crawfurd* II. 133.
[4] *Yule* "Mission" 250.
[5] *Crawfurd* II. 186.
[6] *Cox* 110.
[7] *Crawfurd* II. 186.
[8] *Crawfurd* II. 172.
[9] *Crawfurd* I. 146-7.
[10] Year 1795, *Symes* 326.
[11] *Crawfurd*, *Marks* 160-1, *GUB* II. i. 508, *Westlake* 2.
[12] *TP* 1891 "Les Français en Birmanie" 393.
[13] *Crawfurd* II. 162.
[14] *Yule* "Mission" 302.

from nearly half a *viss* of gold [1] in the case of leading *sawbwas* down to some silver in the case of *ngwegunhmus*. The *sawbwas* in their turn took revenue from the smaller chiefs, usually in kind, such as salt, betel, gold washings, or even a specified number of knives.[2]

Fiefs generally fell to those who were capable of administering them, and many governors concealed under their forbidding exterior a real nobility of character; but only too often the selection was made by favouritism and even bribery, for the king was quite capable of giving charges to anyone who pleased him with a sufficiently large present. What might conceivably happen is indicated by the fact that a servant murdered his master, the governor, intending to seize his property so as to approach the king and buy the province for himself.[3]

Officials who were not important enough to be given fiefs lived by preying on the poor, for they received no salary. A man's whole character frequently changed as soon as he attained power,[4] so much so that the governors and the governed seemed to belong to two different races.[5] A non-official who procured himself a decent competence by his own energy took care to conceal the fact lest he should bring down on his head some trumped up case with a view to confiscating his property.[6] The race possessed much natural ingenuity, but did not exercise it because if a man displayed any individual skill, an official at once pounced down on him and robbed him of the fruits of his labour, or sent him to the palace to amuse the king.[7]

As in Turkey, men were not allowed to build houses of permanent material lest they should use them as strongholds for rebellion;[8] so they lived in discomfort, getting rid of their money quickly on monks and pagodas. Some of the sumptuary laws pressed hard, as for instance one which forbade commoners to use mosquito curtains;[9] and even people who were entitled to decent clothes sometimes avoided dressing up to their station lest some bloodsucker of an official should suspect them of wealth. A poor labourer[10] was heard to say "We are perishing under this government; no security for life, no security for property. If a man is possessed of five rupees to-day, and it becomes known, he is robbed of it by the greedy authorities to-morrow."

The people were constantly rebelling, not because they were a bad people—they were a good people—but because they were in a sort of slavery,[11] and every now and then they would rise against it and sell their lives dearly; hence the land was ever in turmoil, and government instead of being stable was the prey of the strong. Even though

[1] *Crawfurd* II. 184. [2] *Clayton* para. 92.

[3] *Mrs Judson* 33. Cf. para. 15 of despatch dated 25 May 1812 from Governor-General to Court of Directors (*PP* 39).

[4] *Sangermano* 123. [5] *Gouger* 11. [6] *Sonnerat* (1806) III. 20.

[7] *TP* 1891 "Les Français en Birmanie" 394, *Sangermano* 151, *Gouger* 36.

[8] *Hamilton* II. 47.

[9] *TP* 1891 "Les Français en Birmanie" 393.

[10] *Laurie* "Our Burmese wars" 169.

[11] *TP* 1891 "Les Français en Birmanie" 32.

the poor suffered, the race might have progressed had the nobility been allowed to develop a little independence and character; but they had no security of tenure and were treated in the same way. A commander-in-chief, without being allowed to say a word in his defence, was dashed face downwards on the pavement of the palace, men stamped and spat upon him, dragged him two miles by the hair tormenting him with spears, tore out his vitals, and flung him, still conscious, to the elephants; yet all that the unhappy man had done was to acknowledge defeat, ask for reinforcements, and tell His Majesty that the courtiers had deceived him by grossly under-estimating the enemy; and this happened under a merciful king.[1]

The court was the most stupid[2] and conceited imaginable, and did not contain a single man of common understanding;[3] or if there were such, he was afraid to show it, for the government was a sanguinary despotism.[4]

Remote areas, perhaps the greater part of the country, escaped the king's attention; here men breathed more freely, the good qualities of the people asserted themselves, the administration of the local magnates was reasonable, and the peasantry were probably more comfortable than in many other countries, such as India and the backward parts of Europe where the feudal system had outlived its usefulness and had become an instrument of oppression. But the terrible conditions described above obtained, probably throughout the historic period, along the beaten track, e.g. Bhamo, the capital, and Rangoon; and as these were the most important places in the country, the national life was polluted at the source. The great kings were despotic and cruel because they were grappling with a task which was beyond their capacity. The people were taxed but they were not governed, for the kings had not the organisation to deal with a large area covering the Irrawaddy valley, the Shan states, and sometimes Arakan and Tenasserim as well. The function of government is to govern, but it was difficult for the kings to govern when so much of their attention was spent on maintaining themselves in power against endemic rebellion.

White Elephant.[5]—White animals are often sacred—for instance, white horses in Japan, white dogs among the Iroquois, white buffaloes among the Shans of Annam, and white horses among Teutonic tribes (cf. pp. 41, 53, 88, 144, 167, 295, 325). Elephants because of their awesome size tend to be sacred—for instance, in Hinduism eight elephants support the earth; in Africa, elaborate ritual accompanies elephant hunting and the Wambugwe tribes believe the elephant to be the abode of the soul of their ancestors. Therefore it is not surprising to find the white elephant sacred in Enarea, south of Abyssinia, and all over Indo-China. The earliest mention is probably in Aélian who, writing in A.D. 200, speaks of an Indian white elephant ("De Animalium Natura" III. 46). The Chiengmai jungles

[1] Bagyidaw 1819-37, see *Havelock* 331. With *Gouger* 269 cf.[3] Esther VII 8.
[2] *Sonnerát* (1806) III. 20, *Gouger* 329.
[3] Persian's deposition at *Crawfurd* II. app. 125, *Wilson* "Documents" 237.
[4] *Mrs Judson* 5 *et passim*. [5] See p. 274.

were reputed abundant in white elephants. In 1826 the Burmese court was exceedingly hurt when Crawfurd told them that the king of Siam had whiter and more numerous white elephants than the king of Burma. Indeed, when Europeans speak of "The Land of the White Elephant" it is to Siam that they refer. In 1836 the king of Siam spent no less than a quarter of his revenue on his white elephant. See *Razadarit Ayedawpon*, *Konbaungset*, *Jones* V. 538, *Samuel Smith* 41, *Sangermano* 62-5, *BSPC* despatch 25 September 1812 Canning to Edmonstone, *Crawfurd* I. 246-8 and 255, *Yule* "Mission" 135, *Shway Yoe* ch. lii., *Nisbet* I. 203, *Encycl. Religion and Ethics* s.v. "Animals."

Chinese embassies.[1]—See *Konbaungset* 638 *et passim; Parker* "Burma, relations with China" 90-4; *Symes* 285; *RSASB* 1919 18; and *JASBengal* 1837 Burney "Some account of the wars between Burma and China" which gives a detailed account of these embassies.

It is not likely that the Yünnan viceroy represented the girls to be imperial princesses. Cheating by personation of his master's granddaughters (or daughters, p. 291) was high treason and his head would have answered for it. Bodawpaya may have willingly misunderstood the interpreters, as, after the manner of his kind, he had a voracious appetite for self-deception.

The patents of nobility were doubtless like those (gold phylacteries inscribed Thiriyazakyawthu) which were bound on the foreheads of Havelock and his colleagues when they visited Ava in 1826 (*Havelock* 360). The seal of 1792 was worth Rs. 9,000, hardly a sum for which to compromise the status of a kingdom, but the Golden Palace was not wealthy.

The Emperor's letters were sometimes polite, styling the king "Brother"; sometimes they use the haughty language of an overlord to his vassal. The king's 1823 letter studiously refrains from calling the Emperor "brother" and even omits the polite *ba* in verb terminations. But Bodawpaya must have made some serious admissions—e.g. the acceptance of the 1792 seal—for the Chinese were able to convince the English Foreign Office that Burma was tributary, so that England, as successor to Burmese liabilities, consented in the inoperative article I. of the Anglo-Chinese Convention 1886 to send decennial tribute of local produce to China, stipulating only that the envoys should be of Burmese race.

Lehtunmingala,[2]—When Htuntaik 569-82, a traditional chief of Pagan, was performing the rite, the oxen shied at his vestments flapping in the wind, and dragged the plough over him so that he died (*Hmannan* I. 218). The ceremony is described at *Shway Yoe* 255. Cognate ideas underlie the Blessing of the Fields and suchlike local rites in Catholic countries. Actual ploughing as in Burma occurs in Siam, in ancient Attica, and in China where the Emperor himself guided the plough and scattered the seed, similar rites being performed in each province by the governor (*Frazer* "Spirits of the Corn and Wild" I. 108, II. 14). Again, certain fruits in

[1] See p. 280. [2] See p. 295.

Burma could not be eaten until the first to ripen was tasted by the king (*Bastian* II. 105).

Popular Feeling.[1]—I give a few typical statements by residents in the country at the time, who mixed with various classes—

> "From the king to a beggar [the Burmese] were hot for a war. . . . A soldier could be got for five ticals. . . . They were very anxious for war . . . they thought that all the world ought to be slaves to the king of Ava and that it was presumption to contend with his armies. . . . The constant talk of war in the ears of a people who had long been accustomed to a long course of victory and usurpation, inflamed their ambition and rendered it popular. The reports they had heard of the unbounded wealth of Calcutta . . . the general forbearance of [the British] Government for a long course of years, interpreted as timidity, . . . all conspired to lead them to the idea that Bengal would fall an easy prey. It was easy to see that the question of the refugees was fast becoming a pretext. . . . A people so unapproachably wrapped up in the conceit of their own superiority and in a barbarous contempt for the rest of mankind. . . . No doubt was entertained of the defeat of the English; the only fear . . . was that the foreigners, hearing of the advance of the Burmese troops, would be so alarmed as to flee on board their ships and depart before there would be time to secure them as slaves. 'Bring for me,' said a wild young buck of the palace, 'six *kalapyus* [white strangers] to row my boat.' 'And to me,' said the lady of a *wungyi*, 'send four white strangers to manage the affairs of my house, as I understand they are trusty servants.' The war-boats in high glee passed our house, the soldiers dancing and singing, and exhibiting gestures of the most joyous kind. 'Poor fellows,' said we, 'you will probably never dance again.' And it so proved, for few, if any, ever again saw their native home." (*Crawfurd* II. appendix 71, 119, 123; *Gouger* 103, 329; *Wayland* I. 337.)

[1] See p. 304.

GENEALOGICAL TABLES

Chiefs of Pagan.

DATED lists of their progenitors at Tagaung and Prome from the ninth century B.C. are given in the chronicles but are here omitted as being nugatory. Conceivably the three states were contemporary, and the chroniclers arranged the lists consecutively, wishing to portray a continuous lineage stretching back to divine antiquity. Of the data below before 1044, none are attested and many are improbable, see pp. 307-9.

Name.	Year of Accession A.D.	Relationship to Predecessor.	Remarks.	Page.
Pyusawti	167			15, 308
Timinyi	242	son		312
Yimminpaik	299	son		
Paikthili	324	son		
Thinlikyaung	344	son		
Kyaungdurit	387	son		
Thihtan	412	son		
			439-97 usurpers	
Tharamunhpya	494		grandson of Thihtan	
Thaiktaing	516	son		
Thinlikyaungnge	523	son		
Thinlipaik	532	brother		
Hkanlaung	547	brother		
Hkanlat	557	brother		
Htuntaik	569	son		
Htunpyit	582	son		
Htunchit	598	son		
Popa Sawrahan	613		usurping priest	16
Shwe-onthi	640	son-in-law		
Peitthon	652	brother		
Peittaung	660	son		
Ngahkwe	710	brother		
Myinkywe	716		usurping groom	
Theinhka	726		court's nominee, of the blood	
Theinsun	734	son		
Shwelaung	744	son		
Htunhtwin	753	son		
Shwemauk	762	son		
Munlat	785	brother		
Sawhkinhnit	802	son		
Hkelu	829	son		
Pyinbya	846	brother	founded Pagan 849	18
Tannet	878	son		
Sale Ngahkwe	906		usurper, of the blood	
Theinhko	915	son		18
Nyaung-u Sawrahan	931		usurper, the "Cucumber King"	315
Kunhsaw Kyaunghpyu	964		son of Tannet and father of Anawrahta 1044-77	19
Kyiso	986		son of Nyaung-u Sawrahan	19
Sokka-te	992	brother		19

The Dynasty of Pagan 1044-1287.

ANAWRAHTA 1044-77

SAWLU 1077-84 — KYANZITTHA 1084-1112

Sawyun = lady Shwe-einthi

ALAUNGSITHU 1112-67

MINSHINSAW 1167 — NARATHU 1167-70

NARATHEINHKA 1170-3 — NARAPATISITHU 1173-1210

HTILOMINLO 1210-34

KYASWA 1234-50

UZANA 1250-4

NARATHIHAPATE 1254-87

Kyawswa 1287-98
chief of Pagan

Sawhnit 1298-1325
governor of Pagan

Uzana 1325-69
governor of Pagan

On the female side the family passes into the Shan princes who ruled Ava for the next two centuries.

Chiefs of Myinsaing and Pinya 1298-1364.

Name.	Year of Accession A.D.	Relationship to Predecessor.	Remarks.	Page.
Athinhkaya, Yazathinkyan, Thihathu	1298	usurpers	The Three Shan Brothers	75
Thihathu	1312		the youngest of the three. Moved to Pinya	78
Uzana	1324	stepson	son of Kyawswa 1287-98 of Pagan	79
Ngasishin	1343	half-brother		80
Kyawswa-nge	1350	son		
Narathu	1359	brother		
Uzana Pyaung	1364	brother	ruled only three months. Murdered by successor, Thadominbya 1364-8	80

Chiefs of Sagaing 1315-64.

Name.	Year of Accession A.D.	Relationship to Predecessor	Remarks.	Page.
Sawyun . . .	1315		son of Thihathu the Shan Brother 1312-24	79
Tarabyagyi . .	1323	step-brother	murdered	
Shwetaungtet . .	1336	son		
Kyaswa . . .	1340		son of Sawyun 1315-23	
Nawrahtaminye .	1350	brother		
Tarabyange . .	1350	brother		
Minbyauk Thihapate	1352	brother-in-law	murdered by his step-son Thadominbya 1364-68	

Chiefs of Ava 1364-1555.

Name.	Year of Accession A.D.	Relationship to Predecessor	Remarks.	Page.
Thadominbya . .	1364	murderer	descendant of Thihathu, the Shan Brother 1312-24. Founded Ava 1364	80
Nga Nu . . .	1368	usurper	paramour of Saw Umma, reigned only a few days	81
Minkyiswasawke .	1368		descended from both the Pagan dynasty and the Shan Brothers	81
Tarabya . . .	1401	eldest son	reigned seven months, made love to a *nat thami* fairy in the forest, lost his reason and was murdered by an attendant	
Nga Nauk Hsan .	1401	murderer		
Minhkaung . .	1401		son of Minkyiswasawke 1368-1401. He hesitated to accept the throne so his younger brother Theiddat killed a cousin claimant and made him accept it	86
Thihathu . . .	1422	son	murdered at instigation of queen Shin Bo-me	95
Minhla-nge . .	1426	son	poisoned by her	96
Kalekyetaungnyo .	1426		son of Tarabya 1401	96
Mohnyinthado . .	1427		descended from Narapatisithu 1173-1210 and Ngasishin 1343-50	96
Minrekyawswa . .	1440	son		99
Narapati . . .	1443	brother		99
Thihathura . .	1469	son		100
Minhkaung . .	1481	son		102
Shwenankyawshin .	1502	son		104
Thohanbwa . .	1527		son of Sawlon the Mohnyin conqueror, murdered	107
Hkonmaing . .	1543		*sawbwa* of Hsipaw	109
Mobye Narapati .	1546	son	*sawbwa* of Mobye (Mōng Pai)	109
Sithukyawhtin . .	1552		Shan lord of Salin who seized Ava and was overthrown by Bayinnaung in 1555	109

Toungoo Dynasty 1531-1752.

Capitals—Pegu till 1635, thereafter Ava.

- Minkyinyo chief of Toungoo p. 124
  - Tabinshwehti 1531-50
  - lady Atulathiri = BAYINNAUNG 1551-81 = lady Hkinpyison
    - (by lady Atulathiri) NANDABAYIN 1581-99
    - (by lady Hkinpyison) lord of Nyaungyan p. 184
      - ANAUKPETLUN 1605-28
        - Minredeippa 1628
      - THALUN 1629-48
        - PINDALE 1648-61
        - PYE 1661-72
          - NARAWARA 1672
        - Nemyoyegyaw
          - MINREKYAWDIN 1673-98
            - SANE 1698-1714
              - TANINGANWE 1714-33
                - MAHADAMMAYAZA-DIPATI 1733-52

Alaungpaya Dynasty 1752-1885.

Capitals—1752-65 Shwebo, 1765-83 and 1823-37 Ava, 1783-1823 and 1837-57 Amarapura, 1857-85 Mandalay.

- ALAUNGPAYA 1752-60
  - NAUNGDAWGYI 1760-3
  - HSINBYUSHIN 1763-76
    - SINGU 1776-82
  - BODAWPAYA 1782-1819
    - Crown Prince, died 1808
      - BAGYIDAW 1819-37
      - Tharrawaddy 1837-46
        - Pagan 1846-53
        - Mindon 1853-78
          - Thibaw 1875-85

Chiefs of Hanthawaddy (Pegu).

Capitals—825-1057 Pegu, 1287-1363 Martaban, 1363-9 Donwun, 1369-1539 and 1740-7 Pegu.

Name.	Year of Accession A.D.	Relationship to Predecessor.	Remarks.	Page.
Thamala	825		Founded Pegu. Down to 1057 the dates (unattested) are those given in *Shwemawdaw Thamaing*	5
Wimala	837	brother		5
Atha	854	nephew		5
Areindama	861			
A monk	885			
Geinda	902			
Migadeippagyi	917			
Geissadiya	932			
Karawika	942			
Pyinzala	954			
Attatha	967			
Anuyama	982			
Migadeippange	994			
Ekkathamanta	1004			
Uppala	1016			
Pontarika	1028			
Tissa	1043			8
			1057-1287 Pegu is subject to Pagan	
Vareru	1287		Shan adventurer, ruled Martaban from 1281, and Lower Burma from 1287. Murdered	110
Hkun Law	1296	brother	murdered	
Saw O	1310	nephew		
Saw Zein	1324	brother	murdered by Shan guards	
Zein Pun	1331	murderer	murdered at instigation of queen Sandaminhla	
Saw E Gan Gaung	1331		nephew to Saw Zein. Poisoned by his wife, the dowager Sandaminhla, for looking at a concubine	
Binnya E Law	1331		son of Hkun Law	
Binnya U	1353	son	moved to Pegu	111
Razadarit	1385	son		113
Binnyadammayaza	1423	son	poisoned by successor	115
Binnyaran	1426	brother		116
Binnyawaru	1446	nephew	son of lady Shinsawbu, Razadarit's daughter	116
Binnyakyan	1450	cousin		
Mawdaw	1453	cousin	murdered his son and seems to have been murdered	117
Lady Shinsawbu	1453		Razadarit's daughter. In 1460 she handed over to Dammazedi, who was not of the blood	117
Dammazedi	1472	son-in-law		118
Binnyaran	1492	son	grandson of lady Shinsawbu	120
Takayutpi	1526	son	driven out by Tabinshwehti in 1539	120

Chiefs of Hanthawaddy (Pegu)—(*continued*).

Name.	Year of Accession A.D.	Relationship to Predecessor.	Remarks.	Page.
Smim Sawhtut	1550	usurper		162
Smim Htaw	1551		natural son of Binnyaran, executed in 1553	163
			1539-1740 Pegu is subject to Ava	
Smim Htaw Buddhaketi	1740			212
Binnya Dala	1747	father-in-law	conquered by Alaungpaya in 1757, after which Pegu is subject to Ava	215 235 260

Rajas of Arakan.

This list is based on that of Phayre who checked several of the mediæval dates by medalljons. The earlier chiefs, who go as far back as 2,666 B.C., are omitted; there is not much more authority for most of the earlier ones below. For the capitals, see p. 137.

Rajas of Dinnyawadi city 146-788.

Name.	Year of Accession A.D.	Relationship to Predecessor.	Remarks.	Page.
Sandathuriya	146		i.e. Chandrasuriya, p. 137	313
Thuriyadipati	198	son		
Thuriyapatipat	245	son		
Thuriyarupa	298	son		
Thuriyamandala	313	son		
Thuriyawunna	375	son		
Thuriyanatha	418	son		
Thuriyawuntha	459	son		
Thuriyabanda	468	son		
Thuriyakalyana	474	son		
Thuriyamokhka	492	son		
Thuriyateza	513	son		
Thuriyaponnya	544	son		
Thuriyakala	552	son		
Thuriyapabba	575	son		
Thuriyasitya	600	son		
Thuriyathehta	618	son		
Thuriyawimala	640	son		
Thuriyena	648	brother		
Thuriyagantha	670	son		
Thuriyathagya	686	uncle		
Thuriyathiri	694	son		
Thuriyakethi	714	son		
Thuriyakutta	723	son		
Thuriyaketu	746	son		

Rajas of Arakan—(*continued*).

Rajas of Vesali city 788-1018.

Name.	Year of Accession A.D.	Relationship to Predecessor.	Remarks.	Page.
Mahataingchandra	788	son		137
Suriyataingchandra	810	son		
Mawlataingchandra	830	son		
Pawlataingchandra	849	son		
Kalataingchandra	875	son		
Tulataingchandra	884	son		
Sritaingchandra	903	son		
Thinhkataingchandra	935	son		
Chulataingchandra	951	son		
Amyahtu	957		chief of the Myu tribe	
Yehpyu	964	nephew		
Ngapinngaton	994		son of Chulataingchandra	

Rajas of Pyinsa (Sambawut) city 1018-1103.

Name.	Year of Accession A.D.	Relationship to Predecessor.	Remarks.	Page.
Hkittathin	1018		grandnephew of Chulataingchandra	
Chandrathin	1028	brother		
Minyinpyu	1039	son		
Nagathuriya	1049	son		
Suriyayaza	1052	son		
Ponnaka	1054	son		
Minpyugyi	1058	son		
Sithabin	1060		usurper	
Minnangyi	1061		son of Minpyugyi	
Minlade	1066	son		
Minkala	1072	son		
Minbilu	1075	son		
Thinhkaya	1078		usurper	
Minthan	1092	son		
Minpati	1100	son		

Rajas of Parin city 1103-67.

Name.	Year of Accession A.D.	Relationship to Predecessor.	Remarks.	Page.
Letyaminnan	1103		grandson of Minbilu. The date differs from that at p. 45, which is more probable	
Thihaba	1109	son		
Yazagyi	1110	son		
Thagiwingyi	1112	son		
Thagiwinnge	1115	son		
Kawliya	1133	son		
Datharaja	1153	son		325
Ananthiri	1165	son		

Rajas of Hkrit city 1167-80.

Name.	Year of Accession A.D.	Relationship to Predecessor.	Remarks.	Page.
Minonsa	1167	brother		
Pyinsakawa	1174	son		
Keinnayok	1176	son		
Salinkabo	1179		usurper	

Rajas of Arakan—(*continued*).

Rajas of Pyinsa (Sambawut) city 1180-1237.

Name.	Year of Accession A.D.	Relationship to Predecessor.	Remarks.	Page.
Misuthin . . .	1180		son of Pyinsakawa	
Ngayanman . . .	1191	son		
Ngapogan . . .	1193	son		
Ngayahkaing . . .	1195	son		
Ngakyon . . .	1198	son		
Ngasu . . .	1201	son		
Ngaswethin . . .	1205	son		
Minhkaunggyi . .	1206	son		
Minhkaungnge . .	1207	son		
Kabalaunggyi . .	1208	son		
Kabalaungnge . .	1209	son		
Letyagyi . . .	1210	son		
Letyange . . .	1218	son		
Thanabin . . .	1229	son		
Nganathin . . .	1232	son		
Nganalon . . .	1234	son		
Rajas of Launggyet city 1237-1433.				
Alawmahpyu . . .	1237	son		
Yazathugyi . . .	1234	son		
Sawlu . . .	1246	son		
Ossanagyi . . .	1251	son		
Sawmungyi . . .	1260	son		
Nankyagyi . . .	1268	son		
Minbilu . . .	1272	son		
Sithabin . . .	1276		usurper	
Minhti . . .	1279		son of Minbilu	138
			(1374-85 Burmese nominees)	86
Ossanange . . .	1385		of the blood	
Thiwarit . . .	1387	brother		
Thinhse . . .	1390	brother		
Razathu . . .	1394	son		
Sithabin . . .	1395		usurper	
Myinhsainggyi . .	1397		usurper	
Razathu . . .	1397		restored	
Theinhkathu . . .	1401	brother		
Rajahs of Mrohaung (Mrauk-u) city 1433-1785.				
Narameikhla (Minsawmun) .	1404		son of Razathu	87, 139
Ali Khan . . .	1434	brother		100, 140
Basawpyu (Kalima Shah) .	1459	son		140
Dawlya . . .	1482	son		
Basawnyo . . .	1492	uncle		
Yanaung . . .	1494		son of Dawlya	
Salingathu . . .	1494	uncle		
Minyaza . . .	1501	son		
Kasabadi . . .	1523	son		
Minsaw-o . . .	1525		brother to Salingathu	

24

Rajas of Arakan—(*continued*).

Rajahs of Mrohaung (Mrauk-u) city 1433-1785—(continued)

Name.	Year of Accession A.D.	Relationship to Predecessor.	Remarks.	Page.
Thatasa	1525		son of Dawlya	
Minbin	1531		son of Minyaza	140
Dikha	1553	son		
Sawhla	1555	son		
Minsetya	1564	brother		
Minpalaung	1571		son of Minbin	
Minyazagyi (Salim Shah)	1593	son		141
Minhkamaung (Husein Shah)	1612	son		142
Thirithudamma	1622	son		145
Minsani	1638	son		
Narapatigyi	1638		great grandson of Thatasa	145
Thado	1645	nephew		145
Sandathudamma	1652	son		
Thirithuriya	1684	son		
Waradhammaraza	1685	brother		
Munithudhammaraza	1692	brother		
Sandathuriyadhamma	1694	brother		
Nawrahtazaw	1696	son		
Mayokpiya	1696		usurper	
Kalamandat	1697		usurper	
Naradipati	1698		son of Sandathuriyadhamma	
Sandawimala	1700		grandson of Thado	
Sandathuriya	1706		grandson of Sandathudamma	
Sandawizaya	1710		usurper	148
Sandathuriya	1731	son-in-law		
Naradipati	1734	son		
Narapawara	1735		usurper	
Sandawizaya	1737	cousin		
Katya	1737		usurping foreigner	
Madarit	1737		brother to Sandawizaya	
Nara-apaya	1742	uncle		
Thirithu	1761	son		
Sandapayama	1761	brother		
Apaya	1764	brother-in-law		
Sandathumana	1773	brother-in-law		
Sandawimala	1777		usurper	
Sandathaditha	1777		lord of Ramree	
Thamada	1782		In 1785 Arakan was annexed by the Burmese, and in 1826 by the English	149

BIBLIOGRAPHY

Abbreviations :—

* Indicates a vernacular work
B Bodleian Library.
BM British Museum.
IO India Office Library.
OII Oxford India Institute Library.
OU Oxford Union Library.

The standard bibliography is H. Cordier, "Bibliotheca Indosinica," publ. Leroux, Paris 1912, BM Ac.8814.e, OII 8.F.19. It is also in *TP* 1903-6 and *BEFEO* 1912-5.

As the notes in this book mention works only by shortened titles, the list below is unclassified and follows a purely alphabetical order for ease of reference. It does not include every work consulted but only those which are not sufficiently explained in the references; thus under DUROISELLE will not be found his "Stone Sculptures in the Ananda Temple at Pagan" because the reference at p. 41 footnote 2 shows that this article appears in the 1913-4 issue of *ARASI*, which is explained below.

The numbers in brackets are the pages at which the work is cited.

*ALAUNGPAYA AYEDAWBON, publ. Hanthawaddy Press, Rangoon 1900 (219, 236).

ALEXANDER, J. E. "Travels from India to England," publ. Parbury, Allan & Co., London 1827 (354).
B 2.Δ.47 BM 566.g.15.
OII 25.E.9.

ANDERSON, J. "English Intercourse with Siam in the Seventeenth Century," publ. Kegan Paul, London 1890 (203, 272, 314, 339, 341).
B 2351.e.1. BM 2318.h.6.
IO 16.F.F.17.

"A Report on the Expedition to Western Yunnan via Bhamo," publ. Superintendent Government Printing, Calcutta 1871 (353).
B 203.h.172. BM 10055.f.21.
IO 8.K.7 and 8.L.4 OII 25.E.11.

ANNALES DE LA PROPAGATION DE LA FOI, Vol. XXXVI., publ. at Lyons 1864 (346).
B Soc.133.e.589/36. BM P.P. 930.

*ANTHOLOGY. "Anthology of Burmese Literature," publ. Superintendent Government Printing, Rangoon 1921 (77).

ARASI. "Annual Report of the Archæological Survey of India" publ. Superintendent Government Printing, Calcutta (41, 95, 309, 313, 325).

B Per.20638.c.16. BM 7709.t.
IO Room 315. OII 23.F.

AYMONIER, E. "Le Cambodge," three vols., publ. Leroux, Paris 1900-4 (13, 272).

BM 10058.g.33. IO 8.M.23-25.
OII 26.E.10.

BADGER, G. P. "The Travels of Ludovico di Varthema, 1503-8," publ. Hakluyt Society, London 1863 (121, 314, 341).

B Soc.2031.d.4/32. BM R.Ac.6172/30.
IO 18.G.32. OU 323.

BASTIAN, A. "Die Völker des östlichen Asien," four vols., publ. Wigand, Leipzig 1866 (321, 363).

B 203.e.150-1. BM 010055.gg.7.
IO 31.E.9-14. OII 23.C.30.

BAYFIELD, see Pemberton (284, 285, 286, 288, 349, 358).

BEAZLEY, C. R. "The Dawn of Modern Geography," three vols., publ. Clarendon Press, Oxford 1897-1906 (310).

B S.Nat.Sci.226.k. BM 2352.g.1.
IO 18.L.21-23. OU 328.

BEFEO. "Bulletin de l'école française d'extrême orient," periodical, publ. Imprimerie d'Extrême Orient, Hanoi, & Leroux, Paris (9, 30, 87, 100, 111, 115, 308, 313, 315, 322, 333, 334, 337, 338, 356).

B Per.247189.d.5. BM 15235.d.
IO 305.9.D. OII 33.F.

BERNIER. "Travels in the Mogul Empire," edited by Constable and Vincent Smith, publ. Oxford University Press 1914 (147, 344).

B 2064.e.107. BM 10058.pp.16.
IO 23.B.B.5. OII 25.A.2b.

BIGANDET. "An Outline of the history of the Catholic Burmese Mission from the year 1720 to 1887," publ. Hanthawaddy Press, Rangoon 1887 (214, 231, 253, 346, 348).

BOWREY, T. "Geographical Account of Countries round the Bay of Bengal, 1669-79," edited by Sir Richard Temple, publ. Hakluyt Society, Cambridge 1905 (147).

B Soc.2031d.4/N.S.12. OII 26.B.25.
BM R.Ac.6172/87.

BPP = BENGAL PAST AND PRESENT, periodical, publ. Calcutta Historical Society, Calcutta (182).

B Per.20644d.4. BM Ac.8603.

BRITISH BURMA GAZETTEER, two vols., publ. Superintendent Government Printing, Rangoon 1880 (352).

B 201.h.67-68. BM 10057.d.f.26.
IO 64.I.22-23. OII 85.D.

BROWN, see Grant Brown.

BSPC — BENGAL SECRET AND POLITICAL CONSULTATIONS, being the bound annual MS. vols. of Government of India Proceedings, signed by the Viceroy and Members of Council, in the India Office Record Dept. (138, 229, 237, 273, 281, 287, 288, 354, 357, 362).

BUTLER, J. "Travels and Adventures in the Province of Assam during a residence of fourteen years," publ. Smith, Elder, London 1855 (298).
B 203.a.48. BM 10056.d.1.
IO 23.E.9.

CAREY, B. S. "Myingyan Settlement Report," publ. Superintendent Printing, Rangoon 1901 (16, 39, 348, 351).
BM I.S.35/19. IO R and R 9(2670).

CHAU JU-KUA, Hirth and Rockhill, publ. Imperial Academy of Sciences, St. Petersburg 1912 (43, 310).
B Chin.d.116. BM 15234.c.9.

CHINA REVIEW, publ. Hongkong 1872-1901 (310).
BM P.P.3803.bb. IO 300.A.27.P.

CHITTAGONG GAZETTEER, publ. Bengal Secretariat Book Depot, Calcutta 1908 (147).
B 20644.d.6/1. BM 010058.k.
IO 300.A.79.O. OII 85.C.

CLAYTON, H. "Katha Settlement Report," publ. British Burma Press, Rangoon 1906 (4, 262, 360).
B unreferenced Indian blue-book.
BM I.S.35/30. IO R and R 9(3099).

COCHRANE, W. W. "The Shans," publ. Superintendent Government Printing, Rangoon 1915 (308, 323).
B 247188.d.12. BM W.P.3897.
IO 300.A.77.cc. OII 23.B.41.

COEDÈS, G. "Textes d'auteurs grecs et latins relatifs a l'extrême orient depuis le IVe siècle av.J.C. jusqu'au XIVe siècle," publ. Leroux, Paris 1910 (311).
B 24628.d.6. BM 09055.d.
IO 9.EE. OII 26.D.27.

CORDIER, H. "La France en Chine au dix-huitième siècle," publ. Leroux, Paris 1883 (353).
B 2371.9a. BM 9055.e.3.
IO 25.H.27.

"Histoire générale de la Chine," four vols., publ. Geuthner, Paris 1920 (337, 353, 355).
B 24631.e.20. BM 09057.c.19.

"Historique abrégé des relations de la Grande-Bretagne avec la Birmanie," publ. Leroux, Paris 1894 (353).
IO Tract 1051.

COUTO. Diogo de Couto, "Da Asia," nine vols., publ. by His Majesty's Press, Lisbon 1778-88 (158, 162, 163, 310, 343).

B 8°.E.149-63.Art.

COX, H. "Journal of a Residence in the Burman Empire," publ. Warren & Whittaker, London 1821 (237, 275, 277, 284, 290, 315, 329, 336, 340, 359).

B 8°.O.188.BS. BM 1046.c.8.
IO 8.E.5.

CRAWFURD, J. "Journal of an Embassy from the Governor-General of India to the Court of Ava," two vols., publ. Colburn, London 1834 (xx, 82, 205, 236, 248, 251, 258, 260, 265, 273, 277, 284, 295, 298, 299, 300, 301, 303, 304, 313, 315, 330, 331, 334, 336, 341, 351, 350, 354, 355, 357, 358, 359, 361, 362, 363).

B 20653.e.4 and 5. BM 1425.g.19.

CROOKE, W. "Fryer's A New Account of East India and Persia 1672-81," edited by Crooke, three vols., publ. Hakluyt Society, London 1909 (328).

B Soc. 2031.d.4/n.s.19.20.39.
BM R.Ac.6172/93.
IO 300.A.71.D.24. OII 36.A.
OU 327.

CUNNINGHAM, A., and BEGLAR, J. D. "Archæological Survey of India Report," Vol. VIII., publ. Superintendent Government Printing, Calcutta 1878 (330).

B unreferenced BM 2354.g.
IO 35.D.16. OII 20.D.

DAGH-REGISTER. "Dagh-Register gehouden int Casteel Batavia," series edited by J. A. van der Chijs, publ. Nijhoff, 's Hage 1889 onwards (347).

B 23251 d.1 BM Ac.975/12.
IO 7.I.29.

DALRYMPLE, A. "Oriental Repertory," publ. Bigg, London 1793-87 (160, 205, 206, 213, 219, 222, 223, 224, 227, 242, 243, 245, 262, 310, 322, 333, 346, 354, 355, 358).

B Or. Per. 71. BM 148.f.3 and f.4.
IO 84.D.5 and 6.

DE JONGE, J. K. "De Opkomst van het Nederlandsch Gezag in Oost-Indie," series publ. Nijhoff, 's Gravenhage 1862 onwards (141).

BM 9056.gg. IO 7.C.24.

• DINNYAWADI YAZAWINTHIT, by U Panti and U Hpye, publ. Pyegyimantaingpitaka Press, Rangoon 1910 (xix, 185, 210, 280, 282, 327).

BM 14302.b.41.

• DO WE, MS (xviii, 316, 327).

DU HALDE. "The General History of China," four vols., publ. Watts, London 1736 (353).

B 8°.S.123-26 Jur. BM 583.c.27-30.

DUROISELLE, C. "A List of Inscriptions found in Burma," publ. Superintendent Government Printing, Rangoon 1921 (xvi).

BM I.S. IO L.R.2.G.

"Notes on the Ancient Geography of Burma," publ. Superintendent Government Printing, Rangoon 1906 (194, 308).

IO Tracts 999.

ENCYCLOPÆDIA OF RELIGION AND ETHICS, publ. Clark, Edinburgh 1909 (318, 320, 327, 339, 344, 362).

EPIGRAPHIA BIRMANICA, publ. Superintendent Government Printing, Rangoon (xvi, 18, 38, 41, 42, 44, 166, 325).

B Per.Misc.Indic.d.56. BM 14302.c.9.

IO 92.L.3. OII unreferenced.

EPIGRAPHIA INDICA, publ. Government of India, Calcutta (307, 309)

B Per.2461.c.1. BM unreferenced.

IO 315.2.A.23-24, L.R.3.H. OII 21.F.

FARIA Y SOUSA, MANUEL DE. "Asia Portuguesa," three vols., publ. Craesbeeck, Lisbon 1666-75 (188).

B Meerm. 154-56. BM 582.i.20-22.

IO 300.A.76.L.12-14.

"The Portuguese Asia," translated into English by Captain John Stevens, three vols., publ. Brome, at the Sign of the Gun, London 1695 (122, 132, 142, 153, 159, 162, 163, 164, 182, 188, 189, 190, 314, 341, 344).

B 55.b.59-61. BM 582.e.6, 8.

IO 300.A.76.H.10-12.

FERGUSSON, J. "History of Indian and Eastern Architecture," two vols., publ. Murray, London 1910 (46, 325, 330).

B S. Art 94a/1-2. BM 2934.a.

IO 35.v.7/1-2. OII 20.B.2.

FERRAND, G. "Relations de voyages et de textes geographiques arabes, persans, at turcs relatifs à l'extrême orient du VIIIe au XVIIIe siècles," two vols., publ. Leroux, Paris 1913 (10).

B 20657.d.12. BM 09055.d.

FORCHAMMER, E. "Arakan"—I. Mahamuni Pagoda, II. Mrohaung, III. Launggyet, Minbya, Urittaung, Akyab and Sandoway," publ. Superintendent Government Printing, Rangoon 1891 (309, 313).

B 20652.c.1. BM 7701.c.1.

IO 315.2.D.1-2. OII 23.F.18.

"The Jardine Prize: an essay on the sources and development of Burmese law," publ. Superintendent Government Printing, Rangoon 1885 (4, 59, 111, 171, 195, 238, 249, 270, 322, 339, 351).

B Indian Law. BM 14300.g.9.

IO 61.c.30. OII 36.F.37.

FORCHAMMER, E.—(*cont.*).

"Notes on the Early History and Geography of British Burma—I. The Shwedagon Pagoda, II. The First Buddhist Mission to Suvannabhumi," publ. Superintendent Government Printing, Rangoon 1884 (118, 309, 311).

B 20652.c.1. BM 5319.c.14.
IO 315.2.D.1. OII 23.F.18.

"Report on the Kyaukku Temple, at Pagan," publ. Superintendent Government Printing, Rangoon 1919 (17). The 1891 edition is in

B 20652.c.1. BM 7701.c.1(6).
IO 315.2.D.1-2. OII 23.F.18.

FRAZER, J. G. The various volumes of "The Golden Bough," publ. Macmillan, London 1911 onwards, named separately in the notes (45, 144, 187, 316, 324, 338, 339, 362).

FURNIVALL, J. S. "Myingyan Settlement Report," publ. Superintendent Government Printing, Rangoon 1913 (4, 351).

"Syriam Gazetteer," Vol. A, publ. Superintendent Government Printing, Rangoon 1914 (118, 311).

B .20652.e.24[a]. BM I.S.147.
IO 300.A.79.R. OII 15.C.

FYTCHE, A. "Burma, Past and Present," two vols., publ. Kegan Paul, London 1878 (265, 321, 329, 333, 340).

B 226.i.520-21. BM 2354.e.7.
IO 8.c.18. OII 26.B.2 and 3.

GAIT, E. A. "A History of Assam," publ. Superintendent Government Printing, Calcutta 1906 (283, 296, 298, 343).

B 24612.e.35. BM 010058.h.27.
IO 63.c.23.

GERINI, G. E. "Researches on Ptolemy's Geography of Eastern Asia," publ. Royal Asiatic Society, London 1909 (43, 310, 311, 326).

B Soc. 2017.e.336/1 BM 14005.b.1.
IO 305.1.H.1, 1. OII 26.B.28.

GERSON DA CUNHA. "Memoir on the History of the Tooth-Relic of Ceylon," in the Journal of the Bombay branch of the Royal Asiatic Society, 1875 (100, 344).

B Or. Per. 18. BM Ac.8827.
IO 305.4.D. OII 17.B.

GIBSON. "Meiktila Settlement Report," publ. by Government, Rangoon 1900 (275).

BM I.S.35/18. IO R and R9(2553).

GOUGER, H. "Personal Narrative of Two Years' Imprisonment in Burma," publ. Murray, London 1860 (259, 265, 270, 277, 278, 295, 299, 300, 304, 324, 350, 357, 358, 360, 361, 363).

B 210.d.128. BM 10057.b.13.
IO 8.GG.2. OII 38.A.12.

GRAHAME, W. F. "Shwebo Settlement Report," publ. by Government, Rangoon 1906 (348).

B unreferenced Indian blue-book.
BM I.S.35/31. IO R and R9(3064).

GRANT BROWN. "The Dragon of Tagaung," in JRAS 1917.
"The Lady of the Weir," in JRAS 1916 (25, 53).
"The pre-Buddhist religion of the Burmese," in Folk-Lore 1921 (25).
"The Taungbyon Festival," in Journal of the Royal Anthropological Institute 1915 (31).

GUB = GAZETTEER OF UPPER BURMA AND THE SHAN STATES, by J. G. Scott, and J. P. Hardiman, five vols., publ. Superintendent Government Printing, Rangoon 1900 (25, 31, 53, 76, 272, 277, 280, 309, 310, 321, 322, 323, 329, 344, 359).

B 20652.d.10/1(1-2) and 1(1-3).
BM 010055.i.13. IO 8.I.21-25.
OII 15.C.

HAGUE TRANSCRIPTS = the MS. copies of Dutch records in the India Office Record Department (141).

HAKLUYT. "Hakluytus Posthumus, or Purchas His Pilgrims," twenty vols., publ. MacLehose, Glasgow 1907 (140, 175, 176, 179, 180, 184, 237, 310, 312, 314, 315, 334, 336, 341, 343).

B 2031.d.10. BM 2058.c.
OII 37.C. OU 321.

HALLIDAY, R. "The Talaings," publ. Superintendent Government Printing, Rangoon 1917 (3, 6).

B 247188.e.9. BM 0100007.ee.1.
IO 300.A.77.BB.7.

HAMILTON, A. "A New Account of the East Indies," two vols., publ. Mosman, Edinburgh 1727 (140, 147, 175, 206, 345, 346, 350, 360).

B 8°.F.256-57.Linc. BM 793.e.17.
IO 44.c.16-17

HARDY, R. SPENCE. "Eastern Monachism," publ. Partridge & Oakley, London 1850 (277).

B Sansk. 4.492. BM 2217.b.1.
IO 33.c.16 and 19. OII 107.c.

HAVELL, E. B. "The Ancient and Mediæval Architecture of India," publ. Murray, London 1915 (330).

B 173583.d.4. BM 7815.bb.14.
IO 35.v.30. OII 20.F.24.

"Indian Architecture: its psychology, structure and history from the first Muhammadan invasion to the present day," publ. Murray, London 1913 (330).

B 173583.d.2 BM 2034.e.
IO 35.v.28.

HAVELOCK, H. "Memoir of the Three Campaigns of Major-General Sir Archibald Campbell's army in Ava," publ. at Serampore, 1828 (156, 238, 288, 323, 341, 344, 353, 357, 361, 362).
B 226.i.269. BM 9056.e.15.
IO 8.F.9.

HERBERT, T. "Some yeares travels into Africa and Asia," publ. Bishop, London 1638 (345, 346).
B H.8.13.Art. BM 984.f.28.
IO 29.H.11.

HERTZ, W. A. "Magwe Settlement Report," publ. Superintendent Government Printing, Rangoon 1905 (4).
B unreferenced Indian blue-book.
BM I.S.35/36. IO R and R 9(2933).

* HMANNAN YAZAWIN, three vols., publ. Upper Burma Press, Mandalay 1908 (xvi-xix, 16-19, 23, 28, 32, 34, 39, 40, 55, 60, 61, 69, 76, 82, 85, 86, 89, 91, 93, 94, 98, 99, 102, 105, 114, 154, 165, 166, 169, 171, 174, 177, 180, 182, 186, 188, 190, 191, 199, 208, 209, 212, 213, 214, 309, 314, 316, 318, 321, 323, 324, 326, 327, 329, 330, 334, 335, 336, 337, 339-44, 352, 354, 362).

HOBSON-JOBSON. "Hobson-Jobson, a Glossary of Anglo-Indian Words and Phrases," by Yule and Burnell, publ. Murray, London 1903 (5, 6, 310, 311, 342).
B S. Lang.-Eng. 29. BM 2056.b.
IO R.R.27.H.6. OII 9.c.

HODSON, T. C. "The Meitheis," publ. Nutt, London 1908 (239, 317, 322).
B 247182.e.7. BM 10058.e.38.
IO 14.H.H.3, 4. OII 23.B.28.

HUNTER, W. W. "A History of British India," two vols., publ. Longmans, London 1900 (9).
B S.Hist.Ind.3. BM 2386.g.5.
IO 72.c.19-20. OII 27.D.11 and 12.
OU 247.

IA. "Indian Antiquary," periodical, publ. British India Press, Mazgaon, Bombay, and Bernard Quaritch, London (4, 5, 7, 13, 19, 119, 247, 260, 263, 309, 311, 313, 325, 337, 339).
B Or.Per.69. BM 15006.
IO 305.8.F. and 300ᵃ.34.D. OII 19.F.

* INSCRIPTIONS. Six vols., publ. Superintendent Government Printing, Rangoon (xvi, 6, 28, 29, 38, 60, 63, 307, 313, 326, 331, 333, 337).
—— of Pagan, Pinya and Ava, 1892.
—— copied from the stones collected by king Bodawpaya and placed near the Arakan pagoda, Mandalay, two vols. 1897.
—— collected in Upper Burma, two vols. 1900 and 1903.
Original Inscriptions collected by king Bodawpaya in Upper Burma and now placed at the Patodawgyi pagoda, Amarapura, 1913.
B incomplete BM 14302.c.c.
IO 92.E. and 315.2.D.3. OII 20.F.

JADUNATH SARKAR. "History of Aurangzib," four vols., publ. Sarkar, Calcutta 1912-19 (144, 147).

B 24614.e.31. BM 09057.a.a.a.19.
IO 42.B.B. OII 27.A.44.

JASBENGAL.' Journal of the Asiatic Society, Bengal (140, 145, 147, 184, 299, 311, 333, 340, 355, 362).

B Or.Per.17. BM R.Ac.8826.
IO 305.3.A. to F. OII 19.E.

JBRS. "Journal of the Burma Research Society," publ. by the Society, Bernard Free Library, Rangoon (3, 6, 15, 16, 29, 39, 46, 48, 104, 117, 118, 119, 147, 166, 184, 186, 188, 203, 219, 221, 230, 247, 248, 265, 269, 270, 300, 307, 309, 311, 320, 325, 330, 338, 341, 348, 351).

B Per.26121.d.1/1. BM Ac.8830.g.
IO 305.4.E.

JONES. "Siamese history; distinction of sacred and common eras; with historical notices from A.D. 1351 to 1451, the eighth century of the Siamese era. From a correspondent [J. Taylor Jones]," in "Chinese Repository," Vols. V.-VII., publ. at Canton 1836-8 (112, 159, 170, 182, 362).

BM P.P. 3803. IO 300.A.27.0.

JRAS. Journal of the Royal Asiatic Society, London.

B Or.Per.7 BM R.Ac.8820 and 2110.
IO 305.I.A. OII 19.A.

JSS. "Journal of the Siam Society," periodical, publ. at Bangkok (-45, 181, 182, 193, 271, 311, 320, 343).

B Soc. 24718.d.21. BM 759.c.22.
IO 305.4.E.

JUDSON, Mrs. "An Account of the American Baptist Mission to the Burman Empire," publ. Butterworth, London 1823 (117, 236, 278, 358, 359, 360, 361).

B 8°.BSW.62. BM 493.g.18.
IO 78.N.4.

* KO HKAYAING THAMAING, publ. Chaniya Press, Mandalay (xviii, 25).

* KONBAUNGSET YAZAWIN, publ. Mandalay Taing Press, Mandalay 1905 (xviii, 219, 222, 232, 234, 236, 239, 241, 247, 248, 251, 253, 260, 262, 264, 265, 272, 277, 283, 293, 296, 313, 321, 354, 355, 356, 362).

BM 14302.b.35.

LAUNAY, A. "Memorial de la Société des Missions Etrangères," two vols., publ. by the Society, Paris 1912-16 (346).

B 133d.127. BM 04782.i.10

LAURIE, W. F. B. "Our Burmese Wars," publ. Allen, London 1880 (360).

B 226.i.589. BM 9057.a.a.7.
IO 8.D.27-28. OU 4.A.4.

LAURIE, W. F. B.—(*cont.*).

"Pegu, being a Narrative of Events during the Second Burmese War," publ. Smith, Elder, London 1854 (236).

B 226.e.20. BM 9056.c.29.
IO 8.D.25 and 8. E.6, C.20. OU 28.A.2g.

"The Second Burmese War," publ. Smith, Elder, London 1853.

B 226.e.19. BM 9056.c.35.

LINSCHOTEN. "Voyage to the East Indies," two vols., publ. Hakluyt Society, London 1885 (314, 341, 344, 350).

B Soc. 2031.d.4/70-71. BM R.Ac.6172/59.
IO 18.I.3 and 4. OU 325.

LOWIS, C. C. "Tribes of Burma," publ. Superintendent Government Printing, Rangoon 1910 (3).

B 247188.d.9/4. IO Con.267.

MCCULLOCH, W. "Account of the Valley of Munnipore," publ. as Selections from the Records of the Government of India, Foreign Dept., No. XXVII., Calcutta 1859.

BM I.S.358. IO unreferenced.

MACGOWAN, J. "History of China," publ. Kegan Paul, London 1897 (337, 355).

B 24631.d.5. BM 9057.g.12.

MCLEOD, W. C. "Journal of a Mission from Moulmein to the Frontiers of China, 1836-37," publ. by the India Office, London 1869 (355).

B and BM Accounts and Papers, 1868-9.V.
IO 25.I.15.

MCLEOD AND RICHARDSON. "Copy of papers relating to the route of Captain W. C. McLeod from Moulmein to the frontier of China and to the route of Dr Richardson on his fourth mission to the Shan provinces of Burma, or extracts from the same," printed by order of the House of Commons, London 1869 (278, 299, 315, 335).

B and BM Accounts and Papers, 1868-9.XLVI.
IO 25.I.15.

MAJOR, R. H. "India in the Fifteenth Century," publ. Hakluyt Society, London 1857 (99, 121).

B 2031.d.4/22. BM R.Ac.6172/20.
IO 18.G.H.I. and M.

MANRIQUE, S. "Itinerario de las missiones del India Oriental," publ. Caballo, Rome 1649 (139, 144, 315).

B 1332.d.2. BM 1229.e.1.

MANUCCI. "Storia do Mogor," translated by W. Irvine in the Indian Text Series, four vols., publ. John Murray, London 1907 (147, 315, 344, 351).

B 24614.d.17. BM 14005.i.1.
IO 305.2.H.1-3. OU 29.E.7.

MARKS, J. "Forty Years in Burma," publ. Hutchinson, London 1917 (359).

B 1333.E.221. BM 4908.g.5.
IO 8.G.G.4.

MASON, F. "Burmah, its People and Natural Productions," publ. Trübner, London 1860 (321).

B 226.d.48. BM 7002.a.a.a.19.
IO 8.A.13. OII 26.B.5.

ME, NGA. "Maharazawin," MS. (xviii, 145, 280).

MÜLLER, E. "Ancient Inscriptions in Ceylon," publ. Trübner, London 1883 (32).

B Ary.2.203. BM 14165.e.1-2.
IO 92.C.

NAGA HILLS AND MANIPUR GAZETTEER, publ. Baptist Mission Press, Calcutta 1905 (296).

B 20643.d.2/9. BM 010056.i.
IO 300.A.79.P. OII 73.C.

NANDATHARA, Abbot of Kawgo Monastery, Talaing MS. "History of Atha-kumma," written in 1825 (6).

NGA ME, see ME, NGA.

NISBET, J. "Burma under British rule and before," two vols., publ. Constable, London 1901 (329, 362).

B 247188.d.7. BM 010055.e.e.14.
IO 8.H.1 and 2. OII 29.D.14-15.

NOWGONG DISTRICT GAZETTEER, publ. City Press, Calcutta 1905 (298).

B 20643.d.2/6. BM 010056.i.
IO 300.A.79.P. OII 73.C.

PAGAN YAZAWINTHIT, MS. (35, 37, 329, 340).

PAKLAT TALAING CHRONICLE. "Thudammawati-yazawuntha Thihaya-zadiyazawuntha," printed at Paklat in Siam 1910 (xviii, 27, 110).

PALLEGOIX. "Description du royaume thai ou Siam," two vols., publ. Mission de Siam, Paris 1854 (112, 260, 339).

B 246.g.182-3. BM 10055.a.a.17.
IO 8.B.11.

PARKER, E. H. "Burma with special reference to her relations to China," publ. Rangoon Gazette press, Rangoon 1893 (13, 99, 100, 111, 322, 323, 337, 354, 355, 362).

BM 8023.a.a.a.12. IO 8.C.29.

"Précis," being a précis of Chinese imperial and provincial annals and state papers relating to Burma, printed departmentally in Rangoon when Mr Parker was Adviser on Chinese Affairs to the Government of Burma (75, 85, 87, 99, 101, 106, 107, 258, 337, 352, 355, 358).

PARLETT, L. M. "Sagaing Settlement Report," publ. Superintendent Government Printing, Rangoon 1903 (184, 196, 239, 264, 348).
B unreferenced Indian blue-book.
BM I.S. 35/32. IO R and R 9 (2858).

PARSONS. "Minbu Settlement Report," publ. by Government, Rangoon 1900 (347).
BM I.S.35/13. IO R and R 9 (2508).

*PAWTUGI YAZAWIN, publ. Sun Press, Rangoon 1918 (xvi, 188).

PEMBERTON, R. B. "Report on the Eastern Frontier of British India . . . with a supplement by Dr Bayfield on the British Political Relations with Ava," printed by order of the Supreme Government of India, Calcutta 1835 (99, 208, 210, 239, 257, 261, 296, 322, 341).
BM 10057.ee.8. IO 42.F.27.

PÈRE D'ORLÉANS. "History of the two Tartar conquerors of China," publ. Hakluyt Society, London 1854 (352).
B Soc.2031.d.4/17. BM R.Ac.6172/15.
IO 18.G.17. OU 323.

PERKINS, B. W. "Tharrawaddy Gazetteer," Vol. A, publ. Superintendent Government Printing, Rangoon 1920 (315).
B 20652.e.31[a]. BM I.S.147.
IO 300.A.79.R. OII 15.C.

PHAYRE, A. "History of Burma," publ. Trübner, London 1883 (vi, 99, 316, 326, 341, 343).
B 20653.e.2. BM 2318.f.22.
IO 16.F.F.15. OII 29.D.16 and 17.
OU 254.

"Coins of Arakan, of Pegu, and of Burma," in International Numismata Orientalia, publ. Trübner, London 1882 (137).
B Num.24624.c.1. BM 7755.g.26(1882).
IO 84.F.18-20. OII 20.F.3.

MSS., being the collection of Burmese vernacular manuscripts presented by Sir Arthur Phayre to the British Museum, now in the Oriental Students Room (158).

PINKERTON, J. "A general collection of the best and most interesting Voyages and Travels in all parts of the world," seventeen vols., publ. Longmans, London 1808-14 (314).
B B.S.896-912. BM 2059.c.
IO 29.K.2-5.

PINTO. "The Voyages and Adventures of Ferdinand Mendez Pinto, the Portuguese, done into English by Henry Cogan, with an introduction by Arminius Vambery," publ. Fisher Unwin, London 1891 (156, 163, 164, 342).
B 206.d.21. BM 012207.k.7.

PP = PARLIAMENTARY PAPERS, being "Papers relating to East India affairs, viz. Discussions with the Burmese Government," in Vol. XXIV. of Accounts and Papers for the year 1825, printed by order of the House of Commons (277, 282, 285, 293, 302, 358, 360).

PURCHAS. "Purchas his Pilgrimage or Relations of the World," publ. Stansby, London 1626 (190, 324, 346).

B I.1.2.Art.Seld. BM 679.h.15.
IO 29.H.5.

RADHAKUMUD MOOKERJI. "Indian Shipping and Maritime Activity from the earliest times," publ. Longmans, Bombay 1912 (310, 311).

B 23135d. 10. BM 8806.k.23.
IO 47.G.21.

RAJENDRALALA MITRA. "Buddha Gaya, the Hermitage of Sakyamuni," publ. Bengal Secretariat Press, Calcutta 1878 (46).

B Sansk. 2.130. BM 790.l.29.
IO 91.D.14. OII 23.F.12.

RAZADARIT AYEDAWPON, MS. (xvi, xviii, 82, 94, 111, 112, 114, 115, 167, 170, 314, 321, 340, 362).

RIDGEWAY, W. "The Dramas and Dramatic Dances of non-European Races in special reference to the Origin of Greek Tragedy," publ. Cambridge University Press, 1915 (31, 327).

B S.Class.Gr.12.kl. BM 2306.h.3.
IO 300.A.77.E.7.

ROBERTSON, T. C. "Political Incidents of the First Burmese War," publ. Bentley, London 1853 (281, 300).

B 226e.18. BM 9056.c.9.

ROSCOE, J. "The Baganda," publ. Macmillan, London 1911 (356).

B 247214d.11. BM 10006.r.6.

RSASB. "Report of the Superintendent Archæological Survey, Burma," publ. Superintendent Government Printing, Rangoon (3, 6, 12, 29, 34, 39, 44, 46, 57, 102, 119, 189, 253, 307, 309, 311, 312, 313, 316, 322, 326, 328, 330, 337, 356, 362).

B Per.20638.c.30. BM I.S.6.
IO 315 OII 25.F.3.

SAINSON, C. "Nan-tchao Ye-che, traduction d'une histoire de l'ancien Yun-nan," publ. Leroux, Paris 1904 (43, 48, 312).

B Or.Per.78. BM 14003.i.58.

SAMUEL SMITH, see Smith, Samuel.

SANGERMANO. "A Description of the Burmese Empire," publ. Superintendent Government Printing, Rangoon 1885 (205, 237, 263, 264, 265, 268, 270, 272, 275, 276, 277, 278, 349, 350, 357, 360, 362).

IO 8.L.3. OII 27.F.24.

SAN SHWE BU, a précis of Arakanese historical MSS. sent me by San Shwe Bu, Honorary Archæological Officer for Arakan (280, 326).

SAYADAW ATHWA, Burmese translation of his Talaing History of Pegu used by Phayre, now in the British Museum, being manuscripts OR 3462-4 (xviii, 118, 211, 235).

SCHIEFNER, F. A. VON. "Taranathas Geschichte des Buddhismus in Indien," publ. Commissionäre der Kaiserlichen Akademie der Wissenschaften, St. Petersburg, 1869 (40).
B 941.d.2. BM 761.f.37.
OII 95.D.34.

SCHMIDT, P. W. "Slapat ragawan datow smim ron. Buch des Ragawan, der Königsgeschichte," publ. for Kais. Akademie der Wissenschaften by Hölder, Vienna 1906 (9, 116, 118).
B ψ2.102/151. BM Ac.810/6 vol. 151.

SCHOUTEN, G. "Voyage aux Indes orientales commencé l'an 1658 & fini l'an 1665," two vols. publ. Estienne Roger, Amsterdam 1707 (147, 314).
B Douce S88, 89.

SCOTT, J. G. "Burma, a Handbook of Practical Information," publ. Moring, London 1906 (354).
B 20652.e.7. BM 010055.de.62.
IO 8.A.A.2. OII 26.B.4.

SCOTT O'CONNOR. "Mandalay and Other Cities of Burma," publ. Hutchinson, London 1907 (310, 330).
B 20652.d.16. BM 010075.i.3.
IO 8.H.3. OII 29.D.13.

SHWAY YOE (Sir George Scott). "The Burman, His Life and Notions," publ. Macmillan, London 1896 (45, 170, 324, 329, 362).
BM 010057.g.2. OII 23.B.23.
IO 8.A.19.

*SHWEBONNIDAN-KYAN, publ. Hanthawaddy Press, Rangoon 1892 (329).

*SHWEMAWDAW THAMAING, publ. Hanthawaddy Press, Rangoon 1917 (xviii, 119, 311).

*SHWE NAW, MG. "Mun Yazawin," publ. Hanthawaddy Press, Rangoon 1899 (311).

SMEATON, D. M. "The Loyal Karens of Burma," publ. Kegan Paul, London 1887 (3).
B 247188.e.1. BM 10057.bb.4.
IO 8.B.17. OII 38.A.13.

SMITH, SAMUEL. "History of Siam 1657-1767," being reigns of the kings translated by him and printed at his office, Bangkok 1880-1 (197, 200, 214, 241, 254, 339, 340, 344, 362).
B 24625.d.1.

SMITH, VINCENT A. "Catalogue of the Coins in the Indian Museum, Calcutta," publ. Clarendon Press, Oxford 1906 (137).

B Num.2223.d.11. BM 2261.a.
IO 14.A.A. 1, 2. OII 20.C.20.

"The Early History of India," publ. Clarendon Press, Oxford 1914 (310).

B S.Hist.Ind.8.f. BM 2087.d.
IO 44.H.H.12. OII 27.C.

"A History of Fine Art in India and Ceylon from the Earliest Times to the Present Day," publ. Clarendon Press, Oxford 1911 (330).

B 170083.d.6. BM 2263.f.19.
IO 84.C.16. OII 20.F.23.

"The Oxford History of India," publ. Clarendon Press, Oxford 1919 (3, 356).

B S.Hist.Ind.5. BM 2386.a.15.
IO 44.B.B.25. OII 36.A.
OU 247.

SNODGRASS, J. J. "Narrative of the Burmese War," publ. Murray, London 1827 (156, 228, 238, 254, 300, 304, 315, 334, 341, 344, 358).

B 27-709. BM 582.g.21.
IO 8.F.7 and 30. OII 28.A.21.

SONNERAT. "Voyage aux Indes Orientales et à la Chine," two vols., publ. at Paris 1782 (231, 239, 241, 333, 353, 358).

B F.F.69, 70 Jur. Douce S.491.2.

Ditto, four vols., publ. at Paris 1806 (205, 231, 260, 357, 358, 360, 361).

BM 566.d.6 and 7.

STEVENS, see Faria y Sousa.

STEWART, J. A. "Kyaukse Settlement Report," publ. Superintendent Government Printing, Rangoon 1922 (319).

"Pegu Gazetteer," vol. A, publ. Superintendent Government Printing, Rangoon 1917 (311, 322).

B 20652.e.27[a]. BM I.S.147.
IO 300.A.79.R. OII 15.C.

STUART, J. M. B. "Old Burmese Irrigation Works," publ. Superintendent Government Printing, Rangoon 1913 (320).

SYMES, M. "An Account of an Embassy to the Kingdom of Ava," publ. Nicol & Wright, London 1800 (143, 212, 231, 233, 236, 247, 262, 263, 267, 271, 281, 313, 323, 329, 350, 353, 354, 355, 356, 358, 359, 362).

B c.c.123 Art. Seld. Douce S.519.
BM G.2856.
IO 8.M.16. OII 41.F.22.

TAW SEIN KO. "Burmese Sketches," publ. British Burma Press, Rangoon 1913 (308).

BM 012357.m.31.

* "Selections from the Records of the Hlutdaw," publ. by Government, Rangoon 1889 (329).

BM 14302.c.6.

TEMPLE, R. C. "The Thirty-Seven Nats, a phase of Spirit Worship prevailing in Burma," publ. Griggs, London 1906 (19, 28, 54, 77, 80, 91, 93, 95, 105, 161, 168, 315).

B 932.b.1. BM LR.22.b.9.
IO 305.31.G.15. OII 23.F.21.

TENNENT, J. "Christianity in Ceylon," publ. Murray, London 1850 (145, 277).

B 50.520 BM 4765.dd.13.
IO 9.L.16. OII 21.B.18

*THAHTONHNWEMUN YAZAWIN, MS. (xviii, 117).

*THAHTONMYO SHWEZAYAN PAYAGYI THAMAING, publ. Rammapura Press, Moulmein 1912 (309).

TP = "Toung Pao," periodical, publ. E. J. Brill, Leyden (205, 237, 260, 278, 310, 314, 340, 350, 352, 353, 357, 358, 359, 360).

B Per.Or.d.1/1 BM 15235.a.
IO 305/8.B.

TRANT, T. A. "Two years in Ava from May 1824 to May 1826, by an officer on the staff of the Quarter Master General's department [Trant]," publ. Murray, London 1827 (154, 156, 232, 237, 295, 300, 304, 315, 322, 335, 341, 344, 353, 358).

B 27.370. BM 1046.c.9.
IO 8.F.20.

TUN NYEIN. "Inscriptions of Pagan, Pinya, and Ava. Translation with notes," publ. Superintendent Government Printing, Rangoon 1899 (23, 79, 80, 81, 124, 323, 326, 334).

BM 14320.c.c.1. IO 92.c.2.3.
OII 20.c.15.

TWENTY-FOUR PARGANAS GAZETTEER, publ. Bengal Secretariat Book Depot, Calcutta 1914 (143).

B 20644.d.2/31 BM 010058.k.
IO 300.A.79.O. OII 14.D.

VALENTYN, F. "Oud en Nieuw Oost-Indien," five vols., publ. van Braam and Onder de Linden, Dordrecht and Amsterdam 1724-26 (146, 314).

B Fol.B.S.451-8. BM 10028.i.4.
IO 30.I.7-11.

VINCENT SMITH, see Smith, Vincent A.

WARRY, W., a précis of Chinese State Papers, printed departmentally in Rangoon when Mr. Warry was Adviser on Chinese Affairs to the Government of Burma (256, 352, 355).

*WAWHAYALINATTA DIPANI-KYAN, publ. Myammataya Press, Mandalay 1899 (166, 314).

WAYLAND, F. "A Memoir of the Life and Labours of the Rev. Adoniram Judson, D.D.," two vols., publ. Phillips and Sampson (Boston) and Nisbet (London) 1853 (199, 258, 278, 295, 363).

B 210.b.204-5. BM 4985.b.33.

WESTERMARCK, E. "The History of Human Marriage," three vols., publ. Macmillan, London 1921 (313, 325).

B S.Hist.Civ.33y/1-3. BM 2236.d.15.

WESTLAKE. "Kyaukse Settlement Report," publ. Superintendent Government Printing, Rangoon 1892 (359).

BM I.S.35/7. IO R and R 9(2318).

WHITEWAY, R. S. "The rise of the Portuguese power in India 1497-1550," publ. Constable, London 1899 (131, 340, 342).

B 24619.d.5. BM c9057.bb.3.
IO 72.c.10. OU 28.B.4.

WILSON, H. H. "Documents illustrative of the Burmese War with an introductory sketch of the events of the war and an appendix," publ. Government Press, Calcutta 1827 (238, 293, 300, 301, 302, 304, 341, 361).

B Mason B.B.93. BM 583.k.11.
IO 8.M.17.

"Vishnu Purana," publ. Murray, London 1840 (317).

B Sansk.3.37. BM 14016.f.2.
IO 13.L.8. OU 937.

WOOD, a précis of standard Siamese Chronicles sent me by Mr W. A. R. Wood, H.B.M.'s Consul General at Chiengmai (169, 354).

YULE, H. "The Book of Ser Marco Polo," translated and edited by Colonel Sir Henry Yule, revised by Henri Cordier, two vols., publ. Murray, London 1903 (67, 333, 337).

*B 206.d.85-86. BM 2354.f.14.
IO 29.L.27-28. OU 25.D.14-15.
OU 330.

"Cathay and the Way Thither," revised by Henri Cordier, four vols., publ. Hakluyt Society, London 1915 (310).

B Soc.2031.d.4.n.s.38. BM R.Ac.6172/102.
IO 300.A.71.F.10. OU 333.

YULE, H.—(*cont.*).

"A narrative of the Mission sent by the Governor-General of India to the court of Ava in 1855," publ. Smith, Elder, London 1858 (196, 237, 323, 325, 329, 330, 336, 349, 359, 362)..

B	2.Δ.1230.	BM	2354.h.7.
IO	8.M.13.	OU	1136.

*ZINATTAPAKATHANI-KYAN, publ. Hanthawaddy Press, Rangoon 1910 (329)

INDEX.

All place names in Burma are included, but many minor personal names are omitted, especially when they can be searched for under e.g. Literature.
* is occasionally added to indicate a verbatim quotation.